A General Theory of
Secularization

A General Theory of Secularization

DAVID MARTIN

HARPER & ROW PUBLISHERS
NEW YORK, EVANSTON, SAN FRANCISCO

STANDARD BOOK NUMBER 0–06–136179–8
0–06–131935–X (PAPERBACK)

LIBRARY OF CONGRESS CATALOG CARD NUMBER 78–3130

PRINTED IN GREAT BRITAIN

Contents

Introductory Comments

This book is about patterns of secularization and as with most patterns there is a degree of overlap and repetition which allows each chapter to be comprehensible on its own. The key essay is Chapter Two which attempts to organize the material in a general and abstract manner. Chapter Three was originally written as an essay on religion in Europe with special reference to power, and it utilizes the same framework as Chapter Two in a more discursive, descriptive manner and with a different focus. These two chapters are close companions and both follow logically and chronologically from Chapter One, which was a five-finger exercise preluding each of them. Chapter One is the place for the reader to begin. It commenced life by accident as a sketch stimulated by an L.S.E. graduate seminar in 1968 and provided a first approximation for my subsequent thinking. Actually that thinking has run along two lines, one being the conceptual criticism incorporated in *The Religious and the Secular* (1969b) and the other being the attempt at generalization presented here. I may perhaps add that there is also a stylistic difference between the two lines of thinking. In the work on conceptual criticism I have emphasized ambiguity and exploited language; in the present work I have been much more crude and utilitarian. Indeed, I have tried to be plain not only by avoiding any literary artifice but also by eschewing most of the adornments which might be provided by sociological terminology. The book is, I hope, just as difficult as the nature of the argument and material requires, and no more.

I had originally planned five chapters corresponding to each of my categories, but when the two largest chapters were complete I found that two of these categories were constantly referred by way of comparison. I therefore set them on one side as likely to be very repetitive and eventually provided separate coverage for only three of the categories. Of these three the most important is also the largest—that on the 'Mixed' pattern. I find considerable theoretical interest in the problems and implications found in the 'Mixed' pattern i.e. in the special problem presented by areas with bare Protestant majorities, such as Holland. The last chapter was originally asked of me by Professor Ben-David for the International Sociological Conference at Toronto in 1974. It concerns itself with the clergy, and attempts to discuss the current clerical crisis by focusing initially on the Anglo-Saxon variant of the basic patterns and then suggesting how the elements may be rotated for the other patterns. This chapter is a large scale sketch and would require book form for its full development.

The present book is concerned with the 'general' and 'special' theory of secularization in that certain 'general' processes in modern society are funnelled through varied patterns which alter their form, colour, pace and detailed impact. The book which is shortly to follow contains varied commentaries on these broad processes and particular patterns. In that second volume I return to the complexities of the secularization issue as it has concerned me from time to time and more particularly in *The Religious and the Secular*. Ideally the present book should be read in conjunction with *The Religious and the Secular* and with the forthcoming book. Intentional crudities of formulation and definition need to be set against the long-term historical complexities and conceptual problems inherent in issues which have intermittently engaged my attention from the mid-sixties till now. The tensions afflicting this subject need to be held.

I first interested myself in secularization with an essay published in 1965 called 'Towards Eliminating the Concept of Secularization'. Perhaps I should say that I intended to open a debate rather than to banish a word, and I think I have had some success in this. A new turn in my thinking occurred when I wrote 'Notes towards a general theory of secularization'; and an invitation to give the Cadbury lectures in the University of Birmingham provided me with an opportunity to expand those 'Notes'. Certain parts of the programme in the 'Notes' remain untouched, for example the incidence of the Protestant Ethic and of its substitutes, and the Latin American Pattern. Unfortunately the invitation to Birmingham was almost immediately followed by another less welcome invitation to convene my department.

The lectures were thus more of a patchwork than I would have wished. Major unintegrated fragments have been reset within the book which is still to follow.

Time and continued administrative responsibility have prevented me bringing every part of this book up to date. The main argument does not depend on being everywhere up-to-date. The chapter on Europe, for example, was written for a symposium during the Christmas vacation, 1973. It rests, as do most other chapters, on data mostly published between 1960 and 1970. I would like to say in passing that a very large proportion of the empirical backing has derived from Catholic sources and institutes the tradition of Le Bras has my respect and gratitude.

I am very sorry that three important books came my way too late for me to incorporate highly relevant materials: 'The Secularization of Leisure' by E. Katz and M. Gurevitch (London: Faber 1976), 'Godsdienst in Vlaanderen' by J. Billiet and K. Dobbelaere (Leuven: Davidsfonds 1976), and 'Religion in Canadian Society' edited by S. Crysdale and L. Wheatcroft (Toronto: Macmillan 1976).

Since time has been mentioned perhaps I might say I write these introductory comments in August 1976, in Martindale by Ullswater. It seems an appropriate place for me to finish a book.

Martindale by Ullswater
August, 1976

Acknowledgements

My first acknowledgement must be to the Edward Cadbury Trustees who so kindly invited me to give the 1972–3 Cadbury Lectures in the University of Birmingham. My second acknowledgement should be to the Northern Studies Committee of the L.S.E. through the good offices of which I was able to spend three weeks in Scandinavia. I am grateful to *The European Journal of Sociology* for permission to reprint Chapter One, and to M. Scotford Archer and S. Giner for the deployment here of the chapter on Europe which they are to include in a forthcoming symposium.

My secretary, Miss Josephine Johnson deserves my sincere thanks for her help in the latter stages of the manuscript. Miss Judy Strang, M.Sc., was most kind with regard to the early stages, going way beyond the call of secretarial duty. I owe her a tremendous debt. Dr Bryan Wilson was most helpful in offering me the assistance of his secretary in the later stages: I am very grateful to him and to her.

I would also like to thank Daniel Bell and Donald MacRae for reading part of the manuscript and to thank Bryan Wilson, John Whitworth and Tom Nossiter for reading it all. Mr. A. L. Gooch kindly looked over the Spanish references.

My final debts, intellectual and personal, are to my wife, who bore the burden and heat of this particular day.

D.M.

I

Notes towards a General Theory of Secularization

PRELIMINARIES

A general theory of secularization is closer to realization in the sociology of religion than might be expected, in spite of the field being poorly developed. However, the sociology of religion has the advantage of being able to draw in a synthesizing manner on neighbouring areas which are more developed, and in so doing will be able in return to suggest broad schemata of interpretation for use in those fields, especially political sociology. No doubt the notion of a general theory of secularization remains premature, but premature statements do elicit more precise or even alternative formulations incorporating and subsuming wider ranges of material. In any case what follows is less a complete statement of a general theory than a specification of some of its components. Yet in another sense it *is* a theory, since it could be reduced to sets of overarching propositions and their integrally related sub-propositions, with appropriate qualifications and marginal rubrics.

Certain assumptions have been made and certain assumptions have not. It has been assumed that religion affords a particularly important clue to the general character of a given culture, but not that it constitutes the active dynamic, casually prior element in society. A general theory such as is outlined need not pronounce on such questions as the epiphemonenal character of religion.

I have also assumed that certain advantages do accrue from the fact that secularization has been firstly a 'Christian' phenomenon. Some theologians have indeed capitalized on certain congruences between Christianity and secularity to welcome secularization as simply an unfolding of the essence of religion. There is something to this, but less than is claimed. At any rate the advantages for the framing of theory stem from the fact that secularization initially occurs within the ambit of Christian societies. A general theory can be stated for societies within a Christian ambit (or, if you prefer, societies with a Christian historical background) and subsequently be qualified for other societies, just as secularization itself was exported with modifications to other societies. An analysis of the initial 'breakthrough' is usually the crucial part of a theory. The point is that this breakthrough occurred in Christian cultures, whatever the precise relation of Christianity to secularity, and the core of the theory can therefore be stated in relation to those cultures.

It follows that by the term 'religion' in this context I mean Christianity, its characteristic ethos, institutions and beliefs (1), as variously incorporated in Protestant, Sectarian, Catholic and Orthodox forms. This means that I am also assuming for Christianity certain very broad continuities with its own past and a common identifiable core of which different versions remain nevertheless recognizable variants.

So much for assumptions: something now needs to be said about the nature of the general theory. To state a general theory is not to announce some dogma about 'the way things are going' or about irreversible trends. It simply says that in circumstance X this or that development Y tends to occur, or more broadly that in the complex of historical circumstances a, b, c, a development p, q, r tends to occur, with these and these appropriate qualifications, and always allowing of course for adaptations on the part of those who have grasped more or less precisely this development and the best manner of either nullifying it or canalising it (2). In any case some of the component generalizations in the theory of secularization refer to what may be quite limited trends. For example, the dominance of heavy industry (which certainly has deleterious effects on 'religion') may be a diminishing characteristic of modern societies. The stated relation between religion and heavy industry holds, but the extent of the continuing consequences for religion depend on propositions about the development and future of heavy industry.

Certain broad tendencies towards secularization in industrial society have already been fairly well established. These are of the following kind:

that religious institutions are adversely affected to the extent that an area is dominated by heavy industry;

that they are the more adversely affected if the area concerned is homogeneously proletarian;

that religious practice declines proportionately with the size of an urban concentration;

that geographical and social mobility erodes stable religious communities organized on a territorial basis; that it also contributes to a relativization of perspectives through extended culture contact;

that the church becomes institutionally differentiated in response to the differentiation of society, notably into pluriform denominations and sects;

that the church becomes partially differentiated from other institutional spheres: such as justice, ideological legitimation, the state apparatus, social control, education, welfare; and this is paralleled by a compartmentalization of an individual's religious role which may encourage a range of variation in personal religion which contributes to institutional disintegration.

And so on. There is wide variety of such propositions. They are what one would want to term the 'universal processes' of industrial society, not as I've pointed out in the sense that they *must happen*, but in the sense they tend to occur other things being equal. But things are not equal—ever—and it is central to the succeeding argument that they are most conspicuously not equal with respect to the particular cultural (and generally linguistic) complex within which they operate (3). The 'universal processes' operate very differently according to the nature of that complex and I aim to categorize such complexes and note the varying modus operandi of the universal processes in relation to each category. Both the complexes and the characteristic modes within them are now to be designated in terms of certain key components. The general theory is general in that it relates 'universal processes' which are empirically quite well established to a typology of cultural contexts and then specifies the type of refraction which the processes then undergo.

COMPONENT A: '*THE CRUCIAL EVENT*'[4]

Certain crucial events sum up a series of antecedent processes and shape in broad measure the sets of tendencies which fructify over time in a given culture. No doubt a further theoretical statement requires the investigation and summary of their antecedent causes (or if one prefers, prior configurations) but one must select convenient cut-off points and these are best provided by the concept of these crucial events. It is worth noting that such events extend in their effects beyond the culture in which they occur into related cultures where they have some resonance.

Crucial historical event [1]: The success or failure of the Reformation. This is perhaps the appropriate point to note the importance of what for lack of a better formulation one must term 'accidents' whether these be historical or geographical. A geographical accident is the relative security of Protestantism in England by virtue of the Channel, or of Protestantism in Northern Europe by virtue of distance from the main Catholic forces. A historical accident is the Battle of the White Mountain (1620) which was decisive for the fate of Protestantism in most of central Europe.

Crucial historical events [2] are as follows:
(i) The outcome of the English Civil War 1642–60.
This was partially determinative for all cultures in the Anglo-Saxon ambit, currently comprising some three hundred million persons. It must be supplemented by:
(ii) The outcome of the American Revolution 1776, which was determinative for two thirds of the Anglo-Saxon ambit, i.e. the United States. This is perhaps the point to note that the existence of large Catholic minorities and other ethnic groups within a given cultural ambit does not seriously affect the argument[5]. The notion of a crucial event implies that it *is* crucial and establishes a hegemonic power over future developments unless its carriers are decisively displaced, more especially from elite positions and at an early stage.
(iii) The outcome of the French Revolution 1789 et seq., which was partially determinative for Latin Catholic cultures and to a lesser extent their South American offshoots, currently comprising some four hundred fifty million persons.

(iv) The outcome of the Russian Revolution 1917, which was partially determinative for Russia and its East European dependencies—though assisted in some degree by the historical 'accident' of conquest in 1945 et seq. These currently comprise some three hunded million persons.

Certain subsidiary patterns should be noted since, though less important in scale, they had important implications for the secularization process.

(v) The Dutch Revolution, and the Scottish and Swiss Reformations, which currently comprise within their influence some fifty to twenty million persons.

(vi) The *non*-revolution in Lutheran countries (East Germany excepted, which was again a case of conquest) which involved a pattern midway between the English and the Latin. It currently comprises some thirty to forty million persons.

Thus far nothing more has been attempted than a conventional list of what are held to be crucial events. The patterns consequent on each must now be specified.

COMPONENT B: *RESULTANT PATTERNS*[6]

The categories below correspond to those just above, except that (i) and (ii) have been inverted.

(i) The American Pattern. This involves a dislodgement of the relation between an aristocratic political establishment and religious establishment(s). An almost unqualified pluralism becomes associated with an almost universal popularized religious culture. Secularization when it occurs is largely related to ethos rather than to institutions and beliefs. Religion *as such* is unproblematic and non-political, though of course different denominations tend to support one party rather than another and raise issues as between themselves, e.g. nativist Protestant agitations against Catholic immigrants.

(ii) The British Pattern. This involves a *partial* dislodgement of the politico-religious establishment by substantial dissent. Religion *as such* is politically unproblematic, though certain partial alignments of denominations and parties occur e.g. Protestant dissent and the Liberal Party and practising Christians tend somewhat to a disproportionate support of the non-socialist parties. Religious institutions are attenuated but beliefs remain widely disseminated, albeit in a somewhat amorphous manner.

(iii) **The French (Latin) Pattern.** The Baroque autocracies eliminate substantial religious dissent[7] and forces build up within the system towards a revolution with an explicit secular ideology. Such revolutionary explosions become endemic, and religion as such is frequently a political issue. Coherent and massive secularism confronts coherent and massive religiosity, and to the extent that secularism is successful there is a partial tendency to erode institutional adherence and belief *together*. One ethos confronts an alternative ethos, particularly where the elite culture of the secular Enlightenment acquires a mass component and achieves a historicized ideology i.e. Marxism. Obviously ameliorating influences do operate within this vicious circle, perhaps increasingly so since the Second World War. Italy provides clear examples of rapprochement[8]. To the extent that ameliorating influences do operate the end of total theology and the end of total secularist ideology are concomitant tendencies.

(iii) **The South American (extended Latin) Pattern.** South America develops at a time when the European centre of Catholicism shifts from the right to the centre. This provides an opportunity to limit the vicious circles of the Latin pattern and may produce a substantial Catholic left ameliorating the secularist militancy of the left as a whole. At this juncture the organicist element in Catholicism may discover useful congruences with socialism.

(iv) **The Russian Pattern.** This involves a simple inversion of the Caesaro-Papist conjunction by substituting a Marxist counter-orthodoxy. Religion is officially privatized and both beliefs and institutions are subjected to massive attack and massive erosion. However, the internal ethos of the religious institutions is not substantially diminished.

(v) **The Calvinist Pattern.** This involves a liberalization and partial secularization of ethos within the mainstream of the culture, but more especially its elite sections—a process also partly mirrored in the Calvinist section of the American elite. This elicits breakaways to the orthodox Calvinist right (e.g. French Switzerland, Scotland) or to the maintenance of the orthodox 'radical' right in certain situations of embattled isolation (e.g. South Africa). In the long run Calvinist institutions perhaps maintain themselves more vigorously than Lutheran or Anglican ones but not so vigorously as Catholic ones. The Calvinist pattern is discussed further under Component C.

(vi) The Lutheran Pattern. Here, too, there is a liberalization of the centre which however is more exclusively restricted to the elite and which elicits various subjectivist reactions *internally:* pietism and romanticism. The élite becomes open to a historicized enlightenment but perhaps more in relation to nationalism than to Marxism[9]. Eventually religious institutions are partly eroded but religious beliefs are affected only insofar as militant secularism is associated with a substantial Marxist party (e.g. Germany, Finland). This association is *more* prominent than in the Anglo-Saxon patterns, much *less* prominent than the Latin, and is eventually overcome by ameliorating influences acting on socialism itself.

It is important to note that the cultural patterns (i) to (vi) discussed above can form continua with respect to (a) individualism (b) pluralism (c) the salience of their Calvinist element. These continua are as follows, running from left to right, the left marking the positive pole with respect to the phenomenon in question.

Individualism: (i) (ii) (v) (vi) (iii) (iv)
Pluralism: (i) (ii) (v) (vi) (iii) (iv)
Calvinist salience: (v) (i) (ii) (vi) (iii) (iv)

There is, in short, a continuum of pluralism to no-pluralism running from Protestantism to Catholicism to Orthodoxy[10].

It is also worth explicitly drawing out and restating the range of variation which the different patterns exhibit with respect to ethos, institutions and beliefs. These are as follows:

(1) Anglo-Saxon   Institutional erosion, erosion of religious ethos, maintenance of amorphous religious beliefs.

(2) American   Institutional expansion, erosion of religious ethos, maintenance of amorphous religious beliefs.

(3) French (or Latin) Massive religious beliefs, ethos and institutions confronting massive secularist beliefs, ethos and institutions.

(4) Russian   Massive erosion of religious beliefs, ethos
                   and institutions but maintenance of the
                   beliefs and the ethos within the surviving
                   religious institutions.

The other patterns designated are sub-variants within this range.

One may now proceed to a consideration of the two thought systems most central for the secularization process: Calvinism and the Enlightenment (in its rationalistic and historicized variants).

COMPONENT C: *THE CALVINIST AND ENLIGHTENMENT ELEMENTS*

The transition to 'modernity' is assisted by either Calvinism or by the Enlightenment. Calvinism is the less explicitly modern of the two, and achieves an important symbiosis with the rationalistic variant of the Enlightenment especially in the Anglo-Saxon, Scots and continental Calvinist cultures e.g. the Dutch Enlightenment, the Scottish Enlightenment, and in the American Constitution. In Catholic and Orthodox cultures, however, the characteristic symbiosis is between the rationalistic variant of the Enlightenment and its historicized (that is, Marxist) variant. In short the secularizing potentiality occurs *either* through Calvinism plus the Enlightenment *or* the Enlightenment plus its historicized variant.

In Protestant countries, Lutheran, Anglican and Calvinist, two major forms of 'retardation'[11] occur with respect to secularization: these are the pietist-evangelical movement and the 'radical right' of orthodox Calvinism. Both of these have greater resonance at non-elite levels, and indeed positively accuse the elite of religious indifference or 'liberalism'. The social and regional location of the non-cosmopolitan 'old-time religion' of America is particularly well documented. Evangelicalism however has some tendency to liberalization on its own account, and can achieve partial conjunctions with reformist parties.

One further point is worth making. If Lutheranism contains some nationalist potentiality Calvinism perhaps possesses some sense of historical destiny through the notion of 'the people of God'. It too can achieve some assimilation to the historical march of the nation state by translating the notion of 'the people of God' into 'one nation under God'[12]. Thus Protestant countries have their own possibilities of participating in 'history'; this possibility provides the parallel element to the historicized variant of the Enlightenment.

COMPONENT D: *THE RELATION OF RELIGION TO THE GROWTH OF NATIONALISM AND CULTURAL IDENTITY*

This aspect simply involves a series of commonsense relationships, such as that where religion is imposed from above by a conqueror it is thereby weakened, whereas when it is the focus of resistance to a conqueror it is thereby strengthened (unless the conqueror disposes of a total monopoly of educational facilities). These relationships obtain in terms of the persistent 'image' of a religion long after the actual events have taken place. The polar cases are (say) Cuba, where Catholicism remains associated with Spanish domination, and Poland, where it remains associated with national survival. An intermediate case might be provided by Czechoslovakia (strictly Czech Lands) where the official majority religion—Catholicism—is excluded from the national myth, and thereby weakened for the struggle with state sponsored secularism. Other intermediate cases are those like Ireland, Brittany and Wales where a differentiated religion is a source and bulwark of a differentiated culture. There are further types of cases where the religion retains vitality because it is marooned in a sea of alien cultures (Ethiopia) or is at the frontier with such cultures (Lebanon, Cyprus). Further sub-types are provided by the religion of ethnic subgroups dispersed in wider alien societies, the obvious examples being provided by the Irish, Italians, Poles, etc. in the United States, or the communities of the Armenian dispersion.

This is not the place to attempt to translate these 'components' for other world religions. But for instance it is obvious that Islam achieves a symbiosis with a suppressed nationalism (though hardly with the Enlightenment) partly by virtue of the impact of colonialism and the association of that colonialism with Christianity. Or to take another aspect in relation to yet another religion, Judaism achieves a pattern most closely related to the Calvinist one: the centre and elite of the culture partially relates itself to the Enlightenment while two 'retardations' occur; the radical right of the orthodox minority and the 'internal' hassidic revival of Judaic pietism. Put in another way Judaism contains both the radical orthodox right of Calvinism and the internal pietism of Lutheranism.

The foregoing is an attempt to indicate certain components which belong to a general theory of secularization. It aims to relate certain broad social processes to particular historical configurations. This relation is summarized in a typological schema organized around the three distinct areas of institutions, belief and ethos. Clearly the broad social tendencies require more precise statement and a comprehensive articulation one with another. Likewise the historical configurations need a kind of documentation which can put the major 'set' of events within the complex counterpoint of contrary tendencies[13]. But a general theory is after all no more and no less than a sketch of the sort of intellectual architecture required.

NOTES

1. It will be clear that the 'theory' does not adequately specify for these three distinct areas, which are in any case known to vary independently of each other. However I have indicated below something of the range of this variation.

2. These adaptations will include the various sects and denominations as well as changes in 'churchly' Christianity: and sociologists will make statements about their varied viability according to social milieu.

3. Of course they are also 'not equal' with respect to factors which are much more adventitious than those dealt with in this article. Such an adventitious element would be the migration of Catholics to the urban areas of Protestant cultures thereby upsetting to some extent the correlation between large scale urbanization and low practice.

4. An exposition of this notion can be found in Lipset 1969. Cf. the points I have tried to make at the beginning of chap. IV in Martin 1976b and for Barrington Moore, 1966.

5. In Switzerland for example one could treat the Geneva-Zurich axis as the 'active' segment of the society.

6. For a lucid contrast of two of these patterns, the British and the American, cf the essay on Canada in Lipset 1969.

7. Notably the Revocation of the Edict of Nantes, 1685.

8. Presumably the Italian pattern is influenced *for* Catholicism in that the Papacy is Italian, but *against* it in that the Pope was a temporal ruler and opposed to Italian nationalism.

9. The point about nationalism is made tentatively, but Lutheran cultures do have a smaller internationalist aspect than Calvinist ones: at least so Stark argues (1966–72, vol. I). A difficult point arises here in that one does not know whether to categorize nationalistic possibilities as belonging to the original 'essence' of Lutheranism or not. Cf. Kaser 1966.

10. It is arguable whether Orthodox cultures have been less pluralistic than Catholic cultures; Russia has always had substantial dissent.

11. 'Retardation' is not employed pejoratively: they are 'holding movements' expressing some awareness of the weaknesses of liberalism rather than mere reaction. At the intellectual level and in the form of neo-orthodoxy they can mount complex critiques of liberalized Christianity: especially perhaps in alliance with political forces to the left of liberalism e.g. Niebuhr and Barth.

12. This point has been strongly emphasized by Talcott Parsons. Cf. also his valuable essay on Christianity *in* Sills 1968.

13. Cf. Marty 1969a.

II

A Theory of Secularization: Basic Patterns

My aim is ambitious but limited. I want to suggest under what conditions religious institutions, like churches and sects, become less powerful and how it comes about that religious beliefs are less easily accepted. By stating my aim in this particular way I have to sidestep a great many complicated issues about the nature of 'religion' and about the important difference between religious beliefs and religious institutions. In previous discussions I have laid particular emphasis on such issues and in those discussions I argued that sociologists of religion must at the very least indicate how they intend using their key terms, in this case 'religious' and 'secular' (Martin 1969b). By 'religious' I mean an acceptance of a level of reality beyond the observable world known to science, to which are ascribed meanings and purposes completing and transcending those of the purely human realm. I do not intend entering the infinite regress of further definitions of words like 'transcendence'. I simply want to indicate my area of concern not to delimit the precise margin where 'religious' ends and 'secular' begins.

I ought to say that a theory of secularization such as I now propose need not assume that secularization is a very long term or inevitable trend. The segment of human history from which I derive the theory covers a variable depth of about two to four centuries which so far as human history goes can only exhibit a rather local trend. Nevertheless certain tendencies can be noted over that period with regard to the role, power and popularity of religious beliefs and institutions and it is about these I wish to theorize.

'My' theory, if the possessive can be used, is necessarily a synthetic gloss on the work of others. It provides a setting for what is already there. My debts are legion: to Bryan Wilson and those who have worked with him on sectarianism, to the macro-theorists like Talcott Parsons and Edward Shils, to the social historians of religion especially those working recently on the nineteenth century, to the political sociologists, notably Lipset, Rokkan, Dahl and Rose. Durkheim provided the frame and the tradition of Catholic 'sociologie religieuse' provided most of the information. My most important single historical source was the work of the Catholic sociologist Michael Fogarty (1957) on the origins and influence of Christian Democracy in Europe.

I should stress that this is an empirical theory and I believe such theories have an appropriate and honourable place in the economy of science. I have not attempted to touch on the trans-formation of symbols, the shifts of paradigm, or the mutations and revolutions of ideas and I have definitely eschewed any hint of the philosophy of history. For that matter a sketch of a history of ideas consonant with my analysis may be found in Marty (1969a). There is also another highly suggestive account in Chadwick (1975).

There are certain clear costs associated with my approach. Religion is a creature of the realm of symbol, feeling and meaning and I have concentrated on structure. This means I have largely avoided reference to the fact that the 'same' religion, in this case Christianity, adapts and alters from time to time and place to place. Above all I have not attempted to deal with the extensive evangelical renaissance of Christianity which began about 1810 and extended for the most of the nineteenth century (c.f. MacLeod 1974). The elements inside my structural coordinates undergo chemical change over time. And, in any case, my time scale has a cut-off point which is loosely fixed at the period when a country enters modernity. I do not try to explain why the frame which attended Britain's entry is so different from that which attended the entry of France. To do so would be to enter on an almost infinite historical regress. Nevertheless I am reasonably confident that general principles may be located which govern the variety of entrance points into modernity. I am largely concerned with what happens after the entrance has been made and with how the different conformations of the socio-historical net prohibit and allow different variants to emerge with different potencies and trajectories.

Christianity itself is part of that net because it either facilitates or at least does not universally prohibit the passage of essential components of modernity through the net. That is why my theory is ethno-centric or, if you like, centred on the North Atlantic and the West. The West, after all, is where it all began. The patterns I adduce can, if you like, be rotated to comprehend allied developments and other major cultures, of which the principal ones would be Turkey and Japan (c.f. Yalman 1973, and Bellah 1965). Enough is enough, and as William Blake said, enough is already too much.

One last point: empirical theories, whatever their moments of imagination and their appropriate deductive element work by induction from data. Data is what is given, and in this case the given was donated by the indefatigable workers in the tradition of Catholic and Communist empiricism: sociologie religieuse et sociologie atheistique. Thomas Luckmann has rightly pointed to their theoretical failings (1967), but their work is still the necessary condition of theory. Just as the Protestant, and above all the German enquiry into the Bible was a major achievement of the human intellect, so to is the Catholic and above all the French enquiry into the social nature of the Church. The late Gabriel Le Bras, Professor of Canon Law in the University of Paris, requires a salute in passing.

Theory has a purely conditional form: if x and y are present then z is likely to this or that extent. Often I cannot even hope to indicate what that extent is, and there are a lot of situations where it is difficult to be certain how far x is operative or y, or indeed some other factor. In sociology factors merge in a complex gestalt. So in many instances theorization has to be content with sketching the form of an answer, or even less certainly with arguing that such answers as may exist will follow a particular *kind* of form. The attempt at theory is not rendered useless by the fact that the scope of explanation is limited or some things left unexplained. What is needed is some indication of the crucial nexus of relevant factors and some hint as to their likely relationships. Such hints cannot be proved and will sometimes lapse from explanation to description and from generalization to tautology. Nevertheless what I want to argue is sufficiently generous in scope, and it is I hope intelligible. I am trying to present relationships which make intelligible sense of a wide range of data.

Such relationships are not necessarily couched in terms which come as a complete surprise. For a long time people have reflected with varying degrees of rigour on the matters which I want to discuss. They have produced reflections which are more or less plausible and familiar, and which cover this or that sector of my enquiry. Some of the reflections are very familiar indeed and are not at all invalidated by their mere familiarity. The attempt to order these reflections comprehensively on a comparative basis is perhaps less familiar, though again hardly novel. Happily truth and absolute novelty are not highly correlated. The method of approach is also familiar and is I think characteristic of science: an amalgam of induction and deduction. Certain relationships are drawn inductively from the data and certain likelihoods are deducible once an initial pattern has been set up. Of course not all relationships are followed up: they belong to the 'feeder systems' of the present enquiry.

Only one further preliminary is necessary. The kind of explanation I employ must appear both mechanistic and deterministic. The postulate of mechanism is however just a postulate of order. When people argue for example that the divisions of Christians repel potential converts they are making a generalization about what happens, other things being equal, and such a generalization is based on a postulate of order. Such people believe they know what leads to what. Precisely such a postulate underlics the generalizations I want to put forward.

THE FRAME

So much for preliminaries: a theory comes from the imagination and goes to the imagination. I now need to introduce a more directly empirical postulate than the postulate of order. It is that at certain crucial periods in their history societies acquire a particular frame and that subsequent events persistently move within the limits of that frame. There is a contour of dykes and canals set up at a crucial turning point in history and the flow of events then runs according to that contour. It may be that this notion of a frame is simply a subsidiary element in the postulate of order because if events in society 'a' or society 'b' did not have a characteristic tendency then the actors within those societies would be helplessly exposed to random occurrences and therefore to the inexplicable and the uncontrollable. Societies, like human beings, need to repeat themselves, and only very gradually do they succeed in working through various minor variations on the repeats till they arrive at something different.[1]

One form of the near-necessary repeat is so important for the theory of secularization that it merits brief exposition here. Common observation speaks of the vicious circle and the beneficent circle. 'Sets' and 'frames' revolve and evolve inside such circles. The evaluation seemingly implied by words like 'vicious' and 'beneficent' can be set on one side, because all that matters here concerns certain spirals of internal hostility, or repulsion, and mutually antagonistic definition which reinforce themselves, and other spirals of internal compromise and mutual adaptation which likewise reinforce themselves. The fate and form of secularity in any society very much depends on which type of spiral is operative. France for example exemplifies a frame in which the vicious spiral has operated, while Holland exemplifies the reverse. References will tend to focus on France and Holland because they can be used as exemplary instances of the vicious and beneficent circles

Perhaps much depends on whether a nation's revolution is an act which divides internally or unites against something external. Almost every revolution tends to move to extremes, and extremisms directed outwards draws off extremism directed inwards. The frame acquired by America revolting against England or Holland against Spain is one of unity against oppression, whereas the frame acquired by France is one of disunity between one Frenchman and another. There are exceptions: not all revolutions run to extremes whether directed outward or inward; and no doubt generalizations are available to explain why certain revolutions do not generate irreducible hostility. Nevertheless the dynamic instability of the revolutionary condition does play into the hands of irreconcilables, and France is a case where such irreconcilability devastates the internal moral community again and again, more especially from 1870–1940.

The vicious circle affects religion crucially because religion tends to attach itself to one irreconcilable side and to be identified tout court with a particular political position. Initially a revolutionary regime makes limited demands on the Church and part of the Church cautiously and tentatively accepts the regime. But initial suspicion and the use which extremists can make of instability breeds a spiral of fear and mutual repulsion backed by violence until each side feels its very existence endangered by the other. Once this occurs fear is transmuted into reality and the only practical tactic is war *à l'outrance*. From eighteenth century France to contemporary Portugal this pattern has repeated itself and is highly characteristic of societies in which the Church is Catholic and has a religious monopoly. Holland, where religion is duopolistic shows exactly the opposite phenomenon. Each group has accepted certain limited gains and regards the ally on one issue as the enemy in another. Liberals, Catholics, Calvinists, Neo-Calvinists—and later Socialists,—have each needed to concede in order to advance, to give in order to receive. Each compromise and each shifting alliance has reinforced the likelihood and the need for further compromises and further resorts to the pattern of shifting alliances. Where mutual fears do not accelerate and conflicts are not superimposed one on the other to the point where religion is part of one 'package' and irreligion part of the other, there the beneficent circle is established. For no group is secularization a central requirement in final victory.

From what has been just argued it will be clear that generalizations about the progress of secularization must turn initially on a categorization of sorts of situations in which the vicious circle does or does not operate. It will also be clear that such a categorization must turn around the following criteria: whether or not the religion concerned is Catholic, whether or not there is a monopoly of religion, and whether or not the 'frame' of a society is set up through conflict against external or against internal oppressors. For the moment I want to leave the third criterion on one side and set out my categories very simply in terms of Catholicism or not, monopoly or not. I will ask a simple question: is the basic frame of this society forged in a monopoly situation or some variety of pluralism? If the former then certain consequences for secularization follow. If the latter then certain other consequences follow. This perhaps is my first generalization and it is the one on which the categories themselves are based. So let it be formally stated. Where there exists one religion possessed of a monopoly society splits into two warring sides, one of which is dedicated to religion. Similarly where there are two or more religions (or distinct forms of the same religion) this does not happen. What follows will extend that generalization and also explain why in certain societies it does not hold. Indeed, the point about internally and externally directed 'revolutions' already suggests the reason for one group of exceptions. Poland, for example, is entirely Catholic and yet has not split into two warring sides. The reason is that the 'frame' of Polish history was forged in struggle against outsiders, not struggle between insiders.

Perhaps I have confused the issue by saying that the basis of my categorization is Catholic/Protestant, monopoly/no monopoly, internal revolution/external revolution. It is simpler to see the categories which follow as primarily based on a continuum running from total monopoly to total laissez-faire, with duopoly of the Dutch variety somewhere in between. Two warnings are appropriate. The first and most obvious concerns the fact that total monopoly and total laisser-faire are polar terms, rather than real, extant conditions, though seventeenth century Spain and France after 1685 both tried to realize complete monopoly. The second warning underlines the fact that the categories procede in terms of the state of religion when the 'frame' was *initially* set up. The United States conforms to a pattern of religious laisser-faire which is thoroughly Protestant even though large enclaves of Catholics have subsequently altered the religious balance. Moreover, the existence of local establishments in parts of America after 1776 does not alter the overall 'frame' set up by the American revolution, which was one of denominational pluralism. Obviously, all cultures were once monopolistic with regard to religion and almost all cultures now embody substantial pluralism. The categories I present simply refer to the degree of monopoly present when a given society achieved its modern form.

THE CATEGORIES

My first category contains societies based on total monopoly. All Catholic countries have approximated the monopoly model and the residue of this today is to be found in the fact that in many societies insofar as people adhere to any religion at all it is Catholic. Spain and Portugal are the most monopolistic, followed by Italy and Belgium and then by France and Austria. Indeed, all

Orthodox societies have also approximated the monopoly model. Monopoly is not really broken by the extreme sectarianism which from time to time has invaded both Orthodox and Catholic societies. A certain degree of break in monopoly is sometimes due to a shift of frontier whereby an alien church is incorporated inside the boundary of a basically Catholic society: Alsace is perhaps such a case. (Certainly Alsace conforms more to the Germanic than the French pattern of secularization.)[2]

The minor break in monopoly represented by France is perhaps sufficiently distinctive to make it worth further comment. Even the limited instalment of pluralism which occurred in France had distinct sociological consequences. French Calvinism (like English Presbyterianism) began as a 'failed' church and only gradually evolved to denominational status. This is signalized by its concentration in particular territorial enclaves, notably the Cévennes, where Protestants form the local majority.[3] Moreover it was eventually joined by the ethnic religion of Jewry. The result has been that the minority religions in France have persistently allied themselves to the political left, in spite of its militant secularism. This alliance is the precise mirror image of the fact that Catholics in Protestant societies have allied themselves to the political left, except of course that Protestant societies do not breed militant secularism, or indeed a militant left. It is monopoly, above all Catholic monopoly, which ensures abrasive division and militant secularism.

My second category contains societies based on duopoly in which the Protestant Church is the major partner. Breaks in Catholic monopolies are all minor and therefore cannot undo the vicious circle associated with monopoly: French Protestantism now includes only about 3 per cent. This may reflect the fact that an organic church like Catholicism more successfully and vigorously extrudes minorities than do the less organic Protestant churches. (The main counter example of Catholic tolerance is Poland.) At any rate all instances of large minorities consist of Catholics in Protestant societies not vice versa. Such cases lie along the continental frontier of the two confessions and comprise a minority Catholic south facing a majority Protestant north. An important point concerns the qualitative difference made by the size of these minorities, which has been between 30 per cent and 40 per cent over most of post-Reformation history. A qualitative difference is also made by the fact of territorial concentration. A territorial concentration in southern areas has meant that such minorities almost constitute societies in their own right. The sociological consequences of this are quite distinct from those societies where Catholics have by virtue of emigration risen to 10 per cent – 12 per cent (England) or 25 per cent (the U.S.A.) and where they are dispersed geographically throughout the population. This pattern may perhaps be labelled the 'mixed' pattern and it is best exemplified in Holland, Germany and Switzerland. It could also be labelled the 60:40 pattern because this is the kind of proportion that gives rise to characteristic consequences for social organization in general and secularization in particular. The principal consequence is that society is politically organized on a partly confessional basis, but both extremist and secularist politics are rendered less likely because the social position of the Catholic Church inclines it to centre left. There are lots of other concomitant consequences such as a status skew in favour of Protestants and Catholic exclusion from the national myth, but for the moment I only wish to indicate the bare outline of a broad category.

So far then I have described two categories: total monopoly with perhaps enclaves of localized dissidence, and large-scale rival monopolies on the 60:40 model. The next category makes a further qualitative leap in the direction of pluralism. It is exemplified by England and it exists in a modified and even more pluralistic form in Australia, New Zealand and Canada.[4] In England a pattern was early established of a state church partially counterbalanced by a substantial bloc of dissent dispersed in the population at large up to a proportion of about 20 per cent. The prior existence of such a dispersed group meant that even when a residual Catholicism expanded from a low point of about 2 per cent it gradually approximated yet another dissenting denomination. The Protestant dissenters only achieved mild variations in strength area by area and were first concentrated in middle status groups and later, with the onset of industrialization in the 'respectable' working class. The Catholics, being mainly migrants, were located at somewhat lower levels. The fact of territorial dispersal and relative concentration at particular status levels had very important sociological consequences, but at this juncture I merely note a type: a state church confronted by varieties of Protestant dissent variously distributed through the status system, and a Catholic form of dissidence roughly approximating the sociological condition of the Protestant dissenters. The result has been a form of moderate political division, with all kinds of religious dissidence, Catholic, Methodist or Jew, ranged on the centre or moderate left, thus increasing the tendency to moderation and excluding any militant secularism.

The next category exemplifies the final qualitative leap to pluralism: America. The church is finally unhinged from the state and every ex-church approximates the condition of dissent. As in England certain religious bodies achieve relatively greater concentration at given status levels and in particular areas but the basic pattern is one of competing multiple alternatives in every area and at every level. Some ex-churches may be *primus inter pares*, notably the Presbyterians and Episcopalians, but they are much smaller than their lower status rivals. The denominations of the middle ranks, untouched by a history of establishment, like the Methodists and Baptists, form the largest religious bodies, Catholicism excepted. Apart from being concentrated in the middle ranks they also become capable of linking very high status and very low status groupings, an achievement of which they are incapable in the British situation. Catholicism approximates the model of universal competing dissent, just as it approximates the denominational model in England. Competition is established, and perhaps 'established' is the right word because collectively the numerous denominations, especially the Protestants, form a variety of cultural 'establishment', albeit outside the official nexus of church and state. The consequence is that just as competitive pluralism is 'established' in the religious realm so to it is 'established' in the political realm. American society does not split into warring groups but into competing, mutually tolerant parties each differentially supported by the various denominations, with the 'conservative' religion of Catholicism on the politically progressive side of the divide (O'Brien 1969). This further moderates any leftward tendency, which is indeed already moderated by Protestant individualism. The balance thus provided to the overall system is the same balance which marks the English and 'mixed' patterns: in all of them the main 'conservative' church is not the church of the élite or of the majority and

B

therefore reinforces both the left and the moderation of the left. In this way the sociological position of the Catholic Church in all Protestant societies has exactly the opposite consequence to that obtaining in countries where Catholicism is the religion of the majority and the élite. Had the Catholic Church allowed *large* Protestant minorities to remain in, for example, France or Czech Lands, then a balancing process could have occurred whereby Protestants colluded with the left in such numbers that religion as such could not be raised as the dividing issue. In the event Protestants simply walked alongside the left, reinforcing it, but unable to ameliorate either its extremism or its tendency to secularism.

However, there are societies which have no Catholic Church and these have been so far omitted from the process of categorization. These societies are those of Lutheran Scandinavia and the Orthodox countries of eastern Europe. The Orthodox countries are highly monopolistic and represent an instance of extreme collusion between church and state. Unfortunately it is difficult to argue about the characteristic consequence of this extreme symbiosis of church and state, partly because variations of the historic Russian solution has been in some degree imposed on almost all the other Orthodox states and partly because most Orthodox societies are profoundly marked by the external domination of the Turks. This latter factor of external domination is so important an influence that all cases of it, Catholic and Orthodox, must be considered separately later. The difficulty raised by the special position of Russia is insoluble, since it is the sole instance of its class and the sociological consequences which it exhibits could be quite contingent. It is quite easy to ask whether the Russian solution would have been at all as necessary as it now appears in retrospect had the Germans not expedited Lenin's journey from Switzerland. Yet there is a kind of socio-logic about the Orthodox solution. Peter the Great made the Orthodox Church a state department and when the revolution came it simply stood Caesaro-Papism on its head. The Orthodox Church was still treated as a department of state but under the autocratic control of an atheist Caesar. Perhaps this is due to the nature of communism or perhaps to the fact that communism was first successful in a Caesaro-Papist society which in turn donated it the Caesaro-Papist imprint in reverse. Or perhaps, given the anti-pluralist nature of communism, it was relatively likely to make its first breakthrough in a society with an anti-pluralist tradition. The issue cannot be settled, but the logic of the Russian case remains plausible. This logic simply eliminates the possibility of a pluralist political regime, and religion is forced to be the one residual channel of political and psychic opposition. This in turn both reinforces the intransigent attitude of the state and accentuates the theological conservation of the Church. Society is secularized; the Church is not.

The Scandinavian case seems to present intractable evidence against the typical consequences of religious pluralism formulated in respect of previous categories. Of course, Scandinavia, in common with the Orthodox countries, includes countries where religion and repressed nationalism have reinforced one another, most recently in Finland but also in nineteenth century Norway.[5] These might be subsumed under the category of instances where external domination prevents intense internal divisions arising in which religion is a major issue of contention.[6] There would be some justification for this, but there are elements in the Scandinavian pattern which link it with the English pattern. It is in relation to Scandinavia that the existence of a Protestant as distinct from a Catholic church-state nexus becomes an important factor. Protestant churches, especially Lutheran and Anglican ones, are more subject to the state than the Catholic church and for that reason adapt themselves more rapidly to changes in the character of the state. They are also impregnated with an individualism which does not promote organic oppositions or united institutional stands: the attitudes of believers achieve a political dispersal and incoherence rooted in the operations of individual conscience. Hence as the establishment becomes more liberal or socialist the church adapts itself to the new situation and only retains the strictly doctrinal and subjective sphere of faith as its sole prerogative. This adaptibility is reinforced by cells of lay initiative *within* the Lutheran church e.g. Haugeanism, corresponding to the social position of Methodism in the English context.[7] The widespread existence of these cells within a Protestant and incipiently individualistic context make Scandinavia more a weak case of Anglo-American pluralism than a subvariant of the Catholic pattern. The bureaucratic centralism of the basic frame to which the church-state symbiosis belongs does however reassert itself in that social democracy, once successful, has constituted a new establishment and one which likes to control the church in the traditional manner. Anti-clericalism did appear, more especially in Sweden,—an instance where religion had little connection with *repressed* nationalism—but it was rapidly moderated once the church adapted and socialist control was achieved.

So much then for the initial categories which I wish to present. They are, as I have pointed out, based on degrees of pluralism, maximal in the American case, minimal in the Russian (or Orthodox) case. I have by implication suggested that religious pluralism is strongly associated both with the stability of pluralistic democratic regimes and religious monopoly with the incidence of militant 'secular religions'. The analysis has turned not simply on pluralism but on the size of religious minorities, on whether or not they are territorially dispersed and on the nature of their exclusion from the traditional élite. It may however be asked whether secularization is switched one way or another *merely* in terms of such formal social properties as ratios and structural locations. If Catholicism stands on the right where it is the sole religion and the élite religion, and on the centre or left when it is the religion of a minority partially or wholly excluded from the élite, it may seem that social location is all that matters. So before proceeding to a more extended analysis of the socio-logic stemming from my categories something further requires to be said about the inherent character of given religions as well as their location.

The character of a given religion matters a great deal. For example the whole preceding analysis implies that a Catholic or Orthodox monopoly creates a militant counter-image of itself. The nexus of French Enlightenment doctrines resembles a Catholicism inverted and the secular religions produced by France are sometimes a form of Catholicism without Christianity. Moreover though a church adapts to a minority situation it does so by a selective use of its own basic deposit of belief and so doing imprints its character on the minority response. The history of the German centre party exhibits this, and the peculiar resistance of an authoritarian church to all forms of totalitarianism which inhibit its own authority is just one instance of the way the belief or ethos of a church mutates and colours whatever may be the functional logic of its social position. In a minority situation which pushes it towards radicalism the Catholic Church will selectively utilize the universalist aspect of its ideology and translate catholicity into universal rights. In a majority situation high status Protestant churches, which were originally formed in the forge of radical democracy and protest, will selectively emphasise those aspects of belief consonant with individual achievement.

There is more to it however than these potent mirror images and selective mutations. The incidence of pluralism and democracy is related to the incidence of those religious bodies which are themselves *inherently* pluralistic and democratic. Indeed, such bodies sometimes symbolically foreshadow the possibility of radical democracy and pluralism before it can be realized on the political plane. Denominational Protestantism contains varied anticipations of democratic form, which are organizational in the Calvinist instance and more directly theological perhaps in later evangelicalism. The doctrine of election originally framed the psychic confidence of a militant counter-élite but gradually broadened out into an evangelical offer of grace to all. The concept of free grace can run in parallel to the political notion of universal rights. Similarly democratic denominational forms which accept the existence of other varied expressions of the same religious truth are highly consonant with tolerance and democracy. Such foreshadowings and congruences do not lead automatically to religio-political alliances of a democratizing nature but they do create felt and symbolic congruences around which generalized democratic sentiment can form. Democratization is eased even where democratic religious bodies lie partly athwart the political vanguard of democracy. Hence democratic mobilization either does not have to take a secular form (e.g. England) or else may itself take on religious colouring (e.g. the social gospel in America) (Smith 1965). The organizational practices of Protestant nonconformity, even when the disciplined ascesis of such bodies has carried them upward towards the establishment, provide a practical forum of lay participation rhetoric and democratic experience which can be redeployed in the political realm. Semmel (1974) illustrates the kind of congruences, preparations and redeployments I have in mind. So also does the discussion of Arminianism in Lipset (1969).

Such bodies, marked by voluntarism, pluralism and democratic participation, are much more prevalent in the Anglo-American situation than elsewhere. Indeed, their incidence almost runs *pari-passu* with the degree of pluralism exhibited in the categories outlined: universal in America, very extensive in Canada and Australia, fairly extensive in England, and only implicit or else on a small scale in Scandinavia. Perhaps one might also include breakaway neo-Calvinist elements in the Mixed pattern since these both contain implicit Methodist emphases and a heavy strain of political populism e.g. in Holland. Even when Protestant evangelicalism appears on the right, as in Alberta, in the American south, in Northern Ireland and South Africa, it contains a populist emphasis, a stress on equality *within* the group and an anti-establishment charge of some power. This is partly because it recognizes no fundamental authority outside the Bible and assimilates itself to the covenant myth of Israel. The same elements can also appear in a left or liberal context, as for example in Wales and in the Haugean movement. Only one further point needs be made about such democratic and pluralist religious forms: they arrive too late in certain contexts to constitute a crucial factor comparable to the counter-élite mobilization which linked Calvinism to incipient capitalism or to provide the lower-status mobilization that associated evangelicalism with populist democracy. In Russia and in Latin America democratic and individualistic Protestantism arrived late in the process and could not have an important effect, apart that is from the usual consequences of Protestant self-discipline. The importance of the secularization of evangelical Protestantism is that in a wide variety of contexts it enabled the initial mobilization of status groups to occur in a religious framework and could the more easily do this because it was separated from the church-state nexus and congruent with egalitarian populist ideology. Sometimes of course the mobilization of a status group overlapped the mobilization of a regional consciousness, as in Wales, in which case the religious format might extend to cover a wide range of statuses reaching unusually far down in the status system. But that possibility (which Protestant evangelicalism shares with Catholicism and other religions) needs to be explored later in connection with the general analysis of regional awareness and religion. Where regional awareness and nonconformity ally, a whole sub-culture may be democratized. So much then for a necessary aside on the independent impact of different types of religion.

I can now proceed to work out the socio-logic of the basic categories in more detail. So doing I shall inevitably repeat certain of the elements already included in the statement of the basic categories, and some of them must be repeated again when I deal with the differentiation process. Such elements are not just part of a system of formal definitions or descriptions, but bunched causal chains, all playing constantly into each other over time, and it will be clear from the foregoing analysis that I think the degree and type of pluralism attained when the initial 'frame' is set up has a crucial influence over subsequent events. That 'frame' is my cut-off point and another analysis is required as to why a particular frame comes to dominate in a given society. In order the better to expound the internal logic of these various frames I will analyse five universes of relationships: first I take the Anglo-American and Scandinavian group, second the Catholic group, including regimes which have passed through or remain in a right-wing phase, third the communist regimes, fourth the 'mixed' group, and fifth cultures subjected to external domination. One word of warning may be useful. It is that different processes can produce the same consequence in some given respect such as overall level of practice, and similar processes can produce different consequences. A particular condition in this or that society with regard to amount of belief or attitude to religious socialization in the schools cannot be cited as disproof of a particular part of my argument. The whole pattern has to be explained by the application of *all* the facets of my argument and proof or disproof must take all those parts into account.

PROTESTANT PLURALISM: AMERICA TO SCANDINAVIA

The Anglo-American and Scandinavian pattern provides a good basis for comparisons internal to itself. This is because it is Protestant in broad character, especially so with regard to the initial frame and because its differing degrees of pluralism are not *primarily* based on religious enclaves occupying special territories but on religious alternatives differentially associated with different status levels and different politics. The pattern also possesses certain common characteristics of a remarkably uniform kind, even though those characteristics are not exclusive. It is obvious for example that these societies possess fairly stable liberal democratic regimes of a parliamentary kind, and they do not harbour *massive* historic cleavages which have turned in a major way around the issue of religion as *such* or the religious control of education. They exhibit cumulative systems of legitimation rather than alternative systems. They are not marked by anti-clericalism or large-scale secular religions such as communism. Yet within the general characteristics there exist variations of a highly significant kind.

Let me begin the Protestant comparisons with America as the most pluralist culture of all and recapitulate the formal characteristics of American religion. The American pattern is federalist both in politics and religion. Religion is formally excluded from school and state. The number of sects is high and participation is high. Certain denominations are capable of including large segments of the working class and/or of being predominantly working class. The intelligentsia is marginally more left and less inclined to participation than its status equivalents and is strung out along a political spectrum running from the sociological and humanist disciplines to the technical and agricultural disciplines. Successive legitimations, whether initially leaning in a religious or secular direction, are seen as cumulative rather than conflicting. The Churches play a large role in the interstices of society, englobing those institutions for care and welfare which are elsewhere under the aegis of the state. The clergy are assimilated to the concept of rival entrepreneurs running varied religious services on a mixed laissez-faire and oligopolistic model: their status however is usually not high. Religious styles constantly adapt and accept vulgarization in accordance with the stylistic tendencies of their varied markets, sometimes in such a way as to weaken both content and intellectual articulation. Fundamentalist religion retains its grip on the major periphery i.e. the South, and though associated with the right also fosters populist tendencies. So much for the external, formal situation. How do we make the analysis more organic?

Any characterization of the United States must emphasize the fact that it represents a very high degree of differentiation in that church is formally separated from state and even religion from school, and yet the overall social order is legitimated by a pervasive civil religion. The differentiating impulse presses a sociological retro-rocket, and in America this is exemplified by its civil religion as described by Robert Bellah and William Herberg. And just as the civil religion has been described by Bellah so too the differentiation has been magisterially analysed by Parsons (1968)[9] That civil religion also illustrates a basic Protestant tendency, which is the cumulative character of legitimation whatever the logical contradictions of the component parts. In America enlightenment and evangelicalism colluded whereas in France enlightenment and Catholicism collided. But then, of course, the American banner was unfurled against foreign rule not against internal reaction.

America took a British sociological invention, the dissenting denomination, and made it universal: not all at once, since tolerance came dripping slow to the Calvinist elect and establishment remained in many states somewhile after the Revolution. Sociological experiments occur because one or two crucial instances have slipped under the net of the prohibiting factors and the Baptists of Rhode Island were just a crucial instance. The dissenting denomination provided a symbolic anticipation, in its separation from the state, in its implicit pluralism and in the anticipatory hints of democracy. If Christ was head of the Church then the Monarch was not and if the subjects of Christ were his by election then by a series of mutations America was set on the road to subjective choice and free political elections. A change in one order of symbols builds up multiple mutations and a new model is imprinted on man's mind to be taken up and implemented in different circumstance when structural opportunities permit. In this way a change in the doctrine of the Eucharist or a shift in church order has implications across centuries. And this again is characteristic of Protestantism: a doctrinal switch at point A, nameable at this point of time, becomes a switch of feeling and organization in a different sphere to which different names and labels are attached. Not only did the participant democracy of the gathered Church imply democratic political election but the American offer of grace to all universalized salvation. The Wesleyan 'For all, for my saviour died' received a new authorized version in the welcome offered by the Statue of Liberty to the millions of immigrants. This is secularization, but it is also the translation of salvation to take up the idea of a social inclusion and universal civic rights. When everybody is first equal in sin they may also be equal in the tincture of civility. This is how evangelicalism is able to evolve towards the social gospel, though within the limits of individualist understanding. Again the element of subjective choice in the denominational model, as rephrased by Americanism, can become a universal stress on feeling and spontaneity and eventually an emphasis on genuineness. An objection to a particular ritual can be made into a universal objection to manners and codes and institutional constraints. Such objections are by now the common anti-form of English and American culture, but with very different sociological consequences so far as religious participation is concerned. Both cultures share an anti-intellectual populism, but in one the populists are actively inside the churches and in the other largely out.

This is because where denominational dissent is a minor motif as in England, it must acquire a specific status image and this will have to be the image of the first stratum to challenge the old order i.e. the independent entrepreneur and independent artisan[10] I discuss this point below in relation to Britain, but so far as America is concerned the universalization of dissent permits religion to take on as many images as there are social faces. The drug store of religious masks is unlimited. Naturally, there is a marginal sales resistance amongst those most distant from the social apex but this will not develop into the massive rejection found in the continental working class. Furthermore, the single apex is so vaguely defined and so varied from area to area that religion as such cannot be identified with any social or class enemy (B. R. Wilson 1968). In one area Baptists may occupy the perceived apex and in another Presbyterians and Episcopalians and Jews. The overal apex is too high and lost in a vague rhetorical cloud to be easily assaulted. Moreover, as Herberg (1955) suggested, each new migrant group might lose its language in the melting pot, but this gave additional motive to retain religion as badge of identity (cf. also Berger 1961). Thus all the ex-churches, Italian, Polish, Greek, approximated the denominational model. Even the ethnic church of Judaism was remoulded by American culture along denominational lines, and the result is Reform Judaism. Because Britain had had an established church it also retained a largely Orthodox Judaism. A church in America is a denomination. And in the psychic and social space so created the tiniest sect or utopian community may enter in. The model of religion implies infinite variation, even the existence of models which are inimical to the dominant ethos, such as the theocracy of the Church of Mormon. Experimental religion allows all kinds of religious experiment.

By the same token the universality of experimental religion implies a pragmatic, experimental model of political activity. Politicians are judged by genuineness—and performance, not political dogma. Insofar as social alienation exists it can organize behind the mask of religion and when a stratum becomes newly self-conscious it will politicize within a religious format. Thus the apathy of the old-time negro Southern Baptist becomes the political militancy of the new-time Southern Baptist. Even a movement to reject the American dream first takes religious form, as for example, the Black Muslims. Most political movements take religious colouring, though without religion acting as a functional alternative to politics as it sometimes does in European contexts e.g. Swedish revivalism. Even the politics of spontaneity itself finds a mystical religious clothing in meditation, ecstasy and the like, to protest against the domination of the Protestant Ethic and the hard-hat Puritan character structure. In this way major shifts become possible by individual contagion and incorporation, not structural oppositions and overturning. The transition to post-modernity and individualistic self-expression can be made by contagion. And insofar as such a transition is socially premature or unrealistic it will be countered by a reassemblage of Protestant Ethic motifs inside the very vehicle of protest e.g. the Meher Baba cult and the Jesus Movement (Anthony and Robbins 1974). Revolt against Puritan religious parents turns back on itself (as James Richardson (1974) has demonstrated) in the form of the religious commune. Religion accompanies American youth on the way out and escorts them part way back in again. Meanwhile the liberalized denominations are identified not as anti-science and organizationally pre-modern but as having capitulated to science and bureaucracy.[11] American religion then comes to operate a feeder system whereby old-fashioned evangelical denominations pull in new recruits and pass them on to liberal bodies (Glock 1968). These then lose members to mystical cults which in turn eventually reassemble behind the Protestant Ethic. So complex do the locations of religion then become that the characteristic structural locations of European religion are partially transcended and selections of religious style are made on an open market in accordance with variations of intimate personal biography. The laisser-faire of choice complements a model of religious organization based on partial merger and partial oligopoly. This is, of course, entirely complementary to the overall image of American society, except that in religion the old laisser-faire joins hands with the new cult of spontaneity. In American religion the past and the future stand together against the present as well as receiving the imprint of the present. Paradoxically, the religion of the future celebrates the 'now' (cf. Martin 1975a).

I have spent time on the American model because it represents a logically pure type and is one of humanity's possible futures. Britain is a 'retarded' type and one of humanity's actualized pasts.

Now in England by contrast the church-state nexus has been maintained and has been stronger in the mid-twentieth century than the mid-nineteenth. This is because dissent has declined and no longer challenges the establishment. Neverthless a limited dissent coexisted over against the established church and picked up certain groups loosened from the traditional structures: independents, craftsmen, artisans, workers in small scale textiles and in the mines, and in the fishing industry. This dissent has not made large-scale inroads into the working class, outside the 'respectable' sector. As in America the Catholic Church has been the religious carrier of ethnicity for many later—and lower— status groups including a segment of the urban working class. This has meant that Jews and Catholics have been in some degree associated with left parties, thus removing the issue of religion *as such* from the arena of political confrontation. The consequent stabilization of limited political conflict and the exclusion of metaphysical issues from that conflict allow legitimations, both secular and religious, to build up cumulatively rather than in competition. When legitimations are cumulative the crown and church are pulled into the circle of legitimations and are not put in fundamental question. However, the collusion of church, crown and upper status styles *does* prevent religion crossing the status divide to the majority of the working class and prevents it adapting to each status group in the American manner. 'Status images' of particular denominations become progressively more and more fixed and cannot be shifted: Anglican—upper class, middle class and deferential; dissenting—upper working to lower middle, artisan and then—later—social service professions. And up to 1920 these images were affixed to Conservative and Liberal labels, and political and religious fortunes moved in partial accord (Currie and Gilbert 1976). Each fixing of a status image progressively delimits the potential constituency of a given denomination and the practice of religion *in general* is defined as not appropriate to the mass of the working class. So while religion crosses the political divide even as it does in America and is further assisted in so doing by the presence of lower-status urban Catholicism it does not make the massive inroads across the cultural divide(s) which it achieves in the conditions of American pluralism. Religious practice is defined as partly connected with alien authority and alien cultural styles, whereas in America it is set free to run along the complex lines of social geology without the drag of such negative definitions. Moreover, these same constellations have diverse effects on the school system. Because America is *so* pluralist it cannot allow any one denominational influence of educational socialization and also must assert the aspect of social unity in a secular manner through the state schools. Because England only embodies a limited pluralism it can allow its unity to be channelled initially through denominational schools, and the state system can incorporate a modicum of 'agreed' religion within its own schools as these gradually come to predominate over the denominational ones. English schools 'had an agreed syllabus' in religion, at least till recently.

As we turn to Scandinavia we find initially a much stronger state church system with pluralism operative only with respect to 'internal' dissent and (rather later) quite weak free churches. There is no Catholicism to affect the urban working class; and no Anglo-Catholicism in the state church to counterbalance the liberal-free church nexus. The overall result is that the onset of social democracy is associated with noticeable elements of anti-clericalism and of Marxism. A weak echo appears of the 'Latin' pattern of left-right confrontation in which religion is included as a 'package' element on the right. However, various factors ameliorate this confrontation. First, Scandinavian establishments are Protestant, that is they include individualistic elements not amenable to organic confrontations, and moreover they do not elevate the church as a sacred society above the state. Indeed, the

Scandinavian churches adapt to the state and insofar as the state becomes social democratic they adapt yet again. Second, the unitary elements originally expressed by organic, homogeneous religious establishments are retranslated in terms of a new social democratic homogeneity. Third, certain movements of cultural revival and national identity, gave the church a positive relation to the sense of national heritage: Grundvigianism in Denmark and Haugeanism in Norway. Indeed, both these movements contained the Protestant 'seed' of voluntary association and participation, and created a positive image of religion, without however enabling the church to cross the class and status divide so far as regular practice was concerned. So far as Norway was concerned the association of Haugeanism with national revival and liberal democracy created a party of the centre which stabilized the political system in a democratic direction especially so when the left might have gone communist after the first world war. The existence of Haugeanism and of a kind of church-nation sentiment meant that the left needed to appeal to the centre and to such sentiments in order to succeed, and by the time it had succeeded it had accepted its own moderated self-image. Once in control it preferred to control religion in the traditional manner rather than to alienate it. So perhaps one may argue that the limited pluralism of the traditional Scandinavian society allowed tolerances to subsist which repeated themselves once Social Democracy had taken that society over. And since religion was a matter of cultural sentiment not a metaphysic or an ecclesiastical theocracy it remained a tolerable repository of national and historic feeling, which remains expressed for example in a very high practice of the *rites de passage*. What is perhaps particularly interesting is that although industrialization proceeded at various paces, fast and abrasive in Norway, slow and gentle in Denmark, nevertheless the overall political and cultural result was very similar. The figures are startlingly uniform: 95 per cent or so confirmed, 5 per cent or so practising on a given Sunday.

When we place America, England (plus Canada and Australia) and Scandinavia alongside we have a set of subdivisions and also a universe of viable comparisons. A glance at the table given later will assist such comparisons and some of them are worth particular stress. England is allied with Scandinavia in the following respects: a crown, a state church, a social democratic party, a low level of participation, particularly among the working class, and a national sentiment connected vaguely with the national church and the *rites de passage*. Established churches in England and Scandinavia (largely) have a university educated clergy—less so now in England than in Scandinavia—and are liturgically rich and traditional.[12] This is associated with a non-practising working class which remains culturally alienated from the mores and sensibilities of the church-going sectors. England is by contrast allied with America in the fact that religion has been associated with most points of the political spectrum and has never seriously been the bone of political contention as such. Furthermore, this process is assisted in England, the white Commonwealth and in America by a Catholic Church operative in lower status groups and to the left of the politics traditionally associated with Protestants. England is also like America in that its intelligentsia is not particularly anti-religious, though in England it can be argued that the intelligentsia is both less and more believing than status equivalents i.e. attitude to religion are more definitely articulated.

All these varied characteristics, placing England half-way between Scandinavia and the U.S.A. (and Canada and Australia half-way between England and the U.S.A.), are associated with degrees of pluralism. If you take participation and pluralism they run in a direct positively correlated line from the U.S.A. to Canada and Australia, to England, to Scandinavia. Indeed figures are respectively about 40+ per cent, 25+ per cent, 10+ per cent and 5 per cent (or less) per Sunday. If you take anti-clerical sentiment and clerical status they both rise together in the reverse direction *for the same reasons*. Clerks have low status and large congregations in the U.S.A., high status and small congregations in Sweden. Likewise the incidence of Social Democracy and Communism rises along the same continuum. The highest figures for Communist voting are to be found in Iceland and Finland: 18 per cent[13].

Social Democracy is absent from the U.S.A.: present in Australia, Canada, England and Scandinavia; Communism has moderate influence in Scandinavia, more particularly in Finland, Sweden and Iceland. All these consistent positive and negative relationships belong together, but so also do the more complex relationships such as the right wing populism of the American religious peripheries, the left or centre politics of the English religious peripheries, and the centre or right politics of the Scandinavian religious peripheries. The American periphery represent an older and traditional America partly isolated by shifts towards a more sceptical and secular political élite; the English periphery represents ethnic minorities pushed toward liberalism and socialism by the giant conservatism of the Anglican Church and the English 'centre'; the Scandinavian peripheries mainly stay to the centre or right over against the dominance of the social democratic, semi-secular cosmopolitan centre.[14]

We have still to put the linking needle through all these relationships, and it is Protestantism in different degrees of pluralism. Unhinge the centre, make politics and religion federal, separate and dissociate religion from social authority and high culture, let religion adapt to every status group through every variety of pullulating sectarianism. The result is that nobody feels ill at ease with his religion, that faith is distributed along the political spectrum, that the church is never *the* axis of dispute. *But* unity has to be preserved through a school system which keeps religious plurality out and by a national myth which represents a common denominator of all faiths: one nation under God, not under Catholicism or Anglicanism or Presbyterianism. On the other side, retain the centre and even substantial dissent cannot destroy the image which links practice with respectability and conservatism. Crown and church, insofar as they suffuse the society as a whole, are reduced to the level of a vague national sentiment and the *rites de passage*. And insofar as church and state remain unitary there is the possibility of some elements of anti-clericalism, some collusion of religion and the right, and of the church and the crown, some minor eruptions of 'Christian parties', some attachment to a secularist Social Democracy, even marginally a secularist Communism.

CATHOLIC MONOPOLY

I come now to the socio-logic of Catholic societies.

The discussion of each of the subvariants of Protestant pluralism has turned, above all, around the relative ease with which a Protestant society may be stabilized by cumulative legitimation. In Catholic cultures such cumulative legitimations are very much less likely, except in those instances to be discussed later, where *external* pressure or domination has joined Catholic religion and national aspiration within an indissoluble union. I am inclined to attribute this difference to the independent influence of religion itself in that for a society to be Catholic has *this* set of consequences while for a society to be Protestant has *that* set of consequences. But the difference may be re-phrased by regarding Catholicism in the Tridentine period as a kind of 'reaction formation' whereby the 'loose' organicism of medieval and late medieval times is challenged and therefore hardened.[15] The 'natural' union of theology and philosophy, politics and religion, crown and church, religious discipline and social control was thereby turned into a forced and more rigid union. Each attack on this union bred a greater rigidity, which can be seen, not as the true 'intrinsic' nature of a Catholicism possessed of an independent sociological power, but as a sociological consequence of an organic system trying like a limpet to defend itself by clinging with more and more intense desperation to the rock, in this instance the rock of Peter. The wider effect of this 'reaction' was to transfer all the unions of function mentioned above to inappropriate and resistant contexts.

It does not matter particularly for this analysis whether stress is laid on the independent causal impact of Catholicism or on Tridentine Catholicism as a consequence of organicism under pressure, because two developments are abundantly clear which persist throughout the modern period up to recent times. One is the gradual inversion of the symbiosis of crown and church so that the latter becomes subordinate to the former. The rigidity of Catholicism was first a militant posture which became tranformed into a subordinate posture. The most obvious instance of this subordinate posture is provided by the expulsion of the most militant of papal orders, the Society of Jesus, more particularly for political meddling. Enlightened autocracy simply took over the autocracy of the church for its own purposes. In sociological jargon the agency of socialization was thoroughly subordinated to the agency of imperative coordination. This crucial 'secularization'[16] which affected the church philosophically as well as in its institutional role, assisted and made inevitable the next development i.e. the union of church with the political right in conditions where society had split into intermittently warring halves. Since revolution had to break a single system which it identified as one throughout all its corrupt parts, and since revolution included a strong component of individualism which it opposed to organicism *per se*, the symbiosis of Catholicism with the right wing fraction of society was inevitable. The official militancy which had masked the subordinate posture of the church under the heel of enlightenment despotism was now transferred to the right and reactivated as a weapon against the seemingly indissoluble and 'natural' union of radicalism and atheism. In Protestant societies by contrast there was no such 'reaction formation' to carry forward: the church was based on subordination from the start, it had no independent theory of its social paramountcy and it was itself the seed-bed of the individualism loosening the organic structure which in formal terms it might still seem to support.

This digression is necessary because so much turns on the 'nature' of Catholicism and Protestantism, however we may unpack such labels and reassemble them in our sociological kitbags. Had the Reformation triumphed in France, as it nearly did, the sociological and historical consequences for European history and development would have been fantastically different. Few knife-edges have carried such a burden of multiple and vast alternatives. The principal alternative is, of course, the one represented by the Catholic category now under discussion and its system of clashing, rival legitimations.

In Catholic societies there arises a social split, with Catholics and legitimists on one side and other groups, either newly ascendent or previously persecuted, or both, on the other. Even groups which in Protestant societies are mildly religious in nature, such as freemasons, become secularist under the impact of this split and are held up as malignant symbols in Catholic demonology. Even a religious body, such as the French Protestant Church, may ally itself with irreligion under precisely the same pressure. Hence the extraordinary phenomenon of communist voting in some sectors of the Reformed Church. A religious faith like Judaism newly released into the bloodstream of society is necessarily viewed as dangerous and secularist; and may over time conform at least in part to just that image. The radical role played by Catholicism in Protestant societies, sometimes in conjunction with minority nonconformity, is, in this context, inverted, but with the lines of force, tension and repulsion enormously greater. Protestantism, Jewry, freemasonry and indeed any kind of free Catholicism or a philosophy like Krausism, are all thrust to the left of the line separating legitimists and loyal Catholics from the rest. Even attempts from the international Catholic centre to ameliorate such blockages, or ultramontane appeals to Rome on the ground that it represents ideas transcending such merely local alliances, cannot break the pattern until other forces and time supervene.[17] Papalism is stronger than Rome, though the special position of the Pope as a temporal ruler under precisely the same pattern of pressures, may mean that local papalism in France or Spain or elsewhere and the local politics of Rome persistently reinforce each other.

The existence of rival societies within a single social whole creates a violence of expression and clarity of difference absent from the Protestant pattern. The symbols of Catholicism, above all the priesthood, but also the church building, become objects of physical and verbal assault. A Protestant society may allow Llandaff Cathedral to fall down, but local defenders of the sacred ministry and the sacred building in France and Spain have had time and again to prevent violent destruction, and not always successfully, as the fate of Cluny illustrates. Again, while in Protestant societies intellectuals spread along a gentle and un-divided continuum of moderate faith and reluctant doubt, in Catholic societies there is a clear split between militant faith and militant unbelief, with the latter frequently dominant. Moreover the very notion of an 'intellectual' belongs to this specifically Catholic pattern and suggests people given to the elaboration of large scale social and philosophical systems parallel to and in rivalry with Catholicism. Such systems may even reflect Catholicism in inverted form. Saint-Simonianism and Comteanism have borrowed heavily from Catholicism in the very act of opposing it, and Durkheimianism represents the organic idea and an appraisal of it from a secularist point of view (cf. Charlton 1963, and Simon 1963).

All attempts to cross the divide are doomed to failure, because each 'cross bred' individual or philosophy is defined as traitorous and confusing. Those who cross the divide are necessarily too few to break the deadlock or the image of deadlock, and to that extent their number is even further reduced. A Lamennais or a

Father Vincent cannot be successful.[18] Such a split must be end-
lessly reproductive of itself: curé against schoolmaster, even father
against mother. These examples suggest what must be the most
ferocious arena of conflict: socialization. In Protestant societies a
parson may have some mild rivalry with a schoolmaster and a
father may be less practising than a mother, but in general they
cooperate around a melange of religious symbols and vague civil
religion. In Catholic societies it is vital who shapes the image and
controls the loyalty of the next generation; and where that issue
is vital the split must necessarily be transferred from generation to
generation. Only baptism can cross such a divide and the names of
children may still indicate to which side the baptized child has been
truly dedicated—either to a traditional Catholicism or to a secularist civic religion. The attacks on religious orders in Catholic societies are constantly reactivated, less because they are not 'modern'
than because they are the shock troops of Catholic socialization.

The social schizophrenia is transferred to whatever other
fissures appear whether between classes or between regional
loyalties. France, Spain and Italy are, of course, the classic arena
of exacerbated class conflict and in the two former countries
regional conflict is heavily reinforced by religion. Both types of
fissure are more intense than in Protestant societies and the role of
religion more explicit, direct and one-sided. The relationship of
Brittany, La Vendée and Hérault to a secularist Paris has no
parallel in Protestant societies even though the broad tension of
centre and periphery is a sociological constant. In Catholic
societies the sociological constants of local identity versus metropolitan influence, and of class interest, each receive heavy reinforcement, which both strengthens Catholicism where its
strength can spiral positively and weakens it where the reverse
occurs. Indeed, such polarizations and spirals of strength and
weakness can occur within the middle class itself, creating
professions with traditionalist images and others with laicist
images. On the whole those professions having a functional
overlap with religion may turn laicist, whereas in Protestant
societies they are suffused with a vague, religious motivation.
Something here turns on what social 'stage' is under consideration, because very general perceptions of violent divides and
sharply contrary images may over time bring deviant sectors of
rival classes to conform more nearly to the broader image of

association with or dissociation from religion. The bourgeois secularity of one period may gradually succumb to the bourgeois religiosity of the next. By the same token specific categories of the working class may acquire deeply secularist images, as for example in the extractive industries, whereas in Protestant society, more especially in the Anglo-American as compared with the Scandinavian situation, they are more likely to adhere to religious dissent. All macro-conflicts are strongly repeated at the local level. Thus the local hierarchy, whatever form it may take, is isomorphic with religious practice or religious indifference. To take but one analysis, Lison-Tolosana's 'Belmonte de los Caballeros', the economic practices of 'pudientes' and 'propietarios' can be seen as impugning their religious practices. Not even exemplary charity, or more general notions of honour and worth unrelated to class, can really heal this division. From this derives the relative frequency of militant secularization in parts of rural Spain, France and Italy as compared with the rural areas of Protestant societies where mobilization may take the colour of dissenting religion. (I am arguing that in 'alienated' sectors, like extractive industry or depressed agriculture, secularism plays a role in Catholic societies analogous to the role of dissent in Protestant societies).

Other manifestations of the fundamental split obviously occur in the spheres of trade unionism and political parties, insofar as confessional unions and parties make their appearance, or parties which attract hierarchical blessing or anathema. These can be dealt with more appropriately below with respect to differentiation. The object at this point is to establish the logic of a fundamental contrast between the sociological consequences of Protestant pluralism and of Catholic monopoly as these proliferate from sector to sector, above all in the field of global legitimations. In the one instance a reactive organicism carries forward all the multiple functions of religion into a context where they would be 'normally' in partial dissolution. In the other instance a weaker organicism either dissociates from the state (the U.S.A.), or submits to it (Scandinavia), or both (England), and thereby accepts the slow process of loss of function with only 'minor' reactions e.g. the concept of a 'Christian' America as proposed by late nineteenth century Protestantism or the concept of a Christian society as revived by Anglo-Catholicism.[19]

CATHOLIC EXCEPTIONS

There remain two problems: the existence of partial exceptions
to the pattern as outlined and the fact that the vicious spiral does
in the end partially unwind. The former problem can be taken
first. There are two kinds of exception to the pattern as outlined
above. The first occurs where Catholicism is the symbol of a
repressed or recently repressed culture: Eire, Poland, Croatia, the
Basque country, Brittany. In such instances conflict is external,
and internal conflict over religion is muted or obliterated by the
paramount need for unity. The second kind of exception is
provided by Belgium and maybe also by Austria, though conflict
over religion in inter-war Austria was on the classic scale and it
might be more appropriate to consider Austria under the rubric
concerning the more general unwinding of the spiral. If we take
Belgium first it confirms the analysis already made because it
shows (a) the union of Catholic and liberal forces required to fight
external domination, and (b) the continuous power of that pattern
of union once set up when the nation eventually emerged in 1830.
Indeed, it confirms yet another generalization, which is that when
Catholicism is associated with a sub-culture under pressure and in
receipt of metropolitan hauteur the union of church and social
fabric is intensified. Flanders is exactly a case of this kind. So in a
sense there is no problem, because the exception merely illustrates
the rule. The pattern initially set up is one of muted conflict and
even when the crucial issues of church and state, law and religion,
education and confessional socialization enter the arena they fit
within that pattern.

However there is more to be said on the issue because Belgium
is a case of almost evenly balanced bi-polarity, and this creates
divisions so large that unity is imperative. A system on so neat a
see-saw, which nevertheless has historically aspired to view itself
as one system, cannot afford conflicts which tear it apart. In the
French case bi-polarity was heavily skewed—what chance had
Brittany? Each side in the overall social conflict thought victory
possible and believed that victory was coterminous with the
salvation of France. In Belgium bi-polarity is genuine, no victory
is possible and if one side did win Belgium would clearly be
destroyed. The situation is compounded by the fact that until

recently the economic skew which *used* to exist against Flanders was exacerbated by the devaluation of Flemish, but this has the effect not only of entrenching Catholicism further as the symbol of regional resistance but of building up such resistance to the point where it does in fact constitute just that balance of forces which makes unity imperative. Instead of class conflict, with religion as a major issue, there has to emerge something like the Dutch pattern of 'pillarization'.

Austria may be a case of muted conflict or it may be a case of an emergence which is late enough to fit into an analysis of the period of decreasing spirals of conflict. The inter-war period was marked by classic polarization: massively organized political sub-cultures, a Marxistic quasi-religion on the Social Democratic left, para-military action and even, in 1934, civil war. Yet since the second world war Marxism has diminished in influence on the left and the influence of clericalism has diminished *pari passu* on the right. Perhaps the association of Marxism with Russia, and its immediate threatening presence, and the association of clericalism with Dollfuss, each contributed to a loosening of ideological positions and to the removal of the Church as such from the arena of political confrontation. Furthermore the balance of forces both as between black and red strengths and black and red territorial areas made for a balanced hostility within a system of political co-determination. There is one other important element which is the fact that the party of the right is not exclusively identified with 'state bearing elements' i.e. with the natural sources of authority. Indeed in the earlier inter-war phases the leaders of the 'Christian Socials' were neither wealthier nor better educated than their socialist rivals. Thus overall there are various factors which have cumulatively shifted the pattern away from total conflict to a limited contest between rival sub-cultures. Perhaps the key element parallels the Belgian situation in that there is a balance of forces which makes a fight for outright victory not worthwhile. No doubt the shift in the position of the Catholic Church in the international arena assists the process.

The second problem concerned with the unwinding of the vicious spiral is not easily summarized in brief. Given the international nature of the Catholic Church there is a persistent interaction of local and universal considerations, whereby the central tendency of the Church reflects a whole series of cultures at different developmental points and reacts back on them in accordance with the impact of the most crucial pressures. As the church has expanded into more and more cultures where it is associated with minority or third world aspirations it necessarily shifts away from the politics forged by the necessities governing the 'reaction formation' of its classic heartlands. A South Korean[20] or South African situation is characteristic of the new social location crucial to Catholicism and allows theological emphasis to rest on the role of Catholic universality in the onward march of pan-human aspirations. Moreover, the cost of the 'Latin' pattern is increasingly experienced and perceived, and in the South American context, more especially Brazil and Chile, the church sees its survival attendant on dissociation from conservative authority.[21] Indeed in general the church becomes aware that its own specific purposes are endangered by collusion with conservative political pragmatism and its penchant for using the church as an agent of secular apathy. Everywhere the Church moves away from the costs connected with one *particular* political identification, even though the individual faithful may and do retain tendencies more in one direction than another. This generalized perception of 'costs' is an independent sociological pressure on its own account, and is not merely a variable simply dependent on other forces.

Differentiation is itself one of these other forces and must be dealt with below, but there are other local factors reacting back on the overall direction of the Church. One such factor is the widespread discrediting of the right following the second world war. In Italy for example the Catholic Church existed on such a large base that it necessarily included much more than the right, and yet it could only act as the one viable residual legatee of the right provided it leaned in the centre. Again, in France 'Action Française' was destroyed by collaboration; and the association of the Church with patriotic resistance was sufficient to carry it with credit into the post-war period, providing it moved to the centre. In Germany, Catholic opposition to Hitler, reinforced by its centrist traditions, encouraged an alliance of the Church and a very moderate conservatism. So in varied contexts the alliance of Catholicism and the old right was disrupted. The parallel discrediting of the Stalinist left made a shift to the centre less dangerous than it might once have been. Furthermore in each world war, French and Belgian Catholics fought alongside left wingers and old fashioned Republicans and created a sense of common cause overriding political differences. Thus the factor of external threat operated yet again to diminish internal spirals of conflict.

The generalizations applying to the Catholic 'pattern' can be easily summarized. There is substantial social warfare in Catholic cultures to the extent that Catholicism is straightforwardly identified with the antecedent system of authority and to the extent that the balance of forces between regions and generally between opposing strengths is such as to allow either side to think victory possible and worthwhile. On the other hand if Catholicism emerges politically in partial opposition to ruling elements, whether these be aliens or (as in Italy) anti-clerical liberals and if the balance of forces is close, then compromise is more likely. Genuine regional bi-polarity is a further factor in favour of stabilization, precisely because pushing such a conflict too far destroys the nation as a whole. External threats also push internal contestants towards compromise (Germany in the case of France and Belgium, Russia in the case of Austria).

CATHOLIC MONOPOLY OF THE RIGHT

Turning now to statist regimes of the right we encounter again precisely the 'Catholic' pattern, but with the special characteristics found where a pressured Catholic right succeeds in taking over for a period the reins of power. Obvious instances are Spain, Portugal, Croatia, pre-war Fascist Italy, Slovakia,—and, in a sense, the Greece of the Colonels, Hungary under Horthy could also be included. However, a distinction must be made between situations where such statist regimes govern the centre of a large-scale culture e.g. Spain, and where they represent a sub-culture struggling for autonomy as in Croatia and Slovakia. Spain may be taken as paradigmatic of the former situation and a single quotation may indicate in the clearest manner how such a system works itself out on the ground. It describes a town near Saragossa and begins with reference to the practice of upper class women.[22]

In Spain religious practice became a symbol of conformity and a symbol of non-conformity, at least in the period of 1934–1959.

The greater the tension the more Catholics felt the need to show their loyalty and the more covert, repressed tensions displayed themselves specifically in relation to the Church. Now, of course, the Church has partially dissociated itself from the right wing authority, for reasons already partly alluded to. In such regimes the Church tends *initially* to be coextensive at the top with the ruling élite. It is controlled nationally rather than from Rome and is more devotional or 'folk-loric' than theological. The military, who define themselves as national guardians, regard the church as part of the inheritance they exist to guard, and employ it as an agency of socialization and social control. Cadres within the church come into being (the Opus Dei and the Cursillos de christianidad) dedicated to leadership and/or economic development without revolution, and these may have a proto-Protestant ascetic character.

However, various influences loosen the association of church and right-wing state. Often the state desires to use the church in so instrumental a manner that some aspirations to autonomy are awakened. In education, for example, the state may seek straight-forward control rather than one indirectly mediated through the Church. Moreover segments of the Church perceive that there is a cost for its own specific mission in being identified with authority and in representing cultural styles alien to emerging social groups. It responds to differentiation therefore and even initiates it. The priest is the only member of the élite who feels that his role requires an attempt to cross cultural and political divides.[23] In addition the international shifts of the Catholic Church as a whole add new social and intellectual catalysts dissolving the unity of the political right and the Church. The old split between Church and left now reproduces itself as a generation split within the Church itself. However, the Church remains in a quandary since liberalism is historically associated with anti-clericalism, and —more important—offers freedoms which totalitarian movements of the left attempt to utilize for their own purposes. Thus the Church has to edge its way out of the embrace of the right without eventually finding itself suppressed by the left. Where lay democracy is not understood and reform has been long delayed there is a tendency for the first hint of change to engender a rush towards anarchy, and the beneficiaries of anarchy are usually strong men of right or left. The situation in revolutionary Portugal has illustrated all these tendencies. There the Church dissociated itself from the self-defined 'Christian' party, and individual Catholics emerged at most points on the political spectrum. However such opposition to the right as existed in the rather dormant pre-revolutionary hierarchy was of a liberal nature, and therefore confronted by the characteristic dilemmas of liberalism. The growth of anarchy and successive shifts to the left undermined the Church's continuous acceptance of the revolution, especially as the historic spiral of conflict began to appear and accelerate, more specifically centred around a tension between the Catholic north and the more secularist south.[24]

One further point concerning right-wing regimes relates to the place of regional sub-cultures. Where Catholicism is the guardian of a sub-culture within a wider culture it can generally rely on an internal unity induced by the external pressure of the wider society. However, much depends on the political character of the repressive elements in that wider society. If Slovakia feels devalued and dominated by a liberal, secularist Prague it will tend to a right-wing populist identification; similarly so in a Brittany confronting a secularist, radical, homogenizing Paris. On the other hand the Basque movement identified the centre as both inimical to its aspirations and as historically relatively secular. Since the centre was right wing the Basque movement is both Catholic and pushed in a left-ward direction.

SECULAR MONOPOLY OF THE LEFT

The pattern found in statist societies of the right is both repeated and inverted in statist societies of the left. We have seen that in the right-wing pattern the church itself partly initiates the movement towards differentiation from the pressure of authority, but in the left-wing pattern it partly resists that differentiation, which the state pushes forward with 'unnatural' speed. The right wing state endeavours to use religion as a means to a political end and the left wing state endeavours to replace religion by politics. With neither of these aims can religion be fully compliant. The logic of such systems is a logic of power seeking maximization. The Church is at the mercy of secularist élites. In the left-wing state all churches are simultaneously established and disestablished in that power demands they be used as agents of control and also simultaneously deprived of all autonomous efficacy. Religious hierarchy and organization will be tolerated or not tolerated according to this one criterion and the power of appointment and subvention will be used to this single end. The only checks on power are those deriving from the paradox that total control breeds heterodox movements which escape the net of oversight and control. A church of the central regions and the central authority can be used to push against restive peripheral regions. Thus the Russian Orthodox Church has been used against the Uniate areas of the Western Ukraine and the Roumanian Orthodox Church has been deployed against Roumanian ethnic and religious minorities Any church associated with a dissident national sub-culture will bear the brunt of administrative pressure, as for example, Catholicism in Lithuania. (cf. Lane 1974). Thus the Church becomes modern guardian of cultural integrity as well as of individual psychic space.

There are certain sociological constants respecting national identity which are operative in this connection. If the state itself experiences a pressure against its historic unity and identity it will lean on the church to help resist that pressure even though state and church are ideologically opposed. Thus Poland and Roumania both need to retain contact with their historic roots through the Church. A society which *per contra* experiences *dis*unity on account of religion will seek to control and weaken it (e.g. Yugoslavia, Albania) and so too will a society whose religion has been historically cut off from its national myth (e.g. Czech Lands). The above considerations modify but do not weaken the basic impulse of statist societies of the left, which is towards ideological monopoly. Just as the United States represents ideological laissez-faire so left wing societies represent ideological monopoly. This means that all social processes are subject to manipulation, including the formation of values, and it also means that those nearest to the administrative machine will reflect the approved value system most closely. Thus atheism and religion can be measured along a continuum of proximity to and distance from the collective means of administration and control. Administrators, intelligentsia and official agents of socialization are therefore most secular while the marginal and excluded are least. This largely inverts the situation which obtains in statist societies of the right. Faced by such

pressures the official churches tend to remain defensively conservative so far as their internal life is concerned, while the
proscribed and persecuted bodies tend to be eschatological in
outlook, which means in effect that they espouse a sectarian form
of religious conservatism. The religious bodies closest the official
ethos are absorbed by it with relative ease, leaving the other
bodies as channels of covert political dissidence whose vitality
depends on being different and distinct. Perhaps the most successful form of religion is individualistic since the secular metaphysics
of the state tend to provide a public rhetoric rather than a salve
for the individual soul. Such individualistic religion both consoles
and provides a motive for discipline and self-control. The only
open form of politico-religious dissidence may occur where
churches overlap an opposition coming from the extreme left, but
given the very different structural locales of the extreme left and
the church this overlap is not likely to be very frequent or great.
Nevertheless it can occur as a minor motif where there is a
Catholic intelligentsia, as in Poland and Croatia, particularly
in the younger generation of clergy. In east and west alike radical
churchmen link up with post-industrial 'leftism' i.e. the attack
on materialism, bureaucracy, centralism (Lipset 1975).

MIXED PATTERN

Next I come to delineate the 'mixed' pattern. This type of
sociological set is of particular importance because it exemplifies
the relationship between democracy and federalism, and the
conditions under which a beneficent circle operates rather than
a vicious circle. In the analysis of the Catholic pattern stress was
laid on the relationship between an antecedent centralizing autocracy and the breaking of society into mutually antagonistic
sectors. The one instance of a Catholic society lacking such spirals,
at least in the classic form, was Belgium which is inherently
federal by virtue of its basic bi-polarity. (A society like Spain may
appear federal but has a long history of centralization.) So there
is a link demonstrated by cultures of the 'mixed' type and by
those of the Protestant pluralist type, between a loose or federal
structure and the existence of political compromise and consensus. In none of the Protestant pluralist or 'mixed' cultures has

religion *as such* been a major issue, apart from late nineteenth century Germany under the centralizing hegemony of Prussia. Perhaps one may put this in the most abstract and general form by saying that centralization creates a vigorous disunity in which religion as such *is* an issue and federalism creates a moderate unity in which religion as such is *not* an issue. Those Scandinavian countries, especially Sweden, where there have been relatively strong centralizing impulses are also precisely the Protestant countries where religion has, in a minor way, been an issue as such. Unitary agglomerations, political and religious, create alternative unitary agglomerations.

'Mixed' cultures resemble Protestant pluralist cultures in one other respect, which is that the Catholic Church assists in the stabilization of the system by appearing politically on the left or the centre. This again breeds an obvious generalization which extends the generalization already made when comparing the radical role of Protestantism in France and the radical role of Catholicism in Anglo-Saxon cultures. The generalization is this: in *all* Protestant societies, whether Anglo-American or 'mixed', the Catholic Church assists in stabilizing the political sphere and in removing the issue of religion as such from the arena of confrontation, because it stands on the centre-left. As suggested before, Protestant churches would perform the same role in relation to Catholic cultures had not the logic of centralization either eliminated them or else weakened them beyond the point where they could constitute a crucial factor e.g. in France or Czechoslovakia.

A less fundamental but interesting feature which especially characterizes 'mixed' cultures and which nevertheless finds an echo in Protestant pluralist cultures is the appearance of democratic populist impulses within a conservative and religious frame. Sometimes this also has a territorial location and represents a provincial reaction against the secular liberalism dominating the metropolitan centre. Fundamentalism has found links with democratic mobilization in Alberta, in northern Holland, in Dutch South Africa, in Northern Ireland (more especially the Orange Order but also Paisley-ite politics) and in the American South. Such conservative populism is a perfectly genuine popular mobilization with strong egalitarian overtones whatever its conservative and religious colouring. However certain peculiarities are worthy of note which cross our basic categories. The Anglican state church breeds a minor dissident populism of a largely liberal kind, especially so where this finds a territorial base, as in Wales. But in countries where there is a more Presbyterian and Calvinist tone to the Establishment there occurs a stronger tendency to break-offs on the populist right.

Turning now directly to 'mixed' cultures and the beneficent spiral which they exemplify, it is worth stressing again that the existence of conservative religion on the centre-left splits up the image of a unified politico-religious conservatism. The political stance of traditional religion clearly derives from its structural position, and it gives rise to specific Catholic voting habits which have some degree of independence of pure class or status position. In other words the political stance derives from a structure of partial exclusion suffered by the religious community as such and has consequences independent of socio-economic status correlates. The result is a politics of rival religious communities in which the antagonisms of status are both translated into such rivalries and occur inside them as internal strains. The need of the religious community to survive also requires some concession to the lower status participants within its own system. A Catholic religious community placed politically at the centre of the spectrum and playing the role of sub-cultural and regional guardian necessarily assists the forces ranged against the metropolitan foci of power. Its paramount desire for its own centralized control of religious socialization pushes it against schemes for wider centralized controls. Authoritarian systems in opposition, as in Holland and Germany, may curb the authoritarian impulses in the system as a whole.

But the issue of education suggests another element helpful to the beneficent spiral: changing alliances. Catholics originally allied with liberals because their tolerance extended to Catholics. Catholics allied with orthodox Calvinists because liberal tolerance did not extend to 'illiberal' systems of religious education run by Catholics and orthodox Calvinists. The issue of education also suggests the fundamental consequence of a 60/40 ratio between rival confessions, which is massive sub-cultural integration—or 'pillarization'. These 'pillars' conduct the flow of secularization in a dramatic way because they push secular elements into a highly explicit further 'pillar'. On the other hand the pillar of the left must either accept isolation or else prop up the system as a whole; and if the latter then there must be a brake on the kind of secularism which might alienate workers integrated within the other pillars. Hence secularist propaganda is muted and by the same token religious hostility to the left is also muted. So the deals and shifting alliances characterizing Dutch politics from earlier periods are reproduced in the modern system. Naturally, in those areas of relative Protestant homogeneity which are also industrialized the sub-cultural integrations will be less in evidence and a pattern of class politics will occur analogous to that found in Latin systems. But this pattern will be less intransigent and reflect the brakes operative in the system as a whole. This relative transigence may perhaps be attributed not only to the fact that the more organicist and traditionalist religion stands on the political centre but to the fragmentary character of Protestantism considered as a bulwark of the right.

The basic tendency of 'mixed' cultures is towards a liberalized élite centre and to sub-cultural integrations both posed against it and in intermittent alliance with it. A large Catholic sub-culture lies to the centre left with a particular regional redoubt, while an orthodox Protestant sub-culture lies to the right, maybe also with some territorial concentration. The unions and parties belonging to the Catholic sub-culture are *much* larger than the complementary Protestant ones. The deviant case is Germany, at least in two important respects. The tardiness of unification created an issue of religion as such, notably in the form of the Kulturkampf but also in the Nazi period; and the upper middle class was equally tardy in creating the liberalized centre and a power fully independent of the old élite. The tragedy of Germany is based largely on contingent factors of war and depression but both the politics of the later Empire and of Weimar were made more stable by the political stance of the Catholic Church. In the post-war period the Catholic Church avoided accelerating spirals of opposition to Social Democracy and was able in the late fifties to achieve cautious spirals of rapprochement. (The Swiss case is discussed in footnote 25 in the chapter on the mixed pattern.) However, it will have been observed that if nationalist orchestrations of ethnicity overlap religion then there is no beneficent spiral.

On this point two cases are relevant because they are in differing degrees affiliated to the mixed pattern. They are Northern Ireland and South Africa. It should be stressed that the

'mixed' pattern is based on two *churches* not on a single church
vis-à-vis pluralistic, dispersed denominations such as Methodism.
Northern Ireland is an obvious case of rival churches in proportions of 60:40, (or more strictly 66:34). There are two churches
constituting the Protestant majority, and all three churches have
an ethnic and to some extent a territorial base. The Presbyterian
Church is relatively concentrated in the North, the Catholic
Church in South and West, and the Anglican Church in between;
and each services Irish, Scots and English constituencies. The
Presbyterian Church gives birth to a free Presbyterianism of a
theologically conservative kind; and the theological conservatism
of much of Presbyterianism taken as a whole finds expression in
a classic populism within a politically conservative format. The
Catholic Church is equally conservative in its internal life but
stands alongside the movement for Civil Rights and the Social
Democratic Labour Party, while individual Catholics are the
core of political radicalism.

So far the position is very close to the 'mixed' pattern, but the
predicted stability does not and cannot occur. This is because
part of the Catholic population identifies with the adjacent
Republic of Ireland while the Protestant population identifies
with England. This is an expression of the underlying ethnic
difference and of a tradition of historic displacement which
further plays into and reinforces the fear of the majority and its
discriminatory practices. All conflicts are thrust into the religious
channel, creating an accentuated practice and orthodoxy on both
sides. The aspirations of part of the minority go beyond equality
and this creates spirals of fear which prevent even the achievement of equality. Parenthetically almost exactly the same conditions may be observed to apply in Cyprus as between the
Orthodox and Turkish populations, and in the Lebanon, though
this is an instance of infiltration and changing demographic
balance.

South Africa is more loosely affiliated to the mixed pattern
and also shares some characteristics with American pluralism.
But again the predicted stability cannot occur because the distribution of religions lies, as in Ulster, over ethnic differences,
and these are reinforced by colour and culture. There are two
ethnic churches, Anglican and Dutch Reformed, and these are
skewed towards the white population and élite groups. However,

c

both, for different reasons, can feel partially excluded, the Dutch by the impact of Imperialism, and the English by the subsequent Boer hegemony. The result has been an accentuated sense of a pilgrim mission amongst the Dutch. Parts of the Anglican Church by contrast have drawn on the less pressured and less particularistic traditions of England and on the historic presuppositions of Christian mission to support black aspirations. At the same time a classic pluralistic denomination, Methodism, has expanded extensively on the black side of the colour divide, and Catholicism has acted in the sociological role of just such a denomination to expand even further. Added to which separatist churches have appeared on an increasing scale expressing the native sense that the divide is the unbridgeable.

Such a situation does not push politics into a religious channel but it serves to remove religion as such from the fundamental controversy, since each group has a religious expression, and it allows the aspirations of each side to be articulated by spokesmen who are specifically Christian and use a rhetoric which includes religious overtones.

Perhaps the basic sociological point is that where a church is in a major way coextensive with an outgroup it can express the political and civil interests of that group without splitting itself in two. So doing it *may* reinforce the unity of the élite group or groups, depending on how much such groups have to lose psychically and economically. In South Africa and Ulster even lower participants in favoured groups have quite a lot to lose. The specific association of Dutch Reformed religion with that favoured position prevents any extensive theological liberalization, such as occurred in Holland itself, and to the extent that this is the case fundamentalist break-offs are unnecessary. In the Southern States of the U.S.A. and Holland there is less to lose and in these instances the total context of the culture as a whole supports advance and integration. In both South Africa and the American South the extent of Protestant pluralism allows the infiltration of very varied religious forms into amost every part of the cultural system, thus preventing specifically anti-religious alienation.

RELIGION AND EXTERNAL DOMINATION

The final category has already been referred to, for example, under exceptions to the Latin pattern. For that matter some cases within it also belong within the category of left-wing societies. So I repeat for the sake of completeness. It comprises those societies where Catholicism (or Orthodoxy) has stood in for the state under conditions of external domination or external threat. Any pluralism is usually associated with extraneous ethnic intrusions. A dominated society or a society sandwiched between other societies which throw its identity into high relief turns to its religion. Poland, Malta and Eire are instances of the former and constitute the areas of very high practice in Europe. Roumania is an instance of the latter and probably exhibits the highest practice of any Orthodox society under Communism. Cyprus, Lebanon and Israel all experience a reinforcement of their religious practice by virtue of being at a dangerous frontier or having a cultural frontier actually running through their territory (cf. Liebman 1975). The historic role of the church as guardian of a culture and as a substitute state leads to the accretion of further roles and these are carried forward in a relatively un-differentiated form with the onset of independence and/or indus-trialization. Even the advent of classic internal tensions, such as affected Poland between the wars and Malta in the 1960s, does not break this indissoluble union and compromises have to be arrived at much more favourable to the church than in countries like France or Italy.[26] The church constantly experiences the continued after effects of standing against rather than standing for authority.

Allied to the above instances are all the cases so far cited as sub-cultures whose existence is defined by religion. The Basque country, Galicia, Brittany etc. are areas of very high practice, and the Ukraine, Croatia, Slovakia, Wales, Cornwall, Scotland and the Bergen hinterland are each areas of relatively high practice vis-à-vis the wider society. As pointed out above, America consists precisely of numerous sub-cultures each residually defined by religion. The problem of differentiation and alternative foci of identity must be considered below. The simple point here is that all internal conflicts are muted by the existence of alien authority or threat and the paramount need for identity is best nurtured from its historic sources—religion and (according to circumstances) language. Such a need influences the intelligentsia to defend their threatened homeland and religion along with it, most obviously so in Poland and Croatia, least obviously so in Catalonia. It may be that a relatively great emphasis on language relative to religion occurs where a developing urban bourgeoisie is of the same ethnic loyalty as the sub-culture at large; where the sub-culture does not include such a bourgeoisie the emphasis is likely to lie heavily on religion.

FIRST SUMMARY

A number of generalizations have underlain the above analysis and from time to time I have attempted a paragraph or so of summary, notably in relation to the Catholic pattern. These generalizations perhaps deserve to be stated in their most abstract form.

Suppose then a continuum of pluralism and federalism running from near-complete federalism and pluralism to near-complete monopoly. The organic (i.e. Catholic) systems will coexist more easily with the monopolistic sector of the continuum. Or, stated differently, organicism and monopoly will be correlated and symbiotic. However once social change occurs it will be more violent in the case of centralizing organic and monopolistic cultures, and will give rise to competing quasi-organic alternatives. The internal violence of these competing organicisms will only be ameliorated where the system as a whole must unite against external domination and/or where there is a bi-polar balance of forces, more especially if that balance is rooted in a further bi-polarity acute enough to threaten the system as a whole if pushed too far. Anti-clericalism and conflicts over religion as such, especially in the sphere of education will vary positively in accordance with the degree of monopoly.

Federal systems marked by relatively non-organic religious influence (i.e. Protestantism in several varieties) may take several forms each with characteristic sociological consequences. The first is complete pluralism whereby the social and religious hierarchy vary by area and neither authority nor élite culture is associated with religion as such. In such a case varied religious forms adapt to varied cultures and cross the lines of status with relative ease. The second is qualified pluralism where there is a partial association of a particular religious body with the élite and with social authority and this largely constricts active alternative religion to a sector of the upper working and lower middle class. The third is a segmented pluralism where rival churches exist in territorial concentrations. This gives rise to heavy sub-cultural integration. It also gives rise to confessional parties and unions, more especially in the sub-dominant Catholic sector.

Confessional parties and unions exist in the monopoly type of system and in the duopoly type of system. However in the monopoly type of system they tend to be right-wing unless preceded by an élite system composed of anti-clerical liberal elements. In the duopoly system Catholic parties and unions tend to the centre and left. There are almost no Catholic parties in pluralist systems, but Catholicism further stabilizes such systems by setting a conservative theological culture apart from conservative politics. In pluralist systems politics are coloured either by 'liberal' Protestant motifs, or else by populist Protestant motifs in a conservative format, the former being relatively often associated with the metropolitan centre and with the middle class, the latter with provinciality.

Where organicism reasserts itself it does so by commandeering religion, notably Catholicism, since there exists a pre-existent elective affinity. Or else it attempts to extrude religion, more especially Catholicism, because two similar systems cannot exist in rivalry. In the former instance religion initiates some element of differentiation on its own account. In the latter instance religion is made to subserve whatever are the local imperatives of power and identity. If religion can subserve them it can also be an element in preserving identity, more particularly when threatened from outside. If it does not subserve them it is reduced to a minimal role. Either way it is relatively less strong in those sectors close to the central nervous system of power, in which respect its social incidence is the reverse of that obtaining in all the other systems, but especially that of the union of organicism with Catholicism. I mean that the gradient of religiosity varies in accordance with distance from *power*, and that the gradient in communist societies is the reverse of the gradient in conservative organicist (or in Fascist) societies.

All systems organic, or in some degree fragmentary, are more or less culturally homogeneous. Where the overall system is centralizing and organic the sub-cultures exist in a condition of vigorous tension with the centre. Normally such sub-cultures are right wing in political loyalty, but where the centre is of the right they may be of the left. The existence of exterior pressure mutes internal conflict thereby permitting Catholicism to function without division and as undisputed cultural guardian. Where the overall system is less organic and less centralizing the tension between periphery and centre is less vigorous, and the spirals of identification between religion and sub-culture less intense. Given the nature of less organic systems it is more likely that in them the sub-culture will be informed by a fissiparous variant of the metropolitan religion and will be individualistic i.e. have an elective affinity with liberalism or liberal socialism. Such variants, rooted in sub-cultures, stabilize the total systems further by setting up patterns of regional and religious politics located in the centre not on the right. In all systems, organic and fragmentary, the more evenly matched the bi-polarities the greater the need for tolerance of alternatives, including religious alternatives. Per contra the more overwhelming the centre the more it can continuously extend its influence and eliminate all alternatives, whether in the name of tolerance or of totalitarian rule.

Clearly there are a great many sub-generalizations attached to and qualifying the above but these have already been stated at various points and are best brought together in a table opposite.

At this point I must turn aside for two components of secularization theory which can only be dealt with by cursory indication rather than prolonged analysis: the varied incidence and mutations of Protestant Ethic, and the question of religion and politics, especially radical politics, acting as functional alternatives.

EXCURSUS 1: THE PROTESTANT ETHIC

Clearly a complete study would place the social locations of the Protestant Ethic within these patterns. Here however I intend merely to indicate where such a study might begin. In the American instance the Protestant Ethic is dominant. At the same time it constantly reappears alongside the emerging consciousness

	American	English	Scandinavian	Mixed	Latin	Statist (Right)	Statist (Left)	Nationalist
Religious pluralism	High	Medium	Low	High (Duopoly)	Very low	Very low	Very low	Very low
Anti-clericalism	Low	Fairly low	Fairly low/medium	Fairly low	Very high	Very high	Very high	Very low
Clerical status	Low/varied	Medium	Fairly high	Fairly high	High/low	High/low	Low	High
Cultic participation	High	Fairly low	Very low	High	High/low	High/low	Low	High
Internal religious conservatism	Varied	Fairly high	Fairly high	High/low	High/low	High	High	High
Intellectualism in religion	Low/varied	Medium	High	High in the élite	High	Low	Low	High and low
Stability of democracy	High	High	High	High	Low	Low	N.A.	Varied
Communist influence	Low	Low	Low/medium	Low	High	High	High	Low
Catholic political orientation	Centre-left	Centre-left	N.A.	Centre-left	Right then centre	Right then centre	Oppositional	Mostly right
Civil religion	Religiously toned	Religiously toned	Mostly secular	Religiously toned	Tension with religion	Absorbs religion	Anti-religious	Pro-religious
Church–State nexus	Broken	Retained	Retained	Retained	Strained or broken	Retained	Broken selectively	Intimate
School system	Secular	Religious then semi-secular	Secular with religious fringe	Mixed	Increasingly secular	Religious	Secular	Strong religious influence
Intelligentsia	Fairly religious less than status equivalents	More and less religious than status equivalents	Secular and less so than status equivalents	Fairly religious but less so than status equivalents	Less religious than status equivalents	Less religious than status equivalents	Secular	Strong religious influence
Religious parties	Non-existent	Non-existent	Very minor	Influential	Extensive	N.A.	N.A.	Influential

of new status groups e.g. the Black Muslims, and Black Masonry as recently analysed by W. A. Muraskin (1976). It is also dominant in Australia and Canada with certain restrictions related to the existence of an organic Catholicism in Quebec and an Anglican Church in an élite position in both Canada and Australia. The dominance of the Protestant Ethic is also worth noting in Wales, Scotland and Ulster even though certain organic constraints operate within the godly Presbyterian community. In England itself the Protestant Ethic is a counter-élite motif even though it penetrates deep into the élite with the progress of nineteenth century evangelicalism. By this time however the spearhead of the counter-élite is already partly in the embrace of the traditional élite and the Ethic is moving at lower level mobilizations e.g. Methodism. In all the countries with Protestant state churches it is diffused very generally but achieves certain quite specific incarnations as regions or strata make their first emergence with the beginning of industrialism: the 'little people' of Orthodox Calvinist Holland, the Haugeans in Norway, and Pietists everywhere. This emergence may have strong overlaps with nationalist motifs such as clearly exist in German Pietism. The point was put very nicely by Samuel Butler (1918) in his Notebooks: 'When we sing the Hallelujah Chorus we mean "Hallelujah, for the Lord God omnipotent reigneth" and we're no small beer ourselves'. Perhaps it is worth saying that instances may occur where the Protestant Ethic is completely subordinated within the organic bands of isolated tight communities, just as the Jewish Ethic can be similarly controlled by heavy orthodoxy. Some of the potential of the Protestant Ethic is allied with its capacity to make for liberalization i.e. to create self erosion. There is a nice point half-way along the road between the tight godly community and complete liberalization where the Protestant Ethic is socially most potent. Trevor-Roper (1965) has very rightly drawn attention to the limitation on achievement in those remoter areas where the godly community can be completely constricting.

In Catholic countries there exists a Puritanism, as for example in Ireland and Spain, which is too controlled by organic bonds to be released into the social bloodstream. Protestant motifs occur in philosophical movements, like Krausism, in ascetic tendencies in the élite like the Opus Dei and in certain lower level 'sponsored' mobilizations like the 'Cursillos'. Maybe movements of rural cooperation like the Jeunesse Agricole Chrétienne and the recent developments in the west of Ireland should be included under the head of 'functional equivalents' to the Protestant Ethic (McGuire 1975). Clearly Pentecostalism in Latin America, more especially in Chile and Brazil, is impregnated with classic motifs of the Protestant ethos, but it is perhaps only capable of yielding the usual fruits of individual discipline, not of forming any kind of counter-élite (cf. Willems 1965 and 1967). Baptists in the Soviet Union are in the same position for the obvious reason that they are entirely kept within the domain of disciplined personal work. It is interesting that Baptists draw on two pre-revolutionary sects in which Protestant Ethic motifs made a partial appearance: the Molokans and Old Believers. The Molokans were, of course, highly communal in their organization and there was a tight social bond within the Old Believer village. Nevertheless both achieved the fruits of industry. The Old Believers in particular were closely associated with growth of early Moscow industry. Perhaps the point of all such examples is that out-groups of above the lower level who also have a distinctive non-church religion are often structurally well placed to enter upon and achieve the early fruits of industry and industrialization. Further examples outside Christianity are provided in somewhat speculative and psycho-analytic form by Hagen (1962). The point for secularization concerns the internal erosion of the godly discipline, the loosening of the religious casing around the motifs of work and accumulation, and the eventual liberalization of attitudes and controls. Such mutations have been very adequately canvassed elsewhere more particularly in a summary statement by Eisenstadt (1968) and in a critical manner by Feuer (1963).

EXCURSUS 2:
FUNCTIONAL EQUIVALENCE OF
RELIGION AND POLITICS

The other component in secularization theory, which can here only be suggested cursorily, relates to the conditions under which politics provide a functional alternative to religion, or in Marxist terms, the conditions under which hope loses it fantastic guise and gains the clear-eyed unity of scientific theory and political

practice. Obviously this issue is partly parallel to the question of
the functional alternative which language may provide to religion
in the expression of national or regional consciousness. As will be
evident this is a discussion which logically precedes the analysis
of differentiation.

Whether or not politics take over from religion or alternates
with it is partly a matter of the categories outlined here, as well as
of stages of development and differentiation. It is important to
suggest how the functional overlap or differentiation of religion
and politics varies according to those categories. That done something must be said about the specific nature of the politico-
religious interplay, and this I hope to illustrate primarily from
Scandinavian material. There is, of course, a considerable
literature on the English politico-religious mix from Engels to
Halévy to E. P. Thompson.

In the United States religion is the matrix and dominant frame
of political utopia and it provides the mirrors in which each
emerging group envisages its new social self. The political parties
are not now religious, except insofar as they have acted as carriers
of Protestant nativism, but emergent consciousness has all the
same expressed itself in religious terms. The religious element in
this expression has remained alive and active even when a political
correlative has appeared, as for example the Civil Rights Movement. There is no sequence from religion to politics. The Baptists
provide the framework of emergent black awareness, first passively
and then actively; the Civil Rights Movement took up this
activity and translated it into pressure group politics, but without
emptying the churches or eliminating their role. In like manner
the Black bourgeoisie found a religious framework for its aspirations in black masonry and other groups found such a framework
in the Black Muslims (Essien-Udom 1962). The range of religious
masks on offer allowed each new social face to find a religious
persona. Moreover there is a level of cultural sensitivity about
morals, and manners which is always likely to be grounded in a
religious frame of reference. The political movements which
express this sensitivity, more especially provincial and small town
fears of metropolitan manners are inherently linked to a layer of
social defensiveness which is symbolic in form rather than instrumental in intent. The symbolic crusades against alcohol as described by Joseph Gusfield (1966) and the anti-pornographic

campaign as described by Zurcher and Kirkpatrick are both instances of cultural defence i.e. what Wallis calls the 'differential dissolution' of the older Protestant style.[27] And just as cultural defence has a religious face so too utopia acquires religious expression through the Oneida Community or the Shakers, or the Jesus communes or the New Jerusalem of Salt Lake City. These are in John Whitworth's apt phrase 'God's Blueprints' (Whitworth 1975). The politics of the new society here achieve a religious expression without *necessarily* reaching a stage where the fantastic cloak needs to be thrown aside. Religion has after all created those communities most likely to last.

At the other end of the typological scale Catholic societies do seem to illustrate precisely the postulated sequence from religion to politics. And this is because an all-englobing single religion cannot provide enough varying masks for the newly emerging social faces to wear. Certain kinds of millenarian expectation and communal experimentation certainly occur but in the end these are mostly subsumed under the banner of militant secular politics and ideological dogma. Hope becomes political: the primitive rebels, the anarchists and anarcho-syndicalists acquire what appear to be real hard daytime dreams (Hobsbawn 1969). Each emergent group eventually picks up the secularist masks constructed by the metropolitan intelligentsia and moulded for use by secular oligarchies leading the labour unions.

In between there is the Scandinavian and British situation where the politico-religious mix is neither composed of a large repertoire of permanent religious masks nor a straight transition from religion to politics. In Britain at least a very generalized religious rhetoric has been available, more especially that evolved by Protestant dissent but such rhetoric has not been restricted to the moral and status demands of dissenters. Religion has provided a point of rhetorical attachment, alongside other secular rhetorics, and this can happen because Christianity is always conceived as quite distinct from 'Churchianity'. Indeed, a major formulation of new consciousness and new mobilizations took place in a Methodist frame and this has been well-analysed by Bernard Semmel. Whether you regard Methodism as 'work discipline' and 'psychic constriction' as does E. P. Thompson (1968), or as a set of new and internally varied possibilities awaiting different translations, as does Bernard Semmel (1974), is a matter of taste and viewpoint. Certainly major independencies were achieved, certain organizational skills acquired, certain rhetorical styles and skills made available. They might however be used far away from their dissenting origins and to that extent politics took over from religion. The stray spars no longer bore the name of the ship. No religious body expressed the emergent consciousness of the working class as a whole, and once the working class had emerged, the temperature chart of religious awareness began to follow general societal moods and depressions not the fortunes of particular status groups or sectional alliances. Certain of the early unions, such as the miners and agricultural labourers, might have a specific religious tone, but by the end of the first world war, and certainly after the General Strike of 1926, this had mostly disappeared (Moore 1974). The last ripples of nonconformist conscience could be seen even in the Labour Government of 1974—at least in the distribution of denominational origins but it is difficult to see how declining religious bodies can continue to make even this attenuated contribution. At the same time the historic moral style and high seriousness, not to say righteousness, are carried on, and the Campaign for Nuclear Disarmament unleashed every dissenting rhetorical mode and moral pre-judgement. It even incorporated, as Frank Parkin has argued, the primarily expressivist mode in which the new middle class politics were to be couched. Post-industrial politics draws on this well of righteousness even as it rejects the Puritan character structure. The student movement, which is certainly part of post-industrial politics, freely drew on the whole repertoire of religious motifs and modes of expression. These were not damaged, as they were in Catholic countries, by unavoidable association with the ecclesiastical package.

The precise nature of the politico-religious mix is important and it can be illustrated best from Scandinavian examples, even though there is plenty of English material discussing whether enthusiastic religiosity ran prior to political feeling, or after it, or pari-passu with it, or instead of it, or where political action met a blockage. (*All* these relationships have occurred from time to time.) Let us take, in sequence, the relationship of religion to radical voting and the relationship of religion to local cultural defence.

The first example concerning voting and religion is taken from

Sweden. Some preliminary context is clearly necessary. As is well known, Sweden is the least practising of all western societies. The decline has been continuous. B. Gustafsson's *Svensk Kyrkogeografi* (1957, 1971) shows practice in Stockholm declining from 2.4 per cent in 1927 to 1 per cent in 1952 and in Göteborg from 13.1 per cent in 1927 to 4.9 per cent in 1952. Sweden as a whole illustrates a very mild dichotomy of centre and periphery with Stockholm and the central area least practising. The Northern bloc was 2.5 per cent – 5 per cent and the South West plains 5 per cent – 7.5 per cent. As is normal, practice was inversely related to size of town: 9.2 per cent for populations under 500, 6.2 per cent for populations between 500 and 1000, and 1.1 per cent for populations between 15,000 and 20,000. At the same time the paradoxical relation of religion to the axial points of life is also clear: over 90 per cent are confirmed, baptized and buried by the church; and ecclesiastical weddings *increased* in the 1960s from 64 per cent to 84 per cent of the total; presumably as an aspect of family ritual. And these figures for *rites de passage* varied little according to size of town.

Obviously in a society which is relatively homogeneous in terms of religion and in terms of region socio-economic position will predict voting behaviour more than does religion. Yet by using a sophisticated technique of tree-analysis Bo Sarlvik showed that religion retained an effect even after socio-economic status had been controlled for. Social categories inclined to church going were more disinclined to vote socialist and the more they went to church the less they voted socialist. State Church weekly attenders voted 72 per cent non-socialist and Free Church weekly attenders voted 73 per cent non-socialist. The Free Churchmen were however relatively inclined to vote Liberal. That party has traditionally inserted some reference to Christian attitudes in its statements, even though it included a non-religious wing rooted in the urban middle-class. (In these respects it parallels the English Liberals quite closely.)[28]

At this juncture certain interesting points emerge. The first relates to the relative distribution of communist and non-communist voting. The second relates to the appearance of specifically Christian parties and their characteristic support. For the first I rely on S. Rydenfelt's *Kommunismen i Sverige* (1954) and for the second I rely on G. Gustafsson's *Religion och Politik*

(1967), J. Barnes' *The Righthand and Lefthand Kingdoms of God* (1971) and J. Madeley's *Scandinavian Christian Democracy: Throwback or Portent*.[29] These studies show up very clearly the problem of functional alternatives to religion: the linkage is clear and significant, though the causal connection remains obscure.

Communism in Sweden has a varied social location: it is associated with isolated and devalued areas, to which rootless workers have been drawn. In such places it has become the normal, accepted political religion. Communism is also found among certain classes of highly paid worker: miners, shipyard workers, masons, typesetters. Yet there are many areas with identical social characteristics to those where communism is strong, differing only in one feature: religion. Jönköping is fifth among Swedish counties in respect of industrialization and seventeenth in respect of its communist vote. The differentiating factor is religion. The incidence of communism bears no positive relation to unemployment and depression: rather the reverse. Nor is it based on ideological commitment. Communism acts as the available valve of discontent and normative exclusion. If a communist channel is dug as in Italy most discontent flows with it; if the Socialist channel becomes relatively available as is now the case in France it can pick up exactly the same 'negative' social energies. Old-established communities act as a barrier to communism. The ancient trade of fishing, with its self-employed practitioners, is largely immunized against communism; the island of Gotland is slowly secularized but communism remains negligible. The key instances are provided by the two northernmost counties: Vasterbotten and Norbotten. The first has (or had in the early fifties) a communist vote of 2.4 per cent whereas the latter had a communist vote of 21.4 per cent. Both counties had religious revival in the nineteenth century: in one the revival persisted in a moderated form, in the other it died out and communism moved in to fill the void. Both counties had experienced rapid colonization and industrial development: the form of radicalism differed. The religious form is expressed in a Liberal vote, and the political form in a Communist vote. The combined vote received by Liberals and Communists in Vasterbotten was 32 per cent and in Norbotten 30 per cent. Of course, the religious 'functional alternative' is frequently labelled reactionary, but the religious struggle against spiritual and temporal

authority weakened the ancient regime in one way just as he
political battles weakened it in another.

Now, it is precisely in Vasterbotten that the Christian Democratic Union has made its appearance since 1964. It is essentially
an area of Low Church Lutherans and Pentecostals. The most
conservative (according to Dr G. Gustafsson's *Religion och Politik*
(1967)) are the Pentecostals, the least are the Baptists. The latter
fact is related to a persecution of Baptists in the mid-nineteenth
century which served to radicalize them. But the concerns of the
K.D.S. party are essentially centred on 'moral anarchy' and on
a populist reaction against centralization. The fact that they are
continuous with the Liberal Party is important. Liberalism was a
form of expressive politics and it remains such except that the
focus has shifted from the classic issues of Puritan control, like
prohibition, to the post-industrial issues of self-expression. Like
radicalism, expressive politics operate in alternative modes: an-
ciently the disciplines of control, now the rejection of disciplines.
But religious bonds and antinomianism cannot endure together,
even though they are united in a defence of the human and in an
attack on large-scale centralization. So the Liberal Party picks up
the antinomian strand and the K.D.S. the Puritan strand. Such at
any rate is the argument of J. Madeley in his work on 'Scandinavian Christian Democracy'. It is in this context that the con-
gruence of the right of the Liberal Party and of the extreme
Liberal left becomes clear. The enemy for both left and right is
the state. And the participation of Christians on both libertarian
right and libertarian left becomes understandable.

John Barnes describes exactly the same tensions and developments in Bremnes, a district of western Norway.[30] Bremnes is a
stronghold of Haugean pietism and its most widespread political
preference is for the Christian Peoples Party, founded back in
1933. Support for Christian politics in Bremnes means opposition
to cinemas, theatres, dancing, sex education in schools, secular
youth clubs. The main positive policies concern support for
Christian instruction in primary education, for temperance and
disarmament, for prudent state spending, for agriculture and
fisheries and private enterprise. Thus far the programme is part
and parcel of classic Liberalism but under it lies a Norwegian
nationalism expressed in opposition to the state church. The
clergy of the established church were long regarded as instruments

of Danish and (later) Swedish colonialism and of the urban élite
of enlightenment and rationalism. Pietistic politics in Bremnes
therefore stood for faith, for nation, for lay participation, for local
democracy, for local speech and sound rural morality. The prayer
meeting was the symbol of voluntarism and of equality before
God, just as the ecclesiastical hierarchy was part of the worldly
and necessary regiment of men. Thus the religious frame carried
the message of equality, lay participation, nationalism and
localism. It is the intrusion into this of better communications
and of television that has highlighted the peculiar dilemma of
Christian and Pietist politics: the change in the scale of the
relationships with which they are confronted. To resist the centre
is relatively easy compared with the complexities of being required
to rule. To rule from the centre in favour of locality is a paradox
not easily confronted. To translate religious imperatives into
political compromises is equally difficult.

John Madeley has some general comments on the situation
which are worth summarizing. He points out that the new parties
confront the final steps in the secularizing process whereby any
overall ethic is deligitimized and the 'permissive society' inaugurated. What characterizes Scandinavian religion is the internal
variety within the state church and the laicist attitude of the
devout. From the nineteenth century onwards religious authority
has been dispersed from the clergy to the leaders of the semi-
autonomous movements. So there arose a continuum running
from clericalists and churchly revivalists (Laestadianism, Scharta-
uanism, Inner Mission, etc.) to free churchly revivalism and classic
dissent. In relation to the issues of incipient democracy the latter
two types tended to liberalism or even—later—to the left. But in
any case the groupings could hardly agree since they were
divided over clerical authority as well as over democratization.
Thus in Scandinavia the very salience of church issues prevented
the appearance of religious parties just as elsewhere it facilitated
them via the confrontation of secularizing élites and solidary self-
governing churches of Catholic or Calvinist persuasion. However,
the emergence of issues which were culturally symbolic, like
prohibition, united the erstwhile divided Christians. Since the
Liberals (or in Norway the 'old left') no longer provided satisfactory leadership on such issues, or on moral anarchy and the
question of religious socialization, the emergence of a specifically

Christian form of cultural defence was inevitable. Religion defends the integrity of culture. In Norway it began by being coextensive with the state; it ended with defending the local society against the depredations of central authority and the secular élite. The point will be taken up again below in relation to differentiation.

DIFFERENTIATION: GENERAL PROCESS AND PARTICULAR HISTORY

In the final sections of this theoretical essay I am concerned with two universal tendencies of modern society: differentiation and the onset of anomie. The word 'universal' must be qualified because such processes move within the context of the basic patterns. They often break those patterns down but they also stimulate reactions which very much stem from them, as for example the large measure of dedifferentiation which has occurred in eastern countries in the relationship of ontology to legitimation and social control. Differentiation has to be seen partly as a process controlled within the parameters of the basic patterns and partly as a process which loosens them and blurs their distinctiveness. Inevitably some of the elements and instances already referred to above have now to be recycled in the context of differentiation.

Differentiation is much accelarated in modern industrial societies even though it long antedates them. It denotes the process whereby each social sector becomes specialized. The hub is diminished and each social function forms a distinct specialized area. In the case of the family and religion the effect of specialization is sometimes regarded as loss of function and sometimes as a paring down to the 'true' functions. So far as religion is concerned there exists a long history of intimate interaction with the state and legitimation, with political bodies, and with associations for work (such as guilds, cooperatives, communes and unions), with voluntary associations, with socialization and cultural identity. These may now be taken in turn as the impact of differentiation is run through the refracting elements of the various patterns. I begin with variations on the disconnection of church and state, and proceed to politics, unions, voluntary associations and cultural identity. With regard to the church-state connection it is maintained in the Protestant pluralistic societies, with the exception of America. However, as was argued earlier, it is just this explicit separation of church from state that enables a pluralistic religion-in-general to buttress the higher level legitimations of American society. Indeed, since religion has been set free to move downstream with the ebb and flow of sub-cultural change it is more likely to provide generalized legitimations of a more apparently modern kind. Such legitimations must, of course, not only be general but vague. They must be above specific denominations and specific institutional arrangements, whether these be religious or secular. If an ideal is sufficiently broad it cannot be compromised by poor political performance and corruption, but acts rather as a potent point of moral appeal. Of course if an ideal becomes too successful a generation may arrive which expects it to be realized in the proximate future. Then alienation must follow, as for example happened in the 1960s. Broad religious legitimations encounter a limit because their promises must either remain in the long-term future or be compromised by contemporary performance.

In England the continuity of the church-state relationship manages to co-exist with a religious contribution to legitimation which is not much connected with the institutional church, except on such ceremonial occasions as coronations and Remembrance Days. Because religion does not move down the stream of sub-cultural change in the American fashion the contribution to legitimation retains a relatively archaic flavour. The existence of a conservative-Anglican nexus defending the collusion of a specific church with the state initially motivates the liberal-dissenting connection to oppose establishment. Indeed, where the social dynamic of dissent is superimposed on that of Welsh national feeling disestablishment is actually achieved. But the onset of a further aspect of differentiation, notably the separating out of religion and politics,[32] disintegrates the dissenting opposition to establishment, and the established church becomes a *generalized* symbol of a religious presence in the state. Since even in the disestablishment controversy religion *per se* was never at issue most people became willing to stand under the broad umbrella of establishment and its aura of Gothic nostalgia. The established church could provide the imposing west front of civic religion and the objectors were confined to those, like the anglo-catholics, who proposed a more religious function for ecclesiastical institutions, or like Temple, wanted more life and liberty for the Christian conscience. Civic religion of this kind can become compromised by sheer success just as it did in America. Perhaps it was compromised earlier in Britain on account of the moral obloquy attendant on the Empire. Since the middle classes were more socialized into the myth, in England as in America, they were the more susceptible to disillusion. The myth has therefore been more *continuously* successful with the working classes.

Much the same situation obtains in Scandinavia except that the association of minimal pluralism with low practice pushes the institutional church even further in the direction of generalized historical nostalgia and into the role of a social service station. The institutional mediators of a specifically Christian symbolism are just too weak and the religious contribution to general legitimation is the more exiguous. It will be greater however in all those areas where religion played a role in national renaissance: Grundvig and the folk high school movement in Denmark, the Haugean movement and 'old left' areas of Norway, the association of the Church and Finnish nation in the fight against Russia. Sweden exemplifies the weakest church-state association. Yet even there serious moves towards disestablishment have been countered by moves towards the co-establishment of all the churches. Naturally enough, the greater political polarization which once existed over religion as such has eroded the religious component in general legitimations. It is the social service function of religion, especially with regard to *rites de passage*, and the preference which Swedish bureaucrats have for controlling even a weak church, which has stabilized the church in its traditional position.

The Latin pattern contains enormous pressures toward the separation of church and state, of Christianity and civil religion, simply on account of the immense splits over religion *per se*. However, the tension between church and civil religion is restricted both by a desire to retain some national unity through the inclusion of a religious element is overall legitimation, and by the fact that a right wing Catholicism is not easily adapted to a religious position which finally separates faith and nation. Nor is Catholicism easily adapted to what is still the principal opposition to the centralizing impulses of secular bureaucracies i.e. anarchy. The polar cases are perhaps Belgium and Italy in that in the former, Catholicism, Liberalism and the Crown emerged together in the birth of the nation, whereas in the latter Liberalism, the Crown and the emerging nation each faced Catholic, more specifically Papal, opposition. In France the nationalism of the right has been peculiar in that it can become more French than Catholic, thereby creating the kind of religious civil religion of the right from which even the Church eventually wishes to disengage itself. The Church did after all, condemn Action Française.

It is precisely this situation which develops in statist regimes of the right. Such regimes nationalize (or renationalize) the church and assimilate the aura of 'Christian civilization' to their own concepts of organic social order. However there is some difficulty in reducing the church purely to the status of a vehicle for historic continuities, organic unities and social control. Nor is the Christian message entirely translatable into a military-heroic or stoic ethic. 'German Christianity' was the Nazi answer to precisely this problem and was aggravated by the Nazi attempt to control not merely the institutional church but the inner content of its message. Under such pressures, and propelled both by impulses from the church at large and by home constituencies inimical to the feudal-military ethic, the church may attempt to loosen the state bond and achieve a genuine freedom of action.

Statist regimes of the left frequently initiate just this process of differentiation, but in the interests of yet further control rather than freedom. The differentiation of church from the socialization process is the key objective in securing total control and a subsidiary objective is the removal of all independent sources of ecclesiastical wealth. Such issues form the crux of the initial state-church clash. Subsequent developments, such as subventions from the government, further serve the aim of control. Whether or not the explicit separation of church and state occurs depends largely on the logic of the desire for control in this or that historic circumstance. In Roumania, for example, the state may desire to redeploy the historic power of the church as hub of culture and identity to further its attempts at creating homogeneity. If on the other hand the identity of religion and culture is more inclined to fragment national and ideological unity then efforts will be made to prise religion and culture apart, more particularly where an ancient layer of folk rite and folk festival already exists in partial independence from the church. One conspicuous limit on the logic of control arises from the dissidence within the church aroused by total subservience to state demands and by infiltration. Concessions have to be made, by way of freedom for the more conformist elements, in order to counter religious breakaways which pass out of administrative surveillance. Of course, precisely this ideological monopoly exercised by secular metaphysic over against religion represents an extensive dedifferentiation. Only sectors of the technical intelligentsia achieve any measure of ideological neutrality or apathy, though evidence on youth does suggest an increasing component of personal hedonism (cf. Bango, 1968).

Differentiation is also operative in the spheres of politics and associations for work and labour. In the Anglo-American and Scandinavian patterns the situation is clear. The fact that religion as such is not an issue and the existence of religious people at most points on the political spectrum debars any one party or union from claiming to represent religion. Members of one particular religion may be more skewed to this or that party and the leadership of unions may be drawn differentially from this or that denomination, but that is a different matter. For example, members of the non-conformist churches in Britain and Scandinavia have a propensity to vote Labour or Liberal and active members of the state churches have a propensity to vote Conservative. Similarly Catholics are associated with the Democratic Party and the Labour Party and make a contribution to labour union leadership. The political role of the churches will be restricted to the rhetoric of public harmony or else to a broad critique, such as underlay the Catholic Workers Movement in America or Distributivism in England.[33]

Where, as in Sweden, there is no substantial Catholic or even non-conformist religion in the active ranks of the Liberal or Labour parties the role of specifically secular doctrines of an extremist kind is accentuated. Whereas religious influences lay at the tangled roots of American and English reformism it took some decades before a Christian socialist element emerged in Scandinavia. Moreover, perhaps it was only the success of secular political doctrines and of a hedonistic ethos that eventually

stimulated the appearance of small Christian parties dedicated to
local cultural defence (G. Gustafsson 1967). The main instance of
religious political influence early in the process is found in the old
left party (or parties) of southern and western Norway, and even
here the more specifically Christian sector of the party split off
from the rest. This kind of religiously influenced politics originally
approximated the union of non-conformity, liberalism and
national feeling found in late nineteenth century Wales. In all
Protestant cultures the emphasis on conscience in politics tends
to produce associations concerned to promote this or that moral
issue, such as teetotalism (which in the U.S. is sometimes interpreted as symbolic of an older Protestant America under pressure)
or world government or pacificism.[34] The peace issue is endemic
in Protestant liberal democracies and is promoted by a free-
floating political religiosity working through discrete movements
in alliance with varieties of left-wing political alienation. Indeed
it is precisely this type of non-conformist and/or idealistic intellectual middle class sentiment which undermines religion's
contribution to the national myth and actually limits the resonance of the myth itself.

In 'mixed' cultures politics and unionization necessarily follow
the constraints of sub-cultural integration: there is at least a
Catholic party, probably a smaller Protestant party or parties.
The Protestant political pressure is always weaker than the
Catholic because the Protestants are more coextensive with state-
bearing semi-secularist elements and because Protestantism is too
atomized to achieve disciplined political expression. Catholic
unions, being part of a status-deprived minority can act in the
centre of the political stage in a manner not really open to
Protestant unions. In any case the petty-bourgeois concentration
of lower status Protestants is not particularly amenable to unionization. The salient religious majority, much of which is apa-
thetic, does not require organization for the economic contest on a
religious basis.

However even the Catholic parties and unions partly succumb
to the logic of differentiation. Gradually the association of church
and political party breeds a disjunction. Politics operates by the
pragmatic necessities of power with which the purposes of the
Church are not identical. In any case the relative tolerance between left and right assists relaxations of tension and makes

Catholic party political opposition to socialism less necessary. In Germany for example Church and C.D.U. have gradually grown apart, even though Catholic voters retain a residual and declining skew in favour of voting for that party. In a similar manner Catholic unions grow relatively weaker or adopt a stance of secular militancy. Catholic voters loosened from their confessional pillars tend to vote disproportionately to the left.

Since the explicit involvement of the Church in party politics exacerbates the spiral of conflict in Catholic countries it follows that the relative withdrawal of the Church acts as an ameliorating influence. Indeed, the Church may even dissociate itself from parties claiming to be Christian, as has happened in Portugal. Catholics no longer see themselves ineluctably committed to a 'Christian' party and appear at all points on the political spectrum, including the extreme left. In Italy the Church has a further motive to dissociate itself from the governmental corruption of the governing alliances. Religious issues like divorce no longer strictly divide left from right, and for that matter in the Italian context there was always an anti-clerical centre. Divorce comes to be seen more as a matter of the church's internal discipline and in Italy becomes the law of the land. Ancient conflicts over education are gradually forgotten or become arenas of compromise. The end of the differentiation process leaves the church in control of a diminishing minority of schools more especially at the primary level, disconnected from explicit party politics and associated with only a declining minority of unions. Indeed so far as schools are concerned this is the general situation of churches in all the basic patterns insofar as confessional schools exist. Obviously no substantial sector of Catholic schools exists in communist states, any more than there exist religious parties and unions. Only in Poland is there a marginal element of independent church-controlled education, notably the university of Lublin, and a marginal party political presence.

The differentiation of church from the network of voluntary association varies very much in its incidence with the basic patterns. In the U.S.A. the churches, by virtue of their sub-cultural adaptability and ethnic role, constitute the major nexus of association and in that respect partly pre-empt the role of the state. Indeed churches even emerge as substantial entities in the economic field. The limited role of the American state allows churches to expand and fill the interstices of social provision. In Britain by way of partial contrast the churches only expand their voluntary provision in the early period of liberal democracy and then contract it as centralized state agencies and centralized media replace them (Yeo 1976). Religion then becomes one form of voluntary association alongside other forms, each differentiated and with no overarching integral relationship. In Scandinavia the decline of cultic provision actually leaves churches as a local form of voluntary association, and the general tendency to organization by the state gives such voluntary associations a semi-official character (Gellerstam 1971). Perhaps one may observe that in all Protestant cultures the extent of participation in voluntary association of all kinds runs *pari passu* with religious practice.

In 'mixed' cultures each confessional nexus gathers around it a complete voluntary associational system, especially so in the Catholic enclaves. Even the media succumb to pillarization. The effect of differentiation brings about a specific reduction in the scope of the confessional nexus forcing it to evacuate the political and ideological fields in favour of the expression of identity as such. Similar processes operate in Catholic cultures, except that the rival networks are respectively Catholic and secularist, more particularly Communist. In parts of Italy different sectors of the population have been integrated into alternative associational webs. In the rural areas Catholic culture has produced networks of economic association, for example the Jeunesse Agricole Chrétienne in France and recent cooperative movements in the west of Ireland; and in the past there have been confessional trade networks, for example, in the north of Italy (Jemolo 1960). In all Catholic cultures the nexus of association tends to have a more visible ecclesiastical focus, for instance Catholic Action (Poggi 1967) and the Cursillos de christianidad and the Opus Dei, and there is a tendency for these to have political functions. Even an institution like 'Caritas' is more directly ecclesiastical and can be compared in that respect to 'Christian Aid' or 'Oxfam'. Protestant associations for charitable purposes provide a broad banner for men of all faiths and none. Parenthetically the involvement of Protestants in cooperative economic activity, spurred on by the Protestant ethic and the spirit of economic innovation, has now almost entirely ceased, though in the nineteenth century it animated such important movements as Haugeanism and Dutch neo-Calvinism.

DIFFERENTIATION AND CULTURAL IDENTITY

The final layer of possible differentiation concerns culture and it is here that certain complex issues already referred to *en passant* must be dealt with. For example, mention has been made of a possible rivalry between language and religion as the vehicle of identity and of the way left-wing regimes may attempt to use a purely folk-loric type of culture to unlock the intimate union of religion and identity. Reference has also been made to the way religion may be pushed back from a direct ideological-cum-political role to the pure expression of ethnic awareness. Perhaps I might say that I refer here specifically to global ethnic or local awareness, not to the fragmented and partial unions made by dispersed voluntaristic denominations with this or that social stratum.

That religion has been a carrier of identity is axiomatic. The most resistant forms of religion relate to just those *rites de passage*, especially baptism and circumcision, which function as entry visas into a particular natural community. Even in the Russian situation baptism is the residual sign of the union of Russian culture and Orthodoxy, and on peripheries such as Turkestan, the remaining and powerful badge of Islamic identity is circumcision. In Albania where religious activity is forbidden the continuing clandestine form is the rite of circumcision. Put epigrammatically, generation, regeneration and the continuity of the generations work together. Once they cease to do so a profound link is cut.

There are several categories of religio-cultural identity which should be distinguished.

(A) Independent nations where threatened identity and autonomy has had to be mediated by religion: Poland, Ireland, Malta, Greece, Israel, Ethiopia etc.
(B) Separated national enclaves whose identity is similarly mediated: Quebec, Croatia, Slovakia, Brittany, the Basque country, Bosnia, Flanders, Wales, Scotland, Cyprus

(Christian and Muslim), Ulster (Catholic and Protestant), the Southern Sudan, the Ukraine, Georgia, Lithuania etc.

(C) Socio-political enclaves where no ethnic element is present: Dutch, Swiss and German Catholicism, the Lebanon (Christian and Muslim) etc.

(D) Religio-ethnic unions which are dispersed in wider populations without extensive territorial base: British Catholicism, American Catholicism, Australian Catholicism, etc.

(E) Groups whose ethnicity is defined by religion and which are dispersed within their host cultures: the Jewish and Armenian diasporas, the Sikhs, etc.

Category A has received some discussion above and this requires no further discussion here. Category E can be postponed because the Jewish diaspora has a special role in the channelling of secularization. For the moment therefore the focus of concern is Categories B–D. We may distinguish three levels of differentiation: where identity has a religious ideological component, where religion only expresses awareness of kind, and where religion is not the sole or perhaps even the main fount of such awareness.

What then governs the degree of vigour and pertinacity exhibited by religion in relation to sub-culture? So far as categories B and C are concerned, which relate to sub-cultures possessed of a territorial base (whether or not ethnically or linguistically reinforced) a great deal turns on the type of relationship of centre to periphery. How powerful and extensive is the periphery vis-à-vis the centre? Is it devalued, linguistically or culturally, or in terms of status? These relationships in part depend on the greater industrialization of centres compared to peripheries, but South Wales, Belfast, Bilbao and Montreal are not in any way the least industrialized sectors of their societies. The centre-periphery relation has an independent impact which meshes in with the impact of industrialization. (Bilbao is thus more practising than Madrid, but less practising than relatively non-industrial parts of the Basque country.)

Centre and periphery contribute to a pattern of homogeneity and heterogeneity. A very strong centre with tiny resistant margins defines homogeneity, whereas the existence of strong alternative poles defines heterogeneity. In homogeneous cultures, of which Sweden is a good example, there are no strong resistant territorial counter-cultures, though it may perhaps be significant that the Göteborg hinterland is relatively practising. Religion has no cultural base within which to resist the metropolitan influence: the diffuse and distinctive religiosity of (say) Jönköping is not separate *enough* or distinctive *enough*. Something similar occurs in France where Paris forms the focus of a dominating middle area of low practice, but there are strong redoubts of provincial culture: the Massif Centrale, Brittany and La Vendée, Alsace-Lorraine. Spain is multi-polar, for various reasons, partly because there is a pervasive contrast between the higher practice of the historically Christian north and the ex-Muslim south and because there are also strong regional loyalties. Norway too is a bi-polar as between secular Oslo and the relatively religious ethos of Bergen and its hinterland. The point of such examples is not an exhaustive catalogue of centre-periphery relations. It is rather to indicate that where there is any genuine polarity religion tends to be distinctively associated with one of the poles. In some situations the centre is absorbent and gradually erodes the edges of the periphery; in others it simply firms up the resistance of the periphery and acts as a stimulant to autonomy. It is a matter of thresholds whereby indices of autonomy may turn cumulatively up or down. And with these indices will move parallel indices for distinctive religious practice.

There are certain factors which affect the threshold. One relates to the degree to which each distinctive characteristic is reinforced by each and every other distinctive characteristic. Where religion, dialect, geographical and historical peculiarity, political interest and complexion, all cooperat, then impulses from the centre will be more easily repelled. It may also happen paradoxically that where religion is the only distinguishing characteristic distinctiveness may be preserved simply because the one lonely source of definition is coextensive with the preservation of any identity at all. The tiny Catholic area of Bulgaria exemplifies just this phenomenon. Another factor relates to relative evaluations propounded at centre and periphery. A devaluation of the language, culture and status of the periphery, especially where backed by perceived economic exploitation and/ or superiority, will breed vigorous autonomous impulses and defensiveness. Flanders is a case in point. The periphery may even in certain instances be economically or culturally superior and yet remain defensive and separatist because it feels the superiority not sufficiently recognized. Here Catalonia and Scotland are cases in point. Identity is further reinforced by enclaves *within* enclaves possessed of differential economic and social power. The desperation engendered by such a threat makes sub-cultural survival certain: both communities in Ulster are cases in point. An immensely strong union or religion and culture also occurs where the intruding enclave is alien, relatively secular and concentrated in urban milieux and occupations, for example the German community in Poland.

Sub-cultural identity is loosened where there is an antecedent long-term loyalty to the nation as a whole and where processes of social and geographical mobility blur frontiers and lower intergroup antagonisms. Dutch Catholicism for example has weakened for just these reasons, and this weakening has been accelerated by the very efficiency of the internal lines of communication built up as part of 'pillarization'. The weakening of English Catholicism, though real, is less dramatic just because it did not comprise a total organization of life and because there was a base of antagonistic ethnic difference still supporting the religious difference. Sub-cultural loosening also occurs where political aims are achieved and identity recognized. In other words the achievement of substantial autonomy and recognition may weaken those sources of identity, more especially religion, which were previously so necessary to survival.

All the above instances concern unions of culture and religion which remain intact, though at different levels of intensity according to circumstance. The final possibility of differentiation arises where another element, like folk custom or language, can either carry part of the burden of identity or even act as an alternative to religion. As pointed out above folk custom has been encouraged to act as an alternative in eastern countries wherever it has had strong historical roots distinct from religion. I do not presume to suggest the conditions under which language is an alternative to religion, though there is an obvious contingent factor in whether such a separate language (or dialect) actually exists, and an obvious 'necessary' factor in that once a language is used by the majority it becomes indispensable, whereas religion has no such natural indispensability.

The case of Jewry has special interest both for secularization and the differentiation of religion and culture, simply because the union of religion and culture has been so strong and the secular reaction to that union so vigorous. The position of Jewry in the interstices of Catholic and Protestant societies historically involved either conversions, (some forced, some genuine and some prudential,) or else the reinforced solidarities of the ghetto. At the point of Jewish emergence from the ghetto and the onset of 'enlightenment' there also appeared an ambivalence towards religion. Religion was seen as a source of pain, both because Christians were hostile and because without a Jewish faith the hostility could not have arisen. That in itself bred a double resentment, but marginality also made possible penetrating insights into the nature of every bond, including religion. And these insights were not easily compatible with faith. Marginality pushed Jews towards the secularist traditions. Most Jews were in any case concentrated quite disproportionately in the cities and exposed to cosmopolitan and radical influences. Being articulate and intellectual by tradition Jews then greatly expanded and deepened the secularist critique of religion. Their presence in the intelligentsia and the impact of the general secularized critique together shifted the balance of intellectual opinion in a secularist direction. Indeed in all cultures, but especially Latin ones, Jews developed secularism as a specifically intellectual ideology serving the counter-élite sector of the intelligentsia.

So in the Jewish case it might be argued that the relation of religion to sub-culture led to an ambivalent regard for religion and to a considerable expansion of the secularist intelligentsia and its critical stance vis-à-vis religion. However, once Jews returned to Israel and especially with the setting up of the new state, it became more difficult to repudiate religion officially or practically since it provided the historic *raison d'être* of Israeli existence. Furthermore the strength of the religious party was sufficient to make it an indispensable adjunct of the socialist government. These factors were reinforced through the intense solidarities generated by continuous conflict. Hence the older secularist traditions of Jewry were ameliorated, particularly perhaps since the new persecutors of Jews were usually on the left. The trajectory had come—almost—full circle.[35]

Perhaps some summary is appropriate here, not of the varied channelling of differentiation through the basic patterns, but of the factors affecting the final level of religious functioning: the union of religion and sub-culture.

Religion conceived as the source of sub-cultural identity tends to lack any direct ideological expression apart from basic consciousness of kind, more especially so in diaspora situations. Even in Quebec for example there has been no Catholic party. A key element affecting such a unity of religion and local consciousness of kind is the relationship of centre to periphery. This relationship runs along a continuum from metropolitan dominance to genuine bi-polarity. Wherever an alternative pole of consciousness exists, whether massive or marginal, religion is likely to be incorporated as part of its system of defence and may perhaps be the sole source of that defence. The chances of a successful resistance are increased wherever there is historical and geographical peculiarity, a distinctive language and mythology. Where the centre is perceived as according inadequate respect and where this is supplemented by a real or plausible economic exploitation then there is a further strengthening of resistance. If an enclave of the majority or of a different minority intrudes within the periphery then consciousness of local kind may be further accentuated. Indeed if such an intrusive enclave should be relatively secular or of a different faith and disposed to monopolize certain urban occupations the rest of the locality and social structure will embrace religion with redoubled fervour. The political tone of the religio-cultural resistance will in part depend on the perceived political tone of the dominating or oppressive alien centre, as well as on the occupational structure of the region concerned. The achievement of political autonomy or cultural recognition may eventually slacken the tide of local awareness, including its religious component, more especially where social and geographical mobility and shared media weaken the sense of difference and of deprivation. The important underlying point with respect to religion and secularization is that religious practice will in part reflect the constellation of factors just referred to. It is these factors which accentuate the union of religion and culture or grant free passage to the process of differentiation.

CLASS AND ANOMIE:
GENERAL TENDENCIES

I have tried to weave the strand of differentiation according to the patterns of culture shaping the incidence and form of secularization. My final section, which concerns the impact of anonymity in modern society must be preceded by some brief statement of the broad tendencies associated with industrialization, or much accelerated by industrialization. It is fairly well established for example that: —religious institutions are weakened by the presence of heavy industry especially where an area is homogeneously proletarian; that they are adversely affected by the increasing size of urban concentrations especially where these are homogeneously proletarian; that they are corroded by geographical and social mobility especially where these lead to a relativization of perspectives on the world.

These generalizations are, however, not self-explanatory. They need to be made intelligible in relation to the factors which underlie them. These I shall proceed to phrase in terms of a weakening of vertical bonds, (the impact of class) and the weakening of horizontal bonds (the impact of anomie).

Large-scale industry created class in two senses: a sense of a cultural divide between 'us' and 'them' and the weakening of vertical bonds personally binding master and man. Marx referred to these as 'idyllic, patriarchal relations'. Whether the divide is strong or weak and whether it issues in the organization of a revolutionary party depends largely on the patterns I have described. A culture dominated by organic models emphasizing solidarities and dogmatic coherence will breed organic, dogmatic parties emphasizing proletarian solidarity. A culture dominated by weakly organic models will breed mildly progressive socialism; and a culture dominated by myth of individuality and achievement will breed a mild gradient of status levels governed by principles of 'contest' mobility not of 'sponsored' mobility (as used by Turner 1960. What I intend to show is how in the modern situation and especially in Protestant cultures, all organic solidarities, whether of nation or religion or class are partly undermined. To take a hint from the latest British evidence, as reported by David Butler and Donald Stokes in *Political Change in Britain* (1974) the voting constituency operating by models of class or religion is an ageing one. Anomie disrupts the organic solidarities, whether those were actively associated with religion or not.

Obviously generalizations will vary with a wide variety of factors, many of which have been analysed already. They only hold 'other things being equal' and the culture of a new town in the Urals is not 'equal' to that of a town of the same size in Alberta or Galicia. Similarly, on a smaller scale of comparison, the religious tone of a town drawing on migrants from Somerset will differ from the religious tone of a comparable town drawing on such a zone as south Yorkshire. Towns reflect their varying milieux and particular sources of migration. Indeed, 'other things' may be so far unequal in certain circumstances that a town may be more practising than the village or countryside. The *range* of town practice is actually less extensive than that of village practice, since the latter can be anything from 100 per cent to 0 per cent. In parts of southern Spain and Portugal for example where the countryside has been proletarianized and worked by mobile labour forces, and where incidentally there has also sometimes been a long-term tradition of ecclesiastical neglect, the practice of the town exceeds that of the rural areas. Nevertheless all such exceptions, which are perfectly intelligible, do not in any way invalidate the rule. They are simply part of the rubric of qualifying circumstances.

I have suggested that 'other things being equal' these tendencies are particularly associated with modern industrial society. They are not however *uniquely* associated with this type of society, though it is evident that heavy industry does not pre-date industrial society and indeed constitutes one of its defining characteristics. The sort of general social conditions which are accelerated and accentuated by industrial society, such as acute anonymity, social disorganization and the absense of an integrating vertical bond, may exist in non-industrial societies. Modern historians have pointed out that low practice, ignorance of religion, hostility to religious institutions and personnel, indifference and even scepticism, may be located in many of the pre-modern societies of Christendom (K. Thomas 1971). The difference is simply this, that what is possible and indeed quite frequent in pre-modern societies is probable and nearly universal in the modern situation. So, to take the polar case, a pre-modern rural society *can* be marked by hostility to religion or indifference. and a modern industrial city can be marked by high practice and a favourable appraisal of religion. The polar case may even be more frequent than we think, but the reverse polar case is nevertheless much more frequent and depends precisely on the incidence of the factors mentioned. If anomie, depersonalization and other characteristics of contemporary society decline then the erosion of religion may be reversed.

So far the first industrial revolution, and even more the second industrial revolution, have produced conditions of anonymity and depersonalization and the breaking of vertical bonds, and these have been more often inimical to religion than not. Nevertheless certain distinctions need to be made. The first industrial revolution, of which the characteristic instance might be the textile industry, did indeed break bonds of vertical community on an extensive scale, but the impact of this breakage varied according to the patterns of culture already described. Again, it also left substantial sectors of vertical integration (personal service, the small firms) and extensive areas of middle class life more or less co-extensive with the conditions of pre-industrial urbanism. Furthermore major enclaves of artisan and small proprietor community were created which evolved characteristic independent forms of religion, notably Protestant nonconformity. All these aspects, which put a brake on the secularizing impact of the first industrial revolution have been relatively absent from the second industrial revolution.

So the first industrial revolution left standing (a) certain sectors of vertical integration (b) a 'respectable' working class and an artisan horizontal bond which might under certain circumstances include a characteristic religious expression (c) a middle class horizontal bond on a scale not markedly different from the pre-industrial town. There is no need to explore (a) any further since there is a great deal of work available on e.g. the vertical integration present in traditional agriculture, or in the nucleated village as compared with the non-nucleated village or in the small firms and the various kinds of personal service employment. The key factor is the maintenance of a personal bond between *different* status levels which is at least as powerful as any bond at the same status level. Nor is there any particular need to explore (c) any

D

further. With regard to the middle class form of urban community
it saw religion, both for itself and for society as a whole, as a
vehicle of social control. Once the bond weakened under the
impact of fragmentation and mobility and anonymity the role of
religion weakened with it (cf. Rokkan and Valen 1964). The
religion of the artisanate and respectable working class has been
dealt with under the discussion of the Anglo-Scandinavian
pattern.

So much however for the impact of the first industrial revolution. The second industrial revolution, of which the typical
instance might be advent of electronic media, tends to be more
corrosive, and this corrosiveness is the more marked where
religious practice was very much lowered in general by the first
industrial revolution. In other words there is an accelerated spiral
effect added in, so that where religious practice was differentially
weakened by the first industrial revolution its weakness is subject
to redoubled pressure by the second. Where by contrast there is
antecedent strength as in (say) Poland or America adjustments
can be made which limit the downward spiral. In religion as in
other spheres, 'to him that hath not, even that which he hath
shall be taken away'. Furthermore, one of the major effects of
contemporary industrialization and of the communications media
associated with it is homogenization, so that recalcitrant peripheries converge on the norms of the centre. If then the centre, as
in America, is favourable to religion then again the spiral of
erosion is limited, but if not it is that much the more extended.

The point about homogenization may be taken up before
discussing anonymity because it implies a breaking down of
precisely the varied patterns which have been the basis of the
foregoing analysis. Actually, even homogenization will vary
somewhat in accordance with these patterns, but it remains true
that peripheries will conform, at least initially, to the image
promoted by the centre. That centre will be the most cosmopolitan, rootless and urbanized sector of society and the very power
of the impulses sent out to the periphery may stir up a threatened
sense of identity. The old sources of religious variability may
receive renewed strength in proportion to the power of the
external threat. At the same time religious activity as distinct
from identity is diminished both at centre and periphery simply
because modern communications media make for communal

passivity in every sphere of activity. Such communications provide either functional equivalents for religious activity or provide whatever passive religious 'activity' is desired. Either way the strength of religion in the form of active local participation is undermined, and by indirect extension even its role at the level of cultural identity is somewhat weakened. Religion is pushed back to the ancient layers of superstition and basic identity that have always underlain the more active and volatile strata of active Christian participation and evangelization. As I have argued elsewhere this layer of ancient homogeneity is what is left when the homogenizing forces of modern society have corroded the more variable and more active expressions of Christianity. There is a 'correspondence' between cosmopolitan influence and this brute 'religion-in-general', even though the cosmopolis may not be specially interested in such religion. New forces of homogenezation 'accidentally' collude with the most ancient layers of para-Christian superstition and folk wisdom.

This is the point at which to emphasize and analyse the most specific consequence of the second industrial revolution: the breaking of bonds in general. The institutions congruent with modern industry, with bureaucracy and technical rationality, are large, impersonal, and mechanical in their operation. The intimate bonds of horizontal community, working class of otherwise, are broken up; the ecology of the city encourages fragmentation; the small shop gives way to the supermarket; the family firm enters the international consortium; the small farm is rationalized into larger units run by scientific agriculture; the moderate-sized office is swallowed up in large-scale bureaucracy; the community of school is wrecked by education factories operated by mobile teachers. And overall the urban style associated with these developments englobes a yet larger proportion of the population.

Characteristically the horizontal bonds remain only in the form of interest groupings, united by instrumental rather than intrinsic motives. Trade unions cease to operate on the basis of local cohesion and participation but purely as vehicles of sectional advantage. They are built into the impersonal grid of the corporate state. The old rhetoric of community, equality and solidarity simply serves as the convenient cover under which such sectional advantages can be pressed (Pawley 1973). Leaders may be followed not because they are ideologically representative but because leaders with a particular form of intransigent secular ideology can more easily deliver the goods. The interdependent character of modern society makes it increasingly easy to press such demands, particularly in certain key industries, and a secular metaphysic of a Marxist kind then becomes the most useful way in which those in such industries can extract the maximum from the wider society.

Where cities are mere agglomerations of fragmented groupings and where atomization has become the most prevalent social mode even social control has to shift from intrinsic symbols to an appeal based on interest. Each private individual constructs an interested calculus that makes social loyalty simply dependent on how that calculus works out. Thus the religious symbols of community and the notion of an intrinsic morality (which is rooted in religion though not exclusively religious) are both downgraded. There is little consciousness of kind governing the reciprocities of neighbourliness and solidarity at the local level, and civic religion operates less powerfully at the national level. At the expanding centres of modern societies the symbols of national belonging, and the religious symbols partly encapsulated within them, have diminished resonance. At the same time the impersonal nature of the social process and the mechanical character of production jointly make a personal image of the cosmos less easy to attain. Moreover people are constantly thrown from one depersonalized sphere to another: office block to tower block, vast school to large factory, and so cannot easily acquire a coherent approach to living. Hence the world is as incoherent as it is depersonalized. Since religion has to do with social and personal identity and with their coherent relation to a whole it finds its resonance much restricted. Indeed, even quasi-mechanistic but rather individualistic cults like astrology can seem more congruent and relevant than traditional religion, and in any case they fit in with the residual superstition that informs 'religion-in-general'.

Confronted by privatization and fragmentation and the segmented character of his role the individual may strive desperately for reintegration. Where the process is most far advanced certain reactions occur which contain a religious element. The disorganized and anomic sections of the middle class and intelligentsia seek either the securities of commune organization or some form of personal mysticism. They also embrace various cults of authentic personal being and encounter which express the loosening of the social bond and the weakening of its symbols. In this context the direction of the reaction may once again depend on the basic patterns. In America the initial thrust to authenticity and ecstasy often curves back into communes based on fundamentalist religion; in England the activist urge more often relapses into passivity; on the continent there is a move to 'communautés de base' sometimes with a monastic overtone, or else the anarchic radicalism is partly picked up again by communistic organization and dogma. Anarchy in any context is frequently a prelude to totalitarian reintegration, but especially so where there is a continuing parallel totalitarian organization immediately available.

The one form of social organization which remains relatively resistant to binding on a purely instrumental basis is the family. In the sphere of the family intrinsic motives remain comparatively secure.[36] So it is here that religion finds a contemporary point of attachment, because there is some degree of overall coherence and the image of the world remains personal. Whether (or rather to what extent) this familistic form of religion is differentially middle class depends partly on the 'images' set up by the basic patterns. It will always be somewhat more middle class, but in England for example the antecedent image of religious practice as either middle class or lower middle class will constrict this familistic religion to the suburban milieu. Obviously, and in all contexts, the drawing of women into the wider system will weaken even the religion based on the family.

The Church itself must reflect these varied pressures: the bureaucratization and impersonality, and the reaction in the form either of a familistic suburban religion or else in radical celebrations of personal authenticity or community. The rationalization of church organization and liturgy runs *pari passu* with cults of encounter, authenticity and charismatic excitement, all of which leap over the constricting limits of the contemporary organization of roles. Authenticity at upper status levels expresses one reaction to privatization and bureaucratic limitation, which is complemented by Pentecostalism at lower and more provincial status levels. At the same time the fragmented detritus of contemporary social organization is partly picked up by close intimate sects like Witnesses and Mormons, offering substitutes for the experience of the family. At the upper levels of Church organization the bureaucratic form is constantly at war both with the charismatic impulse and also with the staid familistic constituency on which contemporary active religion largely relies.

The alternative to such disintegrations appears to be some secular metaphysic. Along the margins of the west and in most developing societies this can be provided by nationalism, with or without a religious adjunct. Elsewhere secular metaphysic can function in the instrumental pragmatic manner already described though replenished with recruits by virtue of the way the dynamism of modern society is constantly throwing up new disorientations amongst groups previously integrated. These will look for whatever channel challenges the existing order, and where *one* such major channel exists as is the case with the Italian Communist Party they will opt for that, whether or not they are Marxist (Aquaviva 1975). Again the availability of these channels and whether or not they have religious or political colouring depends on the basic patterns. In America only sections of the intelligentsia may embrace a secular metaphysic, since there is no alternative political channel open which promises a major change in the system. America can offer numerous religious channels for the expression of social alienation. In England and Scandinavia there are greater opportunities in the form of left politics, even though these have relatively little resonance for the working class. Metaphysics, secular or otherwise, have little appeal, but lack of metaphysics in conjunction with hedonism gives opportunities for small political sects to control crucial junctures and positions. In Scandinavia there are minor incursions of organized secular metaphysics; and in the old Latin countries, above all Italy and France, these incursions are major. Yet only in Italy do communist parties much exceed 20 per cent and in Scandinavia they rarely exceed 10 per cent at the most. Naturally there is a negative relationship between attachment to such parties and religiosity, in spite of the relaxation of the basic Catholic-Communist antagonism. Insofar as Christians tend to the left they favour the non-bureaucratic forms of leftism i.e. what Lipset calls the 'post-industrial' orientation.

The situation in the east, which can be seen as Orthodoxy stood on its head in a secular form is equally problematic. At present the form, organization and dissemination of secular metaphysic represents an extensive dedifferentiation, at least as compared to the west, though not necessarily as compared with the past of all the 'eastern' societies. Metaphysics and force are applied together as the combined vehicle of social control; and such levels of control are very much higher than those acceptable in western societies. What now transpires partly depends on how much anarchy can be borne in the west and how much control can be borne in the east. In both east and west the state is the organ of unity, but in the west it is dangerously reduced to bare functional necessity and in the east dangerously extended to include over-reaching ontological assertions. For the west religion remains one option in a system of ontological and personal openness; in the east religion is officially cast out by fiat of secular monopoly.

SECOND SUMMARY

In the above analysis I have described two phases of industrialization and the form and extent of their corrosive impact on 'visible religion'. The first phase left all kinds of human-scale structures standing: the family firm, self-employment, the small farm, the small office, the intimate college, and pockets of community, either rural organized around the church or industrial organized around the kin-network. All these were congruent with a family model of society where individuals mattered *in relation* to a constraining structure which could offer meaning. Into the interstices of this society moved the voluntary association, reflecting the same model of the individual in relation to a fairly limited and bounded horizon of meaning. And as life was organized within the frame of national boundaries, defined ethnically and above all linguistically, a sacred centre expanded along with the society as a whole, summing and absorbing the dense network of meanings at all the lower levels. It was divided as I noted by a chasm of class which created horizontal patterns of solidarity but these also rested on conceptions of 'brotherhood' and reflected organic connection.

The second phase attacked precisely these human scale structures: the small home, the medium sized school, the bounded town, the family firm, and replaced them by the structures of large scale bureaucratic rationality. It cut down the urge to limited, varied voluntary association and replaced it by a generalized empathy through mass communication, which easily degenerated into apathy. And the state itself again summed and reflected all these successive, overlapping fragmentations by exhibiting a corrosion of the sense of national identity. Of course, all these processes occur in different places at different speeds, according to the overall balance of sectors. Some societies are just now entering the nationalistic phase without some of the concomitant phenomena listed above and some are into the phase when the sacred centre has ceased to expand and begins to contract.

Now certain consequences follow from the second phase which are partly reactions to and party reflections of the processes as outlined. These reactions have implications for the invisible or visible forms of religion and vary according to basic historic patterns. But because fragmentation is the underlying tendency even the patterns are frayed, and give way to ranges of options partly outside the particular limits indicated by antecedent formations. The consequences are therefore partly derived from the antecedent formations but also share a common atomism.

The consequences can be stated quite simply. The most generalized tendency is towards an apathy which retires from explicit institutional religion, whether as related to the organic rural community or to the voluntary religious associations. This apathy has two elements. The first is an emphasis on formulae in that sheer fragmentation must be countered in some way or another. The most obvious formula is astrological, but all kinds of proverbial wisdom can serve the same end.[37] The other element is a hedonistic consumerism which derives from the fact that the majority of the community has been brought into the active sector of society and citizenship, and out of the dulled acceptance of primordial givens. These newly enfranchised egos are served by a reach-me-down romanticism which replaces the old structures of discipline by a crude search for the realization of the self, through the motor car, private appurtenances and sensation. Images of a greater self-realization seep through in educational ideals and some aspects of advertising and its favourite myths. These images, like reach-me-down romanticism, are associated with destructuring motifs filtered from and by the expressive sector of the middle class.[38] They encounter the traditional structures of discipline in the upper working class and the desire to obtain precisely the middle class level of consumer satisfaction by disciplined achievement. So while the hedonistic fragmented mode makes against traditional religion there remains a social sector for whom religious constraints and disciplines are consonant with both style and aspiration. But it is diminished by the consumer hedonism around about and the expressive mode which descends on it from above and into which it ascends all too successfully. This is quintessentially the Methodist situation.

The second reaction expresses fragmentation and meaninglessness quite directly. It both moves against religion as an expression of structure and discipline and ransacks religion for intrinsic forms of awareness and expansions of consciousness. It is centred above all in the expressive professions, whose life-style inevitably colludes with expressionist tendencies and whose capacity for deriving explicit conclusions from its structural location and logic is unusually well developed. For such groupings the institutional disciplines of family, university or church, are anathema, and the preferred religious mode has to be extra or anti-institutional i.e. mystical. The development of the arts in this milieu is consonant with its social situation: either intense expressionism rejecting every manifestation of structure or an abstracted, random, impersonal mode reflecting the impersonal, rationalized conditions against which expressionism reacts.

The third reaction is not a single reaction but a set, based on a need to restore functional equivalents to the structures which have been lost and the diciplines and socially preferred definitions of self which have been eroded. The most necessary of such identity-confirming structures is the family, and therewith the necessary constraints on sexually inherent in familial organization. In this context the Unified Family is typical: based on brotherly and sisterly agape, on authority and supportive, personalized structures. Other groups provide not only a functional equivalent for the self-definitions of the family but also a functional equivalent for the organic local community. The commune movement is a return to the womb of organic community. The Jehovah Witnesses are an odd hybrid, since they carry familistic relations inside an organizational format based on the economic organization of commercial capitalism i.e. the classic-firm.[89]

In between the heavily structured reactions and the expressions of radical destructuring lies the charismatic movement. The charismatic tendency pursues the search for the ineffable and unspeakable within a strongly bounded and bonded associational form. It is the only form of voluntary association which can expand on the twin base of the search for personal expression and the desperate search for structures of meaning and identity. Since the 'expression' is relatively crude it picks up a social detritus from the older denominations and yet performs the functions of the older denominations in simultaneously 'saving' the disoriented and disciplining them for the inevitable social movement upward. Alternatively it selects out middle class members of the established churches and restabilizes them in a mould which simultaneously gives meaning via structure, and expression through tongues and intimate personal contact. It therefore lies astride all the complex tendencies of the second phase as outlined. By combining traditional and modern elements it is the most viable of all the reactions and the most lively manifestation of the dual tendency to both reflect fragmentation and react sharply against it.

The final point is quite simple. The range, type and form of reactions will vary along a Protestant–Catholic continuum. The organic model as established in Catholic cultures will breed both political and religious anarchism, which then flows into an alternative political model of dogmatic and organic totalitarianism. The pluralistic or semi-pluralistic model as established in Protestant cultures will already have validated fragmentation in some degree and there is no overriding organicist model against which to react and no organicist totalitarian politics to provide a final resting place. Thus excursions into anarcho-mystical cults of a mixed political and religious nature will simply flow back into religious reactions on the model of the family or the local commune.

NOTES

1. Cf. Lipset 1969, Chapter 1.
2. For an interesting account of the French attempt to impose their brand of secularism on Alsace, and especially on its education after 1918 see Paul 1967.

3. For a sociological account cf. Davie 1975, and also Mehl 1965.

4. The comparisons are nicely made in Lipset 1969, and in Alford 1964. Summary accounts of Australian and New Zealand religion can be located in Mol 1969; 1966; 1972.

5. Cf. Rokkan and Valen 1964.

6. I should say that I am treating Germany as belonging to my 'mixed' or 'duopolistic' pattern, even though Prussia prior to unification closely resembled Scandinavia.

7. Cf. Bull 1958, especially with respect to Methodists p. 352 et seq., and Tiegland 1970.

8. There is a nice theoretical work-out of the market model of religion in Berger and Luckmann 1966, and in Berger 1969.

9. A short account of 'Civil religion in America' is provided in Bellah 1968.

10. On the fixing of images cf. Currie and Gilbert 1976.

11. A strong statement of this view is to be found in Roszak 1968.

12. Cf. Flint 1968, B. Gustafsson 1966. This is perhaps the point to mention certain general accounts: Tomasson 1968; Matthieson 1966; Aarflot 1969 and Seppanen 1971. The overall point to stress is that the effect of an established church with an upper middle class clergy is to produce uniformly low attendance, very high participation in the *rites de passage*, extensive extra-ecclesial activity of a pietist or revivalist kind, and (Sweden apart) quite high levels of belief, private devotion and acceptance of the idea of 'being a personal Christian'. About half Norway's population accepted the idea of 'being a personal Christian' according to Matthieson, and Seppanen's data for Finland delineate similar levels of belief and personal religion. A quite extensive layer of superstition should also be noted, as in Ringren 1967. Cf. Seppanen 1966.

13. Cf. MacInnes 1975. 'The Peoples Alliance' gained 18.1 per cent of Icelandic votes in the 1974 elections. Cf. Seppanen 1968.

14. Some idea of the content of religious life at the centre is given in Hauglin 1969. Though active Christianity has lost all the capitals in Scandinavia (as in Europe generally) nevertheless the levels of belief described by Hauglin and others are quite high. There is comparable data cited in Koskelainen 1969, and in Salomonsen 1971, which describes religious life in Copenhagen. An account of interesting and resistant peripheries, (Bjornholm, North Jutland and Smaland) is provided by Kjaer 1971, and by Für 1952, pp. 439–441. Mr Kjaer explicitly sets the free church and inner mission movements of Denmark in the context of peripheral reactions to infidelity at the centre, both historically, and in contemporary Copenhagen. As in England these movements have not made progress since the 1930s. The Free Church tendency in Denmark has in any case always had to compete with Grundvigianism with its emphasis on liberalization, education (the folk high school movement), lay responsibility and Danish tradition. In other words part of the liberal thrust was taken up *inside* the state church.

15. An account of the alternating flexibilities and rigidities of medieval Catholicism is provided in Heer 1962.

16. I mean here that under enlightened despots the church was secularized by being subordinated entirely to the imperatives of secular power and also deeply infiltrated (in Poland, Sweden, France and elsewhere) by deistic or rationalistic doctrines. Secularization in this mode is not merely consonant with high practice: the two go together, sometimes by main force of administrative fiat. But this secularization, reducing the Christian faith and the ecclesiastical institution to the status of a 'ministry' of cults, made the subsequent secularization in terms of explicit rejection of practice so much more likely. A church straightforwardly incorporated in the power structure will be involved in the ruins of that structure. This is the story of liberal–Catholic tension throughout the nineteenth century. It is also the situation out of which comes Kierkegaard's protest against cultural Christianity and philosophical idealism.

17. Cf. Vidler 1954. The appeal of Lamennais to a catholic universal Christianity cannot break either the cultural and political constructions surrounding the local French Church or the constrictions affecting the Pope as a temporal ruler or political temporiser.

18. For an account of Father Vincent, cf. Carr 1966. That of course is at the individual and philosophical level. All the material gathered by French sociologists documents this split at the cultural level, first, as regards the laicist professions and then as regards the working classes. To select at random the latter is cogently illustrated in Bovy 1969. The main writers on this topic are Le Bras, Marcilhacy, Pin, Isambert, Rémy, Poulat, and Boulard.

19. Cf. Handy 1971, and Marty 1970. The slow relinquishment of the idea in England from Gladstone, Arnold and Coleridge onwards is admirably chronicled and excerpted in Nicholls 1967. Eliot 1939 must be almost the last instance of such a conception seriously proposed in England.

20. The radical opposition to right-wing authoritarianism in South Korea is largely concentrated in the Catholic Church, both clergy and laity. This is not to say that the Vatican is entirely happy with such whole-hearted dedication to liberty and justice. The liberal universalism of the Catholic Church in South Africa is well documented; and it was, of course, the White Fathers who first exposed the atrocities committed under Portuguese colonialism.

21. An excellent account for Brazil is given in De Kadt 1970.

22. Lison-Tolosana 1966, pp. 112–115. This is an extremely telling analysis which I quote at length in footnote 13, chapter 6.

23. Not always so. In Cutileiro 1971, one finds precisely the kind of priest who only crosses the divide for ritual functions and otherwise remains on the side of property and propriety, to which he is organically attached by multiple ties.

24. Cutileiro, J., in his account of Portuguese religion given at the Rome Conference, May 1976 (unpublished) stresses that in spite of

these tensions there was calculated moderation on both sides. He suggests that the shared suffering of left and of Church at the hands of the liberal republic 1910–1926 may have something to do with this. Cf. Lane 1974.

25. Since the making of this analysis John Madeley (1975) has argued along lines which are highly congruent. He argues that within the grouping Switzerland, Germany and Holland it is Holland which requires explanation.

He begins by referring to Rokkan's suggestion that 'whereas in the Netherlands the interests of orthodox Protestants were as much threatened by the secular nation-builders as were those of the Catholic Church, in Switzerland the interests of corresponding elements were not challenged—rather that they were brought into the nation-building alliance that was able to defeat the secessionist initiative of the Catholic periphery'. He also refers to Lipset's argument that the degree of political involvement of a state church is directly related to its degree of independence: high for Catholicism, medium for Calvinism, low for Lutheranism. He reformulates this as follows: 'The more a church maintains an independent, wide and responsive authority over its membership the more likely it is to foster collective political action on religious basis.' In the Calvinist case genuine independence and normative scope is weakened by a democratic form which expresses varied secular positions and so prevents centralized action. However, the point of interest here is that while both Switzerland and Holland had Calvinist state churches the former framed its concept of church and state in Erastian i.e. in subservient terms. It was this that enabled Liberals to use the church in nation-building and to encourage the kind of internal doctrinal and normative diversity which could weaken collective cohesion. Hence the issue of religious education in schools was settled by a latitudinarian form of teaching and allowance for parental choice. Orthodoxy was unable to resist the liberalism of the state as it was in Holland. By a further contrast, of course, in England orthodox revivalism and liberalism acted in concert by virtue of the structural position of nonconformity. Discussion of the spatial compartmentalization of religious ghettos in Switzerland is to be found in the chapter on the Mixed Pattern.

26. For an illuminating account of this process, which carries on beyond the period covered by Boissevain. Cf. Vassallo 1970.

27. Zurcher and Kirkpatrick 1976, and Wallis 1976. Wallis emphasizes the role of television in purveying a new metropolitan style and in arousing those who felt this style intruding even on the sacred hearth of the family. The people most opposed to these intrusions are likely to be differentially located in small towns and rural areas, female, and from that part of the middle class not exposed to higher education in the humanities. Basically their protest turns on a religio-political rejection of the values of consumption. A further critique of the whole symbolic crusade approach and its implicit

reductionism or debunking attitude is in the *Scottish Journal of Sociology*, Vol. 1, No. 1, Cf. Tracy and Morrison (1976).

28. Vincent 1966. Cf. also Peel 1971. This contains most helpful sections on provincial dissent.

29. Madeley 1975.

30. J. Barnes 1971; G. Gustafsson 1967; Rydenfelt 1954.

31. Shils 1975, Chapter 8.

32. Currie and Gilbert 1978. Cf. E. T. Davies 1965.

33. Cf. O'Brien 1969, and Hall 1976.

34. Martin 1965a; Mayer 1966; Parkin 1968.

35. These points are developed in Martin 1976c. Cf. Werblowsky 1975 for a penetrating chapter on the Jewish case.

36. Shorter 1976. This book emphasizes that it is a moot point just how long intrinsic motives have been operative in the family historically. There are those who maintain 'family life' is a Puritan invention.

37. For an interpretative discussion of astrology cf. Adorno 1964. Cf. Truzzi 1972, and Hartmann 1976. 'Social dimensions of occult participation, *British J. of Sociology*.

Apart from the kind of formulae deployed in astrology there are other formulaic elements derived from proverbial wisdom and from reiterated folk attitudes. These are brought out according to the particular context and have little overall coherence. Some are very broad attitudes relating to the private individual character of religion while others are wise saws for this or that occasion. I quote from 'Young People's Beliefs', a Report by B. Martin and R. Pluck, privately published by the General Synod of the Church of England, pages 21, 22 and 39.

> 'It cannot be too strongly stressed that a universal individualism was found in the approach of these young people. What you believe is essentially private, it is your own affair, you have the right to believe anything you like. The corollary of this individualism is a strong dislike of having other people's beliefs pushed upon you. . . .'

> 'In a number of cases, especially of boys and at the lower educational level the individualism takes the form of keeping yourself (and your belief) to yourself. . . . Going along with this individualism and privacy of belief is an equally strong and universal insistence on one's own open-mindedness. 'I like to keep an open mind,' must have been repeated as often as, 'What you believe is your own affair.' . . .

> 'Religion operates most of the time as an *implicit* attribution of 'sense' to the way things are in the world, and only seldom orders itself into formal propositions about what things 'mean' and why. Even when something approaching formal propositions has a part to play, it may not take the form of a consistent *single* system of meaning. It is well known that in milieux where there is a folk

saying for every eventuality, these sayings often come in contradictory pairs: 'Him as asks don't get'; 'Him as don't ask, don't
want.' Pragmatism and glaring inconsistency are hidden by the
piecemeal application of whichever ready made saying fits the
particular case. Misfortune can be made sense of by 'God works
in a mysterious way', or 'Be sure your sins will find you out', or
'Bad luck comes in threes', or 'It was just my turn', or 'Men are
like that' and so on. The inconsistencies in the position of many of
our respondents were concealed by this use of commonly repeated
phrases and ad hoc attributions of, if not sense, at least familiarity
to all the situations they encountered . . .'

38. It is not necessary or appropriate to insert here an extended
comment on the role of the expressive middle class in extending their
characteristic destructuring motifs downward through the socialization and communication systems—in which they have key positions.
This destructuring propaganda is part of the war within the middle
class and it contributes to overall psychic instability. It has also been
suggested by Bryan Wilson that a technological society does not
require moral socialization on the old scale, even in the family
Coordination is carried out by the mechanical grid of the bureaucratic structure, which requires specific competences not generalized
moral disciplines. If this is so it provides another push towards
psychic disorganization. Cf. Pawley 1973 and B. R. Wilson 1976.

The contrast between discipline required in the economy and
hedonism released at the level of culture is discussed in Bell 1975.

Comments on the left-wing voting behaviour of the expressive
middle class in many western countries and its 'post-industrial'
orientation is provided by Lipset (1975). One needs to compare the
radical attitudes of this group with the right wing or centre attitudes
of even left-wing voters in the working class. This is shown up in the
work of F. Parkin, R. T. McKenzie, John Goldthorpe and David
Butler among British political sociologists.

III

An Alternative Formulation: Europe

RELIGION AND NATIONHOOD

This chapter provides an alternative statement of the theoretical frame but with a much closer empirical focus. Moreover it restricts its concern entirely to Europe. The previous chapter was a general and mostly abstract statement about secularization. What follows here concentrates on certain key contemporary issues of the European situation. The first of these is the relation of religion to national awareness, and also to regional, sub-cultural awareness. It attempts to provide classifications and generalizations governing religion and the national centre, religion and the regional periphery. The second area of concentration is that of power and the different types of power nexus and concatenations of conflict. This analysis of power links up with an analysis of secular élites, especially Marxist élites but also liberal ones in their pursuit of hegemony. It assumes there is a long standing tension between élite power in the nation state and independent structures of religious loyalty or criticism. The last section is particularly concerned to explore that tension. There are further foci of attention not fully dealt with in the theoretical chapter, notably the impact of migration and the general lineaments of continental practice.

Europe is a unity by virtue of having possessed one Caesar and one God i.e. by virtue of Rome. It is a diversity by virtue of the existence of nations. The patterns of European religion derive from the tension and the partnership between Caesar and God, and from the relationship between religion and the search for national integrity and identity. The solution and dissolution of the partnership between Caesar and God, State and Church will be touched on below but the first task for analysis concerns the relationship of religion to the nation-state. Where Caesar himself does not demand a worship complementing the worship of the deity the nation state itself demands adulation. Christianity may be a religion which rejects the worship of Caesar or the exaltation of the ethnic group but in order to retain even the possibility of suggesting more worthy objects of praise it must be positively related to the national consciousness, particularly as this is highlighted in a myth of national origins. A positive overlap with the national myth is a necessary condition for a lively and widespread attachment to religion: the majority of people cannot bear too sharp a contradiction between their universalistic faith and their group identity. Of course, other factors may affect that liveliness and that attachment in very large measure, but if national myth and religious faith are contradictory the social power of religion is restricted. The religious faith which survives such a contradiction is likely to be composed of refugees from the national myth looking for a sectarian haven capable of creating an alternative society.

In most countries of contemporary Europe it is of enormous importance that the existence of the nation and its heroic folk memory is either rooted directly in religion or positively related to it. If we consider first the northern Protestant nations this is true without exception, although in some cases the original Reformation was more a dynastic decision than a matter of national awareness, which meant that the collaboration of Protestant religion and national self-consciousness was most marked in the period of liberal nation building in the nineteenth century. In Norway and Denmark, for example, the Haugean movement and the Grundvigian movement both, in different ways, accelerated and deepened national self-awareness in the nineteenth century (Breistein 1955). In England and Holland by contrast the events of the Reformation itself and the wars which succeeded it indelibly welded together a land and a people. Both land and people received their founding myths at this time: the defeat of the Armada, the lifting of the siege of Leyden. Sweden's national myth became coextensive with the triumphs of its Protestant conquering hero, Gustavus Adolphus. Switzerland is a little more complicated, since its founding myth of independence against Austria antedates the Reformation, but Swiss national identity was gradually assimilated to Protestantism, particularly as the active sector of Swiss life was Protestant and the active centre of Calvinist Protestantism throughout the continent was at Geneva. Much later the Protestant–Catholic War of 1847 further linked the maintenance of Swiss unity to Protestantism. The most obvious example of the coincidence of faith and nation is provided, then and now, by Scotland. The main organ of Scottish identity was and is its church.

In Catholic societies the relationship is more complex, partly because of the continuing war over the existence of an overarching loyalty to Rome. In certain cases the identity of faith and nationality is absolutely clear. In the Iberian peninsula for example the process of making Catholicism identical with nationality occurred through eight hundred years of war with the Islamic south of the peninsula. In Poland the church was the focus of national unity during the political fragmentations of the twelfth to fourteenth centuries, and then coalesced with romantic nineteenth century nationalism to forge an almost total identity of nation and religion against foreign dominance. Again, in Ireland, though the Church was not necessarily in the forefront of nationalist agitation against English dominance it provided the focus and the symbols around which the sense of Irish unity was maintained. In Belgium Catholics and Liberals together fought against Austrian and French and then against Dutch control, so that Catholicism was very positively associated with the independence which Belgium eventually achieved in 1830. And indeed, sharing this achievement with the Liberals meant that the two forces need not initially polarize or attempt to eliminate each other from the sense of pride in national origins.

In other cases, however, the relationship of Catholicism to national consciousness is more ambiguous: in France, Czechoslovakia, and Italy the Catholic Church had to contend with the myths of liberal, secular nationalism; in Czechoslovakia (strictly in Czech Lands) and in Hungary it had to contend with national roots in Protestantism. In the French case the opposition between the nation as integrated by Catholicism under the old regime and the liberal nationalism proclaimed by the Republic divided the myth between irreconcilable opponents. Clerical and anti-clerical fought over the banner of the nation; an old 'integrisme' confronted the new 'integrisme'. It was fertile soil for secular religions (Charlton 1963). Particularly during the period of the Third

Republic from 1870 up to the separation of Church and State in 1905 the spirit of Jeanne D'Arc faced implacable opposition from prophets like Jules Ferry preaching a religion of the Fatherland (Dansette 1962, vol. ii). Between the world wars there was a characteristically French conflict between the right-wing, Catholic, anti-papal Action Française and Republicans, whether Freemasons, Jews, Protestants or materialists (Weber 1962). In Italy the conflict of secular nationalism with the Church was even clearer. The Pope was an enemy of the Italian nation. The consequence was a secularist liberal intelligentsia and the growing influence of freemasonry and deism in the élite, including the Monarchy itself. On the other hand it was inevitably a matter of national pride that Catholicism was Roman and the Pope Italian. And in any case the attitude of the Church to Italian unity had not been one with that of the Pope.

Czechoslovakia is a different sort of case.[1] The nation was born in the proto-Protestant Hussite movement and persistently in Czech history the baneful influence of Germans and of the Catholic Church were linked together. This sentiment runs all the way from Hus to the liberal Catholic 'Away from Rome' movement and the establishment of the Czech National Church. Hence the success of the Counter-Reformation, though finally assured by the Battle of the White Mountain in 1620, rested uneasily on a base which gave it little support. Since Protestantism was largely eliminated by the Counter-Reformation the national feeling found it difficult to root itself in loyalty to religion whether Catholic or Protestant. Catholicism was disqualified by its associations; Protestantism was largely destroyed. There is perhaps an echo of this in Hungary where the birth of nationalism and the rise of economic development were partly associated with Calvinism.

In the Balkans and in Russia Orthodoxy is plainly associated with national awareness. In the cases of Serbia, Bulgaria, Roumania and Greece the Church was the vehicle of identity during the period of 'the Turkish yoke'. In Russia itself the Church was the soul of nationhood during the early period of domination by invaders from the East. To this day part of the strength of Orthodoxy lies in a feeling that being Russian and being Orthodox amounts to the same thing. The identity of other nations now in the Soviet Union is likewise nourished by churches: the Armenian and Georgian Orthodox Churches, the Uniate

Church of the Ukraine, the Catholic Church in Lithuania, the Lutheranism of the Volga Germans.

Germany itself is a complex case. There is on the one hand the fact that it is the country of Luther's Reformation and there is the important relationship of Luther's Bible to the German language. But the splitting up of Germany into Catholic and Protestant princedoms, respectively concentrated in South and West and North and East (Protestant Württemburg and Catholic Silesia excepted) refracted any direct connection between religion and the overarching myth of the nation. However when national unification came it was under the aegis and dominance of a Protestant power, Prussia, in a situation where Catholicism retained some identification with the national feeling of Southern Germans. The 'secular' religion of German nationalism under Hitler and its war against both Catholicism and the 'Confessing' Lutherans further complicates the picture. So does the fact that a victorious atheist Russia has ever since threatened Germany and divided its territory, thus encouraging a religious counter-definition amongst West Germans.

Cases where it is very difficult for the national myth to coalesce with religion arise where there are several highly distinctive religions within a national border, each with major followings. In this situation no religion can carry the national identity and indeed each religion works divisively against it. In Yugoslavia, Catholic Croatia and Orthodox Serbia both represent unions of religion and nationhood, while Bosnia is largely Muslim. The new state must suppress the divisive element without going so far as to revive aspirations to nationhood by sheer repression, which would in any case be interpreted as favouring one or other of the rival 'nations'. Alongside this cat and mouse policy there has to be built up an overarching secular myth based on the heroic activities of the Partisans, socialist reconstruction and national independence and unity, especially over against Russia and other unfriendly nations. Albania's situation is similar, since neither of its three religions, Catholic, Orthodox and Muslim, can conceivably carry the national identity. Catholicism is in any case compromised by association with Italian Fascist colonialism. However, while Yugoslavia defends its independence against Russian hegemony by openings to the West, Albania did so by association with China.

In the paragraphs above two factors have been mentioned which bear on the question of the efficacy of the association between nation and religion and they ought now to be discussed. One factor is the relationship to Russian hegemony, now and in the past, and the other is the extent to which religion in a given country can plausibly be associated with an antecedent right-wing or Fascist regime. In the case of Bulgaria Russia is the 'elder brother' both historically and now, and the Orthodox Church can be seen as compromised by association with the pre-war regime. Hence the pattern of Russian atheism and severity towards religion is likely to be faithfully followed. Eastern Germany also follows the Russian pattern, partly because its leadership was established to do so. Any connection with the Fascist taint was to be rigidly eschewed and this meant a break with *all* previous continuities, including the Church. The break was the more necessary because the Church was continuous with the culture of a single Germany. Those who could not make the break fled to the West, thereby further weakening any ideological resistance within the D.D.R. The spirit of the new State had to be remade anew and this meant a severe control of the socialization process and the elimination of its religious element. German Communist youth was to worship sport. In short, the old nationalism was unusable and its associations tainted. In the case of Poland, both historically and now, Russia is a source of fear and domination and the Catholic Church, repressed by Russians and Germans, heroically resisted both. One Polish priest in five died in Nazi camps. Hence the association of religion and nation is reinforced and the Russian pattern seen as unacceptable. Roumania conforms more to the Polish situation, particularly since it is sandwiched militantly between Russia itself and pro-Russian Bulgaria. It needs to assert its independence, which partly accounts for its pro-Chinese policy. The Church furthermore represents a Latin culture inserted between Slav cultures and pride in this Latin character assists identification with the Church. Again, though the Church had some association with the pre-war right wing regime and with the 'Iron Guard' nevertheless the Patriarch Justinian established cordial relationships with Communists during and after the war, thus lessening the plausibility of any compromising identification with Fascism.

Czechoslovakia, Hungary, Yugoslavia and Finland provide

intermediate cases. Czechoslovakia's proto-Protestant myth can be reinterpreted as a religious anticipation of a class revolution, especially as regards its radical wing. This myth holds no danger for the régime since the body of practising Protestants in Czechoslovakia is small. Furthermore, when the West acquiesced in the dissection of Czechoslovakia, Communism (and hence Russia) was the only possible source of national recovery for many Czechs. On the other hand Czechoslovakia had been exposed to secular liberalism for which Russia also represented a threat, and this threat was finally realized in 1968. Indeed there was at this time some revival of interest in religion and it is significant that the martyrdom which made the deepest impression was that of a Protestant theological student, Jan Palach. In Hungary there was also a fear of Russian domination, realized in 1956, but the position of the Church, though aligned with Hungarian nationalism, was weakened by association with pre-war right wing regimes and its feudal character and property. Yugoslavia's fears of invasion were never realized; and the Ustasa regime in Croatia, established in the war, was not only right-wing but deeply compromised by the slaughter of large numbers of Serbs.[2] Nevertheless the Church itself was only partly involved in these nationalist excesses, and still remains the one guardian of Croatian national self-awareness. As the regime itself is atheist, Croatian self-consciousness has to rely on its historic religion. Finland was invaded by Russia in 1939 but eventually retained its independence. The Lutheran Church is strengthened by its association with the heroic war of independence, yet weakened by the fact that it had previously largely aligned itself with the right in Finnish politics (Allardt 1964).

The relationships between nationhood and religious identification so far discussed all bear on the present situation, some directly and nearly, some in a more implicit manner. For example in nations like Britain or Holland where the myth of origins is some four centuries old, where the external threats once associated with it have long since receded and where nationhood is not experiencing any other contemporary threat, there the sense of linkage between nation and religion lies dormant. In nations like Poland there has never been a time when the myth is irrelevant: and very similar threats are posed at the present time to those of the past. So the myth is as green and necessary and explicit as ever it was. This is worth underlining since some elements in the above analysis are more plainly of direct relevance to the present; none however has no relevance to the present. The candles burn before Palach's grave in Prague; the audience at the final Promenade concert sings 'And did those feet in ancient time, Walk upon England's mountains green'. Religion maintains itself by songs and candles. As Ireland illustrates, King William's defeat of the Irish at the Boyne is part of contemporary reality. Like the candles it still burns.

Certain conclusions follow from this analysis and these are worth explicit statement. First, an indissoluble union of church and nation arises in those situations where the church has been the sole available vehicle of nationality against foreign domination: Greece, Cyprus, Poland, Belgium, Ireland, Croatia. In such countries bishops have spoken for nations and in Cyprus actually led one in the independence struggle, as well as after it. If the struggle for independence becomes self-conscious at the time of romantic nationalism then the union is a peculiarly potent one, with overtones of a suffering Messianic role. Such one finds in Poland. As will be seen later all the countries mentioned remain areas of high practice and belief: the symbols must not only exist but be seen to be visibly tended. The Greeks must celebrate the Resurrection, the Irish climb St. Patrick's Mountain, and hundreds of thousands of Poles make a pilgrimage to our Lady of Czestochowa. In religion these are present facts. The myth of identity is strengthened further wherever the dominated group have been at the border with another faith: Spain, Austria, Malta, Greece and Poland (at different times) with Islam, Poland with Protestantism and Orthodoxy, Ireland with Protestantism. These are the unions of religion and nation based on suffering and threat. Indeed wherever there is a threat and a border situation the nation is pushed towards its historic faith, even sometimes when it is officially atheist but faced nevertheless with a threat from an atheist country: this is the contemporary situation of Roumania and Poland, and to a much lesser extent of Hungary and Czechoslovakia. Germany and Austria are also the defeated located at a border with atheist victors. And just as there are unions of faith and nation based on suffering so there are unions, *less potent*, based on glory: notably the empires of Holland, Spain, Sweden, Austria and England. These unions are, *ceteris paribus*, much more relaxed: the symbols are less in need of being visibly tended. The most potent unions of all combine past glory and present suffering: once again, Poland.

Ambiguous or negative cases arise under the following circumstances. First, there is an ambiguity where domination restores a religion, as the Counter-Reformation restored Catholicism in Hungary and in Czech Lands, yet has to leave the myth in the hands of a beaten minority. Second, there is ambiguity where a revolution forces the nation to split into two and an old 'integrisme' confronts a new 'integrisme'. This is most likely to happen in Catholic countries since Catholicism is inherently an 'integriste' and organicist system. Third, there is ambiguity where the myths cannot be shared by the whole nation since different areas are dominated by differing religions. This situation is exacerbated where delayed or historically 'late' unification finds these differences a nuisance, irrelevant or positively divisive: examples are Germany, Albania and Yugoslavia. Fourth, there is ambiguity if the ecclesiastical authority explicitly opposes national unification, as in Italy.

IDEAL TYPES OF RELATION BETWEEN POWER AND COUNTER-VAILING POWER

Thus far this analysis has concentrated on religion and nationhood as complementary or antagonistic guardians of overall group identity and of the master symbols of belonging. It is now necessary to introduce a second element: power and counter-vailing power as they relate to patterns of norms. A general discussion of the basic types of relation between power and counter-vailing power is a prerequisite for elaborating a fundamental categorization of sorts of religious culture. The relationship of religion to power arises because it is not only the bearer of identities but a source of legitimacy and of philosophies supporting legitimacy.

Power and alternative power exist in varying relationships: a skewed balance set within agreed limits of tolerable diversity, a confrontation of irreconcilables attempting to skew the balance very heavily one way or the other, an overwhelming monopoly of power. The first comprises a long-term sediment of tolerance, so institutionalized over a long period of time as to seem norma- tively necessary. It generally derives from past situations where each side had to recognize that total victory was impossible and opted for limited tolerances which were susceptible to slow en- largement. The apparently necessary nature of the norm of tolerance acts so as to constrict the exercise of power, and each successful constriction adds to the likelihood of future constraint. Stability thus achieved permits a widening of agreed limits and as limits are widened stability is increased, thereby allowing a further extension of limits. Such a breadth of tolerance, though it must stop short and sharp before the possibility of total freedom, makes extreme opposition or violence appear perverse. If however tolerance presses against these very wide limits it questions legitimacy itself and initiates the anarchic dissolution of society.

The second type of power relationship, which comprises the confrontation of irreconcilables, is composed of rival forces which have had a taste of total authority and desire to taste it yet again. For them the aim is not tolerance and compromise but victory. This unifies both sides and disciplines them amongst themselves because the prospect of a lost battle involves the likelihood of total and permanent defeat. Such an anticipation increases violence and bitterness and creates a tendency to spirals of escalating bitterness. At any point where one side might feel in favour of accommodation it is unlikely that the other side feels similarly; and neither side dare rely on such reciprocity of anticipation. These embattled situations lead each side to elaborate philosophies which commit the soul of the nation into its keeping and define opponents as traitors. Moreover, the aspiration to a philosophy expressing one's viewpoint holistically leads to doctrines whereby each side regards the happy future of humanity as coextensive with its own victory, thereby increasing the likelihood of in- humanity and legitimizing it. The two principles of keeping the nation's soul and anticipating the future of humanity may be yoked together thereby making tolerance of those who resist equivalent to condoning treason and colluding with crimes against humanity's future. Prior to victory opponents are conceived as moral criminals; after victory the law confirms the deliverances of morality.

The third type of power relationship arises after victory, either for those who affirm older principles of 'integrisme' sometimes under the banner of a nationalized Catholic ideology, or for those who affirm new forms of 'integrisme', normally within a Marxist framework. Confining comment to the latter it is clear that any system which proclaims the end of ontological laissez-faire must find the tolerance of error morally offensive and see error and evil as complementary. It may declare an initial confidence in their elimination through natural social processes but faced with the malignant virulence of 'superstition' it will find that these processes need assistance from administrative fiat. Alternatively it may eschew tolerance from the beginning since the toleration of error and evil allows them too great a degree of destructive scope. Hence the struggle must continue to be sharp and bitter. In actual practice policy moves between these two options. Total power aims at producing total peace. Given absolute control of socialization and communication total power will cease to be necessary since the people will act automatically as the rulers desire, and the desires of the rulers are legitimated as the people's will. All contrary wills inhere in the enemies of the people. Legitimacy like power will be total and when both are total both are otiose. Thus the 'sacred canopy' of ideological monopoly is restored.

Now, the above three types, rooted respectively in stable tolerance limits, unstable massive conflict and the stable, massive exercise of power are obviously logical constructs. The first two are based on spirals of stability or instability and the third outlines the logic of total power without such restraints as may arise in practice. Clearly in practice there are often limits to total power just as in practice the stability of systems based on tolerance limits is broken by all kinds of sectional conflicts. What one is pointing to are tendencies either to eliminate dissent, or to institutionalize severe, overlapping conflicts between dichotomous groupings, or to institutionalize conflicts which are merely sectional and usually unconnected. These three possibilities are in fact four since there are two varieties of total power ('Catholic' integrisme and Marxist totalitarian societies), and for that matter there are also three varieties of systems based on tolerance limits. Thus a fundamental classification will incorporate six categories in all, of which five are really operative since the sixth is represented by Europe overseas i.e. the United States.

FUNDAMENTAL CATEGORIES

The fundamental categories can now be formulated and in so doing a whole series of empirical and logical relationships will be implied. From the following analysis it will be clear why the principles of classification should be based on whether or not a culture is Protestant and whether or not it is pluralistic, the two principles being in fact very closely linked to each other.

The first category consists of cultures where Protestantism is dominant, either because they lack Catholic minorities (as in Scandinavia) or because Catholic minorities largely arrived after the pattern had been set in periods of total Protestant dominance (as in England and the United States). For the sake of completeness it is worth indicating the subvarieties of this pattern. The Scandinavian countries are cultures with inclusive state churches largely without Protestant dissent. England is a culture with a less inclusive state church and a very important sector of Protestant dissent. The U.S.A. is a culture where the principle of dissent has been universalized; competing denominations exist within an overall umbrella of general religiosity. *Within* these three sub-varieties of Protestantism is it notable that the degree of anti-clericalism and the extent of practice vary with the amount of dissent. The United States contains the highest amount of dissent and therefore has little anti-clericalism and 40 per cent weekly practice. Everything combines to prevent anti-clericalism. There is no association of any specific religion with the state. The Catholics, by arriving later and taking up lower status positions, have been on the progressive side of politics. Religion has been the *sole* source of migrant identity. And each denomination has moved in flexible symbiosis with various currents of sub-cultural change to that no log-jam associated with religion *per se* has built up across the movement of social development. On the other hand state churches by their continuing association with élite culture cannot vary their style with sub-cultural change, and tend to link up with major blocks lying athwart change in general.[3]

All the cultures concerned illustrate the varied operation of two principles fundamental to Protestantism. The first principle is the notion of the religio-political individual conscience operating outside all ecclesiastical policies. This conscience finds a varied expression according to where the individual is located in the social structure, but is most pervasive in those strata penetrated by nineteenth century liberalism. It is therefore most pervasive in the U.S.A. and Britain where it serves to define politics in terms of morality, and somewhat less pervasive in Scandinavia. The second principle is that of the withdrawal of the church as an institution from any attempt at the independent domination of society. In one sense this may appear to make the church even more conservative than in Catholic countries, but the result is that integrist philosophies propounded by the church as an institution do not become a major area of political tension. The conservatism of Protestant state churches arises because they eliminate ecclesiastical independence and make the Church isomorphic with extant social structure. The avenues of social mobility through the church are closed up and the clergy become more closely linked to the élite both in style and in recruitment, and sometimes in their marked indifference to religion. It is this situation which makes the *cultural* gap yawn widely when the industrial revolution breaks up paternalist relations between upper and lower cultural segments. However, although the Lutheran State Churches were initially opposed to Social Democracy, and although today their active members still tend to cast a conservative vote, nevertheless they accepted the fact that the Social Democratic parties might achieve hegemonic power. In Norway as in Britain there were significant variations on this acceptance, which further lessened tension. In the Norwegian case the 'old left' was originally associated with the religiosity of the Bergen area poised against the Swedish domination emanating from semi-secular Oslo. Thus both democratic and nationalist impulses were channelled through a religious party, and religion was explicitly dissociated from a conservatism which was both secular and inadequately nationalist (Rokkan and Valen 1964). In the British case the whole democratic impulse was initially channelled through an alliance of dissent and Liberalism, but to the extent that this included capitalists as well as craftsmen and the petite bourgeoisie, the conservative party was able to appeal to even lower strata on the basis of a reform of Liberal abuses, notably in the sphere of factory legislation. At the same time the 'integralist' element in the Anglican Church tried to turn the Liberal and dissenting flank by stressing the analogies between medieval organicism and working class solidarity. The result was a form of Anglo-Catholic Socialism in the State Church which could not and did not appear in Scandinavia. Hence not only were all the religious outgroups (Jews, Catholics and dissenting freechurchmen) spread out along the parties of democracy and equity, but insofar as Liberalism and Protestant dissent were successful a section of the State Church joined forces with those to left of the Liberals and the dissenters. Anti-clericalism cannot gain ground where the Liberals have a strong free church support, where Jews and Catholics offer considerable support to Labour, and where the Labour Party itself draws strength from a radical section of the free churches and a medievalist segment of the State Church. The net consequence is a working class separated off less by political opposition or by political solidarity (which in any case it does not possess) than by a cultural distinctiveness which alienates it both from the aristocratic style of the State Church and the liberal styles of the free churches. Sometimes further is said about this pattern below by way of comparison with Holland.

The second category comprises cultures with a Protestant majority but a very substantial Catholic minority: Holland, Germany, Switzerland.[4] As a matter of fact in all such countries at the present time the Catholics are the largest bloc of practising Christians, but the pattern itself derives from a historic ratio of 60–40 associated with a status skew in favour of Protestants, which is in turn associated with greater social dynamism in the Protestant sector. Each culture is sub-divided into Catholic regions and Protestant regions, very broadly south and north respectively. Such societies have developed a *cultural* rather than a purely political bi-polarity and political life has partly turned around the issue of the emancipation and rights of the Catholic sector. Thus the aspirations of relatively depressed groups have been expressed in Catholic organizations, or in parties greatly influenced by Catholics, rather than through parties simply expressing the differences of status and class. The existence of a powerful, if somewhat deprived, bloc, made tolerance and political compromise the most obvious option, more particularly in Holland and Switzerland with extensive traditions of political cooperation. Since Catholics are not motivated to support the conservative parties of the élite the exclusive association of religion

with the right cannot occur. Furthermore, when political polarization is weak some members of both religions are able to take up
positions on the left without adopting a schizophrenic stance. In
all cases the relatively deprived Catholic sector has been more
'organic' and better organized than the Protestant sector. The
long-term complexities and indeed the pathology of the German
case from 1933–1945 cannot be gone into here, but they derive
broadly from the special circumstances of a late national unification and the consequences of defeat in 1918, linked to the
inability of the middle class to push its industrial achievement
through into the political and cultural sector. Hence the deposit
of subservience activated by national disaster.

The Dutch case is particularly interesting in that it offers a
useful comparison with both England and Belgium. The comparison with England arises because the English system involves a
flexible élite, somewhat open to liberal influences yet basically
conservative, facing a counter-culture composed of a partial
conjunction of dissenting religion and liberals of various kinds, the
latter resting on the base provided in the provinces by the former.
The dichotomous basic pattern remains undisturbed even by the
advent of Labour, since a section of the dissenters crossed over
into the Labour Party on finding that the Liberal Party was
sometimes dominated by Whiggery and in any case was losing
the mass appeal which gave it access to power. But in any case
dissenters and other liberals with a 'social' orientation passed
over to the Labour Party and gave it an imprint, which in alliance
with other ideologies incoherently held together, made it an
acceptable replacement to the Liberals as the vehicle of a counter-
culture vis-à-vis élite culture. In the Dutch case both orthodox
Calvinists and Catholics were excluded from the Liberal centre,
the initial reliance of Catholics on the liberalism of Liberals
broke down over the issue of education, while the orthodox
Calvinists were forced to recognize that their national myth was
not safely in Liberal keeping (Daalder 1966). They were therefore
forced into an appeal to the people, which constituted a form of
mobilization parallel to the mobilization of the Catholics (Brunt
1972). The two dissident sectors each mobilized in systems of
social isolation and then talked to each other at the élite level over
the walls of their respective ghettos. This then set a pattern which
is coextensive anyway with a long-term Dutch tradition of de-

centralization and of tolerant accommodation between flexible local élites. The Socialists when they arrived on the scene were forced into a parallel form of protective ghetto and realized that they could only attract the lower echelons within the other ghettos if they ameliorated their rhetoric so as not to prejudice religious loyalties. (This exactly parallels the Norwegian situation in that the extremist tendencies of the new left after the first world war had to be ameliorated to accommodate the regional religious bloc represented by the 'old left' parties, thus laying the foundations of Norwegian political democracy). Eventually, the Catholic Party moved somewhat to the left, recognizing the internal pressure of the lower echelons within it, and engaged in a series of coalitions based on a system of proportional representation which exactly reflected a culture based on a spectrum of positions encapsulated in 'ghettos' (or pillars) rather than on dichotomous alternatives as in the English model.

Thus the 60–40 situation breeds sub-cultural segregation, especially in education, whereby religion is not fully identified with a particular point on the political axis, and whereby the Catholics in particular, who form the largest religious body, move towards the centre-left. The further comparison with Belgium turns on the difference between a cultural discrimination defined in purely religious terms, and a cultural discrimination defined in both religious and linguistic terms. Either way, however, elements of 'pillarization' follow: the Catholic Church achieves an identity separate from the élite, and the politics of status are criss-crossed and stabilized by the politics of cultural defence. Only differentiation eventually weakens the religious-political tie, as is now evident in Holland, Switzerland and Germany.

Whether the advent of higher mobility, geographical, social and in terms of the media, together with elements of secularization in the large cities is weakening the Catholic 'pillar' in Holland is an issue of current debate. Certainly the system has experienced strain as social mixing has increased in the large cities and as very rapid social development has dislocated all kinds of secure definitions. Indeed, the very internal integration of the Catholic pillar has made the conflict between old and new radical middle classes, between administrators and progressive theologians, doubly resonant and violent. And it may be that equality is so close as to render cultural defence more a constriction than an advantage.

Certainly the vote for the Catholic party has been very much reduced since 1967. Where Catholic confessional voting ceases there is first of all apathy and then voting to the left. But so far the system stands and it a direct expression of the 60–40 proportion between the religions.[5]

This is partially reflected in its essentials both in Germany and Switzerland. In Switzerland, of course, the Catholic Church is not associated with the politics of the conservative élite. The political stance of Catholicism in Germany has been central rather than right wing, even though there was an intimate honeymoon with the C.D.U. immediately after the second world war (Kreiterling 1966). In both countries Catholics have suffered some partial exclusion from the military, administrative, educational and commercial élite and have responded accordingly through the politics of the centre and some degree of sub-cultural integration.

The analytic principles underlying social development in these two main categories are worth further explanation. Where dissent is extensive or universal i.e. where inclusive churches identified with the state, the status quo and the élite are weak, as in Britain, or non-existent as in the U.S.A., the varieties of relatively deprived groupings (amongst which Catholics are included) are strung out along the political spectrum in such a way that conflict is not exacerbated by religion *as such* constituting the major differentiating symbol as between left and right. And since religion can be located to the left as well as the right, even if less strongly so, it can ameliorate and constrain the fissiparousness of the left. Common symbols, including those of religion can continue to unite the society above the secondary symbols of conflict. Paradoxically this is achieved in the U.S.A. by the total break between an institutional church and the state, allowing religious symbols to remain a major part of the common vocabulary of legitimation, while in Britain the church can remain established because religion itself has not been at the core of conflicts, and is thereby capable of providing some of the symbols of social unity (cf. Bocock 1974). In Norway the existence of a provincial dissent, albeit formally within the state church, and the association of that dissent with the 'centre' parties of what is called the 'old left' operates in a similar manner. In Sweden the rather limited extent of Protestant dissent, and of the liberalism associated with it, is too minor to affect the situation in this way.

Indeed in Sweden, Finland and Denmark there have been fissions between social Democratic parties and the established churches, and distinct elements of anti-clericalism. But the fact that these state churches are Protestant and believe both in a withdrawal of the church from active political interventions *and* in the principle of the independent religio-political conscience prevents the fission widening into the confrontation of rival blocs. The state churches, by ceasing to be active parts of the operative power structure, can remain part of the common symbolism of the states concerned, along with their respective monarchies. It is significant that, with the exception of Belgium, monarchies only remain in Protestant countries, and for exactly the same reasons that established churches have survived. State churches are not disestablished except in some Protestant cantons in Switzerland; indeed in Sweden it is currently suggested that *all* churches be established. In Switzerland, Holland and Germany the position is slightly different in that the relatively deprived sectors are disproportionately Catholic, and this focuses an extensive area of egalitarian concern on the emancipation of groups whose self definition is largely in terms of religion not status. The 'integrisme' of the Catholic sector thus stands aside from the nexus of church, state, status quo and élite dominance. So once again religion *per se* as embodied in one inclusive institution is not located too exclusively at one point on the political spectrum, and politics are in any case criss-crossed by issues of cultural defence expressed in religious terms. The federalism of all three societies corresponds somewhat to this religious variety, and further breaks down tendencies to dichotomous confrontations in which religion sides too exclusively with one of the polar opposites.

The crucial element in the above argument has been whether or not religion becomes too closely associated with the right wing in politics, thereby explicitly alienating sectors of the population and jeopardizing its place among the master symbols of social consensus and legitimacy. The other element discussed, pluralism, deserves equal stress. As already pointed out it takes various forms: (1) the competition of all denominations with each other in which they are spread out amongst all major parties and are severally associated with most status positions. (2) The competition between a state church allied to an élite culture and dissenting groups in various locations, but found particularly amongst

E

the 'respectable' working class and petite bourgeoisie. (3) 'Competition' within the state church itself, whereby internal movements succeed in ameliorating the élite elements in its culture so as to accommodate democratic or petit bourgeois aspirations. (4) Competition between rival blocs, Protestant and Catholic, in which liberal Protestants ally with latitutarian and agnostic sectors. This results in a kind of 'consolidated' competition between rival oligopolists. (1), (2), (3), are represented by the U.S.A., the U.K., Scandinavia respectively, and (4) by Germany, Holland and Switzerland. The consequences for practice are clear. Type (1) results in an element of overall 'civic religion', complemented by a vast variety of 'vulgarizations' of religion at every status level. Practice is therefore high. Type (2) results in very partial vulgarizations associated with the liberal segments of the population, and it cannot achieve the universal vulgarizations appropriate to the whole range of status groups. The state church remains allied to élite culture. Thus both the liberal, petit bourgeois, and élite social sectors are within reach of institutional Christianity, but the working class is largely outside it. Practice is fairly low, but civic religion can be retained at the overall societal level and an implicit, cultural Christianity is widespread within the working class. The workers' withdrawal is only from the institutional 'style' of the religious sectors. Type (3) results in very low practice because the state church, which is the principal body, retains élite style and connections. But there is a great deal of associational, sub-ecclesial religious activity and the broad cultural identifications with 'Christianity' in a loose sense are not broken. Type (4) is peculiar in that the élite culture becomes explicitly liberal, and latitudinarian, even more so perhaps than in Type (3), and Catholic and (sometimes) orthodox Protestant sectors may organize against it. Religion becomes associated with the politics of regional and cultural defence, and included within the sector covered by that defence there subsist deprived and working class elements. The result is high practice within the organized sub-sectors, and to the extent that these are *highly* organized as in Holland, rather explicit *dis*sociation from institutional religion amongst those not so organized. This type of pattern delays the consequences of social differentiation evident in the other types. But once near parity of status is achieved, cultural defence ceases to overlie the process of social differentiation. The Church then retires from *explicit* involvement in the political sphere to concentrate on the cultural sphere. Thus the connection with the C.D.U. in Germany is relaxed and the Catholic vote in Switzerland and Holland slumps.

The argument as outlined above strongly emphasizes the stabilizing effect of Catholicism where it is a dispersed and fairly small minority, and where it is a large minority settled in a territorial redoubt. However, the effect of Catholicism in its historic heartlands has been quite different, precisely because it has been numerically almost coextensive with the whole society and has grown with the whole structure of status and élite power and culture. Where Catholicism dominates it leads to large political and social fissures, organic oppositions and secularist dogmas of various kinds. This kind of fissure can be charted in Portugal after 1910, in Spain in the 1930s, in France, more especially from 1870 to 1905, and in Italy from the mid-nineteenth century onwards. There are certain partial exceptions such as Belgium and (perhaps) Austria which repay further exploration. In characterizing the third category one draws both on the model of polarizing spirals previously suggested and on the comments made about the organic nature of Catholicism, which at the overall societal level is embodied in national integrisme. The Catholic Church itself is an organic society, dedicated to the notion of unity, and when the Church weds itself to a society any social split threatens its organic character. As a minority, clearly the Church creates for itself an organic sub-culture, a 'column' as the Dutch and Belgians describe it, but as a majority any social division breaks the column in the middle. This makes the issue of the Church a central one, and 'religion' is identified with the Church since religion has been already defined as coterminous with the ecclesiastical institution and with its regulating norms. Thus in societies with Catholic majorities social divisions are coloured and sharply defined by such issues of clericalism, and ecclesiastical rules relating to marriage, and above all by the issue of education, which includes the educational role of the secular priesthood and the regular orders. In 1974, for example, divorce was a major issue in Italian politics; in Belgium since 1968 the question of the revision of the Pacte Scolaire of 1959 (whereby a system of parallel schooling was set up) has been an important issue (Billiet 1973b). The issue of education was of course an endemic crux of conflict in France, with the Second Empire favouring the Catholics and the Third Republic favouring the anti-clericals and expelling the religious orders. Conflicts of this type have persistently converged on the issue of church and state: in France the struggle culminated in 1905 with the separation of Church and State. For the same reason there is controversy over the role of religious symbols in expressing the national unity. Whereas in Protestant societies the secular symbols of res republica and the religious symbols converge, in Catholic societies the symbols of Church and Republic diverge.

Certain other comparisons with Protestant societies underline the nature of the Catholic case: for Protestant societies the issue of divorce in its religious aspect gradually settles into a matter of the *internal* regulation of ecclesiastical bodies and of cultural definitions of the marital bond. The point of Protestant issue with the state, particularly among dissenting groups, has turned either on matters of the regulation of individual morals with regard to (say) alcoholic consumption or the rights of the individual conscience with respect to military service. Occasionally such questions of conscience are also part of the politics of cultural defence as in the 'symbolic crusades' over prohibition and the anti-pornography campaigns.

In Catholic societies, historically and now, the question of individual conscience is rarely raised, being understood neither by Catholics nor secularists. Objections to central authority are however understood and objections to bureaucracy since Catholics and republican governments have a plenitude of both, each reflecting the other. But the individual conscience is a different matter. Pacifist and protest movements in Protestant societies have a high component of religious individualism; in Catholic societies they have a high component of organized politics. By the same token student revolt and intellectual dissent in Anglo-Saxon countries easily take on various religious and quasi-religious colourings, whereas in Catholic countries it easily flows into dogmatic positions and highly organized political cells.

But such spirals of polar opposition do not necessarily pursue their logic to the end, though the difference in 1968 between France and Britain was highly indicative. No British government fell by virtue of fires sparked off in London University. The model presented earlier must remain a model *ceteris paribus*, and external threat brings together erstwhile opponents. The first world war provided an initial break in the polarities of French politics, and the second war both discredited the collaborating right and allowed a Catholic reforming centre to emerge (H. W. Paul 1967). Indeed the dislocations of the war gave a reforming social Catholicism a chance to emerge, throughout western Europe, in France, Belgium, Austria and Germany. Catholicism moved towards the creation of a stabilizing centre and could include openings to the left. This shift was initiated by those Catholics who contributed most to the reconstruction of post-war Europe: Adenauer, Schumann. This was a tradition continued in his own way by de Gaulle. If however the war is not external but civil then the logic of polarization is pursued à l'outrance, and the Spanish and Portuguese reversion to integral Catholicism follows. Should the 'civil war' occur after the overall shift in Vatican politics has partly shifted the Catholic Church away from the right and after the local Catholic Church has itself been partly disengaged and marginally differentiated then religion may well view 'liberal' revolution with benevolent neutrality. This is now the case in contemporary Spain and—perhaps—Portugal.

When the spirals are weakened then the issues of anti-clericalism weakens likewise. If the definition of religion as exclusively on the right is eroded then the left will be glad to be augmented by believing Catholics. If believing Catholics are seen on the left then the definitions in terms of ecclesiastical right and secularist left are gradually relegated to the folk memory. If Catholic education no longer need be viewed as part of the socialization of an anti-republican sector then there is less motive to oppose it. Thus in France the issue of education now barely raises the bogeys of clericalism; and the Pacte Scolaire in Belgium, though once again an issue, was nevertheless indicative of a spirit of accommodation which still exists.

This is the point at which to mention divisions *within* the church corresponding to the relatively greater spread it now achieves along the political spectrum, including the extreme left as distinct from the Communist left. If there is to be religious 'dissent' in Catholic societies it works by parties within the Catholic Church itself and these like the Catholic Church tend to have an explicitly political content. (By contrast the parties within Lutheran Churches, such as the Inner Mission, work by the percolation of a slow cultural stain). These parties actually strain at the institutional character of Catholicism, and at the margins they initiate a free religiosity sitting light to institutional loyalties. This in turn breeds reassertions of institutional discipline, and the resulting struggle is complicated by very general reactions to the institutional constraints of all modern bureaucracy. The spread of the free radical religiosity of Dissenso in Italy was one such movement and it not merely sparked off attempts at ecclesiastical discipline but was complemented by popular archaic movements of a superstitious and eschatological kind. Of course the fate of Dissenso indicates how free radical religiosity can flow eventually in channels dug by the more directly political left. Some Catholics are now standing as independents in the Communist lists. The general post-war shift was recognized by the Vatican and then given a further acceleration by the Council, which both legitimated the opening to the left and provided a context for movements to the right, either stranded elements of pre-war Catholic conservatism or free-floating expressions of archaic and popular religiosity. The former are more prevalent in France, the latter in Italy. One should perhaps note that the possibility of Communist hegemony in Italy from 1974 on has revived Catholic–Communist antagonism: the Vatican strongly inhibited a Communist vote in the 1976 elections.

The French example provides the richest illustration of the shifts and counter-moves which have occurred, and it also merits further discussion of the most important case of the Protestant majority-Catholic minority situation in reverse. As has been said, the old right was discredited by Vichy and along with it the collaborationist bishops of the old Action Française. The Liberals grew in influence; the Mission de France embarked on the worker-priest experiment. The partial absorption of worker priests into a militant working class milieu led to the suspension of the experiment and temporary disarray, but in its place there appeared a new kind of militant Christian social action. This has been complemented by less stress on retreats, rosaries and ritual. The result has been a notable collaboration between militant laity and clergy in social relief and reform, sometimes in company with Marxists, and certainly for a while in dialogue with them. The most obvious instance of lay Catholic action is the Jeunesse Agricole Chrétienne. It began between the wars in rural France and under priestly tutelage. During and after the war it became a form of self-help both in the world of general culture and in the world of farming techniques and organization, and then evolved into a radical instrument of the younger generation and a modernizing influence. (With regard to economic innovation it parallels both Haugean dissent in Norway and Orthodox Calvinist dissent in Holland). Movements and activities of this kind have linked up both with the left and the technocracy. Most extreme have been the manifestations of a new monasticism in the communautés de base, some of which are led by married priests. This, of course, parallels movements towards radical communitarianism in Italy, and in Holland, such as the semi-secularized group 'Shalom' (Van Tillo 1973 and Hervien 1973). This new emphasis on activism at the expense of contemplation and the new clerical, or ex-clerical militancy and politicization aroused various reactions. Even a liberal, such as the Cardinal-Archbishop of Paris appointed in the 1960's, felt it right to use what authority remained. The Church had at least to repudiate the left wing of the Jeunesse Etudiante Chrétienne insofar as there was any suggestion that the Church was corporately implicated in its policies. 'Les Silencieux' form a puzzled centre, perhaps a majority, worried and confused by the new trends. Meanwhile the old integrisme remains, in areas like the Brittany interland or Hérault: it objects to those changes in the liturgy which express a more horizontal sense of community and it has even threatened secession (Ardagh 1973). It now has a rallying point, Eccône.

So far as the Protestant minority (3 per cent) is concerned its link with the kind of social and cultural action just mentioned is through the revival of monticism in association with ecumenical activity at Taizé. The Protestants have traditionally been on the 'left', partly because the Republic consolidated their position in French society, partly because in the late nineteenth century they were influential in the Third Republic (Schram 1954). The 'integrisme' of the Catholics defined them, along with freemasons and Jews, as amongst the alien elements in France and they accepted this role vis-à-vis the Catholics. Their contribution in the 'progressive' sector of French life was not only political but scientific and professional: the 'bar Protestant' is a phrase indicative of their influence. They were tightly knit in familial dynasties, largely in response to their isolation—a factor con-

tributing to a relatively high degree of practice for Protestants.
This inter-linked character has never disappeared. Nor has their
sense of history and martyrdom disappeared. It is the memory of
the persecutions after the Revocation of the Edict of Nantes in
1685, and the memory of the 'integristes' reaction to them which
keeps them to the left. Indeed in the Cévennes, where they form a
regional majority and where the memory of the old martyrdoms
is fiercest, they vote Communist. Their left wing stance complements the labour or progressive sympathies of the Catholic
minorities in Anglo-Saxon countries. Both cases are interesting
instances of the structural position of a religious community
refracting the impact of status: middle class Protestants in France
and middle class Catholics in England cast a disproportionately
large radical vote.

   In Italy there is a somewhat different version of the spirals
found in the French pattern. One has to remember that Italy
experienced unification rather than revolution and that this
unification was one imposed by a liberal anti-clerical and anti-
papal leadership. This leadership worked a system of patronage
and shifting mutations of cabinet personnel: it was able to assume
a high degree of consensus over socio-economic questions, since
the Catholics had left politics at papal bidding and the lower
classes had not arrived. When the latter did arrive, and socialism
with them, the liberals decided to compound with the Catholic
Church over such issues as divorce, the orders and education. By
1919 the Catholics had achieved massive representation through
the Popular Party, a reformist and democratic body, and the
Socialists were in Parliament as the largest single party. As in
Spain, France and Holland, Socialism had important anarchist
roots and support from landless agricultural labourers. The
Catholics were internally divided, though their dislike of the
Liberal state derived more from the temporal politics of the
Vatican than any alienation of Catholics as such. At any rate the
mutual suspicions of Catholics, Liberals and Socialists made
possible the Fascist take-over. After the war all the old symbols
of legitimacy were compromised except the Church. The Lateran
Treaties of 1929 had formalized a reconciliation between the
Church and Fascism and gave some legitimacy to Fascism, but
thereafter Church and Party came increasingly into conflict. The
other survivor into the post-war period was the Communist Party,

which received credit for the resistance even more than it deserved, and reaped a reward in dominant positions in unions and local government. The Christian Democrats now unified all those afraid of communist revolution and eventually became the ruling party to such an extent that it has been possible until the mid-70's to identify Christian Democracy with government and administration. The Christian Democrats attract those of every category who are marginally better off than others in the same category and they draw disproportionately on the practising Catholics; the Communists are the reverse in both respects. Both parties exploit face to face groups, including the family, and insert themselves in the social fabric, often using ideology more as a weapon in intra-party disputes than as a basic resource with the electorate at large. The Catholics have their stronghold in the Venetias and Trentino, the Communists in the central belt of Emilia, Tuscany and Umbria, and both beliefs achieve some degree of closure in their respective social systems: ideological at the top, recreational at grass roots level. The Socialists, for their part, draw on the non-practising Catholics whereas the Communist Party appeals to a sector part of which is explicitly opposed to the Church.[6] Two things are crucial: a marked decline of general hostility towards the Communist Party and decreased deference towards clergy amongst the young.

The system is one which is split in terms of a set of criteria amongst which the Church is very important. Thus far it resembles France. But the Church has not been burdened with the advocacy of a monarchist right: on the contrary it fought the liberal monarchy and when it emerged in politics it adopted a position near the moderate centre. After the war it was associated with a form of Christian Democracy which covered a large range of positions, including the centre-left. Moreover, by the sixties both the Church and the Communist Party had made moves away from total intransigence, some of these moves being pragmatic and some ideological. The Church ceased to be wholly identified with the Christian Democrats, the Communists espoused the 'Italian' way of communism, and a brand of Christian politics emerged highly critical of current social arrangements and unwilling to endorse automatically the Church's position on such controversial matters as divorce. The Catholic labour organizations became more independent of the Church; the Church itself entered the realm of social criticism. Thus some of the spirals which unwound in France also unwound in Italy.[7] And it was no longer possible to impose Catholic marriage discipline on the whole society: in 1974 divorce was accepted. Perhaps the really indicative paradox is here: 61 per cent of practising Catholics still support Democrazia Christiana; and 51 per cent of practising Catholic women voted for divorce.

Two exceptions to the polarities found in cultures characterized by Catholic dominance have been mentioned. They are Belgium and Austria, though the latter only deviates marginally from the classic model. The Belgian case is very instructive. It illustrates first the fact that Catholics are less polarized against 'progressives' if they are fighting a common enemy, in this case foreign control by Austrians, French and more especially the Dutch. The relative unities forged in this struggle for independence set the crucial parameters of later development. The 'set' at a nation's birth has *enormous* constraining force for the future.[8] Furthermore, this set was confirmed and strengthened by the external threat or actuality of German occupations in the two world wars. Indeed, it was this set which not only provided the restrictions on polarizations in Belgian society but made possible a stable monarchy. The monarchy was born with the struggle for independence and was identified both with the struggle against the Germans in the Great War and the conciliatory social policy immediately following it.[9]

Belgian Catholicism can be described as sub-dominant in spite of its numerical dominance. This is because dominance or sub-dominance is not merely a matter of numbers or even of political power but of cultural evaluation. The critical symbol of cultural devaluation in Belgium has been the official attitude to the Flemish language. Until recently Flanders has been economically depressed compared with Wallonia; Catholicism is associated with the small towns and countryside of Flanders and with the Flemish tongue over against French and industrial Wallonia. This deprivation expressed itself in religious and linguistic terms thus providing a cross-cutting criterion for the expression of differences. Since Wallonia is in the French sphere and French is associated with secularism Flanders is forced back on a sharper identification with Catholicism.

Nevertheless the classic polarities did appear in the late nineteenth century and notably over the question of church-state relations, which dominated Belgian politics at the expense of social and economic issues. The crucial issue, as in France, was over education and over the setting up of 'public schools', though in Belgium the net result was more favourable to the Catholics than in France. In Belgium the Catholics retained a larger sector of the education system just as they held a larger share of political support, especially from 1884 to 1914. Being pushed less hard they were in their turn less extreme. Ultra-right Catholics emerged to criticize a Catholic parliamentarianism which tolerated error along with truth. But they did not attack the system as such or hopelessly pursue an outworn system as did those French Catholics who devoted themselves to a royal restoration. As in France, the rationalist societies and freemasons sought to make the church and state independent, to laicize education, welfare and even burial. Furthermore, the two contestants were the sources of each others discipline. Yet the constitutional frame held, but within a pattern of discrete, disciplined sub-cultures. When the socialist party appeared it fitted rapidly into the groove. It partly eschewed ideology, but became sectarian in its opposition to sectarianism and in its creation of a third sub-culture, consisting of unions, friendly societies and cooperatives. So doing it in turn set a pattern for Catholic organizations. Like Holland, Belgium is marked by segregated columns on behalf of which their respective élites meet and negotiate; as in Holland it represents a relatively stable system of sub-cultures which have some tendency to relaxation at their frontiers. If the nation is split it is not so much by the politics of interest as by the politics of culture and language, of which political Catholicism is one living expression. At the same time of course, the Catholic political party has itself been split since 1968 by the language issue: the Christian Socials operate with separate Flemish and Wallonian wings.

Austria is also an instance of verzuiling or Lagermentalität, and the 'columns' retain their perspectives on each other in spite of increasing erosion of status difference and diminution of ideological oppositions. Cultural definitions can not only precede and canalize the opposition and philosophies of class, but can outlast them. In between the wars the two poles were organized as alternative societies, a Black Austria and a Red Austria centred on Vienna, each with para-military wings. The crunch came with the occupation of Red Vienna in 1934, followed by a brief period of Catholic corporatism until Austria was incorporated by Germany in 1938. Thus far the historical situation conforms to the polarization model. But two factors are important in diminishing the polarity. Austria emerged late as a democratic entity, and the strife of the First Republic from 1918 to 1934 was a relatively short episode. When the Second Republic was formed after the Second World War the shift in Catholicism itself had occurred, and the Catholic Church in Austria withdrew from the kind of explicit involvement in Austrian politics which had characterized the pre-war Christian Social Party. Perhaps a third influence is the fact that the party which retains *cultural* links with Catholicism, the People's Party (OUP), is an organization not only of self-defined 'state bearing' elements but of peasants, shopkeepers and white collar workers. This divides the class vote. Hence there is a continuing need for coalition and compromise which exists alongside a continuing tension and suspicion (Engelman 1966).

There are one or two analytic points to be made concerning the pattern in societies where Catholicism is, or has been, the religion of the vast majority of the inhabitants. Obviously, all of them have been afflicted by dichotomous polarizations in which the Church has provided a major focus of contention. The greater the initial friction, the greater the subsequent conflict is likely to be because where oppositions become fundamental, the role of education grows more crucial. Catholics want the right to bring up the next generation as Catholics; Republicans do not want the next generation reared as monarchists. This is the French situation formed in the crucible of Revolution and Restoration, and in the hopes of repeating both which were retained on either side of the fissure.

The French situation has been continually exported via the influence and attraction of French culture and the orientation of its intelligentsia. Nevertheless most other societies provide some important and ameliorating variation on the French pattern. One type of variation relates to the different kinds of relationship of centre to periphery. The French relationship is clearly rooted in the dominance of Paris and Paris is the capital of a vast devastated basin so far as Catholicism is concerned. But Belgium and Austria are made up of eastern and western blocs, with the capital in the western bloc. Of course, that is a gross oversimplification but the crucial point relates to the relative balance of forces. Each side came to recognize the irreducibility of the other and the danger to the nation as a whole should conflict be pushed to the furthest limit (Bogensberger 1972, and Houtart 1972). Even in Spain there was a measure of balance between the Castilian centre and the massive peripheries of Galicia, the Basque country and Catalonia. In Portugal the 'tone' of Lisbon looked towards the more secularist south but the bulk of the population was in the Catholic north. Indeed, looking at Portugal a further factor is evident and that is the ambiguous relation of the Church to the liberal élite which ran the country from 1910–1926. Both in the nineteenth and twentieth centuries the Portuguese liberals were severe on the Church, and between 1910 and 1926 the Church and the nascent socialist movements suffered together. This hardly united the causes of socialism and catholicism, but it provided a modicum of empathy which persisted even through the time of the corporate state 1926–1974. When the revolution came its leaders were moderate in their ecclesiastical policy and the bishops responded with similar moderation. The impact of the ambiguous relation between Portuguese Catholics and liberals is in a way, the obverse of the situation which obtained in Belgium. As has been pointed out above, the liberals and the Catholics were involved together in the struggle to found the nation. This ameliorated their subsequent conflict to quite a significant degree.

In all the societies concerned war had an important effect on the dynamics of unity and disunity. In France after 1870 and in Spain after 1898 the Church was blamed for defeat. Yet the first world war brought even French Catholics and French secularists together to defend the Republic. Similarly in Belgium the fissures closed under external pressure. Indeed, the history of the Christian Social Party reflects precisely the unities forged in the first and second world wars, *and* the linguistic divisions which grew in the 1930s and 1960s. In Austria the second world war gave an opportunity for the spirals of hostility to unwind. The old pattern was disrupted just at the point where the Church had come to realize the danger which explicit political involvement engendered for its structural mission.

Italy is a complex case because of the initial Catholic withdrawal from politics following unification, but it is important that the Catholic Church first stood apart from a modernizing but rather corrupt liberal centre and then refused total identification with the Fascist régime. It was thus able to emerge as a political rallying point for the moderate centre and uncorrupted section of the right, as it did in France.

In general one can say that the Catholic Church, in response to social processes of differentiation and by way of bitter experience, 'saw' the futility of spirals of conflict and the danger of explicit involvement in the politics of a political party, including the politics of the Spanish government. This danger arises because such involvement alienates those whose politics are different from the basic mission of the church. Since the existence of varied self-conscious social sectors is itself an aspect of differentiation, so too the Catholic Church's relative withdrawal from explicit politics especially that of a restorationist right, is equally an *aspect of differentiation*. This is a case of differentiation initiating further differentiation. The war itself assisted the realignments necessary, first producing an alliance of the Church with the centre and centre right, and then a partial withdrawal from all alliances. This fact, combined with the recognition of irreducibility on both sides, reduces the tendency to total conflict and allows some free outriders to appear in both camps, crossing the old lines of conflict. The 'outriders' are likely to be 'free' Marxists, not the Party itself, and 'free' Catholics. The one area where the Catholic Church cannot easily withdraw is where it provides the focus of a regional nationalism, since that nationalism is the *only* significant 'sector' in its own area, or where the system of verzuiling has built up so tight a Catholic organization that its inertias, including political involvement, cannot easily be broken.

The fourth category comprises those societies where the polarizations endemic in a Catholic culture issued in a return to 'integralist' society. This return often involves an appeal to the military, who in Spain for example have historically seen the preservation of the true, Catholic Spain as reverting to their hands after periods of democratic corruption. The importance of the ecclesiastical issue is seen by its key role in the First Republic 1868–1874 and in the Second Republic 1931–1936. It was article 26 of the 1931 Constitution, separating Church and State, confiscating some Church property, restricting the Orders and excluding them from education, which first really focused and hardened opinions against the Republic (cf. Carr 1966). Spain, Portugal and Orthodox Greece belong to or have 'participated' in this third category, as did Austria from 1934 to 1938: outside Europe Chile provides a contemporary example. Such societies normally adopt a corporatist ideology and schemes of 'vertical integration'. It is interesting that in Greece the Colonels explicitly defined themselves as the defenders of Greece's Orthodox heritage. Such regimes attempt to achieve modernization and economic development without cultural radicalization or the political and the personal fragmentations of liberalism. In Spain, 'Opus Dei' is—or was—a major vehicle of this: an ascetic lay order of élite personnel which has played a considerable role in government and is dedicated both to modernization and tradition.[10] And indeed in Spain the economic transformations achieved have been remarkable.

Such régimes are obviously authoritarian: their hierarchical principles complement those of the Catholic Church. Again, like the Catholic Church they condone moderate cultural deviance and repress explicit opposition. They allow intellectual dissent provided it does not organize; and Protestantism has had to exist against some legal restriction and cultural constraint. In any case Protestantism consists of tiny minorities dating mainly from the nineteenth century (Almerich 1972). Authoritarian regimes of the right are less all-embracing in their control than communist societies, since for the latter cultural deviance is as dangerous as organized opposition. Catholicism is defined as the source of the national tradition and is supported in that specific role: as with the absolutist rulers of the eighteenth century there is no tolerance of ecclesiastical independence. The principal technique is the control of the higher appointments, which usually ensures a compliant official voice. The manipulation of the appointment of the sometime Archbishop of Athens by the Colonels was one important example.[11] However, the very recognition of the church and of its traditions allows those traditions to be used as vehicles of opposition. The Church can become a funnel for opposition once it is freed from the overwhelming fear of being crushed and persecuted from the left. Thus the Spanish Church from about 1960 onward has proved a source of opposition to the regime, particularly where this opposition is linked to the historic Spanish aspirations towards regional autonomy in Catalonia and in the Basque country. In the Basque country Catholicism is a major carrier of a radical separatism; in Catalonia the separatism is expressed more in cultural and linguistic terms. Both areas have moved to the left: Catalonia before the Civil War, partly because the Republic granted some autonomy, the Basque country after the war because the new regime denied it.

In any case, the Spanish Church is open to influences from international Catholicism, either the Second Vatican Council or the French Church, which reflect developments in the Church as a whole and its partial rapprochement (aggiornamento) with the situation in Europe and the world at large (Duocastella 1965). Nationalism cannot convert a church into a pure expression of the Nation. Nevertheless there are obviously a variety of elements in the Spanish Church (Marcus Alonso 1965). There is a layer of local superstition pre-dating Christianity itself. There is the kind of Catholicism that believes Spain more Catholic than the Pope and rejects outside or modernizing influences, whether derived from him or elsewhere. Then there is a generation affected by the Council and by the ferments of the sixties which finds the integrisme, authoritarianism, the psychic constriction and role-bound character of the older Catholicism not easily tolerable. Thus there arises a generation gap, particularly with those whose priestly formation took place in the conformist period from 1940 to 1960. Young priests have been shown to nourish surprisingly radical opinions; they also sometimes work with local Communists. This gap in itself leads to tensions, fewer vocations and defections. Indeed, it is characteristic of this 'liberated' Catholicism, in Spain as in Holland, that once the conservative dykes are breached after a long period of holding back the waters of modernity, then there is a tendency to react to extremes, politically and existentially. Hence the suspicion with which the regime views the Church from time to time, hence maybe the 1970 proposals for a state monopoly of education, and the tension with the Vatican even under the very moderate policy of consolidation inaugurated by Pope Paul. (A parallel opposition to the authoritarianism of the state exists in the Brazilian Catholic Church.)

On the other hand, the role of the Church in relation to the regime is symbolically represented in the building of enormous edifices and the mausoleums created for General Franco and the fallen in the Civil War. At the level of state symbolism church and state are forced to be one; organizationally the church can and must be controlled; culturally it can funnel opposition, including opposition which has (or had) no other legitimate outlet. In this last respect it plays the role of the church in authoritarian societies of the left. The church building has time and again been chosen as the best venue for radical demonstrations.

A short note is appropriate on Portugal since the revolution of 1974. Prior to that time the upper clergy had been quiescent and their appointment controlled by the regime. Protest and political dissidence came largely from Portuguese Catholic missionaries in the overseas territories. The Church inherited a tradition of anti-clericalism and middle class indifference on the one side and support from the smaller proprietors of the north and centre on the other. There were exceptions to the record of quiescence, notably the Bishop of Oporto, who protested from a liberal viewpoint. Being a non-theological body the Portuguese Church found the winds of change from Rome not entirely to its liking: it stood rather by the Pilgrimage to Fatima and the mystique of Empire. The movement of dissident priests back from Africa to Portugal imported revolution, just as happened in the case of the military.

With the coup the bishops published a pastoral praising democracy, but the increasing leftward trend alerted ecclesiastical uncertainties, especially with respect to the control of Catholic radio. The Catholic population itself is spread along the political spectrum, less so in the Communist party, but everywhere else including the close ally of the Communist party, the M.D.P. Perhaps there are proportionately more Christians in the non-Marxist Social Democratic Centre and the M.P.D. than in the Socialist Party of Mario Soares. The Social Democratic Centre has a member of Opus Dei as its secretary; and there are also Christian Democrats who have been banned from elections. Based on Braga and more traditional Catholic areas the C.D.S. used explicit Christian symbolism and ecclesiastical connections, partly to the embarrassment of the Church. The banning of the C.D.S. was probably advantageous. Clearly the Church laity have been coexisting with the new Portugal, even in part enthusiastically, but that coexistence, particularly so far as the hierarchy are concerned, is threatened by Communist attempts at hegemony and the atheistic philosophy inevitably associated with it. Since then democratic forces and the Church have been in practical alliance: the freedom of Catholic radio and of the official Socialist newspaper have turned out to be the same cause. (This material is taken from various sources, but particularly *The Times* and Adrian Hastings, *The Tablet*, April 12 and 19, 1975). There is little doubt that the influence of the priests and parish weeklies, more especially in the Catholic north, prepared the way for the defeat of left extremism in November 1975.

The Greek situation exemplifies a clear pattern with local variations of truly Byzantine complexity. Basically the Colonels violated the laws of the Church (and of Byzantium) by trying to retire any democratic or non-compliant bishops and leaning on the sometime liberal but now reactionary Archbishop of Athens, Hieronymos. They even had in mind the use of the Church as a mini-Vatican of the eastern Mediterranean fostering pan-Hellenic ambitions in that area. The resultant tensions and the eventual overt conflict with Makarios plus the mainland unrest signalized by the 'polytechnic events' in Athens led directly to the desperate throws preceding the Cyprus debacle and to the division of the island. Once the Colonels were deposed the hierarchy was again in part retired, but not before the image of the Church had been seriously damaged amongst the young. What remained however was the union of the Church and the Greek Spirit, and the pattern of rural rite and festival intertwining the Church and the café as twin foci of social existence.

Authoritarian societies of the left provide our fifth category, one in which the immanent possibilities of societies are overprinted by the fact of Russian hegemony and the imposition of communist governments. History is full of contingencies of this kind from the Battle of White Mountain to the Battle of Stalingrad. As has just been remarked, the Church must be controlled organizationally, by the manipulation of appointments, the infiltration of government agents and by subventions of money which are dependent on compliant behaviour. In authoritarian societies of the right the Church must act as it does because it is forcibly united to the state; in authoritarian societies of the left it is often forcibly separated from the state (Bociurkiw 1973 and Cviic 1973) Churches are reduced to the level of private associations for religious deviants, who are usually allowed no more scope than is required for the bare performance of worship, and often less than that. Freedom of cultic behaviour is frequently interpreted to mean that active evangelization amounts to interference with the rights of others while atheistic propaganda is part of the liberation of the backward and psychically deviant. In Russia, indeed, religious socialization under the age of eighteen is forbidden. As evangelization is forbidden so too is political comment. The public voice of the church can be raised no higher than a request for its rights under codes of 'socialist legality', in itself often a dangerous operation. It is also allowed and encouraged to support the 'peace' conferences of the eastern bloc and to perform certain political roles through ecumenical organizations.[12] Participation in such organizations is conditional on obedience to governmental policies, and on a reciprocal silence from other churches in the West who desire such participation. The overall impact of this is threefold. First, the church is totally excluded from the official symbolism of the nation. Second, its public voice and symbolic presence can only be deployed in total obedience to national policy. Third, it must accept complete privatization in that it cannot explicitly form a sub-culture or contribute to debate on public issues. As an association of private persons it operates under a Ministry of Cults, with which it must be registered, and which, in the Soviet Union at least, defines the minimum local numbers necessary for registration and the opening of a church.[13]

All the above follows from the fact of the end of ideological laissez-faire. Error cannot be allowed open competition with truth, and truth requires active administration action. This administrative action operates through total control of the media and means of socialization, which means that there is an inverse relationship between the number of believers in a given milieu and exposure to media and the socialization processes. Since the administrators must themselves be untainted they are necessarily part of the Communist party, which is the vanguard of truth. And since administrative power is the chief focus of power and status it follows that the élite are almost entirely non-religious. Given that this is the situation in the power élite and given the differential impact of media and socialization it follows that believers are concentrated amongst the relatively powerless, the relatively uneducated and those least integrated into the social and economic process. Whether they are least integrated because they are believers or vice versa varies from case to case. In this way the relationship of practice to education and status is the reverse of that obtaining in western societies. Religion is pushed to margins, geographical and social.

Since the aim of communist societies is to exorcise culture of all contrary or recalcitrant elements it cannot afford even the cultural deviance found in authoritarian societies of the right. A Solzhenitsyn is a peculiar offence, particularly when his opposition is twofold: to the mistakes and the theory of the regime and to the subservience of the Church. But just because the thrust of communist policy is towards the comprehensive redemption of culture as well as of structure this means that churches and sects are symbols of opposition without needing to do more than actually exist. Since politics are proscribed, except in the form of inner-party pressures, political opposition is pushed down to the level of culture, either literature or religion, particularly as passed from hand to hand in samizdat form.

Restriction to the private sphere leaves religion a resonance within the axes of the individual life-cycle, and these axes are not covered by the formulations of officially certified truth. Nevertheless they must be discouraged and displaced by functional equivalents in the form of socialist rituals for birth, confirmation, marriage and death. These rites, more especially baptism, are the most tenacious aspects of religion in communist as in western societies since they touch the person most nearly. They set him in cosmic space, carry forward the subterranean continuities and nostalgias of culture, and focus familial pressures for the symbolic expression of those continuities (Aptekman 1965, and Krianev and Popov 1963). Hence the need to refurbish all the non-religious elements of folklore in order to cover up the discontinuity which could be left by the demise of religion. In Russia at least this policy has been partly successful, especially in relation to the marriage rite.

Policy is in fact variable, moving between periods of relative tolerance and vigorous repression, but the aim is unchanging. This is because a scientific prediction has been made about the demise of religion and about the triumph of 'science' by administrators who are self-defined as the only philosophic guardians of social science. If the facts do not 'naturally' conform to their prediction then the reality must be forcibly manipulated, else science and its priesthood are discredited. On their own premises they have no option but to persecute.

Under these kinds of pressure the churches themselves remain conservative in their ethos: to adjust theologically is to concede the last bastions of independence. On the whole dialogue does not ensue between Marxists and Christians, except in Catholic Poland and Yugoslavia, merely because Marxist truth can gain nothing by commerce with error. The relationship is an endurance test not a discussion. Even churches must repeat the public rhetoric of communism, since he who is not publicly with communism must be against it. This is not to say the rhetoric is entirely believed either within churches or outside them. An acceptance of the 'sacred canopy' of Marxist dogma in the population at large is accompanied by a very widespread pragmatic scepticism. Yet this is not the same as disbelief but runs parallel to the distinction made in western societies between 'real' Christianity and the extant institutional church. It allows dissidents to hanker after the 'real' Marxism of a libertarian or Trotskyist left. 'Marxism has not failed; it has never been tried'—to adapt the defence of Christian apologists.

The aim of all such systems is unity and ideological monopoly, and it is even possible to use the old state churches as interim vehicles for suppressing deviance. Orthodoxy in Russia and in Rumania is used to suppress Uniate and other deviants. Religious nationalism such as exists in Catholic Lithuania and the western Ukraine can be suppressed as mere 'bourgeois nationalism', whereas Russian nationalism is 'loyalty to the socialist fatherland'. Philosophical annihilation goes hand in hand with repression. Yet unity is not achieved because total control even of Orthodoxy itself or the Baptist churches breeds vigorous schisms within both, and the schismatics accuse the official leadership of being state puppets. Thus the puppets sometimes need and ask to be allowed some marginal leeway in order to prevent breakaway movements of untraceable, uncontrollable, unregistered schismatics. In certain cases, notably the Jews, language and culture have to be suppressed along with religion in order to prevent sub-cultural diversification. Where even this fails the state may eventually prefer migration, since this weakens the resistance of those left behind. Even so, migration, which was used freely by Russian sects under Tsarism is not now a right but an occasional privilege.

In fact the only major instance of religious independence exists in Poland, where the Catholic Church is so strong as to constitute an element of semi-recognized political opposition, even indeed of limited criticism.[14] Each side warily watches and treats the other within agreed norms and uses the fact of rivalry to discipline deviants within its own ranks. Only here, in the most Catholic land in Europe, does the central issue for Catholicism—education —recur as a major question within the eastern bloc. The communist concessions in Poland are purely pragmatic and display the usual alternations between strong pressure and relative relief, especially in the crucial fields of education and socialization. The Catholic Church, for its part tries to escape from the consequences of a Vatican policy geared to the situation in Eastern Europe as a whole—since this gives too much away. The Church also minimizes the impact of the Vatican Council because this could create divisions for the government to exploit.[15]

Something more must be said about the relationship of ideological monopoly and of the newly-revived 'sacred canopy' to Baptists, eschatological sectarians, groups like the Old Believers, and communitarians like the Molokans. Molokans, by virtue of forming separate communities, economically and socially, were clearly offensive to social unity, and were further endangered by their very rationalism and progressivism. They were so close to communism; therefore they were otiose and should be disbanded (Klibanov 1970). Many of them turned to the Baptists, who were representative of the classic Protestant ethic, and who asked only for the right to be good, sober, disciplined workers on some other basis than the imperatives of 'socialist morality'. They were allowed to exist narrowly within these confines and they form a 'constituency' (as distinct from membership) of about 1 per cent of the Russian population. Most Baptists are in the interstitial, moderately educated sectors of urban life, whereas Orthodoxy is concentrated in the lowest (and largest) sector of the peasantry. Nevertheless, the subservience which is the price of Baptist survival has led to the appearance of the 'Initiative Group', itself comprising the best educated and younger Baptists, and those most fully integrated into the Soviet economy.[16] The Old Believers, who were themselves at one time the functional equivalent of representatives of the Protestant Ethic are in relatively tolerated decay. The Witnesses usually define the regime as anti-Christ, and they are repressed with rigour because they are clear channels both of alienation and religious fantasy, as well as contaminated by a capitalist organizational style and American origins. The Pentecostals suffer only slightly less and for the same reasons. Such sects become visible by virtue of their dogged attempts to socialize their children in their beliefs. An index of repression and fear is provided by the desuetude of sectarian pacifism: military service is defined by socialism as central to loyalty, and opposition to it carries enormous costs in visibility and vulnerability. So much for the utopianism of Tolstoy or of the Doukhobors. (It is one of the paradoxes of liberty that self-defined progressive states treat military service as *the* obligation. Switzerland is just such an instance of 'democratic' intolerance, and so in some degree is the United States.)

It is worth noting that the sectarians and traditional Protestant denominations are present in any numbers only in Russia. The other religious minorities in Eastern Europe are 'churches' such as Catholicism in East Germany (8 per cent), Calvinism in Hungary (20 per cent), and Islam in Yugoslavia (12 per cent) and Bulgaria (8 per cent). Given the antagonism between Catholicism and the regime in Hungary, relationships between the Calvinist Church and the regime have been less acerbic. Catholicism in East Germany is heavily pressured and also more lively and resistant than the Lutheran Church.

Jewry is repressed as a source of deviant culture, religiously and ethnically defined,[17] though it can also be repressed by relatively liberal communists as in Poland because Jews who escaped to Russia returned as a key element in the post-war Stalinist élite. The same criteria for repression apply to any religion which has an ethnic base potentially at odds with the imperatives of overall Russian unity. Any such fissiparous union of autonomous national sentiment and religion is labelled as 'bourgeois nationalism' by contrast with the true nationalism of the 'socialist fatherland'. Catholic Lithuania, and to a lesser extent, semi-Catholic Latvia and Lutheran Estonia are each countries where religion has some association with nationality, particularly so in the case of Lithuania (Marshall 1971). Hence the severe and partially successful pressure to which the Catholic Church in Lithuania is currently subjected. The resistance of the one-time established Lutheranism in Estonia has been quite weak: the Church does not provide a very effective focus of national

feeling. Interestingly enough, both Lutheranism and the Mennonite faith provide vigorous foci of ethnic identity amongst those
Germans scattered in various parts of Russia.

RELIGION AND REGIONAL IDENTITY
AND AUTONOMY

At this point the discussion of the five basic categories can be
concluded, and a subject taken up which from time to time has
arisen during the course of analysis: the question of regional
sub-culture. It is never quite clear of course where a genuine
nation exists as distinct from a regional tone and sense of belonging. La Vendée is a region, Brittany and Catalonia are somewhat
more than regions, Lithuania and Croatia are nations incorporated in other nations. The discussion of regions must necessarily
overlap with what has previously been said about national myths
and the attitudes towards cultural diversity which vary according
to our five different categories. Regionalism introduces a particular aspect of power: the power of the centre versus the periphery.
The centre may dominate politically and/or numerically; or the
situation may be bi-polar. Regionalism also introduces a particular aspect of identity: the problem of the shading off of one
identity into another, and the overlapping and subsumption of
identities at margins and borders. Some general principles arise
with respect to the specific questions of periphery and centre,
however much these overlap with other issues of status difference
or economic deprivation, both actual and perceived. Furthermore,
there can even arise some overlap between a regional religiosity,
geographically defined, and the kind of dispersed sub-cultural
sector normally represented by Protestant nonconformity: Wales
is the obvious example. I mean that Protestant dissenting denominationalism, normally dispersed in a wider society at rather
specific status levels *can* constitute a regional religiosity.

If regions and areas with a specific religious tone attached to
them are listed they are plainly of various kinds, though often
at the border with another country or pressed against the border
of the sea. Examples are: Lapland, the Bergen hinterland, the
Göteborg and Jönköping regions, North Jutland, Friesland,
Wales, Scotland, the Western Isles, Northern Ireland, Cornwall,

North Lancashire (the Fylde), Flanders, Brittany, La Vendée, Alsace, the Jura, the Cévennes, the Basque country, Catalonia, Malta, Croatia, Serbia, Bosnia, Cyprus, the Calvinist and Lutheran regions of Hungary, Muslim Southern Bulgaria, Lithuania, Estonia, Georgia, Armenia. These variously involve (1) areas where the religious frontier is marginally different from the national border; hence, presumably, the 1 per cent of Orthodox Christians in Finland whose national affiliation lies athwart their religious affiliation. (2) Relatively remote and usually rural peripheries which retain and then emphasize orthodoxies once dominant at the centre: hence Friesland with its orthodox Calvinists split off from the liberalized Dutch Reformed Church, and North Jutland, characterized by a kind of piety now practically extinct in Copenhagen. (3) Alternative poles to the official centre, where the centre can be defined as relatively secularist: the area of Bergen poised against the ambience of Oslo, or Slovakia set against Czech Lands and Moravia.

(4) An area of different language or dialect where religion supports identity over against a relatively secular capital: Flanders vis-à-vis Brussels, Brittany vis-à-vis Paris. (5) An area where language is a *relatively* weak defining element, thus thrusting the onus of definition on to religion: the Basque country and to some extent Wales. (6) An area where a language has died out making religion the *only* possible source of renewed identity: Cornwall. (7) An area originally defined by conversion to a different religion which must retain that religion if it is to have any contemporary source of identity: the 'island' of Catholic, 'Italianate' culture in Bulgaria. (8) Islands, like Malta and Cyprus, for whom religion has both provided the sense of internal belonging *and* a sense of external affiliation, plus on occasions the role of buffer or strategic point vis-à-vis different and hostile religions. (9) A Protestant Island or peninsula in a Catholic Sea or vice versa: Württemburg, the Cévennes, Silesia, the Jura, the areas of Upper Austria to which Protestants retreated at the Counter-Reformation. This is quite close to (7). (10) Areas retaining the old religion after the new religion has taken over the heartlands of a culture: the Fylde and some of the western isles which escaped the Reformation. (11) Areas which have acquired a specific religio-ethnic character by virtue of the clustering of migrants: semi-Catholic Preston, Liverpool. (12) A 'plantation' defined and sustained by

the hostility of the relatively dispossessed: Protestant Ulster. (13) An area where the national church or a free church acquires relatively greater strength and achieves some self-consciousness because of it: the Göteborg hinterland with its Lutheran awareness, Jönköping with its noticeable colouring of free church adherents. (14) Ex-nations or proto-nations for whom a major (or the major) source of identity is religion: Scotland, Estonia, Croatia, Lithuania, Armenia. (15) Areas with national sentiment which are principally defined by culture, language and politics but which also need religion to be congruent with that definition, especially as regards clerical personnel and language: Catalonia. (16) An area of mixed religion placed at a linguistic junction, which paradoxically gains some self-awareness and increased religious self-consciousness by virtue of internal rivalry and being alternately in one cultural sphere and then another: Alsace, partly Protestant and partly Catholic, and using two languages. (17) An area of weak ethnic consciousness and a depressed and dispersed mode of life for whom expressions of identity can only occur in some minor variant of the metropolitan religion. The influence of Laestadianism among the Finnish and Swedish Lapps is an instance of this, the principal symbol of identity being a difference in clerical dress.[18]

Certain characteristics of these several different types of identity are worth underlining. Many are remote or in some way cut off: this makes both for distinctiveness and definition as well as preventing the latest waves of culture corroding the local way of life too quickly. If they are also rural then this makes for dispersed communication and weakens impulses from the metropolitan centre. Some are placed at borders and either draw strength from the presence of co-religionists across the border, or from the fact they are the last outpost of one religion before the territory of the infidel begins.

One of the kinds of special area and region listed above is based on migration, i.e. the movement of people from a regional or national culture to another national or cultural context. This has varied implications for religious practice and identity according to whether or not certain conditions are fulfilled. As is well-known, foreign migrants tend to cluster at the cultural centre rather than the periphery, and so may increase the alienation of periphery from centre.

The conditions which bear on the maintenance of religious identity and practice with respect to migration can be rapidly stated. They are: whether or not the migration is seasonal; whether or not whole families are involved; whether or not the roles available in the host culture allow clustering in given urban sectors; whether or not the religion of the host culture is significantly different from that of the migrants; whether or not there are historic mutual perceptions as between members of the two cultures which are hostile or involve superiority and/or inferiority; whether or not religion has been a major focus of such perceptions; whether or not adequate numbers move to form a supporting environment; whether or not other foci of identity like language have to be dropped; whether or not the group achieves forms of social mobility which break down endogamy; whether or not historic 'peculiarities' (like the role of women or wearing of turbans) are defined as *jointly* crucial for the identity of the religion and of the culture.

If one considers some of the varieties of movement from national cultures into migrant areas one can see how these conditions apply. West Indians, with Anglican, Catholic or Methodist backgrounds have moved to Britain, so have Catholic Poles, Maltese, Italians and Hungarians, and Orthodox Armenians, Russians, Cypriots and Greeks; so also have Muslim Pakistanis, and Bangladeshis, Sikhs and Hindus. Algerian Muslims and North African Jews and Russians have moved to France; Spaniards have moved to France and Switzerland; Italians have moved to Switzerland and Germany; Turks have moved to Germany, Portuguese have moved to Germany and France. Two of these are classic cases of diaspora where there is no indubitable region to which they may return: Jews and Armenians. Jews may, of course 'return' to Israel, but that is not where they come from.

We may take those cases which illustrate the application of the conditions outlined above. The West Indians come from a practising culture to a non-practising culture; they are of the same religion as the inhabitants; they are defined by themselves and others as inferior; their religious 'style' is different, i.e. enthusiastic. The result is a tendency to form groups belonging to an enthusiastic variant of the Christian religion, Pentecostalism, which can provide a sense of protective enclosure and catharsis for migrants. The Scots and Welsh came from practising cultures to a non-practising culture; they are not self-defined as respectively so superior and so inferior that there is a sense of important difference. The result is an accommodation to the English levels of practice and eventual loss of identity. The Irish came from a practising to a non-practising culture; there is a historic perception of England in which religion is the major focus of difference; the religious difference is considerable; the Irish feel they are regarded as inferior; they achieve relatively little social mobility, at least until very recently. The result is that they retain a fairly high level of practice and religious identity. The Poles came from a practising to a non-practising culture; they concentrated overwhelmingly in London and were involved in little geographical mobility; they mostly came together in wartime conditions of crisis requiring mutual support; they came from a culture where religion was defined as the source of hope in difficulty. They therefore maintained a high level of practice. The Pakistanis came from a 'practising' to a non-practising culture; their religion was very different and defined as indissolubly wedded to their culture; they felt themselves regarded as inferior and different and were easily discernible as different; they had specific customs regarded as essential to their identity which clashed with the customs of the host culture, such as the place of girls in schools. The result was the setting up of institutions of cultural defence and demands for special treatment. Jews came (largely) from eastern and then from central Europe; they achieved social mobility, but geographically they shifted in a regular sequence from certain specific areas of a particular status to other specific areas of a higher status, thus retaining some cohesion. They were defined by themselves and others as different; they had specific customs which defined that difference and they tended to hold that some minimum adherence to their customs was essential to the retention of identity; *but* their mobility within the education system made endogamy difficult to apply and a relatively friendly environment corroded symbolic acts designed to distinguish and mark Jews off. Hence on the one hand Jews retained a high proportion of adherence in terms of synagogue affiliation, but let peripheral customs go and achieved a lower level of practice.

These processes, illustrated from British examples, can be applied to continental examples. The practising Breton moving to secular Paris sinks to the level of practice amongst those in his new group; the Italian in France does likewise and then returns to whatever was his original practice on going home; the Italian in Britain in a Protestant environment is likely to practise. The Italian in Switzerland is in a relatively practising environment. He is likely to practice. And incidentally he succeeds in altering the religious and linguistic balance of the country. The Russians and Ukrainians in Paris, as in London, are likely to practise and lay stress on the church as the resonating memory of their culture, because their diaspora includes specifically religious reasons for flight. But with the next generation one cannot be sure. The Protestants who fled from Eastern Europe to Austria and Western Germany are likely to find in the church a spiritual home which is also a cultural one, especially perhaps where surrounded by Catholics, as in Austria, the Palatinate, etc. Flemish people going to Brussels do as the Bruxellois do. The operation of some of these same principles has been common observation concerning all those Europeans who migrated to America: deprived to the possibility of retaining culture through language they carried their past forward through religion.

We must now examine certain key examples of regional cultures, notably where religion is related to proto-nationalism, but also where a strong regional sense is mediated by religion. Croatia and Flanders have already been discussed, and so too has the Bergen hinterland.

At this point I want to take three examples of regional sentiment which are right wing, two which were to the right and have now moved to the left, one which has been persistently left, and one which remains to the right but has a left wing. I will discuss Slovakia, Brittany and La Vendée; the Basque country and Catalonia; Wales and Ireland.

Slovakia may be regarded as an instance of bi-polarity: it includes about a third of the population of Czechoslovakia and is much the most practising area of that country. It has always been on the wrong 'foot' and that foot a right one. This has come about by a mutual process of definition by Slovak nationalists and by those for whom Slovak nationalism was dangerous. The first step in the 'wrong' direction was taken because Slovakia was a satellite of Hungary which in turn was a satellite of Austria. When the Hungarian liberals rose against Austria in 1848 the

Slovaks rose against the Hungarians hoping to gain favour with Austria. They did not. And with the liberal state of 1918 they became part of one Czechoslovakia. National awareness fed on three sources. The first was the belief that they were economically exploited so that their pattern of industrialization was distorted to provide feeders for eventual processing by Hungarian and later by Czech industry. The second was that their intelligentsia and white collar workers were relatively unrepresented in the administrative élites, most conspicuously the Czech army. This exclusion ran parallel to a relative devaluation of the Slovak language. The third source of national awareness was religion: Slovaks distrusted the Hussite and atheist traditions of the Czechs. So when the Slovak People's Party was founded in 1913 it was led by a priest Hlinka and it expressed religious and status and economic devaluations. It declared itself 'For God and People' and advanced the slogan 'In Slovakia speak Slovak'.

During the liberal republic the government coalitions always had a majority in Czech Lands and were a minority in Slovakia, where the Slovak nationalists constituted the largest single party. The next wrong step occurred in 1938 and 1939. Hitler leaned in the Slovak direction as part of his overall plan to destroy Czechoslovakia and in 1939 an independent Slovakia emerged under his protection and under the aegis of German economic pressures and dynamisms. The new Slovakia became a one-party 'clerico-fascist' state with a Catholic priest, Tiso, as President. One has to remember that Slovakia was strongly Catholic, though there was a small autonomist Protestant party, and that the priesthood was a widely available channel of advancement for every level of society. The new regime developed *pari passu* with the Ustachi regime in Catholic Croatia.

In this situation the Communist Party (together with Russia) had come to be regarded as the champions of Czech democracy against Hitler. After various tactical tries and turns in the war the Communists eventually returned to this position, adopting their pre-war anti-Munich, patriotic policy. In the National Coalition governments after the war the Communists were strongest in Czech Lands, where they secured 41 per cent of the vote in 1946, and only a minority in Slovakia where they received 30.4 per cent of the vote, as compared with a vote of 62 per cent for the Slovak Democratic Party. This pushed them towards a centralist policy. They had to undermine the Slovak party as a nucleus of reaction and successor to 'clerico-fascism' and simultaneously claim that Slovakia had 'nothing to fear from the Czech working class'. After February 1948 the Communist takeover was complete—the Stalinist leaders of the 1950s regarded autonomism as a purely Slovak affair and purged the Slovak intelligentsia accordingly. At the same time a combination of economic development and repression of Catholicism made nationalism more overt and self-conscious, particularly over the issue of Slovak migration to Czech Lands. The Prague Spring proposed some degree of devolution in every sphere towards local economic decision, workers' participation, and Slovak autonomy. The re-opening of churches and recovery of religious life at this time was most obvious in Slovakia. The Russians invaded, but Slovak autonomy was retained, and Husak, who had been imprisoned as a Slovak patriot, now presided over the new State.

Brittany and La Vendée have in the past clung to a militant Catholicism, and have seen their regional identity and faith mutually threatened by a secularist Paris. In the case of Brittany the language has been downgraded and the use of Breton names discouraged. So, for various mutually supporting reasons, Brittany and La Vendée are areas of devout practice and right wing voting. The Basque sentiment began similarly. The desire for autonomy looked back to medieval popular forms of foral democracy. The language was in decline, throwing the onus of identity on to religion. Yet at the same time the Castilian Spanish which made inroads in the Basque tongue was defined as the tongue of a neglectful centre associated with liberal secularists. So Basque nationalism was fiercely Catholic and right-wing. But given a situation in which Madrid was taken over by right-wing exponents of centralism it moved to the left, taking its fervent Catholicism with it. So there appeared the phenomenon of the guerilla priest. Catalonian sentiment began partly in a symbiosis of republican and federalist sentiment and partly in a conservative movement of linguistic and cultural revival which was successful.[19] There was less need of a religious vehicle of identity; and in any case Catalonia was the emporium of refugee radicalism and European political influence. During the dictatorship of Primo de Rivera the achievements and aspirations of its autonomous regional and middle class culture were slighted. It moved further to the left,

and, when a measure of autonomy was granted by the Republic
in 1931 the move to the left was sealed. The sociological generalizations which follow are simply stated: if the language and
culture of the periphery can carry identity alone and if the centre
is not perceived as religiously very different then religion is not
likely to be the focus of regional sentiment. If language is less
viable as a source of identity and if the centre is perceived as
different, whether it is secularist or of another religion, then
religious nationalism is the likely outcome. It depends on who is
responsible for trying to curb the urge to autonomy: whoever it is
one adopts the opposing political stance. The Irish case can be
understood in the same way. Ireland was subject to perceived and
actual neglect and expropriation; it was dominated by a small
Protestant élite; it was a geographical unity but suffered from the
'wedge' made by Ulster Plantations of the late sixteenth and
seventeenth centuries; the language gradually gave way to
English, in spite of its retention in certain western areas of the
Gaeltacht; it relied first on the Liberals and then on the Labour
Party for support in the British Parliament. Overall, the national
sentiment belongs to a predominantly rural society, with only one
important urban cultural centre, Dublin, and it is therefore
conservative in tone; but given the historic role of the Conservative Party in relation to Ulster Unionism and the complex fissions
following the Irish civil war, its militant segment includes very
left wing elements. These left wing elements include the specifically Marxist I.R.A. which has been under heavy Catholic
displeasure for 25 years.

Wales has been the obverse of Slovakia: always on the left foot.
In the eighteenth century much of Wales embraced a localized,
democratic religion, the Calvinist variant of Methodism. The new
faith appealed to those slightly removed from the system of social
pressures and sanctions: the yeomen, artisans and shopkeepers.
The gentry and to a lesser degree the Established Church were
isolated by these changes and faced a vigorous, independent
movement based on the chapels promoting land reform and
political and civil liberties. Democratic religious organization and
rhetoric and democratic choral singing came to provide the
dominant ethos; and the chapels were in explicit alliance with
Liberalism. At the same time the educated man took precedence
within an overall egalitarian system: he was the major influence

in the chapel and became the manager in the colliery. Indeed, nonconformist traders and managers created a new professional class through which they dominated the schools and local politics. Its greatest triumph was when a Welsh Baptist lawyer, Lloyd-George, became Liberal Prime Minister in 1916, and its symbolic success was signalized by the disestablishment of the Church in 1911.

With the emergence of a large working class in South Wales and the advent of socialism the chapels severed their explicit Liberal connection. Chapel-goers now mostly voted Labour, and there appeared a strong trade-union-chapel axis. Depression, unemployment and migration deepened the Welsh attachment to Labour and produced Communist enclaves. At the same time erosion occurred: the effects of mobility and new centres of entertainment diminished the life of the chapels. English began to replace Welsh and an English middle class took many important industrial positions, not to mention Welsh country cottages. The cultural penetration alerted the guardians of Welsh language and identity, more especially in the nonconformist, Welsh speaking, professional middle class. A Welsh nationalism emerged to challenge the dominance of Socialism and Liberalism, as well as the dominance of England. Its roots were religious and linguistic the politics of cultural defence. Nevertheless nationalist politics could not be conservative: that remained part of the definition of English economic and cultural hegemony. Wales continued to counter-distinguish herself from England by egalitarianism rather than deference, Welsh rather than English, chapel rather than church, even though both chapel and language were on the decline. Indeed, the fact of decline was the stimulus of renewed identification. England, taken on its own possessed an in-built conservative majority, bolstered by the unionism of the Ulster Protestants; Scotland and Wales provided the possibility of a Socialist Government and fragments of Liberal opposition. The mutually antagonistic political and religious definitions of the English centre and the Welsh or Scots peripheries were reactivated by the very process of homogenization.

Since the discussion has turned on issues of centre and periphery the special position of Ireland can be used to illustrate just how complex and important the questions of centre and periphery are. After all peripheries can be centres, or represent and stand for

F

centres, while centres can be peripheries. Ireland is peripheral to England but England is peripheral to Europe and to Rome. The Roman centre at its moment of weakness before the barbarians, was strengthened on its distant Irish periphery, from which the faith returned to Scotland and England, moving first from peripheral island to peripheral island: Iona to Lindisfarne. So Ireland like Poland is the hard circumference of the Roman centre of the circle. Since Ireland is indeed peripheral to England and England defines its marginality in relation to Europe through Protestantism, Ireland is strengthened in her Catholicism and in her relation to England's historic enemies, Catholic Spain and France. This in turn strengthens the fear and prejudice of Englishmen with regard to Popery, and justifies repression. Indeed it justifies the 'planting' of a Protestant people from another periphery, Scotland, on the N.E. periphery of Ireland. Once there the plantation dominates *and* needs the local population. And when this situation leads to partition as in 1922 the local Catholics in Northern Ireland find themselves a people of the centre still pushed to the social periphery of a periphery. The historical scene is set for violence, intransigence, fear and religious bigotry. In Southern Ireland where Catholicism and the State are one, the historical enmity no longer obtains. The Protestant cause is defeated without any doubt; but the Protestants remain in positions of relatively high status and constitute a declining 5 per cent of the population concentrated in the Dublin area and the S.W. coast. Five per cents are rarely dangerous, ratios of 60–40 often are, and especially so when set in a wider pan-Irish context of 75–25 which makes a minority of the local northern Protestant majority.

Just one isolated query remains over the analysis so far provided before we proceed to a discussion of the consequences of industrialization and modernization in the context of the five basic categories outlined. This query concerns the relationship between the incidence of free churches dispersed through the wider culture and the incidence of regional sentiment relying on religion as a vehicle. Religious dissent of the free church kind is a Protestant phenomenon, except for its efflorescence in Russia since the revolution, and latterly in Brazil and Chile. It is at its maximum in the U.S.A.; it is powerful in Britain; it is of a minor importance in Sweden and Germany; and insofar as it exists in Scotland and Holland it consists of movements towards a restatement of Calvinist orthodoxy.[20] The free church principle overlaps regional sentiment only in Wales, Cornwall and Friesland, unless one includes internal parties within Lutheranism, in which case it also overlaps regional sentiment in the Bergen hinterland. Clearly, the free church principle is largely characteristic of Protestant cultures and then only under highly specific conditions which cannot be enumerated here; and it has a very limited association with regional awareness.

CORRELATES AND CONSEQUENCES

This article has been concerned with power at the level of the state, with power through the agency of systems of meaning, and with their interrelationship. It is now necessary to turn to the contours of practice and belief as observed on the ground, exercising power and having power exercised upon them.

The European map of religious practice consists of a dark heartland at the European centre of which the hub is Switzerland. An arm moves down towards Venice and a thick tongue stretches along the Rhine up to Southern Holland, with a fork downwards into Flanders. Isolated blocks lie like dark continents separated by some movement of the continental plates: Slovakia, Poland, Brittany, the Massif Central, Ireland, Northern Iberia, Greece. England and Russia are shaded lightly: England greys somewhat to north and west, Russia lightens as the eye travels east. Scandinavia is the area least tinged by religious practice, constituting a region of off-white across the north of the continent, which also stretches down deep into Lutheran Germany and especially Protestant East Germany. Along the underside of the continent below the Tagus and through the marches of S.W. Spain there is another area scarcely darker, cutting patchily across southern Italy, into Albania, Serbia, Montenegro and Bulgaria. Most of these southern areas have been regions of disaffection for a long time, and indeed their borders correspond curiously to the rim of Islam's advance into Christendom.

Perhaps some figures may indicate what levels of intensity underlie the relativities just indicated. I would estimate that on any given Sunday those present in church constitute about one person in four of those over seven and able to attend; perhaps the figure should be a little higher. The figure for East Europe is about the same, but it represents a sharper recent decline from higher levels existing prior to the advent of communist governments. In Russia perhaps about 5 per cent are regularly in church (where the buildings are available) with maybe somewhat higher proportions at the margins, as for example the Ukraine and Armenia in the south and Lithuania and Latvia in the north-west. In Scandinavia the percentages vary between 2 per cent and 4 per cent, and this is repeated for the Protestant state churches taken *on their own* in Holland, Germany and England. If the overall proportion rises (as it does in the U.K., to some 12 per cent) this either derives from a Catholic diaspora or the existence of substantial dissent, e.g. the nonconformists in England and the neo-orthodox schisms in Holland, or both. In dissenting Wales and (sociologically) dissenting Scotland and Northern Ireland, Protestant weekly practice rises to about 25 per cent; and a mild reflection of this is seen in Norway in the religious form that regionalism takes in the Bergen hinterland. Protestant practice also rises to the 25 per cent level or higher where it is a minority as in France or is at the border with Catholicism as in Switzerland. But in general Protestant practice on any given Sunday is about 5 per cent and Catholic practice (overall) about 35/40 per cent. However, this varies from the 95 per cent of Eire, and the 75 per cent of northern Spain and Poland, Bavaria, Western Austria and southern and central Switzerland, to the 10 per cent of southern Spain, southern Portugal and the Paris basinic[21] areas of large scale industry with industrial proletariat, or of latifundia with rural proletariat.

Catholic weekly practice is at its optimum where it is the expression of a repressed nationalism (Poland) or of a repressed regional nationalism (the Basque country) and in these circumstances it achieves majority practice: Eire 95 per cent, Poland 75 per cent, the Basque country 80 per cent, Brittany 75 per cent. Then it achieves good levels of practice where it is either a moderately sized minority of (say) 10 per cent as in the U.K. or 20 per cent as in the U.S.A., or a very large minority as in Germany, Switzerland and Holland. In these latter it is assisted by heavy regional concentrations, and whereas in the U.K. and the U.S.A. Catholicism creates a purely cultural integration, in Holland, Germany and Switzerland it builds up 'pillars' covering most aspects of life. The consequence is practice of 40 per cent and over. However recent data do indicate falls in the U.S., U.K., Holland, Germany, Austria and Flanders from the mid-sixties on. Poor conditions exist for Catholicism in those whole societies where it is the official majority faith and where this has given rise to dichotomous splits in the society such that Catholicism is largely identified with one side of the split. This has been the case in France, Italy and Spain and leads to an overall weekly practice of 20 per cent, 30 per cent and 35 per cent respectively. The weekly figures for France show a drop even between 1971 and 1975: 21 per cent to 17 per cent. Spain and France are also marked by steep gradients of practice in relation to status.

Protestant practice has special characteristics which should be noted. It involves a quite substantial amount of seasonal and occasional conformity, so that between a third and a half of Protestants have contact with the church from time to time: this type of practice is relatively low in Sweden but quite substantial in England.[22] Second the penumbra of belief is high (60 per cent believe in God in Sweden, 70–80 per cent in England, 90 per cent in Germany) and the practice of prayer is very widespread. Private prayer is a practice of at least half the population in most Protestant countries; and there is in addition a web of religiously toned associations which generally covers about one person in three. Confirmed indifference in Protestant societies generally affects only about a third of the population, while confirmed piety is characteristic of only about one sixth (cf. Salomonsen 1973).

In Orthodox societies the resistance to secularization is weaker so that Serbia, Bulgaria and Russia probably achieve little above 5 per cent practice, and that more sharply concentrated in older groups than elsewhere. The variations occur where Orthodoxy can retain a positive relation to nationalism, as it does in Greece (40 per cent plus?), and in Roumania (25 per cent plus?). Roumania uses the church as one element in the national counter-definition of an isolated Latin culture. Catholic societies in East Europe are probably in the range 20 per cent–30 per cent with the exception of Poland; Catholic enclaves are in any case always stronger than the surrounding Orthodox or Protestant areas whether in Croatia and Slovenia or in the D.D.R. Firm practice in the youngest generation rarely characterizes more than 10 per cent, again Poland excepted.

But the relevant category here is communist government and this has certain general consequences. The first is that the area of explicit atheism is very much larger than in western Protestant societies and considerably larger even than in those Catholic societies of the west where large communist parties exist. Grass roots communism in the West is mainly non-ideological, but in the East ideological conformity is officially propagated within the state education system and the media. It generally claims about one third of the population, though in Orthodox Bulgaria and Russia and Czech Lands it may amount to two-thirds. Furthermore the intermediate third, between believers and non-believers, possesses a vague inchoate belief, often hesitant, which is supplemented by occasional conformity to the rites of the Church. Specifically ecclesiastical religion, where religious and priestly authority is fully accepted, is pushed back so that it accounts for about a third of the believers.[23] It seems the rite has a continued appeal analogous to the appeal of prayer in the Protestant west.

The social location of religiosity in communist countries is very well illustrated by recent surveys conducted in Slovenia. Nine peasants out of ten are 'religious' and five workers out of ten are accounted so. By contrast with West the white collar stratum is less religious than the workers. Both migration to the towns and increased education diminish religiosity. The younger workers are *more* religious than the older since they are of peasant origin: this conforms to the Polish pattern rather than (say) the Bulgarian pattern and the pattern of other Eastern European states where religion declines among the younger working class groups. It is interesting that these surveys mention the danger of Christianity becoming the ideology of the lower, deprived strata, a position to which the younger clergy are already moving. (One may perhaps recollect that Slovenia is one of the few areas with a pre-war tradition of Christian Socialism). In other words, Christianity in the East returns to the sociological condition originally noted by St. Paul: 'not many wise, not many mighty but the offscourings of the earth'. Other researchers note the possibility of a hardening core of Christian witness centred on faith in Jesus Christ.[24]

The most tenacious aspect of religion east and west is the rite of Baptism: it is relatively weak in Russia (45 per cent), Bulgaria, East Germany and England (60 per cent) but it is normally practised by at least 90 per cent of the population in the west, including those countries with large communist sectors. And it is a majority practice in most East European countries. Ecclesiastical marriage is much less universal, especially in countries where there has been a tradition of laicist militancy. In countries like West Germany it is perhaps seen as an aspect of administration and widely practised on that account. In Eastern Europe ecclesiastical marriage is sometimes a minority practice, particularly in view of the fact that it makes the participants visible to the authorities in a way Baptism need not. Confirmation tends to be a majority practice where it is associated with initiation into adulthood, so that in Scandinavia over 90 per cent of the population is confirmed.

Various important changes underlie these static figures. First, practice is generally in decline. Second, it is tilted towards the older generation, but much more sharply so in eastern Europe than in the West. Poland is quite exceptional in this since the state can not deprive the church of institutional access to the young. Third, where practice is poor in Catholic countries there is a greater degree of participation and personal communion among those who *do* practice. Fourth, where Christianity is under pressure there emerges a core, of which perhaps faith in Christ is the key element, and this becomes relatively irreducible and perhaps more coherent as the vague and uncertain elements are shorn away. Religion also acquires, where this is allowed, some capacity for social and political criticism. Fifth, ecclesiastical religion in terms of priestly authority and the regulation of familial morality is everywhere diminishing. Sixth, superstition is probably in decline but remains as a substantial free-floating element in most Protestant societies (supplemented by soupçon of reincarnation and spiritualism); and it also remains as an element embedded in the life of the Church and outside it in undeveloped rural areas, e.g. in parts of Spain, Portugal and Greece. Indeed in these areas there is a very substantial extra-ecclesiastical religiosity. Seventh, alongside superstition there lies a very widespread folk religion based on decency, limited reciprocity, and belief in 'something' which is often accompanied by a respect for the ritual forms of religion in church and in state but without any great understanding of their meaning. This folk religion and this civic religion are particularly widespread in Protestant societies and they are not eroded by the recoil of ecclesiastical religion and institutional practice. It is perhaps most significant that in the Orthodox east the core of resistance is the rite, in the Protestant west private prayer.

This leads to a consideration of the internal condition of the church. In this connection one must be aware of cultural layers which are encapsulated in Catholicism: para-Christian and pre-Christian manipulative magic, semi-christianized systems of mediation, expressing local loyalties and providing sources of personal consolation and assistance, the religion of the Council of Trent and the religion of the Second Vatican Council. The last-mentioned makes more progress where the Catholic Church is decreasingly isomorphic with the social order, where the level of literacy is increasing, and where the incidence of the new middle class is high enough for them to regard authoritarianism and priestly prestige as a constraint. It makes much less progress where there is an external threat against which unity is essential, as in Poland, or where the majority of Catholics are of low status or peasants or of the old middle class.

The changes of the last decade or so which have occurred in conjunction with the Council have been most dramatic in the U.S.A., Holland, Spain, and, in lesser degree, Germany. They include a devolution of authority expressed in schemes of participation: lay consultation, episcopal collegiality, democratic procedures in monasteries and priestly associations. Ecclesiastical roles have become more specialized, they demand more expertise and are less programmed by rigid socialization. Priests are organized in groups in relation to larger areas. Liturgy is a dialogue of priest and people based on joint celebration, with a premium on clear communication and personal encounter rather than the invocation of the numinous. In all this one sees the triple operation of rationalization, specialization and the urge to personal contact which is bred by large scale bureaucratic structures. Private confession declines as corporate communion increases. Thus the new 'personalism' is corporate in its emphasis rather than individualistic. The Cursillos de christianidad of the early 60's exemplify just such a personal religion: a corporate 'Protestant' feeling resembling the Wesleyan class meeting. Indeed, in its most radical manifestations it results in free communitarianism, where the participants translate the gospel into communal anticipations, sometimes with a direct political content. These openings to the communitarian left are paralleled by associations of traditionalists, as well as archaic folk movements, to the rural right. The majority in the middle are often confused and disoriented. Hence in part the decline in practice and hence, in particular, the defections of clergy and falling numbers of vocations.

The process of differentiation which dissolves the all-round role of the clergy also separates the church off from other spheres. In the east it becomes simply a private and privatized association, though there are exceptions: Poland where it provides the soul of the culture, and Roumania where church and state still collaborate. Nevertheless, in most East-European states, church and state have been separated, and since there are no parties, the church is similarly separated from politics. This separation from politics can be seen operative in many contexts. In Spain the Church edges out of the system of legitimacy. In France and Italy it moves from right to centre, loosens the spirals of mutual antagonism and therefore of anti-clericalism, and gradually disentangles itself from direct support of a political party. The same is true of Germany. More Catholics appear on the left, the traditionalists and integrists become a minority wing, and the Church itself becomes a vehicle of political and social criticism. Bishops move to the centre-left.

At the same time the mechanisms of sub-cultural integration also weaken, particularly where Catholics come very close to overall parity with Protestant majorities. This again is more likely to occur where there is a large new middle class able to use the electronic media to spread its viewpoint, as in Holland. Nevertheless, though there are moves to universal schooling within state systems, the Catholic Church retains a heavy commitment to separate schools, since these are the sole key to distinctive socialization. The socialization provided by Catholic schools in countries once dominated by anti-clericalism and by struggle over education often becomes less rigid, so lessening the fear of the state that such schools train up in the next generation of the right. Certainly this is the case in France. Protestants, on the other hand, are happier to accept the highly general religious 'instruction' usually provided in state schools, unless they belong to neo-orthodox breakaways. And in one or two Protestant countries, Sweden for example, the religious element is largely deprived of any tincture of commitment. Britain seems to be moving in a similar direction. Indeed, such education often simply initiates into the folk-lore or the minimal morality or the basic classics of Christian civilization. Insofar as religious education is provided on the media it becomes less static, less dominated by ritual or church sources, more open to the dramatization of basic existential situations and political and social debate. In the interesting phrase of the recent report (1976) on religious education in Britain: it 'explores life stances'.

As has already been remarked official Catholic social morality concerning the family is often disregarded, especially by educated and student Catholics and this is congruent with widespread moves to separate the norms of Christianity or the Church from the legal norms governing family life. This again makes familial life a matter of Christian conscience not external regulation. Broad ideas of personal fulfilment partially replace rigid legal and social categories and prohibitions. Indeed, in eastern countries there is even an attempt to replace wholesale the religious element in the celebration of the family life cycle: birth, adulthood, marriage and death.

The final section of this brief summary must be concerned with the impact of industrialization and modernization on the churches, and the best focus for this is a review of practice in relation to occupation. Certain categories of work may be listed which lead to low practice. First, there are steel workers, metal workers, and people in all large and highly mechanized industrial complexes, especially when these are located on their own and with no admixture of other categories. Second, there are large scale farming enterprises, employing seasonal hired labour, or in eastern Europe state farms. These categories are marked by size, impersonality and the pervasiveness of the mechanical. They subject men rigidly to process in the case of industry, and to uncertainty in the case of large scale capitalist farming. Then there are groups which vary: in Catholic societies the extractive industries and fishing are often likely to be dechristianized, while in Protestant societies they are more likely to be influenced by dissent.

In all cases the intelligentsia is likely to be more explicit against or for religion.

In Catholic societies they generally have a lay secularist viewpoint which also extends to the health and perhaps legal professions. In Protestant societies they are either humanistic or they have a free personal religiosity, often tinged by medievalism, anarchism and communitarian nostalgias. In communist societies intellectuals barely exist, except as a sector of administration and ideological control—hence their rigid atheism, except where humanistic and Christian traditions have some partial resonance, as in Czechoslovakia, Poland and Catholic Yugoslavia. This is where some dialogue has occurred, now largely silenced by increasing state pressures on the churches.

Workers in administration necessarily vary according to the basic ideological leaning of the state: in Spain highly practising, in Protestant countries moderately so, and in communist countries barely practising at all. 'Independents' are largely confined to western societies and tend to practise at whatever is the local level of church attendance. Technicians are rather similar to administrative workers: indeed they also are an aspect of control. In eastern societies they are relatively uninterested in ideological questions, and where there is a strong Catholic Church as in Poland they are not as markedly non-Christian as philosophers, literary men and other heirs to humanism. In the west they also have tendency to be non-ideological or to exhibit a naïve acceptance of some world view, such as fundamentalist Protestantism which they conceive of as an 'explanation' analogous on the religious level to their own scientific explanations. This religiosity links with a greater conservatism than is found in the humanist intelligentsia. Indeed, the humanist intelligentsia, aided by the new middle class in the media, education and the expressive arts has become partially radicalized by a rivalry with, and a distaste for, the technicist mentality, which they associate with the concept of pollution and exploitation of the world. Everywhere in Catholic or Protestant societies the new middle class is less practising than the old.

This brings us to groups prone to high practice. First, there are the western administrative and business élites, who are in any case always disproportionately Protestant, except of course in southern Europe. Second, there are the white collar workers and lower echelons of the personnel manning the education system. Third, there are the petit bourgeois sectors: shopkeepers, small business men. Fourth, there are small farmers in traditional areas impregnated by deference and hierarchy, medium sized farmers owning their own land under settled agricultural conditions, the gentry themselves and (within the limits set by large distances and isolation) those engaged in herding and shepherding. Insofar as both the growth of industry and the industrialization of the countryside tend to draw people from country to the towns this has implications for the proportion of those practising in a given society.

Indeed, in general the disorientations of industrial society in terms of conceptual, geographical and social mobility, all militate against the roots and the sense of the familiar and familial which support Christian images of the world. But alongside this general mobility certain fundamental facts stand out: insofar as work takes place in a personal setting where people own their homes, or their farms, or their own individual skills and professional abilities, in contexts which are familiar and on a human scale they are more likely to practice Christianity and be sensitive to it. Insofar as they are submerged in a mass, dominated by vast enterprises and large scale private or state undertakings, subjected to a soulless process based on mechanism, they are less likely to practice Christianity or to be aware of its meaning. The intelligentsia varies. If sensitized to forms of control inimical to its own expressionist sensitivity it may revert to highly personal religiosity, in particular either a free, unbounded mysticism or aesthetic ritualism. But if the intelligentsia is deployed as the agent of technical exploitation carried out under the aegis of state power it succumbs to a materialistic ideology.

So long as these conditions outlined above continue so long does religious practice decline. It is possible to sum up the rival ecologies of practice and non-practice with two contrasting models. Imagine first Dimitrovgrad in the east or Bilonsville in the west: towns recently invented and rapidly developed around a huge complex based solely on heavy industry. They lie within the general area of a vast city and are surrounded more immediately by an agricultural region of either capitalistic or state farms. The labourers recruited from the capitalist farms come from an anomic, rootless rural proletariat, used to one agricultural crisis after another. Imagine, second, Marcester and Marislava: towns dating from Roman or early medieval times, expanding slowly around the employment provided by small light industries or services, or shops and provincial administration. The tone is civic: the building materials are organic, the shapes rounded and human in scale. People mostly own their homes and the size of the houses varies only slightly according to income. There is little unemployment; families rarely break up in divorce or separation. No great roads slash through or over the old streets; bells sound through tree lined avenues. People stay put; relationships of dependence, when they exist, are personal; different professions and avocations mix; long established craftsmen consort with the members of old firms of solicitors and family business men. Round about are moderate sized farms, personally owned by those who run them, and there is a long tradition of modest, steady, agricultural prosperity. Other things being equal, according to the given political culture and its history, Marislava and Marcester practice and believe, Bilonsville does not practice, Dimitrovgrad neither practices nor believes.

POST-SCRIPT

A post-script is necessary to the above in view of certain salient facts: the total manipulation of culture in Eastern Europe in the interests of power and of intellectual theory and the concomitant reversal of the relation of religion to status obtaining in Western Europe. This forms the essential frontier of the contemporary world and the most crucial element in the situation of religious belief. It requires summary comment.

Western Europe exhibits partial conformities under varying degrees of strain; Eastern Europe exhibits residual impulses to non-conformity under immense pressures toward total conformity. The stepping up of restrictions on the churches are expressions of this pressure. Western Europe is a system illustrating tendencies to a limited pluralism; Eastern Europe is a system illustrating a tendency to a total monism. Why? How? Why should the 'sacred canopy' retain a secularist guise and with 'scientific' pretensions?

The ruling ideology of Eastern Europe is an intellectualist formation originally expressing the position of intellectuals, especially of those who possessed ethnic or religious marginality in a state of partial disintegration. This ideology served the power interests of these intellectuals in the course of confronting the old administrative élites and it also helped to mobilize and solidify the hitherto untheoretical sector of the deprived insofar as these had already achieved positions of *relative* power and affluence within the current system. Whether intellectuals were able to achieve their ends depended on a variety of factors, among them the speed of industrialization and resultant disorientation of meaning systems, the relative prestige of intellectuals, and the existence of situations where society had *already* split into warring poles. In some cases the power impulses of certain sectional oligarchies in the leading sectors of the proletariat were also subserved by this intellectualist ideology, although it was grasped in a vulgarized and rigidified form.

Once in control, for a variety of reasons which require no elaboration here, the intellectuals and the sectional working class oligarchies found themselves confronted by the remorseless imperatives of power, made doubly remorseless by their own ideology, which disallowed conflict and claimed a monopoly of power and ontological rectitude. Thus armed and constricted they set about total control in terms familiar to them: the manipulation of culture through socialization, education and the rejection of all verbal dissidence. Creatures of the word they feared the word more than the rite. Like Puritans in the past the metaphysical aura of the ideology served to cover the impulses to power, economic in the Puritan case, but political and cultural as well in the intellectual case. The twin aspects of this power were exploitation of the population in the interests of domination, and exploitation of the natural resources and of technique to provide enough rewards for selected sectors to make the domination secure. Power did not need to be shared, but rewards needed to be meted out to key sectors. Trapped in the technicist requirements of statism they needed to reorientate education in modes antagonistic to the expressionistic and traditionalist elements in humanism, and this had the double pay-off of limiting access to the past and diminishing the range of persons open to notions of intellectual dissidence. Intellectual dissidence in its turn had to fight to hold on to these traditions, and included in the traditions was some access to older concepts of freedom embodied in the religious past. Older style humanists were doubly inclined to this in cases where they belonged to those sectors of the older élite now persecuted by the new élite. At the same time the technicist mentality had its usual consequence of ideological indifferentism, insofar as socialization was incomplete; but mere indifference could not generate a charge of ideological resistance on a large scale. One element of syncretism between old and new had a paradoxical consequence: the older integrisme had created the marginality of part of the radical intelligentsia, notably a déraciné Jewry, but it now passed on identical tendencies to the new integrisme, so that after the first period of power the same marginal sectors of the intelligentsia came under pressure, and were thrust out or pushed towards dissidence vis-à-vis the new regime. Another element, equally paradoxical, is not due merely to syncretism with the older systems of integration but to the logic of monistic systems: schisms between doctrinal élites controlling different territories, heresies within territories defined by overt verbal dissidence or variation, reference to sacred scriptures, a class of committed ideologians, and rites of ideological reinforcement. The only limits on the logic of total power are temporary and pragmatic: where the old integrisme was extremely powerful as in Poland, where rival integrismes might diverge and disintegrate the state, as in Yugoslavia, where the old integrisme might be *used* against marginal groups as in Roumania, and where external threat suggested the utility of a temporary union of old and new integrismes as in the Russian patriotic war against the Germans.

In the West, as has been suggested, all power is partial and socialization is fragmented somewhat by religious and linguistic sub-cultures and sub-cultures based on status. Certain points are salient. The humanist intelligentsia still has interests in confronting the old administrative élites, especially when these ally themselves with the rising group of manipulative technocrats. But now it fears most of all the logic of total control. Its expressionist ideology pushes it towards the sources of power in the communication system where is spreads discontent with the old legal-military-clerical élites, but largely in the name of expressionist ideologies deriving from extreme liberalism rather than in the name of disciplined revolution. The liberal option is strengthened in those countries with Protestant traditions which also lack disciplined revolutionary forces. The technical élite itself is largely subordinate to the administrative élite by virtue of specialization since it has no special ideological axe to grind and few sources from which to construct one. It simply conforms to the religious tone of the immediate élite, often indeed in a naïve form. In West and East it conforms: its indices of belief *and* unbelief are those of its immediate milieu. The imperatives of industrialization and the need to satisfy popular aspirations in the interests of stability force the old administrative élite and technocratic sector forward on courses which disorientate and weaken the traditional meaning systems of Europe. This disorientation and the extension of pluralism can create the conditions under which either the older forms of integration will try and re-establish themselves in control, or the pluralistic tendency will be pushed dangerously close to anarchy and atomism, or the monism of the Eastern European system will come to seem attractive by virtue of the ideological vacua and disintegrations which have been created. Indeed, the first two of these options *can* combine to assist the progress of the third. Which of these options, singly or in combination, will be taken up is not clear; what *is* clear is that the alternative eastern form of integration cannot loosen without massive internal contradiction.

NOTES

1. Cf. Steiner 1973, on which I have drawn extensively. I am also grateful for conversations with E. Gellner on these topics.
2. Alexander, forthcoming, Chapter 1, section B.
3. From this derives the relative status of clergy in the different types of Protestant pattern: high in Sweden, considerably lower in the United States. Other related consequences are to be located in the prestige of humanistic life-styles, the slower pace of popularization in education and so on. Lipset brings out such differences in his comparison between the U.S.A. and Canada (1969). The distinction he outlines between the U.S.A. and Canada marks an intermediate point between the American and British sub-variants of the Protestant pattern.
4. Cf. Fogarty 1957. This provides a particularly useful analysis of the religious organizations, unions and parties in countries of mixed religion.
5. Thurlings 1971. Cf. also Larkin 1974. It is interesting that where Catholic voters cease to vote confessionally their left voting reflects degree of previous church attachment.
6. Galli and Prandi 1970; and Hazelrigg 1972.
7. S. H. Barnes 1966. Cf. Mackie 1975.
8. For an exposition of this notion which is assumed throughout the present chapter. Cf. Lipset 1969.
9. Lorwin 1966. Cf. also Verdoot and Rayside 1975.
10. Opus Dei is currently (January 1974) not powerful in the Spanish government. Cf. Artigues 1971.

11. 'Shadow over the Greek Church', in *Greek Report*, April 1969.

12. One should study in this connection W. C. Fletcher's contribution to the Carleton Conference (1971), 'Religion and Soviet Foreign Policy', in Bociurkiw and Strang 1975. One has to remember that the World Council of Churches takes two pressures particularly into account. It defers to the third world, including Arab states where Israel is concerned; and it desires to retain the participation of the Orthodox, partly to widen its ecumenical front vis-à-vis Rome. The first pressure leads it to emphasize the racialist issue and the second pressure leads it to play down offences against liberty (including religious liberty) in the East, and emphasize the colonialism of the West. To some extent it carries forward the position of the Christian Peace Conference centred on Prague. Since Peace descended on Prague in 1968 this particular organization has become useless for the purposes of Russia foreign policy. However, the C.P.C. was very active in the condemnation of American foreign policy. What was involved for a pro-Russian Christian of goodwill is best illustrated from the autobiography of the Czech Protestant theologian, J. Hromadka. One may say that the Russian episcopate is totally responsive to the Soviet government; over Czechoslovakia for example, and recently in its attitude to Solzhenitsyn.

13. For a general survey, cf. Stackhouse 1968. One should consult in particular the work of A. I. Klibanov on the Russian side and the writings of Ethel and Stephen Dunn (e.g. Dunn and Dunn 1967). The most succinct general survey of the Russia situation in particular is B. Bociurkiw's contribution to Marshall 1971.

14. 'Znak', the lay organization of Catholic intellectuals is of some importance here, cf. Swiecicki 1973.

15. Staron 1969. Something of the danger of divisions between older and younger Catholics can be seen in Croatia. The hierarchy feel that 'openness' and participation are easily misunderstood by the uneducated, while younger priests support greater specialization of function, lay involvement and the optional character of celibacy. This division now takes place, of course, in a situation of increased pressure on the Church following accusations that it is involved in Croatian nationalist propaganda. Cf. *Absees*, April 1973, p. 275; and Hickling 1973.

16. I am grateful to Dr. Christel Lane for information about the 'Initiative Group' in a paper read at the L.S.E. Seminar on the sociology of religion (Lane 1974). Her paper has been most useful, together with brief summaries of the contents of Russian theses and surveys cf. Millar 1971.

17. It is interesting that the only Jewish community to survive the Nazi period more or less intact was in Bulgaria, which has no important anti-semitic tradition. Jews mostly left for Israel in the early years of the Communist regime; some 150,000 Muslims similarly left for Turkey. Polish Jews have from time to time left for Israel, no

doubt encouraged by the anti-semitism which the post-war left shares
with the pre-war right.

18. For highly interesting material on geographical sub-cultures
in Britain, France, Belgium etc., cf. Gay 1971; and Boulard 1960.
An important aspect of both studies is their emphasis on the extra-
ordinary persistence of patterns over centuries. In 1978 there will
appear the most detailed of productions in this field: F.-A. Isambert's
atlas of religious practice in France.

19. For the symbiosis of republicanism, refugee sentiment and
federalism cf. Fag 1976; and for the centralizing pressure of eighteenth century absolutism cf. Hargreaves-Maudsley 1976. There is
an interesting study to be done of the role of radical choirs in
regional sentiment, for which cf. W. Weber 1975 and Raynor 1976.

20. Northern Ireland is not made up of dissenters but of three
semi-territorial churches: Roman Catholic, Church of Ireland and
Presbyterian, corresponding to the Irish, and to the English and
Scots founding communities. Cf. Rose 1971.

21. For all such materials one should consult the relevant chapters
in Mol 1972. There is a fair amount of evidence bearing on the
decline of Catholic participation since the mid-sixties, which though
—or because—it starts from a higher base line is more noticeable
than Protestant declines over the same period. The decline from 21
per cent to 17 per cent per Sunday in France 1971–1975 is noted in
the text and derives from polls of French public opinion quoted in
The Times. In this poll carried out by Sofres for the first French TV
channel 26 per cent said they went to church once or twice a month
or occasionally and 68 per cent said they prayed from time to time.
The average practising Catholic is aged 65 or over, lives in towns of
2,000–20,000 inhabitants, is or has been a senior manager, an important shopkeeper, an industrialist, a doctor or a lawyer. *Doxa* (Nos.
17 and 18, 7/9, 1973) shows Italians divided into about $\frac{1}{3}$ regularly
practising, $\frac{1}{3}$ occasionally and $\frac{1}{3}$ non-practising, the proportion of
practising dropping sharply amongst males and somewhat among
young people (30 per cent in the age group 16–34). This lower level
was concentrated among those aged 25–34. Some 45 per cent of
Italian received communion in the course of a year. Australian
Gallup shows an overall decline of churchgoing per Sunday 1961–
1972 from 44 per cent to 31 per cent, to which Catholics contribute
disproportionately. The dip in American church-going over this
period was largely Catholic. In the U.K. A.E.C.W. Spencer writing
in *The Month* for April 1975 describes a Catholic recession from
about 34 per cent per Sunday in 1965 to about 25 per cent in 1973.
If we take these varied indices, including declines noted elsewhere
for Holland and Germany, their import seems to be that there is a
general decline in regular Catholic participation, which is particularly noticeable in Protestant cultures where hitherto practice has
run at a high level. There was also a decline of $\frac{1}{3}$ in Flanders.

One further point of particular interest may be mentioned and it is that Catholic conversions in the U.K. have been noted by R. Currie and A. Gilbert as running parallel to the vitality of Protestant churches and that these in turn run parallel to very broad indices of confidence and 'vitality' in the society as a whole. The confidence of the early fifties and the decline from 1960 onward is early noticeable in the data. Such findings clearly have relevance to the general European situation and the loss of morale since the high points of the 1950s. The same authors also document the variations in free church and Anglican vitality in relation to the fortunes of the Liberal and Conservative parties; at least up to the first world war. The direct impact of political confidence, societal or sectional, and the negative effect of wars are factors that all need transferring to the European context. 1968 for example saw a universal trembling of the indices. Cf. Currie and Gilbert 1978.

22. Tomasson 1971; and *Religion in Britain and Northern Ireland*, London Independent Television Authority, 1970.

23. Cf. Roter 1971; and Cimic 1971. The English Summary of H. Kubiak 1972 is useful in showing the decline in specifically ecclesiastical religion in a Polish steel works. M. Jaroszewski (1965) makes similar points. These Marxist views need to be set against the work of such scholars as V. C. Chrypinski and J. Majka. It is helpful to consult Majka 1968.

24. *Absees*, April 1973, p. 270, for material on Slovenia. For the possibility of a 'hard core' emerging, cf. Kadlecova 1972.

I should note two recent papers: A. Swiecicki 'Situation de la Sociologie des religions en Pologne comparée à celles des autres pays socialistes d'Europe' and S. Urcan 'Working Class commitment to church and religion in Yugoslavia', both in the 'Acts of the 14th Conference of the Sociology of Religion', C.I.S.R., Lille 1977. The first paper provides a table of Eastern European differences, with some further bibliographical material to that noted above, especially as regards Hungary. The second paper describes religion in the Yugoslavia Catholic working class. It shows that nearly all were baptised and the vast majority received their first communion. Yet only half were believers or engaged at all in religious practice and about one third were unbelievers. Eight per cent attended weekly and a further 8 per cent monthly. Urcan underlines differences by social level: peasantry (97 per cent believers, 98.3 per cent children baptised) self-employed craftsmen (57.8 per cent believers, 92.1 per cent children baptised), workers (53.3 per cent believers, 87.7 per cent children baptised), clerks (40.2 per cent believers, 68.8 per cent children baptised), intelligentsia (25 per cent believers, 51.1 per cent children baptised). He notes that these variations relate to level of education, skill and freedom from pressure of existence and that these same factors have the *reverse* consequence in the West.

IV

The 'Mixed' Pattern

The term 'mixed' religion here refers to the presence of major rival confessions, which form alternative natural societies resting, to some extent, on a territorial base. It does not refer to the type of pluralistic situation obtaining in the United States where a wide variety of denominations are mixed cheek by jowl, with only minor enclaves of territorial concentration e.g. German Lutherans in the mid-west. The rival confessions of the 'mixed' variety are in effect 'churches' of the old kind with a confessional frontier between them and areas of partial diaspora on either side of the frontier. The existence of such churches often runs *pari passu* with a tendency to political pluralism, which recognizes that extensive sub-societies exist within the global society. The German *Länder* are such sub-cultures, and so are the Swiss cantons.

The problem of sub-societies placed under one global umbrella gives rise to different axis of discussion and analysis from that obtaining in genuinely pluralistic or fully monopolistic societies. The pressure of one territorial church to maintain its own internal lines of communication and its integrity results in a build-up of interlinked sub-cultural institutions and interactions. The more contact there is by migration and by diaspora the more tightly the bounds are drawn, at least in the earlier stages. The crucial fact of social existence becomes the process of internal integration within the sub-culture and external confrontation between sub-cultures. This need not be violent but it will be institutionalized and express itself politically. The need to concentrate on sub-cultural integration differentiates the 'mixed' position from others in that these others must be approached with quite distinct axes in mind. A 'Latin' pattern contains two organic societies very strongly polarized over the whole area of the country, though obviously one will be dominant in some sectors and territorial areas, and the other dominant elsewhere. This creates an axis of discussion based on rival party (or ideological) allegiances. An Anglo-American pattern is internally very much looser and the distinctive gradations of allegiance alter by gentle and implicit differences associated with the culture of status and region. Religion scarcely seems to matter because it is an adjunct of this or that cultural style and is not used to define and reinforce conflicts. So the axis of discussion is status and culture. In all statist societies, the core of the system is imperative co-ordination i.e. the power nexus, and this means that the issue is one of church and state, or of the tension or the collusion between 'power' élites. Obviously all the various elements, status, party, power, and sub-cultural integration, have to be considered in every case, but there is an emphasis which differs from pattern to pattern. Religion is seen to count in the mixed pattern precisely because it runs along the lines set by sub-cultural integration.[1]

Holland provides the most interesting example among societies conforming to the mixed pattern. This is why the emphasis of what follows lies on the Dutch case. It provides a dramatic instance of sub-cultural integration and an equally dramatic instance of partial breakdown in this integration. It also allows and suggests certain comparisons with cultures possessing roughly equivalent proportions between rival confessions (Ulster, the Lebanon, Nigeria, and even Cyprus), other cultures with a semi-Calvinist élite (South Africa, Wales) or societies with an extensive Calvinist sub-culture (Protestant France, Hungary). These are not comparisons that I intend to pursue here, although it is interesting to note how some kinds of boundary maintenance between sub-cultures can lead to a highly institutionalized and stable peace-within-the-feud, while others break out into open warfare. A further possible point of comparison could be provided by Belgium. In Belgium, the secularist-religious confrontation of France is superimposed on a division by territories rather like that of Holland, and these are defined by language as well as by degree of religiosity. The result resembles the case of Holland in terms of processes of sub-cultural integration, except that the axis of conflict is not Protestant-Catholic, but French/secularist-Flemish/Catholic. Belgium is thus territorially and sociologically half-way between France and Holland, between the Latin and the mixed pattern.

The main elements in such comparisons concern the range of elements included in sub-cultural integrations and the extent to which crucial defining elements are constantly reinforcing each other at one and the same social border. Another major element concerns the locus of liberalization and its relation to secularizing élites. In most situations the major partner of a two-sector society can allow itself some secularization at least amongst the élite, but this sparks off a religious reaction among some of its followers, particularly those outside the nexus of cosmopolitan and élite power. Thus, in Scotland, Holland, Ulster, and elsewhere part of the élite has relaxed its religiosity, with varying degrees of reaction. A populist and rigorist element has arisen in association with the non-élite segment of the major religion, and this has contributed to an association of populism, of the radical right and orthodoxy in a hard amalgam of forces. In other situations, the élite itself has not felt able to afford such a relaxation or such a weakening division within the major religion, as for example in South Africa. An echo of the combination of populism and old-time provincial religion can be found in the small-town Protestantism of America, and something of its 'progressive' potentiality is illustrated in William Jennings Bryan. Whether popular impulses express themselves in 'left' or 'right' format or in what mixture of liberal and non-liberal elements, depends very much on the precise concatenation of groupings and histories. By the same token, the exact placing of Protestant Ethic elements—Methodism in England, old-style Protestantism in the United States, Haugeanism in Norway, the Opus Dei in Spain, the Old Believers in Russia— also depends on the interrelation of groupings and histories. At any rate, in the Dutch case, the populist impulse has been partly encased in the Re-Reformed movements of the theological and social right, and so too have important expressions of the Protestant ethic.

On the other side of the conservative fraction lies a parallel set of schismatic tendencies to the left, associated in this case with a weakening of integration within the authoritarian, Catholic sub-culture. This has, of course, been the subject of enormous speculation, because the disruption in the Dutch Catholic Church provided an example of a Church once more papal than the Pope which suddenly became more conciliar than the Council. The process of charismatic enthusiasm followed by a religious trough is already clear and permits some reflections on the role and future of neo-traditionalism.[2] Moreover, reflections are also in order concerning the reasons for such an outburst in Holland when, for example, the Roman Church in England remained relatively unaffected (McCaffery 1973, Larkin 1974). 'The openings to the left', widely characteristic of disintegrating Catholicism, whether in Spain or France or elsewhere, can be observed in a number of embodiments: the left voting of ex-confessional voters, the 'communautés de base', communitarian experiments, and politico-religious pressure groups like Shalom (Van Tillo 1973). These pressure groups often involve a translation of religious into political perspectives complementary to the reverse translations going on amongst the flotsam and jetsam left by the political and experimental failure of the student movement in Anglo-Saxon societies, e.g. the Jesus Movement.[3] Alongside these are the varieties of eastern cult found amongst Metropolitan youth, whether in Los Angeles, Amsterdam or London. The openings to the left and the possible slackening of sub-cultural integration, together with the very rapid progress of industrialization and urbanization in Holland, have led to restructuring and psychic readjustment throughout the institutional Church. Thus the parish has been restructured, the role of the priest or minister adapted, the intentions of the monastic orders reshaped, and theological perspectives infiltrated by a variety of humanistic personalism. All these changes now endemic in the churches of advanced industrial societies are best discussed in the Dutch context.

Before discussing Holland in extenso I turn to two 'weaker' cases of the mixed pattern. Switzerland and Germany are federal societies and their federalism rests in the one case on the cantonal system and in the other on the fragmentary princedoms and electorates of the Holy Roman Empire. In both societies there is a high correlation between the borders of constituent elements in the federation and areas of different religion. The relative proportions as between Protestant and Catholic have been traditionally something like 60/40, though the migration of Catholics into Switzerland and differential birth rates[4] have altered the proportion significantly; and the excision of E. Germany has also altered the proportions for Germany. Very roughly these are now societies where the two religions are of equal nominal strength, but since

the Catholic sector is more integrated and its institutional participation in better shape, the 'active' religion in both societies is
predominantly Catholic. This makes, at least in Germany, for a
fair degree of ecumenical dialogue at the upper levels between the
relatively weaker and relatively higher status Protestants and the
stronger, lower status Catholics.

In Switzerland the Reformation claimed the urban cantons,
and the rural cantons mostly adhered to Rome. The Protestant
organizational structure paralleled the political structure, though
eventually church and state parted in most Protestant cantons
whereas they remained united in the Catholic ones. In Catholic
cantons schools stayed denominational. There are also free
churches which arose during the nineteenth century revival
(Plymouth Brethren, Methodists and the like) and these were
concentrated in French-speaking Switzerland. These reflected an
opposition both to certain cantonal governments and to the state
churches. Some have now reunited with the state churches. The
Eglise Catholique Crétienne is recognized by the state and is
a part of the Old Catholic schism after the first Vatican Council
which also had some influence both in Holland and in Czechoslovakia. It is a recognized church but comprises only 0.5 per cent
of the population.

In Switzerland about 99 per cent are baptized, 96 per cent
confirmed and 91 per cent married in church. Alongside this high
rate of conformity to the basic rites some 27 per cent have given
up regular church attendance: 34 per cent of Protestants and 18
per cent of Catholics. According to Campiche (quoting Boltansky)
practice fluctuates according to region, the denominational com-
position of a canton, and size of town.[5] Thus the level of attendance, vocations and candidatures for the ministry or priesthood
is higher in the mountainous Catholic areas, lower in the Protestant areas, especially so in the large towns. Protestants practise
more in cantons where there is a Catholic majority. In 1958 in
French Switzerland about 85 per cent of Catholics in the high
valleys were present at Mass on any given Sunday; in the towns
of the Catholic cantons the total dropped to 20–30 per cent while
in urban areas with a Protestant majority it dropped to 15–20
per cent. The rate for Protestants in the large city of Geneva is
about 6–7 per cent. In a sector of Lausanne about 16 per cent of
the population were present every Sunday, 13 per cent two or

three times a month, 10 per cent once a month and 30 per cent a few times a year. 22 per cent never attended and 3 per cent could not. In short, about one third are fairly regular attenders and over a third occasional attenders. As has frequently been noted, at least with respect to Protestant countries, those who do not attend in the large cities very frequently pray (one half of the population daily in Lausanne) and/or attend to a radio or television service. Practice decreases until the mid-twenties in the life cycle and tends to rise slowly again after the age of forty. Congregations consist largely of minors, married people of the same denomination and the widowed; by contrast the divorced and those with partners of a different religion have very low rates of practice. As regards occupation workers have the lowest degree of practice: according to a Lausanne survey (1962) 27.3 per cent of skilled Catholic workmen practised and 15.1 per cent of unskilled Catholic workmen, as compared with 68.9 per cent of Catholic executives. Practice rises with level of education. However, although the churches are culturally alien to the urban worker and sometimes conceived as sympathetic to the propertied classes, there is no violent rupture or antagonism between the churches and labour. In Catholic areas the rate of practice decreases the broader the occupational spectrum within the Catholic sector, indicating that the factor involved is probably cultural difference, not political antagonism. Again, the difference between men and women increases the lower the general level of practice. Practice is an element in general integration: those who participate in social and political life whether in town or country are more likely to practise, though Catholics are less affected by the absence of tight-knit structures in towns, presumably because they have a comprehensive structure of their own. Commuting and social and geographical mobility affect practice adversely. One cannot help noting how nearly all the data summarized above are the exact mirror image of the situation obtaining in Eastern Europe, in particular as regards the relative practice of administrators, clerical workers, skilled and unskilled manual workers. Each step away from the 'centre' defines a step down in degree of religious practice, or conversely, in communist societies a step up.

Campiche states that only a minority of the population defines the task of the churches as they themselves define it. This finding is hardly peculiar to Switzerland. Swiss consider the church along the lines indicated by Glock in his study of American Episcopalians as existing to console and to guarantee morality. Opinion holds that political challenge is outside the ecclesiastical province and clergy are not even allowed a local political role. Many opinion leaders in any case have moved towards an irreligious moralism, a post-Christian humanism or syncretism, sometimes mixed with eastern mysticism. However, educated people are on the whole inclined to accept definitions of the churches' role more in accordance with the churches' own teachings and are able to integrate their faith more easily into their private lives. Protestants and Catholics differ little in their attitude to work: the Protestant influence has indirectly affected the Catholic minority both as regards the acceptance of national asceticism and the national mythology. The skew in status favouring Protestants is frequently remarked on by Catholics, particularly as regards the higher élite positions. Protestant predominance in the élite does have some overall societal impact.

Regular church goers vote more frequently than non-church goers (which is another index of integration) and more frequently choose the radical and liberal parties, unless they are Catholics in which case they vote for the Christian Social Party. Protestants from time to time have made attempts at organized trade unionism, particularly after the first world war when evangelicals were repelled by the anti-religious, anti-national and class war attitudes of the Social Democrats, and they also formed a small rather right-wing Evangelical People's Party which still exists. There has also been a Catholic trade union movement, but the majority of workers are organized in unions under Social Democratic aegis. The Catholic Social Party, which developed a social policy without being socialist tends to take the centre of the political spectrum, acting to stabilize political life and inclined from time to time to the Social Democratic left or the right.

The role of Catholics, who were an integrated but relatively deprived sector, in tempering the illiberality of liberalism is quite important. The Catholic revolt of 1847 was based on a fear of overweening state centralization under liberal aegis and of interference in the internal affairs of the Church. This resistance tempered liberal zeal and although ideological warfare recurred in the 1870s, the settlement eventually made by the liberals was a moderate one. Moreover, although Protestants were at this time allied with the liberals, they began to recognize their own need of a socially integrating conception of 'the Church', and built up their own associations, notably in the field of youth.[6] This is an echo of the reaction of the theological right in Holland, which recognizes the disintegrating effects of liberalism and the need for strong conceptions of the overarching social group as a precondition of survival. It is interesting that where the church is menaced by pagan illiberalism, demanding integration under pagan auspices, e.g. Nazism, it develops a high doctrine of the Church and of divine transcendence and judgement in association with left-wing ideology. Karl Barth is the major example.

The Swiss case is important because it presents important contrasts with Holland: its church polity is Erastian and the problem of 'pillars' is solved spatially by the technique of progressive localization. So far as ecclesiastical polity is concerned S. M. Lipset has pointed out how type of polity affects the likelihood of a religious incursion into party politics. A theocratic, proudly independent, multi-bonded church organization makes for just such an incursion since it has a militant doctrine and can mobilize multiple ties. In Switzerland however ecclesiastical polity has been Erastian and this has meant a degree of subservience to the state similar to that obtaining in Lutheran and Anglican societies. Hence orthodoxy has not mounted the kind of rebellion against the manipulations of the secular élite which occurred in Holland.

This relative quiescence of the orthodox Protestant sector has focused the issue of 'pillarization' solely around the Catholic Church. It is interesting to observe the specific form taken by differentiation in the Swiss context and the Swiss variant of the secularization of politics. The hinge on which differentiation turns opens earlier and more slowly than in Holland. In Holland differentiation waited for the equalization of the pillars and in Switzerland the appearance of socialism weakened the anticlericalism of the old élite enough to allow a relaxation of Catholic integration. Happily the language issue and the religious issue rose and fell according to different tempi, allowing each to be dealt with separately rather than in conditions of mutual reinforcement. (This temporal phasing of problems was of course important in Scandinavia. Too many problems at once are fatal: one thing at a time and not too fast is always best.) In Switzerland the watershed came with the first world war. H. H. Kerr (1974) points out how the rivalry of France and Germany sparked off linguistic identifications in Switzerland. The old religious differences were now partly re-canalized into identities based on language. And this was made possible by the advent of socialism. The Radicals who had exercised a long liberal hegemony felt it prudent to give up their anti-clericalism and work with the Catholic Conservatives against the new Socialist parties.

Once the threat of liberal anti-clericalism was shifted, free passage was granted to differentiation. In spite of retaining the religious loyalty of all age groups the Catholic Church became less and less able to mobilize in party political terms. At the same time the institution of proportional representation froze politics at the point of their post-war alignment. Since then the shifts of varying coalitions have taken place in the post-war format.

It is interesting to note that although Switzerland belongs to the 'Mixed' pattern it experiences overflows from the tidal forces sweeping around it. The allemanic areas evidence the gentle polarizations of the 'Mixed' pattern, as indeed does Alsace, but the Swiss Romand is characterized by a heavy Latin polarization. The Communist Party is largely confined to the Swiss Romand and is represented by the French speaking middle class. In any case, as Jonathan Steinberg has pointed out, the heterogeneous micro-formation of nineteenth century Swiss capitalism made for an anarchist rather than a communist response. But even here pillarization had its impact: all Anarchists were Protestant. Religion defines and counter-defines even the lines of secular force. Why did the overarching issues and overarching pillars sink less deep in Swiss mountains than in Dutch polders? The answer is partly ecological: Switzerland is split up spatially and has less dynamic population density. Cultural frontiers are less exposed— *so far*. And the bearers of centralization and of decentralization have switched identities over time: once the Swiss Romands supported centralism, now they ally with some smaller Catholic cantons against centralizing impulses from German and more especially commercial interests. But the key is the localization of issues and meanings. The Dutch had to put up social dykes: the Swiss already had mountains.

Jonathan Steinberg's account of Jurassian separatism allows

one to understand the continuing role of religion as a bastion of cultural defence, even after differentiation has loosened the tie with party politics (Kerr 1974). The question of the Jura resembles the question of Ulster. Like Ulster it began with the Reformation, when the Prince-Bishop of Basel was forcibly retired to rule the poor remote valleys of the eastern Jura. It continued when Napoleon eliminated him and his jurisdiction in the name of reason and revolution. In 1815 the sometime domains of the Prince-Bishop were given to the Bernese in compensation for the loss of Vaud. The Protestants of the southern Jura were glad to be joined to a powerful Protestant canton; the poorer Catholics of the northern Jura were not. The arrival of German-speaking Protestant immigrants complicated the issue: Catholic separatism revived and was viewed by Protestants and by radicals alike as clericalism. After the second world war in the 50s the issue came to a vote and the line of division was sharply geographical and religious. For example, certain old Catholic communes 'sous les roches' which had once belonged to the Prince-Bishopric voted overwhelmingly 'Yes' while villages 'sur les roches' which had never been part of the Bishopric and were Protestant voted overwhelmingly 'No'. Since the separatist Catholics were not a majority and since they felt they could not win by democratic means they turned to violence. A Catholic para-military force appeared and then a Protestant one. After a further plebiscite in 1974 which favoured the separatists there emerged an anti-separatist movement; and a Third Force for Jura unity was ground to pieces between separatists and anti-separatists. The complex manoeuvres which followed are an index of the logic of cumulative localization. As Steinberg shows the solution to Swiss pillarization is a cellular structure, focusing issues in ever smaller and more precise geographical units. This is what confirmed *all* Jurassiens as adherents of the Swiss national religion: to localize and to split is the sacred way of Switzerland. Had they joined France there would have been no nonsense about decentralization.

Yet there is a final paradox to be observed and it has come to the fore only in the last decade. Switzerland lives by a mountain myth and the idea of a hardy citizenry ready to repel all onslaughts. The myth is one of locality but it depends on unity in the defence of disunity, on authority in defence of freedom, on a refusal to tolerate disbelief in the myth of Swiss tolerance and

Swiss innocence. It therefore draws a sacred boundary around freedom's mountain redoubt. Trouble and sin lie across that boundary outside of Switzerland's Eden. Everyone must be ready to defend that boundary: where so much is local something must be supremely unifying. The core of unification is provided by the army, and the army has embodied a quasi-religious myth. It has lived off the 'lucky threats' of Nazism and Communism but as these have receded it has become exposed to the acids of modernity and the general challenge to authority. A mobile generation moving across permeable borders is reckless of every kind of border: personal, cantonal, national; and it rejects the vertical borders of seniority and hierarchy. Swiss democracy is deeply sedimented and it is so long standing as to be complacent. National sentiment, which stands guard over the myth of Europe's oldest revolution is now under pressure. The paradox is illustrated in the fact that Swiss freedom includes the military obligation of every citizen; and the army of freedom is a stronghold of the *status quo*. As in the city state only slaves do not serve. Switzerland *is* the myth of freedom: the conscientious objector is barely recognized. If the quasi-religious myth of democracy were less strong compulsion would also be less vigorous.

So Switzerland is a clear case of tendencies to be examined below in Holland. A federalist, 'loose' centre is integrally linked to alternative religions occupying different territorial bases. These alternative religions are not pluralistic denominations competing in society at large, but churches guarding distinct sub-societies. This distinction is fundamental as between the mixed pattern and the Anglo-Saxon pattern. The Catholic sub-society fulfils two roles. It tempers the hegemonic tendencies of liberalism. And it prevents non-liberal religion from being entangled exclusively in a social nexus which defines it as politically conservative and which could lead to political divisions over religion as such.

In medieval times and later Germany possessed a tradition of local sovereignty. With the coming of Reformation the strong impulses to radicalism and to individualization were rapidly absorbed by the drive to autonomy and religious homogeneity which animated the various territorial states. Religious heterogeneity had to wait for the indifference of absolutist enlightened rulers and more especially for the dissolution of some of the old borders by Napoleon. The united Germany which eventually emerged in 1871 was officially federal but the Catholic areas were treated as an alien and even potentially disloyal minority. Bismarck's 'Kulturkampf' was the most obvious expression of the tension between Prussian and Protestant dominance and the Catholic Church. Prussians still thought in terms of the necessary union of religion and territorial loyalty. Catholics felt themselves under pressure from the state and opposed to both the liberal bourgeoisie and the Protestant landowners. The 'Kulturkampf' stimulated Catholic voting for the Centre Party: in the 1870s confessional voting reached its highest point. Insofar as Catholics did not support the Centre Party they became more inclined to the left than Protestants. Indeed within the Centre Party itself there gradually emerged a labour and a trade union wing. Catholics stood with the left against all the assaults of right wing nationalists and refused to accept Bismarck's laws against the socialists. The most religious among Protestants were firmly conservative. But as in Holland, the growth of 'Kulturprotestantismus' provoked orthodox Protestant opposition and affinities of interest were discovered with the Catholics, more especially over the issue of education.

The Centre Party and a para-political network of association provided a 'pillar' of strength for Catholics. In the varied coalitions which characterized German democracy the Centre Party was an essential ingredient and it could therefore act as a channel for patronage. With the inauguration of the Weimar Republic after the first world war it became the principal element in alliances of liberals, Social Democrats and others against communists, nationalists and National Socialists. It made its principal contribution to social and economic policy and reform in this period At the same time it had to incorporate the regional sentiment which animated some strongly Catholic areas. In the 1920s the old regional feeling which had once lain behind the Bavarian Patriotic Party reasserted itself and Catholics became divided between those promoting social improvements organized from the centre, and those standing for local autonomy. (I draw my account both above and below largely from Gunter Kehrer (1972), Michael Fogarty (1957) and Gerhard Lehnbruch (1975).

National Socialist policy towards the Catholic Church was a

new version of the 'Kulturkampf' and a typical totalitarian bid
for control by a new secular élite. The new authoritarianism
initially attempted to harness the churches but immediately ran
up against the old authoritarianism of the Catholic Church. As is
usual only an authoritatively integrated body can resist authoritarianism viz. the Communist Party in Spain. Nazism grew
steadily more anti-Christian and split the Lutherans into the
'German Christians', and the 'Confessing Church'. The Nazis
therefore reactivated some of the older affinities between devoted
Protestants and Catholics. Bonhoeffer is, of course, the symbol
and martyr of the Confessing Church. Political Catholicism and
Lutheran opposition to Hitler together laid part of the base on
which a new, united and moderate conservative party might
emerge once Germany was defeated. After the war the older
conservative parties, which were mostly Protestant, had ceased
to exist and the Centre Party now formed the nucleus of the
C.D.U. The C.D.U., according to Kreiterling (1966) not only had
an absolute majority under a convinced Catholic leader, Adenauer, but also served to reintegrate Catholics into the mainstream
of German society. To be a Catholic was an excellent recommen-
dation for a key post, even though the party was not explicitly
confessional. Catholics even saw the way open to a rechristianiza-
tion of society, to be undertaken in ecumenical alliance with
believing Protestants. They were 'the majority in the majority'
and the politically dynamic sector of the society at large. Initially
they maintained traditional attitudes towards their principal and
(to begin with) only rivals, the Social Democrats. But in 1959 the
Social Democrats adopted the reformist 'Bad Godesberg' programme and dropped their own traditional opposition to religion
and the Church. The way was now open for the spirals of
antagonism to weaken. The Social Democrats offered to respect
the 'special mission of the churches'. Catholic organizations were
initially sceptical, as was the Social Democratic left, but a serious
dialogue nevertheless developed and with the coming of the
Vatican Council Catholic enthusiasm for their politico-social en-
gagement with the C.D.U. decreased. They came to feel after
many years of C.D.U. rule that they were the creatures of a
neo-liberal profane dynamism at odds with Catholic social doctrine. They had in any case been discontented with the over-
representation of Protestants at higher party levels. This had been

part of an effort to retain a non-confessional image and this same effort had seriously blunted the edge of Catholic social doctrine.

In the Rhineland and the Ruhr, where the dynamic of industrialization was particularly strong, the votes of the Catholic majority began to shift towards the S.P.D. from 1956 onwards. Practical improvements took precedence over older ideological conflicts; specifically religious issues became dormant; the new morality appeared. Between 1956 and 1965 the shift of Catholics to the S.P.D. accelerated: 76 per cent of practising Catholics voted for the C.D.U. in 1953, 61 per cent in 1961. From 1963 on the active elements in Catholicism proposed to cooperate with social democracy within the C.D.U.–S.P.D. coalition, and by the late '60s the Catholic hierarchy publicly stated its political neutrality and unwillingness to recommend how a Catholic should vote. This gave the Church a greater freedom of action, and maybe also an augmented moral authority vis-à-vis the almost purely political drives behind the C.D.U. Catholics were simply encouraged to be active in both parties, as were Protestants, thus ending a tradition of direct political action by the Catholic Church in Germany. Specifically clerical influence on political decision making declined. This situation certainly bears on the general lack of violent anti-clericalism and the fact that the S.P.D. was able to drop its anti-religious bias.

This does not mean that religion no longer affects party choice: the liberal Free Democratic Party is predominantly Protestant *and* relatively secularist in image, as also is the new nationalist party: it contains small independent business men and, in some areas, Protestant farmers. Predominantly Catholic areas (Bavaria, South Baden, the Saar, the Rhineland) still vote mainly for the C.D.U., while *strongly* Protestant Schleswig-Holstein also adheres to the C.D.U. The more a man participates actively in the church, of whatever denomination, the more likely he is to vote for the C.D.U. In urban areas Catholics tend to vote for the S.P.D. and in rural areas Protestants and Catholics tend to vote for the C.D.U. The strongly industrialized Protestant areas such as north Hessen provide strong support for the S.P.D. In other words the usual variables of industrialization and class are operative, and the effect of a *specifically* Catholic political influence in the state has declined, though the influence of participation in the church, in Germany as elsewhere, remains, as also do some of the local

G

traditions of Catholic political loyalty. Overall, there is a significant deconfessionalization of politics and a relatively increasing
salience of social class: a situation to be observed again in Holland.
There are however certain relationships between participation
and occupation which are to be described below.[7] The principal
sources are Kehrer 1972 and Greinacher 1963.

Since membership of the churches in Germany is a matter of
birthright inheritance the baptismal rite is nearly universal,
though it is coming to be seen as a private occasion, primarily
for the immediate family. Here we have the symbolic hint of
privatization and family-based religion. The proportion of church
weddings has decreased somewhat from the near-uniformity of
the last century, but it has stabilized round about 85 per cent after
dropping to 60 per cent during the late thirties when the National
Socialists put pressure on the churches. As regards divine service
perhaps some 15–20 per cent of Protestants attended regularly
in 1972 as compared with over 30 per cent doing so a decade
previous. Trends are somewhat better documented for Catholics.
It is probably the case that in the first quarter of this century
about three out of four Catholics were regular attenders. After the
war, in the period of Catholic confidence described above, the
percentage rose from 45.1 per cent in 1946 present at Mass on
Sunday to 51.1 per cent in 1949, 40.9 per cent in 1967 and 32.3
per cent in 1972. (The decline around the year of trauma, 1968,
is almost universal in West Europe.)

Easter duties follow the same curve but at a level about 5 per
cent higher. These percentages alter according to whether practice
occurs on a traditional area of Catholic dominance, or in an area
of mixed religion or in an area of Catholic diaspora: the total
decreases from the first to the last. This is in interesting contrast to
the situation apparently obtaining in other countries. Where
Catholics are in a diaspora situation in a largely Protestant country they generally experience pressures to increased internal
integration, but where they have a massive traditional sector such
as exists in Germany the traditional areas are more integrated,
and the diaspora situation more open to alternative influences.
Or it may be that the diaspora in Germany exists in heavily
industrialized areas. The differential influence of the variables as
between the dynamics of majority–minority status and industrialization is not clear from the data. At any rate, Greinacher is able

to report the usual variations according to sex, marital status and age: the drop in early adolescence, the low point in the first decade or more of marriage, the faithfulness of the unmarried and widowed, and the marked unfaithfulness of the divorced. He also underlines the usual increase in personal faith which runs alongside the decrease in social conformity, signalized by the proportionate increase in personal communion. One aspect of the statistics he cites is of particular interest. The class he labels 'independents' are in fact peculiarly subject to the local religious tone: where practice is high, as in Trèves, the 'independents' follow suit, where low as in Munich they do likewise. On the other hand functionaries and 'employers' are relatively stable; similarly so workers, but at a much lower level which hardly ever exceeds 20 per cent. Of course, all the figures he cites are quite high by general European standards and indicate that the situation of Catholics as a large minority marginally deprived as to status, income and education, is religiously advantageous.

The status skew in favour of Protestants is connected with many factors, historical and contemporary, and requires a very complex analysis: the factors of different motivation and anticipation, operative in relation to status and urban background, mesh with 'religious' factors in a most complicated manner. Where Catholicism is the dominant religion e.g. in Cologne, the status skew does not appear, but in Germany overall it does and is no doubt related to the leading role in the federation played by Prussia and even further back to the fact that it was the free cities of the Empire which first went Protestant at the Reformation. Certainly professors, generals and higher civil servants, and the business élite are all quite disproportionately Protestant, suggesting the persistence of older modes of recruitment in the élite, in spite of the more favourable political atmosphere with respect to Catholics in the post-war period. It is also of some interest that Catholics more nearly achieve parity in the arts faculties, while the disparity in the scientific, technical and medical faculties is considerable. This slant of Catholic populations towards the arts is a widespread phenomenon, in spite of the anti-religious traditions which also exist in the humanities. Indeed, one might say that in the humanistic faculties of countries of mixed religion there is a Catholic tendency *and* an anti-religious tendency, while believing Protestants are rather fewer. The believing Protestants may easily be concentrated in such faculties as engineering and medicine. These, however, are observations rather than proven facts.

Since education has been rather a focal point in other discussions, and since it is relevant to sub-cultural integration, something further must be said on this score. Clearly neither in Switzerland nor in Germany does 'verzuiling' exist on the Dutch scale. Germany was one of the earliest societies to adopt an overall schools system, and the vast majority of schools are under state control. Nevertheless education is not religiously neutral. In the first place, as in Britain, there is a religious instruction in all state schools (except in Bremen) and in the second place, as in Britain, a large proportion of teachers are educated at denominational institutions. In the third place, there are schools with relative denominational bias within the overall state system, and this depends on local federal governments which is in turn related to the precise mix of denominations in any area. In the Catholic Saar denominational schools are normal, in Hessen not, and in mixed areas parents tend to prefer to have non-denominational schools (cf. Fogarty 1957).

Kehrer emphasizes the administrative nature of German institutional religion and this comes out not only in schools policy but in the sphere of welfare and the relationship of churches to mass media. The sector of welfare administered by the churches is very large, but in practice this amounts to the existence of a religiously 'toned' part of *general* administration. It does not feed segregationist tendencies on the Dutch scale. Churches are subsidiary elements of administration; and in the sphere of the media this means, simply, that their upper echelons operate as a mild pressure group of not very visible 'advisors', again as in Britain. Thus there is an affiliation to a pattern of denominational pluralism as well as to the pattern of confessional 'pillarization'. Germany belongs to the mixed pattern, because it contains rival territorial churches with concentrations by area which leads to quite extensive sub-cultural integrations on a religious basis. But the general overarching societal frame is also strong, perhaps precisely because it was once weak.

We now come to Holland where the sub-cultural integration noted in Germany and Switzerland achieves much more pervasive manifestations. This necessitates some historical background. In the course of detailing the key moments and aspects in this background it is clear that in its slow, stable extension of political rights and its absorbent looseness of structure Holland resembles England, however much England differs on account of its relative religious homogeneity i.e. a greater state church preponderance and a *Protestant* dissent.[8] Holland is the classic case of a pattern established early and constantly fed into by new elements which it moulds in its own image. Just as England achieved a pattern in 1660 of a preponderant élite poised against moderate and massive dissent so the criss-crossing pluralities, complex balances and congeries of interest in Dutch politics were set up early on, even before the Reformation. The Dutch case is best analysed by constant reference to England, since in this way both the fundamental difference in pattern and the striking similarities can be brought out.

Dutch medieval traditions successfully resisted central authority. In the later centuries power was oligarchical, dispersed, and rooted in alternating factions, as indeed was power in eighteenth century England. These were the core elements in the pattern: decentralization, a system of ins and outs. When most of Europe moved towards absolutism in the late sixteenth century the Dutch sought to arrest the growth of central government, as did the English fifty years later. The same decentralization prevented the growth of autocratic monarchy, of a central bureaucracy, or of a centralized, independent military establishment. Holland, even more than England, possessed a civilian establishment. Like England in the mid-seventeenth century, it lived by perpetual debate and pamphleteering.

The French overran Holland in 1795 and provided a unitary administrative framework, later utilized by the only king to resemble an absolutist monarch: William I. This gave rise to organized opposition against the centre and to debate on a national scale, and it is this crucial transmutation of local factioning into varied and differently based attacks on the centre which has set the tone of politics and religion since then. There were regional interests to be set against the centre, and the successive and overlapping oppositions found their strengths in various important regional settings: Catholics in the south-east, Orthodox Protestants in the north, Liberals and Socialists in the north-east. Again, as in England, the bourgeoisie early gained an important voice, and gradually mixed with the aristocracy rather than destroying it. This coalescence created a permanent respect for élite values which led to a high degree of security and a high respect for law. The élite therefore felt able to concede without danger and to allow wide areas of private autonomy. Furthermore, the élites were never fully identified either with the political apparatus or the state church: the tightly concentrated agglomerations of power which give rise to alternative agglomerations never came into existence. Tolerance was normative and the orthodox Catholics or Calvinists had to fight a battle against a pure latitudinarianism at the centre, which was also a fight for their own emancipation. Thus emancipation was a fight to have the freedom not to be totally latitudinarian, as well as a fight to change the skew of status against the centre.

Orthodox Protestants were initially indistinguishable from the Conservatives and shared their horror of the French Revolution; Catholics were initially well-disposed to the Liberal establishment because it tolerated Catholic demands. Calvinists first denied the representative character of the Liberal establishment. Then, when they realized that they were gradually being shouldered out of the Liberal establishment in terms of a liberal rejection of *their* traditional values, they appealed to the people. Only a section of the people responded to them, so creating a variety of fundamentalist populism very similar to the populism of William Jennings Bryan and the fundamentalists of small town America. There are also parallels with the Orange Order in Northern Ireland, as perhaps the name of that order suggests.

As the Liberals grew more secular and anti-clerical they also touched off Catholic opposition, particularly with respect to the schools issue, and since this issue affected all the other issues relating to religion and sub-cultural integrity it inaugurated mass debate. In time both Calvinists and Catholics were to recognize that they shared a community of injustice if not of religious values. Both were eventually to agree on a common interest with respect to confessional schools, so that—again as in England—schools became divided between the confessions. However, here lies a difference: in England the centre was educationally stronger, and the nonconformist sub-culture was much more weak than the Anglican Church, which retained a secure relation to the hub of

English society. It is also interesting that the Calvinist Anti-School Law League was modelled on the English Anti-Corn Law League, also a movement with much dissenting support. Both societies sustained traditions of organized moral-cum-political causes.

The development of orthodox Calvinist dissent must be dealt with below since it bears comparison with Methodism in England and Haugeanism in Norway, as well as with the populist movement of America. Suffice to say at this point that from the 1880s till 1913 Dutch politics, in common with much political life throughout the continent, from Spain to England, witnessed a classical alternation, except that the alternation was between religious cabinets and Liberal ones. Counter-élites extended upward and then downward towards the mass, and respect for authority within the Calvinist groups eventually resulted in a division between the non-populist group, the Christian Historical Union, and a populist party led by aristocrats, the Anti-Revolutionary Party. The Christian Historicals straddled the more conservative elements *within* the Dutch Reformed Church, whereas the Anti-Revolutionaries preferred the safety and the focused (if limited) power of sub-cultural isolation. The Catholics, as the largest bloc, preferred to be relatively passive in their pressure group politics lest they awake the latent Protestant prejudices of the overall majority. In this way each minority became introverted and the lines of political opposition became roughly co-extensive with denominational sub-culture. The nearest English approximation to this is the partial identity of Liberals and Nonconformity, but again the contrast is illuminating. Both Liberals and Nonconformists could conceive themselves as confronting a centre focused on a union of Conservatives and Anglicans: it was a dichotomous system with one of the religious groups allied not to ancient orthodoxy but to the values of freedom, conscience and civil rights. In England the Liberals could not be as élitist as in Holland, but had to rely on provincial, popular Nonconformity. It is quite clear that the two situations had to lead to different systems of representation: dichotomous alternations in the English case with an overall conservative bias, and sets of coalitions in the Dutch case, rooted in proportional representation. Thus, it can be argued that the relative positions of religious groups in a given culture help determine whether the system is one of proportional representation or not.

As in England, sub-cultural political emancipation preceded
organized working class politics, but in the English case part of
the forces of nonconformist emancipation flowed over into the
channels provided by the working class movement, partly because
the political efforts of lower-status nonconformists were for a time
blocked by the Liberal élite. In Holland both the newly emanci-
pated groups were initially anti-socialist and although they lost
some working class support in the industrializing cities they also
retained enough workers to become internally more democratic.
In any case, many workers were not proletarian but based on the
crafts, and these strengthened radicalism *within* the Liberal Party
and Anti-Revolutionary Party. In England they first provided a
radical element in the Liberal Party and then a moderating
element in the Labour Party. Furthermore, agricultural depression meant that Radical and Socialist deputies first appeared in
agricultural constituencies, a situation perhaps paralleled by the
agricultural workers union in England, led by a Methodist
preacher Joseph Arch. Revolutionary anarchism also appeared in
Holland, especially amongst canal and peat diggers. So when the
proletariat did develop it was exposed to the whole range of
socialist ideology and became rather fragmented. The earlier rise
of the British movement and its links with craft and nonconformist
elements gave it a tone of radical moralism which muted the
schisms and dogmatisms of ideology, except among the intellectual fringes. English radicalism was a moral unity not a dogmatic
dissensus, a reflection of the non-dogmatic character of English,
as compared to Dutch religion.

Initially socialism was anti-clerical, but becoming conscious of
the need to attract Catholic and Calvinist workers it ameliorated
its stance and accepted the notion of subsidies to religious schools.
(This amelioration parallels that of the Norwegian left after the
first world war on finding it must make some adjustment to the
power of the religious parties of the 'old left'). After various splits
and schisms a Communist party appeared rooted in the residue
of an anarchist strike and on the electoral base originally held by
the anarchists. (As in so many contexts, totalitarian movements
easily root themselves in anarchistic ones.) Socialism was not
immediately incorporated in the national system and began to
build for itself a sub-cultural ghetto parallel to that of the religious
sub-cultures, and with the same consequences in terms both of

integration and of constriction. In 1932 the leftist element was ejected, at exactly the same time as the leftist Independent Labour Party was ejected in England; and as in England the Socialists adopted a planning technique on Fabian lines. Again as in England there was a considerable pacifist element, with some roots in anarchistic tendencies and reflecting an alienation from the national consensus, but with the war and Nazism this petered out: so too did its English equivalent (cf. Martin 1965a). In 1939 the coalition between Catholics and Anti-Revolutionaries broke up because the Catholics had moved left and the A.R.P. to the right. So the Socialists entered a cabinet of Catholics, Christian Historicals and assorted Liberals. As they did so they explicitly abandoned dogma with respect to religion and the class struggle, partly on the ground that it was otherwise impossible to attract the clientèle of the religious parties.

In Holland and in England the end of war brought Socialists close to power: in England as a majority and in Holland as the leading element in a coalition. And in both countries pro-Russian sentiment had created a communist vote nibbling at the left of socialist strength. Socialism retained its position in Holland due to the coalition system, seven years longer than in England, and then left the government in 1958, returning to it in 1965.

It is this system which has given rise to the phenomenon of pillarization: several integrated sub-cultures in which the élites of each negotiate, combine and recombine over the walls of the ghetto. As Goudsblom puts it: no other social division outside the 'pillars' has yielded any lasting and preponderant issue (Goudsblom 1967). The stability of such a system when contrasted with the centralization, polarization and instability of France is very clear. Neither generation gaps nor female emancipation have disrupted this stability. There is not even the dichotomy presented by the Walloons and the Flemish in Belgian society. As in America the political parties, especially the religious ones, have taken up conflict *internally*. And like those who reject the caste system in India, the Liberals and Socialists by virtue of their rejection of pillarization only build yet another pillar. Because socio-economic and religious matters criss-cross they confuse the issues and assist stability and this is further assisted by an element also traditional in England: civility and the tradition of public orderliness.

The question arises as to whether the system is in decline. While it retains its power amongst trade unions and makes gains in education, it sustains losses in the field of sport. By contrast with Britain each pillar has its own access to the media but some Liberals, Socialists and latitudinarian Protestants have pleaded for a more 'national' system on the BBC model. However, the election of 1965 restabilized the position against open commercial television. At the same time the widening of perspectives provided by the media and increased secularity, plus greater mixing in leisure, has partly eroded some aspects of 'pillarization'. However, this leads to a further question, which is a consideration of two crucial elements in the system of pillars: the Orthodox Calvinists and the Catholics.

The possibility of a decline in the strength of 'pillarization' is normally set in the context of three factors, leaving aside for the moment the 'factor' of secularization: the integration of élites at the top of the system, the slow permeation downwards of objections by intellectuals to the system, and the successful conclusion of the emancipation process, making isolation unnecessary. The last argument is put forward with respect to the orthodox Calvinists, the Gereformeerden, on the grounds that they have acquired religious and social power and prestige. Emancipation is thus conceived in terms of an accepted honoured place in the social structure.

Brunt has argued that such an approach leaves aside the fact that the Orthodox Calvinists are in any case not a unified pillar.[9] Indeed, in terms of overall unity they are a 'pillar' shattered into fragments by schism. Before the question of emancipation is discussed the principal fragments need to be examined. The unity of neo-orthodoxy is defined in terms of shared confessional formulae, not in terms of a common organization. To that extent it resembles evangelicalism in Britain and America, which exists not only in fundamentalist churches but also within the state church. All neo-orthodox churches vest authority in the godly community, or congregation: the differences turn on *degrees* of orthodoxy, of severity and separation from the enticements of the world, and of devotion to the inner witness of the heart. This 'heart-work' gives them an affinity to Wesleyans, in spite of their Calvinist orthodoxy and their insistence on human powerlessness and divine election.

Really doctrinaire Calvinists are represented by a small political party for which only heads of households vote. They number about a quarter of a million persons. The less extreme neo-Calvinists are much more optimistic and active in the world and they derive from a later secession which took place in 1886–8. They number over three quarters of a million persons. The orthodox in general are often confused with the 'kleine luyden' or 'little people'. But who, in fact, were and are the little people? Nowadays they are the straight-laced among the poor who cannot fit in and who are thought of as religious fanatics. The 'little people came into existence in the 1830s with an attack by Kuyper and a number of aristocrats on the liberal establishment which also appealed to the lowest strata of society: manual labourers, farmworkers, small craftsmen and traders, peasants. This parallels the movement of the Plymouth Brethren in England at the same time, similarly led by aristocrats and followed by many 'small people', including fisherfolk. The later schism of 1886–8 was rather differently composed of well-to-do farmers. These took the initiative in founding an agrarian-industrial network of factories, banks and insurance companies within an environment domin-ated by autarchically organized small family businesses. In this respect the parallel is with Norway and the agrarian industrial reforms of Hauge and his followers. These farmers also called themselves 'little people' but were far from being in the deprived groups associated with the earlier schism. Those who derive from the earlier schism have shared in the emancipation which has been partially achieved by those who made up the later schism and who reformed agriculture, succeeded in the struggle for denominational schools, founded the Free University of Amster-dam and formed the core of the Anti-Revolutionary Party. No doubt both groups would sustain comparison with the great disruption in the Scottish Church of 1843 and other schisms within the Scots Presbyterian churches in the nineteenth century.

Emancipation and its effect on the Catholic column as analysed by Thurlings provides a somewhat different kind of story.[10] Until 1960 Dutch Catholics were renowned for uniformity, orthodoxy, a high birth rate and numerous vocations to the priesthood. Between 1860 and 1960 they built up a colossal structure con-stituting their own social 'pillar' which can be seen as part of a massive attempt, not only to safeguard their specific values and faith, but also to change the criteria of allocation in Dutch society in their favour, though of course amongst themselves they encompassed a large variety of status positions and were only deprived on the average. Initially cultural defence had resulted in an immense burgeoning of Catholic organizations; not only schools, trade unions and a party, but libraries, social welfare organizations, cooperatives and (eventually) a broadcasting station. These were maintained not merely by the need for cultural defence but by an internal momentum provided by the existence of bureaucratic machinery and its workers, by the development programme itself and the efficiency with which it was carried out. Being so successful, indeed too successful, the system led to a degree of self-contained closure which when combined with readjustments in Catholic status led to demands for a greater degree of openness, especially after 1945. In 1960 the turning point came: the Catholics had now achieved substantial equality and felt capable of a more open dialogue not only with the world but with their own past and traditions. Theologians took the lead in this, and initiated a fierce controversy with the old administrative élite, which first of all aroused great enthusiasm and then brought about a general slackening of Catholic identity and practice. The intellectual élite of theologians were supported by other intellectuals and new middle class groups like journalists, and by labour leaders and young people generally, whereas the administrative élite turned for support to the traditional leaders of profane organizations in agriculture and commerce and members of the older middle class, like shopkeepers. Bishops, being both theologically minded and concerned with administration, endeavoured to maintain communication with the progressives and keep the ties with Rome endangered by such issues as clerical celibacy. In short, the Bishops were forced to referee *a civil war within the middle class*, paralleling the civil wars elsewhere e.g. England and the U.S.A.

Catholics have been distinguished by their attitude to authority, and in a conflict which includes the question of authority their identity is more threatened than that of other groups. Furthermore, both sides in the controversy claimed optimal commitment, and this differs from the traditional position of Rome in which there was always tolerance towards the weak and erring. Conservatives were now obliged to defend official norms explicitly and progressives to attack them. The new personalism and communitarian fervour of the progressives was, in fact, only an élite option, and once immediate enthusiasm waned a variety of less exciting possibilities remained, apart that is from the drift to political extremism. Either people sank into a frustrated refusal to participate or they diverged into separate social sectors where a kind of Catholicism developed varied to meet different types of demand. One group had one type of liturgy, another group yet another type. The gains of universality were lost: differentiation, which in Catholicism is always quite subtle and under a clear overarching umbrella, became uncomfortably explicit. Indeed the progressives had the choice of the sectarian cell or accepting an authority which they disputed and which is even so their only badge of identity. Or they could become extremely ecumenical, as many did, and simply become lost and unidentifiable in Dutch society at large. The marked decline of Catholic confessional voting is an index of this weakened identity.

These are the options and this the situation: are there further reasons why it has occurred in Holland? Why, for example, has the explosion been so minor by comparison in England? There is, of course, the fact that mobility in general disrupts the stability of segregated sub-cultures and Dutch society has undergone great and rapid changes which require considerable mobility. Then there is the combined impact of internal cohesion and strong lines of communication allied to a high level of literacy. This means that when the kind of issues raised by the council cracked the authoritarian structure the resonance of the subsequent debate was considerable. Previously the system had echoed loudly to the tune of one message; now it resonated doubly with several conflicting messages, especially so given the progressive sympathies of media operators. Knowledge of being watched by the world acted as a further accelerator.

The youth of the middle class was at the forefront of the conflict, which in any case overlapped the much broader student explosion against bureaucratic authority, of which the Roman Church was an obvious instance. This led to radical Christian groups in all three religious parties, not merely the Catholics. The personalism and existential perspective of these radical groups stressed the historicity and relativity of truth, (e.g. the contextual character of morality) in a way quite inimical to ecclesiastical authority. In England the intellectual Catholic middle class was small and the level of theoretical literacy low. This meant that innovations succeeded each other slowly enough not to cause confusion. Furthermore Catholics were separated not only by religion but by ethnicity. Catholic mobility was not yet so high as to take them deep into the latitudinarian sectors of English society and in any case the urban concentration and geographical mobility of Catholics was of long standing. Thus English Catholics were less separated by the walls of the ghetto, yet more distinct in terms of ethnic background and lower average status. In short, there were fewer ghetto walls to break down and more genuine social distance (cf. McCaffery 1973, Larkin 1974, Goddijn 1973).

Part of the controversy engendered turned on the role of the priest and the traditional view of life in the orders. Many of the orders had become fossilized, duty-bound and constricting. Now, with a fall in vocations and an increase in defections there is a slope in the age structure towards the older groups which further complicates the path of change. After 1965 many religious joined small communitarian groups, attempting to renew the original aims of their orders in small private houses. One study of a congregation showed that more friars than fathers and more fathers than novices were traditionally minded; the young in general were more inclined to change (Baan 1966, Verdonck 1971, Stoop 1971). A similar study of priests showed a parallel division between those whose orientation was to the rite and those who were primarily concerned with 'witnessing' and caring (Poeisz 1967a and 1963). The broad outlines of the clash of modes lies in the distinction between the goal of personal sanctification pursued in a context of partial or total withdrawal and of roles rigidly specified by authority, and an open, free witness to the love of God whereby rules subserve specific ends and within a context of free choice and and communal democracy. So far as the exponents of the latter are concerned rules such as the rule of celibacy should vary according to personal choice and specific spiritual objectives. The challenge to authority and uniformity is as clear as the challenge to rules: the group is to be self-determining, self-socializing, capable of elaborating its own mechanisms of control. The result would be a Catholic Church deprived equally of hierarchy and of universality, deprived of all boundaries setting it off from the world or other communions and committed to following the dynamics of each local culture wherever they might lead. And alongside this breakdown of the 'external' authority and boundaries, of the otherness of God and the otherness of people, there went a pervasive spiritualism which eroded sacramental doctrine. The sacrament was converted from a realization of the transcendent and an objective focus of the sacred within specific boundaries and under given conditions into a meal based on total encounter and absolute unity. With the disappearance of the 'other' there went the disappearance of the private. Indeed, this was signalized by the diminution of purely private devotions at mass and the increase in communion and in free, inter-personal exchanges. The verticality of church architecture and of the rite gave way to a roundness pointing towards a common centre. Various devices symbolized this: the position of the priest facing the congregation, the celebration of the Eucharist in the middle of the People of God, the informality of the language, the anthropological emphases of the new catechisms, the diversification (not to say confusion) of forms. The weakening of boundaries also smudged the distinction between clerical and lay, church and world. The aspiration to encounter and community was oddly complemented by bureaucratic rationalization: e.g. in liturgical reform, not only in Holland but elsewhere. In England for example shaking hands symbolizes encounter, 'We believe' indicates community, and the flatness of the language represents the bureaucratization of prose.

Naturally such radical innovations, more Protestant than Protestantism, more enthusiastic than sectarianism, more radical than representative democracy, more communitarian than extant communities, gave rise to conflict. The older generation were confused and then horrified, the younger generation initially delighted and then confused. 'Dialogue' became Babel. Attempts were made to put more conservative persons in positions of authority; numbers of priests constituted pressure groups on the authorities.[11] The confusion led to a drop in the number of candidatures to the priesthood, and presumably those who did candidate were relatively conservative. Indeed this last is a phenomenon highly likely wherever there is a crisis in vocations, and it is accentuated by the age structure of those who remain. Restructuring, however, went on, not so much in the existential direction indicated by enthusiasts, but in the bureaucratic direction indicated by wider thrusts in society at large: expanded units, 'group practice', specialization of function and professionalization. The aspiration was to do away with managerialism; the reality was more bureaucracy. In this the reform of Dutch Catholicism went the way of the reform of Dutch and English Universities.

The more extreme form of the communitarian enterprise mentioned above can be illustrated by the group called '*Shalom*', since it suggests a very typical sequence in openings to the left initiated by young, enthusiastic Christians. It represents an attempt to maintain perpetual self-renewing group charisma by mechanisms designed to prevent the normal tendencies to stabilization and rigidification. It also illustrates the tension between the moral imperatives of the gospel and a realistic appraisal of the elements of power and coercion required in revolutionary activity. *Shalom* began in the ecumenical aspirations of young Christians who were also activated by political and social concern and who operated within the context of the neo-Marxist enthusiasms of many in the student population. It was originally part of a whole series of ecumenical groups, whose concerns had shifted to general social questions. It celebrated the Last Supper ecumenically and converted it into a form of Love Feast freely invented and containing a great deal of contemporary political comment culled from newspapers. Gradually, all other barriers collapsed in a pan-human aspiration to unify east and west, rich and poor, church and world, Christian and non-Christian. All distinctions were eliminated by the aspiration to universal 'peace': Shalom. But meanwhile, there was to be conflict, not merely with the Churches, which soon became irrelevant, but with the entrenched structures of the social world, above all exploitation and violence. To do this 'Shalom' became activist and at the same time tried to organize in such a way that democratic participation was continuously possible without either losing the original character of the movement through dilution or succumbing to inertia and to formulae. This meant selection, socialization and such restrictions on the development of internal structure as might allow a dynamic policy. Ecumenism had become cosmo-politics, the last questions had given way to the next-to-last questions, and ultimate peace to immediate warfare. Not peace but a sword.

The activities of Shalom can be put in the context of the

characteristic life of the very large cities, where the latitudinarian agnosticism of a professional upper middle class, especially those in the business of education and communication, is complemented by a burgeoning of mystical and oriental cults. Amsterdam may serve as an example of this take over of the 'centre' by non-belief *or* irrationalism of various kinds. Amsterdam here provides a paradigm of London or New York or Los Angeles (Nuij 1973). One may note in passing the special situation which arises for the church when the most powerful media of modern society are in the hands of a left-liberal establishment, since this means that those from its own ranks who take up such work are disproportionately inclined to the expressivist progressivism of media men in general, and favourably disposed to the ideology of change. A society which lives by newness can promote changing fashions in dissidence but not the repetition of what are believed to be ancient truths. Hence there is a rapid succession of kinds of cult, and indeed of bizarre forms of counter-cult reaffirming tradition and discipline in ways sufficiently odd to be satisfying to the participant and curious to the observer. A vigorous example of the latter is the syncretistic cult emanating from Korea, the Unification Church, which affirms the traditional values of the areas in which it takes root.[12]

The special radicalism of the humanist intelligentsia and its hatred of the technicist mentality and large-scale bureaucratization has had considerable influence in Amsterdam. Amsterdam itself illustrates all the major tendencies of modern society: accelerated 'industrialization', concentration of population, the movement to the suburbs, the process of commuting, rapid mobility, the increase in purely functional relationships. It is one of the most secularized areas in Holland: only 4 per cent of the population attend the Protestant churches on Sunday and these are concentrated in the petite bourgeoisie. The 'pillars' are no longer operative. At the same time the city is besieged by minor cults.

There are first the cults which have reclaimed many from the drug culture and operate in the downward curve of student radicalism: the Jesus people and the Children of God. Such are often concentrated in petit bourgeois sectors and combine spiritual individualism with communal ties replacing those of the family. Then there are forms of eastern mystical cult, at various levels.

Amongst intellectuals there are partisans of Zen, the major Indian philosophical systems, Transcendental Meditation, and Yoga. Many of those participating in these movements seek some kind of psychic harmony and release. At a somewhat lower intellectual level are more exotic groups like Hare Krishna and Maharaj Ji: amongst these one encounters the same replication of the functions of the family together with a recoil from the sexual licence and general indiscipline of the counter culture. Amongst the followers of Maharaj Ji and those adhering to the Korean 'Unified Family' authority is very strongly re-established. In short, these movements either translate disorientation into messages of personal release or illustrate a sharp recoil from the counter-culture. They carry forward universalism but revert to self-control inside the bounds of the primary group.

Just as candidatures for the priesthood have declined so too there has been a parallel decline in practice and some confusion as to belief. Here I rely largely on the data provided by Laeyendecker.[13] As regards practice one must begin with the census data on affiliation. Disaffiliation does not necessarily imply that the person concerned disbelieves or does not attend church, any more than affiliation necessarily implies belief and practice. From 1889 to 1960 Catholics increased as a proportion of the population from 37.1 per cent to 40.4 per cent, an increase partly reflecting their higher birth rate. From 1889 to 1960 affiliation to the State Church dropped from 48.7 per cent to 28.3 per cent, while affiliation to neo-orthodox Calvinism rose from 4.0 per cent to 9.3 per cent, this last increase being only very partially related to the undoubted high birth rate of the neo-orthodox. Non-affiliation has increased from 0.1 per cent in 1889 to 14.4 per cent in 1930 and 18.4 per cent in 1960, and has lately undergone a deceleration. Non-affiliation is least in the southern Catholic provinces (2 per cent) and greatest in the north and urbanized regions, where it rises to just under or just over a third. The figures for the large towns are very instructive: the industrial west of Amsterdam (50–55.7 per cent), Amsterdam itself (48 per cent), Rotterdam (34 per cent), The Hague (30 per cent) and Utrecht (21 per cent). In the agrarian north there are also small communities where non-affiliation is above 40 per cent. The occupational distribution of disaffiliation is significant and should be compared with the reputed practice of similar professions in Spain: intellectuals, those in liberal professions, workers and the new middle class (clerical workers, civil servants, etc.) are above the national average, while farmers, business men, retail traders and artisans are below it. These facts presumably need setting in a context of the distribution of Protestants by occupation and the existence of specifically Catholic areas pulling up the overall average of affiliation. Moreover a Catholic 'pillar' probably reduces the level of non-affiliation amongst sizeable sectors of workers, reducing the contrast between them and the middle class. The distinction between old and new middle class is very important and is constantly reflected not only in differential rates of religious practice but in political preference. Academics, journalists, media men, publicists, practitioners of the arts, and some sectors of the liberal professions and service professions, tend to be over-represented on the left given that they do in fact belong to the middle class.

With regard to the non-adherence in the northern agrarian sector it is perhaps again appropriate to recollect the southern European data on low participation in certain agrarian areas. Labour relations in large-scale agricultural undertakings were similar to those of the urban proletariat and discontent was fanned by agrarian crises 1880–1895 and 1918–1930. The opposition by organized labour which followed was condemned by the churches, and to this day one of the consequences is not only massive non-affiliation but villages with communist majorities. It is worthwhile observing that no occupation is *intrinsically* traditionalist. There are situations where even the petite bourgeoisie is likely to become communist.

A factor affecting non-affiliation which should be emphasized even though it is part of more general processes is the diminution in social functions experienced by churches, since this attenuates the motives for gathering together in a church context. Church-going used to be a medium of news, contacts and recreation and churches were vehicles of welfare and charity. With the development of the press, even a religious press, and of non-religious social clubs, and with the secularizing of charities, the incentives to attendance have declined. At any rate non-affiliation is higher than it is in neighbouring west European countries where it rarely rises above 5 per cent. This suggests that the 'pillars' not only define and hold people within the churches but ensure that whoever is outside those pillars is highly secularized. Thus there is a polarization at the level of culture and of its meaning systems which complements the lack of polarization at the political level. Overall one may estimate that about a third of the population are fairly securely in the secular pillar.

Occupational variations as between churches are of interest. Neo-Calvinists tend to avoid academic and artistic avocations and concentrate at their élite level, on positions of power. In the Dutch Reformed Church the middle classes are over-represented, though not the intelligentsia and higher professions; and farmers and agricultural workers also have an over-representation. Within the Catholic Church labourers slightly exceed their proportion in the national population. It is interesting that the age structure is skewed towards the old in the Dutch Reformed Church and towards youth in the Roman Catholic Church.

As to church attendance, in 1966 a survey showed that some 64.4 per cent of Catholics over seven fulfilled their Sunday duties and since that time there has been a distinct decline. Indeed, other sources quote a lower figure for the mid-sixties, but the crucial fact relates to a decline in the late sixties complementing the rapid decline in priestly vocations. The proportion was lowest in the big cities, where over a third of Catholics are present on any given Sunday: it was highest in those areas where Catholics are a tiny minority. This contradicts the German data in the practice of Catholics in a diaspora situation: the reasons for the contradiction are unclear. Easter duties are fulfilled by over three-quarters of the Catholic population, and with regard to them it is the homo-geneous south which has the highest proportion (say, about 90 per cent). With respect to the Dutch Reformed Church only about 4–5 per cent of all 'adherents' attend weekly, which brings it close to Anglican and Lutheran levels of non-participation. 4–5 per cent is the level of participation for all state churches in Protestant societies. The trend is towards further decreases. The differences noted for Catholics in Amsterdam and Utrecht are repeated for the Dutch Reformed Church. Of neo-Calvinists about 80 per cent attend regularly, which means that they contribute about 6 per cent to the overall total amongst the population at large. The total for church participation per Sunday is probably between 25 per cent and 30 per cent.

The diminished respect for ecclesiastical moral doctrine and discipline noted elsewhere is also found in Holland. The increase in the number of Catholics marrying non-Catholics and the decrease in the Catholic birth rate are perhaps both indicative. Those who belong to the Dutch Reformed Church are least bothered about the possibility of a son or daughter joining another denomination while neo-Calvinists are most bothered by it. Laeyendecker sums up the total situation as a decline in participation, integration, identification and normative control, and this is considerable in the Dutch Reformed Church, noticeable amongst Catholics and marginally visible even among neo-Calvinists. Nevertheless the vast majority of Dutchmen believe in God, including half of the non-affiliated, and about 70 per cent believe in a life to come. Faith and church have undergone some partial separation which is perhaps why those who inquire into Dutch religion have a lively interest in the highly personal perspectives of individuals. It is in such a milieu that Thomas Luckmann can locate his notion of an 'invisible' religion.

In commenting more generally on the category of cultures with mixed religion certain important points shrould be re-emphasized. One is that in every case, and this incidentally applies also to cultures where Protestants are minorities, Catholics suffer some relative deprivation in terms of status. In Holland it is as true as it is in Germany that Catholics are under-represented amongst scientists, academics and the business élite. Another point concerns the varied consequences of a ratio of 60/40. First of all the minority culture, partially excluded from the status system and the national myth, adopts the tactic of pillarization: political, cultural and, in some cases, vicinal segregation. In Northern Ireland all three types of segregation exist; and the high degree of vicinal segregation in Belfast and elsewhere may reflect the fact that regional segregation is very partial (cf. Jones 1960 and 1956). The Dutch segregation system, though less total and certainly less violent, may also reflect the rather partial extent of regional segregation. Perhaps the total size of the area also has an impact. Taking Germany and Switzerland as a whole the blocs of religious near-homogeneity are large enough to constitute something quite close to regional segregation, thereby obviating the need for pillarization. In any case in their own areas the local Catholics have a traditional status system which makes them less defensive about the skew at a national level. The same point may explain the high practice of Dutch Catholics in diaspora and the relatively low practice of German Catholics in diaspora. In all countries where 60/40 conditions obtain the Catholics move politically to the centre (except maybe in the special circumstances of Northern Ireland) and constitute a party, thereby crossing the politics of status with the politics of cultural defence. This weakens any left-wing movement based on class warfare because the left has part of its base pre-empted, because conflict has been incorporated *inside* the confessional parties, and because the parties of the left have to present themselves in such a way as to tempt Catholic voters. In so doing they first alter their external image and then conform to it internally. Other things being equal this leads towards stable democracy. In Germany other things were not equal due to Lutheran subservience, late unification, absolutist traditions, a deferential middle class and, above all, defeat in war and its appalling aftermath.

The reasons why Northern Ireland does not fit the generalization about stability are themselves instructive. First, although it is a case of a 60/40 mix within its own territory the proportions are 75/25 in Ireland as a whole. This heightens the fears of the Protestant majority, since it is also a minority, and gives the Catholic minority, which is also a majority, a sense of mission and ultimate confidence.[14] Thus both sides are doubly intransigent and, being intransigent, the slow adjustment towards equality which occurred in Germany did not occur. Discrimination was reinforced, frustration heightened. The fears raised by a differential Catholic birth rate were only mildly ameliorated by differential Catholic migration. When adjustments came they upset a very rigid *status quo*, thus violently alarming the Protestants, and then reviving the old mythology of the Catholics. Both sides thus became totally imprisoned by their ancient rival myths. At this point there occurred a development that will be noted in connection with a discussion of regional nationalism. The regional nationalism of Northern Ireland now includes a left-wing sector of some importance, paralleling the drift of some European right-wing nationalisms towards the left. This may lead us to a formal generalization: where Catholics are a large minority, regionally based and suffering only a slight status skew they stabilize the politics of the centre, and when they shift to the left, as recently in Germany, the shift is only marginal and gentle. If however Catholics are concentrated in a culture activated by a frustrated nationalism then an initial impetus towards the right often leads first to fissures and then to a movement on the extreme left.[15]

Something further must be said about the recent process of 'emancipation' of Catholics, not only in Germany and Holland but also in the U.K. and the U.S.A. In the U.S.A. and the U.K. Catholics have come as migrants to a culture with a Protestant 'set' already totally dominant. It is true they have risen from 5–25 per cent in the U.S.A. and 5–12 per cent in the U.K., but this is not large enough to disrupt the politics of status by the politics of cultural defence. Moreover, they have gone into the large towns in both cases. The Catholic 'region' has been the large town, and rural or small town areas are relatively Protestant. So far as the U.S.A. is concerned Catholics have often taken over local political centres and then extended this success in the direction of a nationwide political adjustment, up to the point where a Catholic was first a candidate for the Presidency and then eventually elected. They concentrated in the more progressive of the parties, thus further stabilizing the dichotomous system. This latter development also occurred in Britain, though no doubt in both countries the small movements of the extreme left recruited disproportionately from Catholics and ex-Catholics. In sum, where Catholics are a minority in Protestant culture they almost invariably contribute to democratic political stability, either by setting a large segment of religious voters in the centre or the 'progressive' wing of politics, as happens in cultures where the proportion is 80/100 or 90/100, or by criss-crossing the politics of status by politics of cultural defence located somewhere towards the centre, as happens in the 60/40 situation.

One may note in passing that no cases exist of cultures where the proportion 60/40 is in favour of the Catholics, simply because wherever Catholics were dominant and in power they had a cultural definition of unity and of integral religiosity which led to a much more systematic resocialization programme of Protestant areas, e.g. in Czech Lands, in Hungary and France. Catholic religion is more integral and this is the reason why it tends to reduce rival sectors, and why when in a minority it is so successful in building up associational networks for cultural defence.

The 'emancipation' of Dutch Catholics has given rise to the explosion of theological radicalism and restructuring already noted. The forms taken by the radicalism are paralleled in a significant way by developments in Quebec over exactly the same period. Hence some comparative comment is in order. Naturally, the differences are important: in Quebec the religious division is enhanced by a linguistic division and the regional segregation is *very* considerable, even *within* the province. On the other hand it is a total functioning society, potentially autonomous, and the process of differentiation can work within the whole society without running up against internal lines of pillarization. The common element is a separating out of religious leadership and administration: in Holland the sub-cultural leadership and the religious specialists clash, in Quebec the general leadership ceases to be locked together with the religious specialists, including those who lead and administer the specifically religious institutions (cf. Caldarola 1975 and Lemieux 1973).

There is indeed a spectrum of comparisons to be observed within which Dutch Catholicism and Quebec take adjacent places, and the crucial elements in the spectrum are domination and degree of regional concentration. At one end of the spectrum is Cyprus (1973), which is heir to a tradition whereby the Islamic conquerors made the Christian Church into the secular authority, responsible to it for Christian populations. Thus the Church was both the *only* source of identity for the self-consciousness of the subject population and the vehicle of administration. Here the church constitutes the whole body of society within itself. So when the independent national body emerges it is headed by the Archbishop. A separate nationalist type of politics tries to assert itself but is not yet successful. Next along the spectrum is Quebec, where for long the Catholic hierarchy was isomorphic with the élite structure and in conjunction with that structure spoke for Quebec. But Quebec was a complete society, albeit within the general ambience of Anglo-Saxon dominance. It had experienced internal differentiation and it had further sources of identity in its language which were signalized by attempts at linguistic purification. Politics took over and the hierarchy ceased to be the crux of legitimation, and lower echelons in the Church moved towards social criticism. In the Dutch case the Catholics belonged *to* a wider society with which they shared a language and were mixed with Protestants as well as regionally concentrated. Hence they attempted to organize a sector which was *part* of the wider politics of the nation and the *whole* of politics for the sector itself.

Once however the major aims of identity and equality were achieved the differentiation working in the wider society and within the separate sector itself became potent and operative, causing a split between a radicalized religious sector and the agencies of bureaucratic inertia. In the German and Swiss cases these problems had largely been solved antecedently by federalism so that differentiation and near-equality simply loosed the Catholic Church from the specific political commitments which were part of its original strategy of cultural defence. In the American and British cases the proportion was too low and the mixing too great to permit pillarization and the differentiation already too far advanced in the general society. The Church simply attempted to retain mechanisms of integration at the level of socialization assisted by the fact that it carried the ethnic identity of its members.

The developmental point underlying the Dutch example and the others adduced for comparative purposes can now be restated Differentiation, conceived as a process of separating out the specifically religious from other spheres, occurs in all societies to some degree, but is affected in the manner described by the politics of cultural defence, and by whether those politics concern a complete functioning society, or a regional sector with partial diaspora, or a total diaspora consisting of migrants. If we are dealing with migrants the union of religion with other sectors is *purely* cultural, but in *that* sphere it is enhanced. Religion doubles for cultural identity, and hence the vigour of sub-cultural migrant religion in the U.S.A.[16] It does not disturb and is not disturbed by integration with the wider society. Differentiation is accomplished immediately and the links with the political sphere are entirely indirect. Where we are dealing with a total functioning sub-society, as in Quebec, religion and politics are initially pushed together and then, with industrialization, urbanization and differentiation, there occurs a separating out which arouses no special clash, because religion has to remain a main source of identity without being the prop of established power. As in America it becomes a cultural fact, without massive alienation by virtue of identity with established power. In Holland, however, differentiation has to occur *within* the religious format provided by the 'pillar' and the clash comes when the specifically religious element combines with the powerful influence of *general* social integration to challenge the administrative inertias sustained by the process of pillarization. In Holland the proccss of separating out is difficult to achieve because the inertias of the single pillar are reinforced by those of other pillars, formed in contradistinction to it, and the end result is not yet clear. In Germany the result however is much clearer: the church cuts its links with a specific political stance and retires to the level of culture. Its political consequences then become indirect, working through the average tendencies of individual Catholics. It is this retirement onto the bastion of culture that is the most universal tendency following from differentiation, even though the mixed pattern is inimical to it in the ways described above.

NOTES

1. Cf. Alford 1964 for a discussion of the conditions under which the religious variable has more or less direct impact.
2. Goddijn 1974 covers the period of the 'great disruption'. A review of it by Thomas Gannon points out that it ignores the 'Hawthorn effect' brought about by the watching world.
3. Cf. Richardson, Simmonds, and Harder 1975; and Richardson 1974.
4. There is a higher rate among Catholics in agricultural areas and among Catholic immigrants; as is usually the case in other countries, the birth-rate of Catholics in towns moves very much closer to the Protestant level, socio-economic group by socio-economic group. Migration has also led to an increase in mixed marriages, especially in urban areas, and particularly between Protestant males and Catholic females. This favours the Catholic Church.
5. I rely here on Campiche 1972; Campiche 1971; and Campiche 1975.
6. Cf. Steinberg 1976 and Fogarty 1957. I draw heavily on Steinberg here.
7. I rely on Kreiterling 1966 for the above comments.
8. Cf. Daalder 1966. I rely on Daalder and Goudsblom 1967 for this background.
9. I rely here on Brunt 1972.
10. I rely here on Thurlings 1971.
11. Cf. Goddijn 1973; Steeman 1967; Kusters 1971; and Poeisz 1967b.
12. Cf. Beckford 1973. Many contemporary cults are interesting in that they are reactions to the excesses of the 1960s, in so far as they restore the secure boundaries of the self and defined limits of conduct, especially in the sphere of sexuality. Indeed, they often represent notable recoveries of the Protestant Ethic. At the same

time they carry forward the attempt to transcend certain boundaries, but within the religious context. The Pentecostals, including those inside conventional churches, leap over the limits of language and the limits on expressiveness. The Unified Family attempts to leap over denominational and national boundaries. Indeed, its whole theme is unification. The syncretism of many of the new cults is in part an expression of the ecumenical tendency at grass roots. What they illustrate sociologically is that impulses to unify which ignore a base in a bounded self and a basic social group (the family or functional equivalent) are heading for trouble.

13. Laeyendecker 1972a; and Laeyendecker 1972b, and 1967. Cf. Schreuder 1970.

14. Roberts 1975, is very helpful and underlines both the extra-ordinary esoteric elements parallel to freemasonry, and the elements of internal democracy. Cf. Roberts 1971.

15. Boserup and Wersøn 1967; and Jenkins 1969. Cf. Rose 1971, and Elliot and Hickie 1971.

16. Cf. Herberg 1955, for the classic statement of this process. Cf. also Herberg 1964.

17. I have not intruded a discussion of South Africa into this chapter but it may be worth emphasizing that the Dutch neo-ortho-dox ghetto or 'pillar' was exported to South Africa together with a total ideology deriving from Abraham Kuyper. Just as Kuyper led the Calvinist orthodox out of liberal bondage, and conceived them as the real kernel of the nation, so the Boers were led out of the liberal ambience established by Britain into a land which the Lord their God should give them. The British were viewed as mere Laodicean Deists.

However the twin movements of neo-Calvinism have since been separated by their different structural positions and by contrary interpretations of the ambiguous deposit of faith laid down by Kuyper. The Afrikaners converted divine election into racial élitism, the power of God into their own earthly authority, and vocation into their superior mission. The Orthodox in Holland could have no such illusions about God-guided authority, especially after the German invasion. So whereas the Afrikaner Brotherhood harboured semi-Nazi tendencies the Orthodox in Holland put up a remarkable resistance to Hitler.

Both the closed ranks of Afrikanerdom and the resistant unity of the Dutch Orthodox stem from the multi-bonded character of Calvinism and its drive to unify all aspects of culture under religious categories. The difference between the Dutch Orthodox and the Afrikaner Orthodox shows how structural position can either bring out the radical democratic possibilities latent in Calvinism or leave them entirely unexploited. A threatened and encircled élite cannot allow itself any scepticism about its national mission, and the South African ruling caste therefore constitutes almost the only instance in the modern world where the categories of cultural debate, of political discussion (and schism) are theological. Only very recently has urbanization created a powerful modernizing schism within the ranks of Israel and made possible a responsive echo to the criticisms of Christians elsewhere. Of course the shift *inside* theological categories from criteria of faith to implicit biological criteria can be viewed as a form of secularization.

I rely here entirely on an unpublished manuscript shown me by Charles Bloomberg.

V

The Pattern of Secular Monopoly

As we turn to Eastern Europe to look at societies under the control of secularist monopoly it is quite clear that not all the countries concerned can be examined in any detail. A comparison between Poland and Russia is perhaps the best recourse, for a number of reasons. The material for these two societies is much greater in volume and quality than that elsewhere. Furthermore, the two countries offer the maximum opportunity for bringing out important contrasts: between a dominating and a dominated society, between Orthodox and Catholic, between total state power and elements of constitutional opposition, between total disruption of the countryside pattern and limited disruption. Nevertheless, other countries warrant mention insofar as the evidence they offer differs markedly enough to warrant a query or an explanation and insofar as special developments have occurred in them from time to time. For example, there is some interest in the current situation with regard to church–state relations in Hungary and Yugoslavia.

It is worth noting that the type, source and volume of material in the differing societies is indicative of the conditions therein. In Russia, the clearly stated aim of most research is to bring out the optimal conditions and apply the best techniques for eliminating vestiges of the 'idealist' world view. In Bulgaria the same applies. In Albania there is no research: only anathematization.[1] In other countries the Marxist, polemical and political intent is less strident, particularly so in Yugoslavia and Poland. Poland is notable for numerous Catholic studies centred on the University of Lublin (the only non-state university in the East) and for Marxist studies, like those of Kubiak (1970) and Jaroszewski (1965),[2] which cautiously assess the limited degree to which religious ideology has disappeared or been transformed under 'the new conditions created by socialism'. There are other sources outside the countries concerned, usually written by those whose primary interest is the fate of religion in Russia, notably in the work of Ethel and Stephen Dunn, Michael Bourdeaux, Christel Lane, and Professor Bociurkiw. In spite of the work of those outside and inside the Soviet Union hard facts are still often difficult to come by.[3] The assessments made by William Fletcher (1972) for example simply illustrate the contradictions between the sources. Somewhat less uncertain is the important work done on the history of Russian sectarianism, particularly the two volumes by A. Klibanov.[4]

In societies where culture is directly manipulated in the service of ideological monopoly the relationships of church and state are crucial. In Poland the antecedent power of the church helps to conserve its power. In Marxist states existing power gives continuing relative power, weakness breeds further weakness. The Polish state is unable to crush the church without enormous upheavals and unacceptable breaks with the Polish past. Hence it works at undermining the church without confronting it, at expanding control of the media, and at creating an atmosphere and a state of opinion whereby the church can only speak within a restricted range of issues. Since the church must be admitted as potent in the symbolic realm then every effort must be made to keep it solely within that realm. The Church for its part underwrites the aims and rhetoric of communist policy in order to retain the institutional avenues of survival, and avoids as far as possible any direct confrontations or any attempt to create anti-state opinion. Thus it is reported that Catholics are no less committed to the overall aims of the state than non-Catholics. Protests are made only by the upper hierarchy and are carefully coordinated to secure the safety afforded by numbers and public prominence. Each side utilizes the existence of the other to maintain discipline in its own ranks. Thus the hierarchy is able to exert pressure against those who break ranks over the issue of 'traditional' versus 'transformed' Christianity and to mute the divisions consequent on differing receptions accorded to the Vatican Council. The Party naturally tried to exploit these divisions. A highly indicative incident was that provided by the Episcopal letter, inviting Germans to share in the celebration of one thousand years of Christianity in Poland in a spirit of *mutual* forgiveness. A campaign of vilification was launched and the letter itself publicized in distorted form.

The minor element of loyal opposition which it to be found in Catholic policy, and the range of differing positions taken, can be seen in the existence of very contrasted Catholic lay organizations. *Pax*, for example, has attempted a rapprochement between religion and communist ideology which was too far reaching for either side; and it was in addition utterly servile towards the Communist Party. *Znak*, on the other hand, cooperates on pragmatic grounds, and its five deputies speak for a considerable segment of the Catholic intelligentsia: it both engages in occasional, indirect criticism, e.g. when it came to the defence of student demonstrations in 1968, and supports further democratization, by which it means individual ownership in land (still over 85 per cent of cultivated land), decentralization, more scope for independent workers, and workers' (rather than party) control (cf. Swiecicki 1973).

The intelligentsia has other traditions aside from *Pax* and *Znak*. Most lively and adaptable are those which descend from such pre-war Catholic organizations as 'Iuventus Christiana', 'Odrodzenie' and 'Marian Sodality'. Such viewpoints embody a search for a more profound realization of Christian imperatives, the furtherance of which may include criticism of the Church for its sentimentality, inflexible moral doctrines and intellectual superficiality. Then there are traditionalists, mainly of the older generation, such as those originally attached to 'Eleusis', who are orthodox in attitude but who are less interested in Catholicism as a doctrine than in religion as a cultural and historical bastion of Polish awareness. This was the traditional view of the gentry. Finally, there are those who find it awkward to acknowledge their Church connection or who have put themselves at odds with ecclesiastical regulations (cf. Chrypinski 1975 and Majka 1972).

The Polish intelligentsia has never been wholly loyal to Catholicism and has from time to time entertained important humanistic and positivistic traditions. Indeed, between the wars, when the Church showed some signs of institutional alliance with the right, the anti-clericalism so normal in Catholic societies elsewhere made its appearance. But the time was too short for this to become a major force or, indeed, for substantial alienation to arise in the working class. As for humanism the older traditions have been attenuated by the diminution of the humanistic faculties within the universities. The way in which partial access to the older scepticism has been shut off may be illustrated from a survey quoted by Majka in which younger teachers (18–24) had a higher rate of practice (75.2 per cent) than older teachers (30–50 years and older) amongst whom only 49.6 per cent admitted to practice (Majka 1972, p. 420). The same survey showed the usual inverse ratio between *amount* of education and extent of religious practice. Positivism is important because it links with the special position of the new technical intelligentsia vis-à-vis both Catholicism and Marxism. It is claimed that the new technical intelligentsia is interested in instrumental aims and the pleasures of technique, rather than in unverifiable, unquantifiable dogmas. However in the west this has often led to a rather naïve religiosity outside the boundaries of the specific technique; and in Poland it has meant not only an incapacity to understand or take an interest in Catholic philosophy but a complementary incapacity to criticize it (Jaroszewski 1965, p. 95ff.).

Evidence in this important area is ambiguous. An enquiry in 1959 among Warsaw students produced results which showed that believers were much more numerous in science faculties and technical faculties than amongst students of the humanities (Pawelcznska 1961). This is explained by Swiecicki by the fact that natural scientists derive their attitudes from their families and students of the humanities from their teachers; which, if true, would provide two paradoxical illustrations of the power of tradition. This data fits the western evidence which shows e.g. philosophers more prone to positive disbelief than engineers. Nowakowska's study of the belief and practice of scientific research workers by various disciplines shows believers best represented among those in technical and agricultural sciences, moderately represented among doctors, chemists, lawyers and literary men, and worst represented among biologists. The importance attached to teaching and its crucial relation to ideological control is indicated by the fact that 35 per cent of teachers are party members, a much higher proportion than obtains in the 'free' professions.[5] The reported variation by disciplines is partly congruent with western experience, in particular the fact that *convinced* atheists were most to be found amongst literary men. It also appears that the practice of physical education is highly antithetical to the practice of religion. It is important to note the sharp divergence from the norms of Catholic morality amongst the intelligentsia, since this has already been noted in the west, for example in Spain. Assiduous practice and conformity to Catholic moral teaching by no means go together. Furthermore, this divergence reappears, though less acutely, in other sectors of Polish life than the intelligentsia, and is particularly marked over such matters as divorce and family planning. To conform to a rite is not to assent to a moral doctrine, especially where that doctrine relates to the family.

The attitudes of Polish schoolchildren are of interest particularly in the view of the Abbé Majka's claim that the advent of universal compulsory schooling initially assisted the church. Catechism classes were originally given in school. When this was forbidden in 1959, catechetical instruction took place in after-school classes for which parents had to 'contract in'. In rural dioceses 'contracting in' is the norm, though in some large cities the pattern is less well established, and attendance sometimes drop below 50 per cent amongst older children. Indeed, in later adolescence there is a tendency for religiosity to be markedly less in evidence, particularly amongst males. This once more conforms to western tendencies. Religion is for the young and the female. An enquiry amongst young people of after school age conducted by Polish Radio showed that four out of five regarded themselves as Catholics and one in twenty as atheists (Skorzynska and Szaniawska 1960). It is interesting that studies of Polish youth in general show no alteration in religiosity from 1959–1968.

One further consequence of the extension of education is that wider sectors of the peasantry have been brought to the level where they are capable of sustaining studies for the priesthood. This doubtless lies behind the curious fact that the faculties of theology are comparatively representative of the social structure in terms of social origin, whereas other disciplines show something of the differentials obtaining in the West (Clifford-Vaughan 1972). In general, the supply of priests relative to population is inadequate and maldistributed. However the crisis of recruitment to the priesthood has not been so marked in Poland as elsewhere, though the rise in vocations from 1945 onwards ended in 1956. As is generally the case the patterns of female vocations have been relatively stable, though again the rise ended in 1956 (Majka 1972). The prestige of the priesthood in Poland has traditionally

H

been high, and remains so, particularly in rural areas, where one study showed most people consider the priest a *necessary* intermediary between man and God.[6] On the other hand, and especially in the towns, his role is increasingly seen as reduced to the specifically religious sphere.[7] This inverts the situation in the west, where the role in terms of the traditional social structure has diminished but in terms of communal activity has increased. However, this is part of the overall eastern European situation, where even when the church and its priests are strong, they are pushed back to the sphere of the religious or of cultural symbolism at the local level.

This is the point at which to comment on rural religiosity, since the cultural role and prestige of the priest is highest in rural areas. In spite of the vast changes in the direction of urbanization nearly half of Poland remains rural. Many observers have characterized Polish peasant's religiosity as superstitious, embodied in material objects, emblematic, proverbial and bound up with his own specific practicality (cf. Czarnowski 1956, W. J. Thomas and Znaniecki 1958). Like all Polish Catholicism it is Marian, non-eucharistic, para-liturgical and resistant to intellectual formalization. Superstitious practices have decreased, but in some ways traditional religiosity has even shown an increase. The indifferent and partially indifferent are found in older age groups. All major Catholic practices are performed by the vast majority of the population: baptism, Sunday Mass, first communion, Easter duty. The Lenten Missions attract even larger numbers than Sunday Mass. The postponement of baptism noted in Spain, which is indeed a universal tendency, can also be observed in Poland. In sum something over 70 per cent regularly attend Sunday Mass, while some 85 per cent perform their Easter Duty. The rites of baptism, first communion and ecclesiastical marriage are nearly universal.

A very important point to remember in reviewing Polish rural religiosity is that the land was handed over to the peasants, not collectivized. Thus though there was an economic transformation in terms of the structure of ownership, there was no corresponding cultural disruption. State farms constitute only about 10 per cent of the area of total land holdings; it is on them that the level of religiosity is less high (Pawelcznska 1966). How far the rural sector is both believing and practising can be judged from the large number of areas where there are not enough persons for basic party organization.

Over the past thirty years people from the rural areas have migrated to the towns in great numbers. However, the church has provided a nexus of organization within which that transition may take place. Moreover, in many cases the migration is not a long distance one and contacts are retained with the rural base. Thus continuities can be maintained. Of course, a great deal depends on the antecedent religiosity of workers in the areas to which peasants migrate and the relative proportions of the two groups. In the working class districts formed during the first period of industrialization at the end of the nineteenth century the dynamism of the Catholic Church varied: in the zone of Russian occupation state policy restricted the Church much more than was the case in the zone of German occupation. Nevertheless, the general consequence of the first industrialization, occurring as it did under conditions of foreign occupation, was not widespread dechristianization. Thus the new wave of contemporary industrialization does not flow automatically into secularizing channels laid down during the first stage of industrialization. Only in Warsaw, Lodz, and the area of Zaglebic are religious practices notably below those of the rural areas. In Warsaw, weekly practice is overall perhaps about 50 per cent and an enquiry sponsored by the Polish Academy of Sciences suggested that in long-established worker areas about one in three were at Mass on a given Sunday and in areas of 'new' workers about one in two. An investigation of workers' hostels in Silesia of workers from 16 to 30 years of age, coming mostly from small towns or the country showed about one in two practising regularly, one in three practising irregularly, and one in ten unbelieving. Pawelcznska's researches confirm the claim that the degree of difference between town and country is *not* very great, especially so with regard to beliefs as compared with practices. She points out that religious practice increased in the country from 1960–1965, without any alteration in beliefs (Pawelcznska 1966). Public opinion studies show that there is some slight difference in belief between skilled and unskilled workers: 75 per cent of the former were believers and 82 per cent of the latter. This difference merits comparison with Russia, where it is very much more marked. It is worth noting that the religiosity of third generation workers is less

deferential towards priest and hierarchy. The study by Kubiak
is interesting in this context, since it examined mainly manual
staff of the Integrated Steel Works in Cracow and compared
them with their relations who had stayed in the villages. Amongst
the migrants unbelievers numbered one in five, whereas they were
negligible amonst the villagers. The largest category shifted from
regular practice to irregular practice. The migrants were also
more inclined to see the Church as properly restricted to a private,
associational sector, particularly as regards social questions outside
the local and personal spheres. Decency was no longer regarded
as dependent on religiosity. The believers amongst the migrants
were older, less educated, and less integrated into professional,
political, secular and cultural activity. This again corresponds to
a great deal of Russian data, which documents the 'marginality'
of the believers in Russian society (Kubiak 1970).

It is now appropriate to turn to Russia in order to bring out the
general situation and then compare it with conditions in Poland.
In Russia as in Poland the treatment of the Church and religion
by the State has gone through various stages, but the Russian
measures have been very much more severe. The crucial legal
provision is the prohibition of religious socialization under the age
of eighteen. This is supplemented by administrative harassment
which was greatly stepped up after Khruschev's inauguration of
the final campaign to eliminate religion.[8] The war, the national
unity it created, the patriotic attitude of the churches and the
promise of services in the sphere of foreign relations, led to a
relaxation of restrictions until the late fifties during Khruschev's
period as First Secretary. Since in other fields Khruschev was
relatively liberal it was useful for him to demonstrate communist
orthodoxy with regard to religion. Thus the churches have now
passed through a long period of pressure comparable in severity if
not brutality with the campaign during collectivization from
1928–1832 and the attacks during the great purges in 1937–1938.
During this time anti-religious propaganda has pervaded the
media and schools, social pressures have been stepped up, legal
and administrative measures tightened, discrimination against
believers heightened, secular rites installed, seminaries and monasteries sharply reduced in number—and sociology encouraged to
investigate the sources of such religion as still manages to remain
in being.

It should be stressed that the survival of religion is an ideological problem for Marxist science given that the dominant ontology allows it no right to exist. Hence the official ideologians have recourse to explanations designed to nihilate contrary realities: lag, external influence, the war, personal pathology and insecurity, poor and casual propaganda work, the marginal position of believers, and—most dangerously—the gap left for feelings of alienation by the difference between Soviet theory and practice. Only when that which is perfect is come will that which is in part (i.e. religion) be done away. This last view is not really satisfactory from the Soviet viewpoint. It weakens the ontological nihilation of religion by suggesting that religion survives for reasons not so very different from those operative in capitalist countries. At the back of this is a fear that the secular religion of Russia, though widely accepted, does not arouse much interest. If one scans an 'honours list' of those who read their atheist literature it probably shows in reverse order the sectors where believers are relatively strong.[9] Teachers come first, followed by Government employees and cultural workers, engineers and technicians, students, workers, pensioners, housewives, invalids, and community service employees. Here we have a measure of the degree to which the élite of a secular religion, which is based on the imperatives of centralized administrative power, total socialization, and scientific and technical control, concern themselves with the ideological orthodoxy underpinning the regime. Education is, as ever, crucial: four out of five teachers read their atheistic bibles; one out of two workers, pensioners and housewives do so. Women are 70 per cent of the believers, 27 per cent of the Council of the Union. Communist power is largely masculine power.

Clearly socialization, communication and administration, plus science, are the key elements in an ideologically monopolistic society and it follows not merely that those who service these sectors will display most overt loyalty to it, but that believers will be both shielded from the communications and socialization systems and attempt further to shield themselves from it. In general, therefore, believers are most concentrated amongst those with least education, least contact with state dominated media and least to lose.[10] 13 per cent of believers attended the cinema; 72 per cent of non-believers did so. Housewives, the lowest grade of peasants, unskilled workers and the retired make up the great majority of

registered sect numbers and church goers.[11] A soviet source sets
out the position as follows. The huts of collective farmers are one
and a half times more liable to have icons than the huts of those
employed in state institutions: 47 per cent as compared to 30 per
cent. These farmers are less 'integrated' into the state system;
they are in addition less well educated and on the average somewhat older. The Dunns sum up the situation derived from surveys
rather similarly. Believers generally quite often work outside the
public economy, are poor, gather together for mutual help and
psychic support, are independently employed or employed in
small and medium sized enterprises. They are the old, the female,
the rural, the uneducated and the backward. Thus believers in the
Orenburg region were mostly 'seamstresses, hall porters, cleaners,
shoemakers, nurses and, more rarely, mechanics and welders'.[12]
The church is the functional equivalent for the old of the club for
the young; for some it is also a source of local patriotism. If people
outside these alienated or backward sectors are attracted to
religion it is likely to be for aesthetic satisfactions, especially as
found in rituals and *rites du passage*, or because they need relief
in personal tragedy (cf. Krianev and Popov 1963). The most
notable exceptions to these generalizations exist among new dissenters, especially the Baptists. The older type of dissenters,
especially the Old Believers, retain a relation to culture and
Russian awareness rather like the Orthodox, whereas Baptists and
other new dissenters are rather different. Information on this is
largely drawn from the work of Christel Lane.

The Baptists are the largest group of non-Orthodox Christians
and provide above all a moral community and discipline such as
Orthodoxy cannot provide. They include a larger proportion of
workers and white collar groups than the Orthodox and have a
somewhat higher level of education, as well as of religious knowledge. Their vigorous work-discipline makes them relatively acceptable to the authorities, and their close internal ties provide a
strong defence against the anomic effect of migration and rapid
social change. These characteristics carry them into the newly
developed territories where Orthodoxy is particularly weak. Adventists and Pentecostalists share the social and religious tendencies of the Baptists, with perhaps a socially lower recruiting
base and a stronger anti-Soviet tinge among Pentecostalists.
Among both Adventists and Baptists a schismatic sector has

syphoned off those who reject total ideological control and this same tendency is paralleled, indeed heavily reinforced, among some of the Orthodox splinter groups of a mystical and eschatological kind, which appeal to young but poorly educated people, and among certain Old Believer splinter groups, such as the 'Wanderers'. The most explicit political opposition comes from the Jehovah's Witnesses and they constitute a sectarian end of the road in so far as Baptists recruit from Orthodox, Adventists and Pentecostalists from Baptists, and Witnesses from Adventists and Pentecostalists. All the sects provide defences against anonymity, all are reinforced in their conservatism and resistance to denominationalization by external pressure, and some act as channels of political or social alienation or at least of ideological independence. The most alienated are the Witnesses, the most independent are the Initiative group who split off from the Baptists. All are conservative religiously, as indeed are the older and decaying sects of pre-revolutionary times and the Orthodox church itself. Heavy pressure and a chosen or enforced isolation make for conservatism. The overall constituency of dissent, both archaic and recent, is perhaps some six or seven million people among whom the Baptists have much the largest following. Insofar as the older sects aspired to a distinctive community life, such as was achieved by Molokans, Dukhobors, and even to some extent by Old Believers, they necessarily decay for lack of social and ideological space in which to move. In so far as Baptists carry a moral community about in their individual heads, they pick up the remains of the older sects and penetrate into the new areas of industrial development (Lane 1977, 1974, 1975a and 1975b).

Soviet analysts, perhaps correctly, emphasize the role of religious ritual at the turning points of life and with regard to the meaning of one's own intimate, personal existence. Soviet 'civic' religion also lacks cosmic resonance. Thus the baptismal *rite de passage* has a particularly tenacious hold in Soviet society, which is strengthened by the fact that many people think it coextensive with being a Russian. It is also strengthened by social pressure, particularly from the older generation. For some it is done just in case', since not all who have recourse to the rites are firm believers. Aptekman's (1965) study of an industrial raion in Leningrad is instructive. Skilled workers in heavy and metal-working industry had their children baptized the least; workers in light industry, especially small, poorly mechanized ones, baptized their children somewhat more; construction workers, who were intermittently in Leningrad and possessed low skill and education, baptized their children most—37 per cent in 1963. Only 1 per cent of doctors had their children baptized, and 7 per cent of engineers. In terms of education it was found that of those with higher education only 0.6 per cent had children baptized, of those with seven years schooling 51.4 per cent and of those with four years schooling 23.3 per cent. The people who had children baptized were normally reported on by civic organizations as follows: 'Satisfactory worker. No gross violations of labour discipline. Doesn't participate in civic affairs'. Survivals of petty bourgeois individualism are also blamed: in areas where most people own their own homes the percentage of baptisms is three times above the average. It is worth noting with respect to baptism and other *rites de passage* that in the Riazan oblast, in which only 61 out of 991 churches prior to the revolution are operating, Orthodox baptisms, marriages and funerals accounted for 60 per cent, 15 per cent, and 30 per cent of the total respectively (1961 figures). In the Penza oblast the comparable figures were 48.5 per cent, 20.9 per cent and 64 per cent.[13] The figures given do not reflect the countrywide average: they over-represent weddings, which are highly secularized, and under-represent funerals, which are often conducted religiously 'by correspondence'. Nevertheless, baptism is probably practised by some 50 per cent of Russians, and is regarded as a primary index of being a Russian.

Work done on peasants as a social class is also highly indicative and gives some insight into rural religion. One must remember that 40–45 per cent of Soviet citizens belong to the rural sector. The kolkhoz members are divided into four classes, each allotted a different standard of housing and remuneration. The top group is infiltrated by urbanized, professional men who assert governmental control over any tendencies to local community sentiment. They, if you like, are the tentacles of the central ideological system, the managerial and cultural representatives of the over-arching secular 'canopy'. The lowest social group, however, which is also the largest, maintains its own sub-culture, quite strongly penetrated by religion. Overall, about 38 per cent— maybe less—of kolkhozniki are believers; in the lowest group very many more are so, especially amongst the over forties (who have little hope of advancement) and amongst the women. In the average kolkhoz 95 per cent of working women are in this lowest group, and their vertical mobility is almost nil. They are isolated. These are the believers and they provide a social base for the persistence of religion. Women in the kolkhoz system as a whole are five times more likely to believe than men; they are concentrated at a low level in a specific sub-culture; and they socialize the next generation, and the generation after that, since they have very frequent links with their own female children. In short, religion passes along the depressed female underside of the Soviet system. But that is not the whole story, and it is interesting that there are some sectors of the intelligentsia, brooding in traditional Russian manner on the life of the countryside, and also brooding on the religion that belongs to it.[14] The extent of this intellectual interest can be exaggerated, and its active nuclei are very small, but it nevertheless exists.

How many then are believers within the Soviet system as a whole? In the (suppressed) Census of 1936 some 56 per cent were reported as believers. This figure has probably been halved, and it may vary according to area from between 10 per cent to 50 per cent. Believers certainly increase as one moves westward, especially in the areas of German occupation in the war and in the newly acquired territories, above all perhaps in Catholic Lithuania. In Lithuania the combination of a relatively short exposure to repression and to indoctrination plus the association of religion and national awareness leads to vigorous resistance and equally vigorous attempts at suppression.[15] The Ukraine is probably relatively more believing than other areas; so also, perhaps, is Soviet Armenia. The Georgian Church was too russified and too associated with social oppression to retain much influence into the Soviet era.[16]

How many of the third of the Soviet population who believe also practise is hard to determine. According to some Russian materials between one fifth and one third of those who believe attend church regularly, and over half episodically, more particularly on feast days. This means that between 6 per cent and 10 per cent of Russians in the sometime Christianized areas are fairly regular attenders at church and perhaps 15 per cent or more irregular attenders, i.e. about 30 million persons.

The work of Christel Lane points towards generalizations about religion and national awareness highly congruent with my own broad argument. In Lithuania, the Ukraine, and Armenia, the church has deep roots in national awareness and is relatively strong. In Estonia, Latvia, and Georgia, the church, though national, was connected with foreign cultural influence, in the case of Estonia and Latvia, a German influence. This led to a rapid post-war disintegration much accelerated by German defeat. On the other hand, the dispersed and frightened German communities of Russia have latterly returned to lay Lutheranism or to a revived Mennonite faith, which gives vigorous, if archaic, expression to nostalgia and identity. Indeed, so strong is this sense of religio-national identity that it tends to exclude younger members who lack the language, and pushes them towards the Baptists. It is, in a general way, important that national awareness is less well served by a largely intellectual state church like Lutheranism or by a largely ritualistic church like Orthodoxy, than by Catholicism. The union of vigorous intellectual and ritual dimensions in Catholicism, plus the range of multiple associations it builds up with culture and with the international community, give it a unique power of resistance, and make it a unique focus of totalitarian attention.

When one compares Russia and Poland one compares a system in which one integrisme has *replaced* another with a system in which two forms of 'integrisme' have to maintain uneasy *coexistence*. In Russia the power nexus exercises total dominance and religions exist precariously in private associational form as the only visible chink in the fabric of ideological conformity. Its only counter-vailing power lies in the threatened fissiparousness of its own members should subservience be seen by them as absolute and servile. This is the weapon offered to the official churches by the breakaway groups of Orthodoxy, and by the schism amongst the Baptists caused by the 'Initiative Group'. Religious continuity cannot lie through the major organized forms of socialization, which ceaselessly inveigh against it, but in the continuities and inertias of culture at the lower levels and margins. In Poland by contrast religion has a massive voluntary and organized presence in the form of institutional socialization which the state may inhibit but dare not prohibit; and most of the cultural continuities of Polish life can flow through it. Yet state power can gradually press it back to the sphere of culture alone and into the realm of the family: Polish practice is familial.

The possibility of influencing the young through well-organized institutional presence represents the crucial difference between Poland and Russia. The second most important difference lies in the relative lack of disturbance in the Polish countryside. Whereas the Russian countryside and its culture were violently uprooted the Polish countryside was mostly allowed to remain intact. Of course in both cases formal education is controlled in the service of the regime and this results in believers being concentrated in the least educated sectors, but this inverse relationship between education and belief is gentle in the Polish case, very sharp in the Russian case. Poland has a strong Catholic intelligentsia; Russia has an intelligentsia overwhelmingly anti-Christian and it barely recognises the right of such Christian intellectuals as there are to exist. There is yet another difference, which is historic and yet has contemporary significance. Poland has one church; Russia has many sects as well as a church. The repression of the church and the suppression of the older communitarian sects pushed many members of both the church and older sects towards a less visible form of individualistic religion: the Baptists.[17] The official privatization of religion by the government can be complemented by the private, ethical, individual religion of the Baptists. Baptists and affiliated sects are not rooted in the old continuities of culture only but are mobile carriers of religion in the more urbanized and collectivised sectors, and through the Iniative Group affect even the younger people and the relatively well-educated. The fact that it is the most 'alienated' forms of religion that are most energetic and successful suggests that they act as carriers of moral revulsion towards the régime, in its actuality if not its theory. And moreover their geographical distribution corresponds to areas generally associated with dissent: Ukraine, Belorussia, Modviya, the Baltic provinces, and the areas of exile—Siberia and Central Asia. This further suggests that religion of a personal kind represents a final attempt to resist the total domination of individual life by an omnipotent state claiming omnipresence and omniscience. This is not necessary in Poland: the church itself is a visible enough alternative to total domination to allow personal and cultural life to flow with some degree of independence through the channels it provides.

In both countries the most resilient form of religion is embodied in the rite, especially those marking the life cycle and the crises of life. Yet in Russia there is a pool of inchoate, ill-formed belief which does not (and often *cannot*) find expression in the rite, while in Poland there are varieties of ritual adherence which are compatible with partial unbelief as well as with sharp divergence from the moral doctrines of the church.

This difference, which may relate to the highly depressed and disorganized condition of religion in Russia, especially the sheer lack of buildings, may however suggest a more general comparison with the West, more particularly the Protestant West. In an acted, ritual religion the rite is most tenacious; in a personal religion individual prayer is most tenacious. There are many hints in the evidence that this is so.[18]

It has already been argued that the crucial relationship of church and state defines the limits of the possible for institutional religion in all statist countries, especially where they aspire to manipulate and direct the intimacies and inertias of culture, as is the case in all countries dominated by Marxist élites. This is the whole point of the comparison between Russia and Poland. Bulgaria and Roumania provide a similar contrast and much of the above analysis is straightforwardly transferable, especially so in the Bulgarian case. In Bulgaria there was an initial period of strong tension up to 1953, with growing conflict between the Patriarch and the Communist leader, Dimitrov, ending in the Patriarch's removal and a modus vivendi established under a new Patriarch. Such clashes, ending in the removal of the recalcitrant ecclesiastic, are of course common form in the early stages of church-state conflict. The losses of the church both in the early and later stage were heavy, and the partial shift to the Protestant sects which took place in Russia only occurred on a small scale. The check on Protestant expansion may have been partly the consequence of the 'Pastors' trial' on charges of spying. But in any case the Baptists, who provided an open channel in Russia, were and are weak. Such lively sectarianism as exists in Bulgaria is to be found amongst the Pentecostals.

Ochavkov's study found that about one in three of the population were in some sense 'believing': one in five attended church on occasion, about a quarter of them regularly. Of the believers about one in six were strongly so, and the rest are divided about equally between the passive and the hesitant. About one in five or so say household prayers, celebrate All Souls' Day and have an icon corner. Religiosity varies with age and education. Of those between 18 and 23 some 12 per cent are 'religious'; of those over 69 some 78 per cent. Of the illiterate 81 per cent are religious; amongst the best educated 7.75 per cent are religious. Amongst social groupings associated with relative prosperity in pre-communist Bulgaria, Kulaks, industrialists, merchants, craftsmen, over half are religious; amongst the other groups, peasants, workers etc. about a third. The religious are concentrated much more among private farmers and craftsmen than cooperative farmers and craftsmen. Clerks and officials are least religious; the workers come after them second in line. Amongst the youngest group 3.23 per cent of white collar workers, 9.40 per cent of workers and 17.85 per cent of cooperative farmers were religious. The religious are everywhere less likely to relate to the general culture and more likely to avoid membership of political organizations.[19] The conclusion can be stated simply: religiosity is least where state control, exercised in terms of property, education and administration is greatest. This is bound to be the case, in varying degrees, throughout eastern Europe. The variable is the degree of control: least in Poland, most in Bulgaria. One other conclusion is absolutely universal: the resistance of the Orthodox is more vague and evanescent than that of Protestant sects, Catholics and Muslims. This latter point must be taken up again later.

On Roumania information is sparse.[20] Two aspects are worthy of emphasis. First, the Church led by Patriarch Justinian trimmed its sails in time to be associated with the anti-Nazi movement rather than with General Antonescu, and it adapted itself rapidly to the national communism of Ceasescu. Along with the Party it became co-guardian of Roumanian identity: a role dependent on total obedience. There was, and is, no dialogue, merely a partial coalescence between two hubs of national unity. The result is a church which flourishes institutionally, with monasteries active and sometimes operating as collectives, and many vocations to the priesthood. Children wearing the uniform of the Communist Youth Organization are sometimes to be seen in church, civil servants, even party officials, occasionally attend discreetly.

Second, so far as sociological evidence is concerned, data collected in 1971–2 show the strongly religious as about 10 per cent, the slightly religious, indifferent and wavering as about 50 per cent, while non-religious and atheists constitute the remainder.[21] As is usual, the Orthodox are less resistant than Catholics and Reformed, while the Protesant sects are most resistant. Religious belief and practice are twice as frequent in the countryside as compared with the towns; and the usual differentials occur as to age and sex. Perhaps the main function of religion is 'moral-cum-traditional', though the function of the Protestant sects probably lies in the creation of a small-scale alternative form of social integration.

At this point it is useful to turn to neighbouring Yugoslavia which has been more liberal than Bulgaria but in which the logic of total control seems to be gradually reasserting itself. In the case of Yugoslavia one may summarize the religious situation before considering church-state relations. The Census of 1953 provided interesting data in that though the average number of atheists was 12.6 per cent it was highest in the areas of largely Orthodox nationality (Montenegrins 32.5 per cent, Serbs and Macedonians 15.8 per cent), low among Catholic Slovenes and Croats (10 per cent) and lowest of all in Muslim areas. Some half of Montenegrin males were atheists, reflecting a long term pre-war tradition of religious neglect in the sometime Prince-Bishopric of Montenegro. Indeed this parallels the areas of traditional religious neglect in the south of Spain, Portugal and Italy. With respect to age atheists were concentrated in the age group 20–34; above fifty years of age they were negligible.[22]

Certain more recent surveys are worthy of note. Amongst all Yugoslav students nearly half declared themselves opposed to religion, about a quarter were non-practising unbelievers, 3 per cent were practising believers, 4.5 per cent non-practising believers, 5.4 per cent believers who practise periodically and 15.8 per cent practising non-believers! Perhaps this last group provides another hint about the role of ritual.[23] Similar results were found amongst secondary school teachers, but it is interesting that whereas 39 per cent of males were consistent atheists, only 18 per cent of females were so. Amongst workers in Bosnia-Herzegovina declared atheists were most numerous among the skilled (56.3 per cent) and least numerous amongst the unskilled (30.7 per cent). 72.4 per cent of the highly skilled never went to church; 44.9 per cent of the unskilled never did so. Thus the higher rate of unbelief and non-practice amongst the skilled found in Bulgaria and Russia is also found in Yugoslavia.[24]

Data exists for people over eighteen in Slovenia which is relevant to the relationship of religion to type of milieu, whether urban or rural and in particular to the decline of a specifically *ecclesiastical* form of religion.[25] Those who were faithful to the *church* were about one in five, and growing less numerous over time; those who were religious but partially detached from the church were somewhat less than half of those investigated. Religiosity varied according to locality: in the countryside about nine out of ten were religious and about a third of them showed a traditional attachment to the church. In middle sized towns irreligiosity was enormously increased, more so indeed than in the major cities. However, such middle-sized towns are traditional working-class centres, and have also been part of the rapid industrial development which has taken place since the war. The same study shows the usual decrease of belief with increase in the level of education, though curiously and maybe significantly, those regularly at church are drawn somewhat more from the most educated (9.6 per cent) than amongst those with only secondary education (7.1 per cent). As regards the different elements of belief, about a third of believers have a strong anticipation of a future life; and it is interesting that a number of the strongly attached are unbelieving or uncertain concerning this aspect of faith. Two or three per cent of the *un*believers also remain hopeful. With regard to the general teaching of the church about half of those believing take up a more or less independent stance: again this links with findings in Poland and Spain and elsewhere. Only one in five *fully* accept the authority of the church.

A footnote is in place here concerning the important role of the family since it undoubtedly applies elsewhere, though less strongly in Russia where attempts are made to reduce its role, and more strongly in Poland where such attempts cannot be made and where even school cannot be organized in direct contradiction to family beliefs. Bahtijarevic notes (what is generally recognized) that the influence of the family is most operative up to early adolescence, at which point uncertainties increase and peer-group or school pressure may play a greater role. In his study of schools

in the Zagreb region Bahtijarevic shows convinced believers decreasing from 50 per cent in the fifth form of the elementary
school to 25 per cent in the eighth. In the secondary school the
believers decrease from 21 per cent in the first form to 16 per cent
in the fourth. However, the point of transition was at the change
from elementary to secondary school i.e. mid-adolescence, and
after that convictions did not alter much. Now, believers are
characteristically children of the less well educated believing
parents. Where both parents are peasants or craftsmen religiosity
is greatest; where they are both clerks it is least. The influence
of the father on the whole is greater than that of a mother, a result
which may conflict with western evidence. The 'atmosphere' of a
home makes no difference to *belief*, which depends on socialization, but where poor it does tend to produce fanatics either for or
against religion. About one in three believers are quite orthodox
as to belief and practice: beliefs in God and to a lesser degree Jesus
Christ are relatively secure as compared to precepts concerning
sexual morality; baptism and worship on feast days have a much
firmer lodgement than household prayers. Overall, strong consistent belief and attachment to the church accounted for some
seven out of a hundred secondary school students. *All* came from
families with a strong attachment to the church (the vast majority)
or a partial attachment to it. In short, family socialization is
almost a condition of institutional religion. (Bahtijarevic 1971).

Ø. Gaasholt's study of the distribution of local-cum-traditional
attitudes has a certain theoretical interest. His focus is on the
extent by which religion may impinge on the formation of the
secular, countrywide, values on which the new Yugoslav state is
built. His work shows the usual negative relationship of religion
to level of education. But apart from that it indicates that at the
lower levels of status and education religion is an embedded
element in a general parochial and traditional attitude. Those
within that level whether atheists or believers share that parochial-
ism. At the higher levels however although religion declines the
existence of belief is very positively associated with the retention
of general traditional values. The only important exceptions to
this are amongst partisans. Partisans are rarely believers but even
when they believe they do not hold traditionalist attitudes. To a
lesser degree this is also true of the intellectual élite. Presumably
such results point to the wartime crucible in which the new élite

of Yugoslavia was born and the corrosive dissolutions associated with that wartime experience. For other members of the élite, however, religion and traditionalism move in conditions of mutual and strong support.

Data of this kind lie within a context of state decision and manipulation of culture and socialization. The first decade after the war was one of quite severe persecution. The party initiated compliant priests' associations, conducted many trials, confiscated most ecclesiastical properties, brought pressure to bear on believers not to give their children religious education and made it impossible for schoolteachers or officials to have any overt connection with religion (cf. Alexander, forthcoming). Relations took a considerable turn for the better with the signing of the Belgrade Protocol which happened to coincide with a weakening in the power of the secret police. The Catholic Church then extended its activities, though the Serbian Orthodox Church appeared more nervous and (for example) only really attempted to carry out the religious education of children in two of its dioceses. The revival of interest in religion plus reviving elements of Croatian nationalism then coincided (by what causal sequence is not clear) with a new assertion of total ideological monopoly. The Croatian party leadership was vigorously purged and the Church accused of complicity in nationalist agitation. On the whole, however, the Catholic Church kept at a distance from this agitation, partly because of the dangers involved in it for the church, and partly because of the complex conflict within the church itself turning around issues raised by the Vatican Council. The conflict turns on such matters as collegial decision making, lay participation, celibacy and more specialized roles for the priesthood (cf. Petešić 1972). Indeed one may say that partial normalization of church-state relations assisted the relaxation of discipline within the Yugoslav Catholic Church, together with some diminution in vocations to the priesthood, which had previously been more than numerically adequate to its task. Now, however, discipline in both party and church may be restored, though while the party itself is in turmoil it is unlikely to launch into a head-on conflict. Drives to total social control are normally halted until inner-party conflicts have been worked out. It must be stressed that all halts to social control in communist societies are in principle *tactical* halts en route to total control.

The three remaining communist societies, Hungary, Czechoslovakia and East Germany may now be rapidly reviewed, and
only such points emphasized as distinguish them from the others,
or are worthy of particular note.

Czechoslovakia and especially Hungary are societies marked
by initial conflict between the regime and the Catholic Church.
In East Germany overt conflict with the Lutheran Church has
been less in evidence except for a period of arrests 1950–53 and
1958–59, and the party policy has concentrated on restriction and
social pressure. In Hungary up to 1945 the Catholic Church
wielded massive power and possessed great wealth, notably in
land. From the outset there commenced a long confrontation over
such measures as the legalization of civil divorce, the making of
religious instruction in schools optional rather than compulsory,
the confiscation of church property and schools, the prescription of
Catholic trade unions, the elimination of the church press and the
banning of voluntary associations connected with the Church.
Furthermore church people were subject to harassment and im-
prisonment, including Cardinal Mindszenty; church personnel
were closely scrutinized and appointments manipulated. The Calvinist Church was the first to sign an agreement whereby the confiscation of property was to be balanced by payment of salaries and
upkeep of buildings. After a government threat to deport all the
monks and nuns in the country the Catholic Church signed a similar agreement, though a much greater degree of tension remained
than existed between the Protestant Churches and the government. After a pause following the rising of 1956 pressure was
again stepped up in the early sixties in spite of an 'agreement'
reached in 1964, and by 1966 some 12,000 priests were banned
from their duties. The difficulty was partially resolved with the
reluctant departure of Mindszenty to Rome in 1971.[26]

The situation of the Churches in this period of fairly continuous
pressure is not entirely clear, though the Calvinists were clearly
more resilient, both in their regional stronghold east of the Tisza
river and amongst the urban ex-bourgeoisie. A global figure for
church attendance was given in 1963 by the Ministry of Church
Affairs of 25 per cent each Sunday. There are hints that the
Catholic Church provided a broad umbrella within which political opposition was focused and that this opposition was strengthened in periods of political and economic difficulty. Furthermore,

indoctrination could sometimes be counter-productive among students and intellectuals. A survey by Varga of late adolescents in Budapest secondary schools in 1967 provided rather curious data.[27] The first curiosity is the degree of disjunction between thought and practice: well over half the young people were atheists and six out of ten were to this or that degree practising. Similarly, though members of the Communist Youth League (the only permitted youth organization) were less religious in their thinking than non-members, the difference was negligible as regards religious behaviour. Over a third of the sample desired a church wedding: one in four of these because it was more beautiful, and one in four because they thought it was proper that marriage be blessed by the Church. As in Poland and elsewhere there was a sector of the believing who separated questions of faith from assent to ecclesiastical moral doctrine and who did not view morality as uniquely tied to faith. The second curiosity is the fact that though girls practised more than boys their religious thinking barely differed, in spite of the fact that of the older generation some 43.5 per cent of mothers were 'overtly religious' and only 25.9 per cent of fathers. Varga also studied youth in three villages, industrial, agro-industrial and traditional. Overall about one quarter of the youths were traditionally religious and one quarter atheistic, with the former concentrated in the traditional village. Varga also noted a large segment in town and country whose outlook was simply *non*-ideological and directed more towards stability and prosperity.

Both the oddities just noted have echoes in the East German materials.[28] Marsula points to a decreasing difference between male and female religiosity and to a disjunction of belief and practice amongst the young. With regard to the latter, although practice declines with each step downward in age it rises again in the age group 14 to 25. The reasons for this are obscure but it is worth noting that in East Germany the institutional aspect of religion now tends to occur only in *semi*-public form at the level of discussion groups and in house groups sometimes organized by criteria of age and vocation, and that within these fluid groupings there may be operative a youth culture outside the immense pressures of conformity wielded by the official organizations.

Other conclusions are those familiar in other contexts: the least religious are white collar workers (43 per cent 'religious'), closely followed by blue-collar workers (45.5 per cent 'religious'), and followed at a distance by collective farmers (77.8 per cent 'religious'). It is noteworthy that the Lutheran Church, having experienced a recession in defection rates 1933–46 now shows higher rates than Roman Catholics. There is, however, an overall recession: of a population of about 17 million 31.80 per cent declared themselves without religious affiliation in the 1967 Census, compared with 8 per cent in 1950, the declining figures for Protestants being 80 per cent to 59.35 per cent and for Roman Catholics 11 per cent to 8 per cent. About a quarter of this decline may be attributed to the flight to the West. There has been a sharp decline—a halving perhaps from 1954–63—in confirmations and church weddings and even in baptisms, especially in industrial areas and above all in East Berlin. There is a Youth Consecration Ceremony intended to rival and parallel confirmation, and the pressures concerning this are complemented by others affecting employment (especially in administration), entry to university and religious practice within the Army.[29] Overall the weak resistance of the 'state' Lutheran Church parallels the weak resistance of Lutheranism in Latvia and Estonia.

The relationship of the churches to the state is determined by the fact that churches are the only exceptions to the ideological monopoly attempted by the government, and are in no way exceptions to its monopoly of power. The Party has endeavoured to penetrate the churches through 'Christian Work Circles', a group called 'Encounter Catholics' and 'The Association of Protestant Clergy', all of which chorus assent to East German policy towards West Germany and the West generally and can be used against church authorities. The aim of the Party is the breaking of Lutheran and Catholic contacts with West Germans, a weakening of Catholic connections with Rome especially in the sphere of appointments, and clear Catholic acceptance of and participation in the Republic. Legal uncertainties also leave room for manipulation and arbitrary action. Each year charitable work is further restricted, leaving only the handicapped and sick children in church care. Of all groups the Lutheran Church is the most compliant as it has also been the most quickly eroded; Methodists and Protestant sectarians along with Catholics have been much more resistant to this erosion. The decline of the

Lutheran Church is most evident in the sphere of vocations: since 1954 divinity students have continuously decreased in numbers, which has been a factor in the creation of the role of pastor and the acceptance of women ministers.

In Czechoslovakia, or strictly in Czech Lands, the process of alienation from the Church began very much earlier, in the period of persecution and discrimination from 1620 to 1791, which led to some indifference amongst Hussites forcibly converted to Catholicism; and then after the First World War there were mass withdrawals from the Roman Church on account of its Hapsburg associations. The subsequent Catholic attempt to relate to Czech thought and culture was complicated by the Second World War: part of the Catholic clergy supported by the Fascist regime, more so in Slovakia than elsewhere, but the majority sided with the resistance, thus partly restoring the national image of the Church. The Church clearly preferred a liberal to a Communist regime and after the Communist take-over in 1948 there was a clash which resulted in the confiscation of church property, vigorous control of appointments, and an arrangement whereby the state took responsibility for the expenses of worship. Such arrangements were more acceptable to non-Catholics, who possessed no lands, than to the Catholic Church. Tension has never been absent however and is currently intensifying, a tendency symbolized in the recent dismissal of two pastors of the Czech Brethren. The Church of the Czech Brethren (about 7.5 per cent of the population) is interesting both as continuing the radical traditions of the Hussite Revolution and as associated with the 'Prague Spring' of 1968. One of its leaders, Professor Hromadka, a lifelong friend of the Soviet Union and participant in the Communist-inspired 'peace' conferences, protested against the invasion. Since then several pastors have been imprisoned and more forbidden to hold office. Their fate provides an illustration of the role of state subsidy vis-à-vis the church and suggests why in some areas churches refuse that subsidy.[30]

Religion in Czech Lands, for the kind of historical reasons noted, as well as on account of greater industrialization, is much less strong than in Slovakia. Those claiming no religion constitute 31 per cent amongst Czechs, 13 per cent among Slovaks and 9 per cent among Poles. This differentiation is an important index of the impact of national traditions. Investigations are few but a

1963 survey in Moravia, the most industrialized of the regions, does allow some comparison with an investigation carried out for the whole country in 1947. In this particular area, firm belief in God dropped from 64 per cent to 34 per cent and firm atheistic convictions rose from 12 per cent to 38 per cent. Firm belief in Christ as the incarnate God dropped from 35 per cent to 25 per cent and the category of the doubtful dropped from 18 per cent to 10 per cent. Firm belief in a life to come dropped from 38 per cent to 24 per cent. As to practice: regular attendance dropped from 28 per cent to 16 per cent and irregular attendance dropped from 42 per cent to 28 per cent. Prayer in private, often or occasionally, dropped from 70 per cent to 44 per cent.

More Protestants believe in God, read religious literature and consider life from a religious viewpoint than do Catholics; more Catholics believe in eternal life and partake of the sacraments. The National Czechoslovak Church continues to express an 'alienated tradition' consonant with its schismatic origins. It has many more atheists in its younger generation than have the Protestant and Catholic Churches. It has no influence in Slovakia. Several points emerge from all this: first, the disjunction between rite on the one hand and belief and prayer on the other; second, a relative consolidation of belief amongst a committed core in which faith in Christ is perhaps the key element. Otherwise quite normal data were adduced: believers decreasing with increased size of town, with extent of migration, degree of youthfulness and amount of education. Thus believers were 41 per cent in places of under 2,000 population and 13 per cent in towns of over 50,000 population. The extent of clear belief increased progressively from intelligentsia (15 per cent), to white collar worker (21 per cent), to worker (30 per cent), to pensioner (38 per cent), to housewife (45 per cent), to farmer (73 per cent).[31]

These varied results complete the survey of religion in eastern Europe and permit certain generalizations of some importance. Since in statist societies everything depends on governmental pressures and manipulations the church-state connection must first be summarized, more particularly since it usually reflects the specificity of different histories and cultural patterns. Professor Bociurkiw notes three stages: transition, confrontation, and accommodation, though evidence cited above suggests that governmental pressures are now making the accommodation increasingly tense.[32] Some countries, like Yugoslavia, with communist governments established in the war, had no transitional phase, since this phase normally existed while coalition governments still remained prior to the final communist take-overs, e.g. in East Germany and Czechoslovakia. Confrontation largely coincided with the Stalinist 'cold war' periods and *temporarily* lapsed either with internal relaxations or eruptions, e.g. Prague 1968, Hungary 1956, Poland 1956, East Germany 1953. Crucial areas of control were and are those of church appointment and access to religious socialization: Russia and Albania provide the most repressive examples in these respects; Poland is the least repressive. In other words communist regimes have a hold on the internal power structure of the churches via control of appointments (supplemented by fifth columns like priests' or lay associations) and can restrict the influence and independence of the church by separating it from agencies of socialization and through the power of the purse. In most countries, churches are reduced to purely private associations whose political voice is confined to the repetition of governmental policy—especially in foreign policy and at the W.C.C.—and whose internal press is heavily censored. The principle of church-state separation is most clear in Yugoslavia, Albania and Russia; the principle is not adopted in East Germany, Czechoslovakia and Roumania, and indeed in Roumania the church has quasi-established status. Religious groups, except in Albania and the U.S.S.R., possess the rights of a juridical person, but in general need to be 'recognized' by the state before these rights can be exercised. Only Albania and Russia forbid organized religious education of the young.

Resistance to secularization, whether occurring by social process or administrative fiat, varies by denomination. Lutheran state churches are not very resistant, e.g. in Estonia, Latvia and East Germany. Nor are the Orthodox state churches resistant in Serbia, Russia and Bulgaria. Only the Roumanian Orthodox Church manages to be compliant *and* vigorous. The Catholic Church is highly resistant and has been the centre of major clashes in Hungary, Czechoslovakia, Yugoslavia and Lithuania. Where a small minority it forms a tight-knit core of believers, as in East Germany and Bulgaria. The 'free' Protestant denominations are also quite tightly knit vis-à-vis the social majority, e.g. the Baptists and Adventists in Russia, the Methodists in East Germany. So too are the sectarians (above all the Jehovah's Witnesses) and these maintain relatively young age structures compared to other churches. Muslims are also resistant to secularization, not only on account of the collusion of religion and nationality, though that exists in the U.S.S.R., but because their religion is quite undifferentiated from the customs and mores of the culture itself.[33] The fabric of culture resists the tearing of its seamless web.

Everywhere (except in Poland) the young are more likely to be more irreligious than the old. The religious are less well educated and less well-represented in industrialized areas, especially the sectors of heavy industry and of high manual skills. Religion has little influence in the ruling élite, the intelligentsia, and the bureaucratic apparatus; it has moderate influence amongst workers and collective farmers; it is strong amongst independent craftsmen, those with some private property, the lower peasantry and wherever the countryside is not too much given over to state forms of production; and amongst the marginal groups in service and small-scale industries. In other words, religion is relatively unsuccessful wherever socialization and communication processes are under full state control. Only in Poland and Yugoslavia is there an important Catholic intelligentsia. The larger the town, the smaller is the belief and practice, unless the smaller towns are places of old worker traditions or of recent state-initiated development and migration, as in parts of Yugoslavia. Women are usually more religious than men, and this is an aspect of inequality of role: heavy in the U.S.S.R., relatively minor in East Germany and very attenuated in specific sectors, e.g. among certain categories of students socialized together. Everywhere religion is channelled through females, though less successfully in those cultures where males are allotted defining roles, e.g. Bulgaria and Yugoslavia.

Although in Russia belief exists outside the churches, in many countries there is an attachment to the rite over and above specific belief and the practice of private prayer. There is also, maybe, a relative consolidation of hard-core believers in certain areas, e.g. Czechoslovakia, although this is clearly not universal. The attachment to the rite as distinct from the practice of private prayer contrasts with the western or, at any rate, with the western Protestant situation. The element of consolidation or at least of heightened resistance within the religious minority may however have some parallels in the West. Dogma is less resilient than is the rite, and ecclesiastical moral doctrines clearly less resilient than either. Indeed, there is a widespread corrosion of specifically ecclesiastical religion and authority, and religious experience is somewhat subjectivized. Presumably where the priest's word and his sermon are the principal source of people's world view then we have a specifically ecclesiastical form of religion, and the evidence is that such occurs only amongst strata whose educational level is low. Specifically ecclesiastical religion remains within the countryside, especially in Poland but also throughout Central Europe. In Russia religion is not so much ecclesiastical in this sense (though it takes place in church where it can) as it is sub-cultural. Sectarian religion everywhere exhibits a counter-integrative function and a rejection of total state control of personal moral life. Finally atheism as the state 'religion' everywhere has its organized cadres, often constituting 20–30 per cent of the population, but in between the old believers and the new is a large group of the uncommitted who care neither for old nor new metaphysic as compared with creature comforts and a quiet life. Here 'secularization' east and west is one and the same.

The pattern of secularization in the eastern countries has a considerable degree of unity derived from the fact that many of them have been Orthodox, all of them have been overprinted by the fact of Russian domination, and they have in addition been relatively undeveloped. What varies most of all is the relation of nationalism to religion, and the degree to which repressed nationalism is informed by a genuinely *internal* religious culture. The areas marked by strong and vital churches are those where a religion has linked itself to the sense of identity by multiple ties: Lithuania, Armenia, Poland, Roumania, Croatia. This relationship precisely reflects parallel phenomena in the West: Ireland, the Basque country.

So there is a unity in the eastern pattern which goes beyond the common element of communist superimposition after the Second World War. And at the same time there is a historic variety illustrated in differing degrees of vitality and in differing solutions to the church-state problem. The common condition of under-development—Czechoslovakia excepted—gives rise to certain imperatives for which communism offers a characteristic solution. These are the provision of a Puritan ethic, which substitutes for the drive, militancy, and constricted psychology of Protestantism in the West; and the provision of a totalitarian frame which can both speed up the process and eliminate either opposition or deleterious anarchy. This means that religious Protestantism is relegated to the sphere of cultural 'services', notably a reinforcement of work discipline such as one sees among Russian Baptists, and a strengthening of a mobile, moral community under conditions of very rapid social change. It provides these services equally in Russia or Brazil. But in Russia it is prevented from forming the base for a serious individualistic culture or from continuing the relationship of Old Believers, i.e. old-fashioned dissent, to incipient capitalist development.[34]

The overall imperative of rapid change entails unity, and that unity is achieved by the elimination of all intermediate corporations and all alternative ideologies, especially those with a non-utilitarian, aesthetic, or mystical range. This development again represents a functional equivalent to capitalist utilitarianism but without the adjunct of political liberalism. An ontological laisser-faire is replaced by ontological monopoly. Neither facts nor people can be allowed to speak 'for themselves'. In a way, the constant push towards unification resembles the earlier movement of enlightened despotism, in which control was a prerequisite of development. The enlightened despot subjugated the church to the imperatives of unity and thereby made it an adjunct of established power. This made it an automatic enemy to the secularizing élites of the liberal period, for whom it was an awkwardly resistant sector. When enlightenment and despotism were resumed under the auspices of the historical myth of Marxism, the secularizing élites again saw the church as a barrier to total control. Thus the church passed through three phases: as an adjunct of total control; as an irreducible resistant element within the hegemony of liberalism; and a recalcitrant enemy of total control, reinforcing the sector of liberality and freedom and independent national identity. Differentiation was imposed so rapidly that the church was either immediately thrown structurally into that sector of social forces which might press for freedom and psychic space, or its extensive cultural power was immediately reimpressed to serve the needs of national unity over against external pressure. In short, the church was either pushed into constituting a sector of dissidence or independence inside a country, which made liberalism an ally, or it was pushed into constituting the base of a dissident or independent nation, which made nationalism an ally. The two forces against which the Church fought in the nineteenth century, liberalism and nationalism, thereby became its allies in the twentieth.

NOTES

1. Information on Albania is exiguous and derived from party literature (*Zeri i popullit* 1 November 1972 and 8 July 1972, and *Bashkimi* 17 December 1972). These documents say religious influence is alive in the north, especially the Mirdita and Mat regions, in Shkodra and the mountains. It operates through baptisms, circumcisions, burials, feast days celebrated under the guise of family reunions, and services conducted under the pretence of social visiting, especially in highland areas. The institutional life of the churches has been almost entirely repressed. Cf. Prifti 1975. Travellers' accounts of the period prior to repression seem to indicate a lively institutional life. Cf. Richard Clogg (T.L.S. 25.2.77) for a discussion of the direct relationship of repression to the Albanian imitation of China's cultural revolution and of the accentuated anti-clericalism which arises from the intellectual character of the Albanian communist leadership. Clogg points out the difference which originally existed between the patriarchal mountaineers of the north and the more fertile south ruled by Muslim landowners and worked by landless labourers, many of whom were Christian. The Orthodox Church in the South was relatively open to Greek and international influences and the South provided many of the nationalist and communist leaders. In the interwar period there was a brief experiment in democratic government under the orthodox Bishop Fan Noli, followed by the Zog regime and accelerating Italian penetration. The communists were able to use their position in the resistance to take over after the war and they were later greatly aided in their struggle for survival by the Sino-Soviet split. China was their bulwark, political and economic, against Russia, and the repression of religion followed in the wake of a carefully manipulated cultural revolution, directed against bureaucracy and 'feudal survivals'. All places of worship (some 2,000) were closed, religious holidays replaced by Miners' and Printers' Days and there was an attempt to eliminate religious names. The last Patriarch of the Orthodox Church died in prison in 1973.

2. Piwowarski 1971. For a discussion of the sociology of religion in Poland, cf. Majka 1963. A useful source of information from time to time is 'Le Chrétien dans le monde', *Cahiers ODISS*. More general discussions may be found in Majka 1968; and in the chapter on Poland in Beeson 1974, Staron 1969. Material on Polish Catholic

intellectual life may be found in Zatko 1967. A general discussion of all kinds of dissent is provided by Bauman 1971.

3. The most up-to-date and comprehensive work is to be found in Lane 1977, and in Lane 1974, 1975b, and 1975a.

4. Klibanov has a work on religious sectarianism published in Moscow in 1965 and a further work published in Moscow in 1969. Cf. Klibanov 1970, and 1965. A careful review of his 1965 book is provided by E. Dunn in *Slavic Review*, 1, 1967, and there are relevant further materials in Dunn and Dunn 1964.

5. Nowakowska, 1961. This spectrum of disciplines runs quite close to the left-right spectrum in the United States, described by S. M. Lipset.

6. Cf. W. Piwowarski, cited in Majka 1972.

7. Kubiak 1970, and Jaroszewski 1965, p. 92. Cf. Zdaniewicz 1968.

8. Cf. Kolarz 1962, and Bordeaux 1968, 1965, and 1970; and Fletcher and Lowrie 1971.

9. Quoted by B. Bociurkiw in Marshall 1971.

10. Pivovarov 1967–1970 documents this in his study of a parish.

11. Cf. the chapter on 'Peasants as a Social Class' in Millar 1971.

12. Cf. B. Bociurkiw in Marshall 1971, and the work of the Dunns cited above, and more especially Dunn and Dunn 1975.

13. Cf. the chapters on 'Peasants as a Social Class', and 'The Soviet rural family' in Millar 1971.

14. Cf. the chapter on 'The countryside in Soviet Literature' in Millar 1971, and chapter 8 in Marshall 1971. Lane (1977) gives lower figures for believers among Kolkhozniki.

15. Cf. Stanley Vardys 1971. It is interesting to note in S. M. Lipset's comments on pre-Soviet electoral behaviour in the Baltic Republics that parties with a religious element were essentially a Catholic phenomenon. Classical Reformation Protestantism does not lend itself to political expression, and the history of the Baltic Republics since sovietization also shows how easily it succumbs to repression. The condition of Lutheranism in Estonia and Latvia is parlous, although it may be that Methodism has picked up a small part of the Lutheran losses. Cf. Veinberg 1971.

16. Cf. the chapters on Georgia and Armenia in Marshall 1971, and Bordeaux 1965.

17. Cf. Zlobin 1965, and Klibanov and Mitrokhin 1974. Lane 1975a on the Molokans suggests that Baptists have picked up some remnants of the once extensive 'progressive' sect. It is interesting that the new revolutionary government initially tolerated the sects either on grounds of having been persecuted or being like the Molokans, proto-communist. Once in power, however, the government found proto-communist manifestations otiose, and the Protestant sects to be too much identified with bourgeois individualism.

18. Lane 1975b describes the disorganized inchoate state of Orthodox religious consciousness. She stresses the emphasis on forms of prayer which concern worldly benefit. However, personal prayer

is relatively rare among Orthodox believers. She also emphasizes the lack of any secular extrapolation from religious premises: Orthodoxy implies little for the socio-political realm. Superstition is of course deeply intertwined with Orthodoxy even though the priesthood has officially fought it. Superstition has proved remarkably strong and is constantly noted in Soviet works on religion. Cf. Tazhurizina 1974, and Alekseev 1974. Alekseev notes that farm equipment operators are peculiarly resistant to religion; being educated and in command of technology they don't need God's assistance. A table is provided for women and for men indicating degrees of religiosity. Among women it runs from housewives and pensioners through those concerned with animal husbandry and service personnel to administrators; among men it runs from pensioners and general labourers through those concerned with animal husbandry and service personnel to technicians and administrators. Alekseev's article stresses the role of women of relatively little education and the impact of tradition with regard to village festivals, birth, and death (but not marriage), and the keeping of ikons. Family ties and the need to communicate with people are both blamed for the importance of religious holidays.

19. Cf. Ochavkov 1972; and the chapter on Bulgaria in Martin 1969b. Supporting indications of Bulgarian secularity are given in an international comparative survey of family life and religion, reported in *Social Compass*, 18, 2, 1971.

20. Cf. the article on Roumania in Beeson 1974, and K. Hitchins' essay in Bociurkiw and Strong 1975. Hitchins concludes both that the importance of the Church in civic affairs is increasing, and that it depends as never before on the state's domestic priorities and the vicissitudes of international relations. Cf. Frend 1971. Frend says that the Orthodox Church represents the will to national survival, and cites 'national pride, protection against the invader, whether Russian or Latin ...'. Paradoxically there is also an element of pride in Latinity: Roumania is Orthodox *and* Latin.

21. This is taken from H. Culea's survey in *Viitorul Social*, 1, 1973, reported in ABSEES for July, 1973. The journal, *Religion in Communist Lands* provides some material from time to time, especially on the plight of dissidents. The fortune of the Orthodox is complemented by the parlous situation of Baptists and Uniates. As in Russia, the relative preference for the Orthodox is connected with the problem of ethnic minorities. Cf. J. Hale 'Ceausescu's Roumania', London: Harrap 1971 for information on the ethnic-cum-religious minorities more especially the Germans (Lutheran) and the Hungarians (Catholics, Reformed and Unitarian). The Germans initially suffered after the war but their economic contribution has led to relative prosperity; the large Jewish community initially gained after the war and then suffered, to some extent at the hands of Moscow-trained Communist Jews. The community is today much reduced in numbers and many Roumanian Jews are now in Israel.

22. Cf. Fiamengo 1972, and M. Brocic and B. Denitch in Bociurkiw and Strong 1975.

23. Cited in Fiamengo 1972.

24. Cited in Fiamengo 1962. All the data in the studies cited stress the relative vitality of the Catholic Church.

25. Cf. ABSEES April, 1973. In the article concern is expressed lest religion becomes the ideology of the poor, and promoted in that role by the younger clergy. Perhaps it is worth recollecting that Slovenia once had a Christian Socialist Movement which was assimilated by the partisans under the pressures of the war. For material on Slovenia and the general problem of nationality and religion in Yugoslavia, cf. Alexander, forthcoming. The unrest in Croatia since 1971 has contributed to the tension between churches and state. Cf. Hickling 1973.

26. I am relying here on material supplied by the late Michael Hickling as part of his Ph.D. thesis on Church-State relations in Eastern Europe, which he prepared for the University of London. There is a chapter on Hungary in Beeson 1974, ad an article by L. Laszlo in Bociurkiw and Strong 1975. Laszlo concludes that the regime wants to be beloved by all the people, including the believers, and so wishes to normalize relations with the churches. It also desires international respectability and diplomatic relations with the Vatican. At the same time it feels bound to shackle the churches and to control religion. Laszlo cites (p. 313) a poll of working and student youth showing one third as believers. Other researches to which he refers endorse a rather characteristic distribution: 15–20 per cent firm believers; 25–30 per cent Marxists, and the rest hovering.

27. Varga 1972. Cf. also Bango 1968. Bango's study of students begins by reference to the two salient facts: the rapid urbanization of Hungary and the forced attenuation of Catholic organization. If parents wish they may attest that their children desire to take a religious course: in 1967 some 12–13 per cent did so at primary level, 1–2 per cent at secondary level. Believers accounted for some third of those interviewed, of which considerably less than half were practising. Nearly one third were uncertain materialists and nearly one third atheists. Believers largely cited habit and parental wishes as lying behind their religious practice. One other finding was important: most young people were 'materialist' in the sense that their main concern was with personal achievement. Socialism was approved in general but the adult world and its politics were observed with passivity and cynicism.

28. W. Marsula, cited in Stackhouse 1968. Stackhouse also summarizes material from other eastern European countries; and there is a complementary article by Norman Birnbaum dealing with similar issues.

29. Wilhelm 1972. For the political aspect, cf. G. Brand in Bociurkiw and Strong 1975.

30. E. Kadlecová 1972. What the situation meant to a pro-

Russian can be gleaned from the autobiography of the Protestant theologian J. Hromadka. Cf. Kadlecová 1965.

31. Kadlecová 1972; P. A. Toma and M. J. Reban in Bociurkiw and Strong 1975 mention a 1970 study (p. 281) showing 70.7 per cent in Slovakia as believers. The same authors refer to the existence of a Christian intelligentsia.

32. B. Bociurkiw in a lecture on Church and State in Eastern Europe, delivered at the London School of Economics.

33. Cf. A. Benningsen on Islam in Bociurkiw and Strong 1975, and material in Marshall 1971. Benningsen stresses *un*official and nationalist opposition channelled through Islam. In Islamic areas, circumcision has the role of conferring national and religious identity. One should also note the resistance of the Uniate Church in association with Ukrainian nationalism, as documented by V. Markus in Bociurkiw and Strong 1975.

34. I have not tried to do more than hint at the varied forms of the 'Protestant' ethic which arise in the process of industrialization, although plainly there are two forms: ideologically constricted, in Spain (Opus Dei, etc.) and in Russia; and psychically constricted, in Anglo-Saxon democracies and Scandinavia. Protestantism itself is a major, if ambiguous, agent of capitalism, democracy, and science, in Protestant countries, more especially where dissent and an 'open' social structure is possible. It is confined to the provision of small-scale moral communities and work discipline in the context of totalitarianism. The point about the Old Believers mentioned in my text indicates just one of the variant channels whereby analogues of the Protestant Ethic achieve partial linkage with democratic and modernizing impulses. I quote Blackwell (1965): "Many of the private industrial entrepreneurs in Moscow were Old Believers. The focus of their business activities was the textile industry. Here the peculiar beliefs, way of life, and organization of the larger communities of the schismatics seemed admirably suited to the accumulation of industrial capital, the provision of incentive for master and worker alike, and the mobilization of the lower social strata of Moscow and the surrounding countryside into a factory labor force.' (p. 407). 'In the case of the Moscow schismatic enterprises, the institutional aspect was more important than the ideological in the accumulation of capital and the organization of production. Not individual capitalists moved by a wordly ascetic 'calling' in the accumulation of wealth in business affairs so much as a group capital through legacies, contributions, and a communal way of life and enterprise determined the economic expansion of the Moscow Old Believers. The Russian communal tradition, glorified by Slavophiles and the *narodniki* asserted itself, although not for long. Money and commerce brought with it materialistic individualism, property consciousness, and the appearance of a class of secularized, private entrepreneurs.' (p. 424).

VI

The Pattern of Reactive Organicism

The discussion of statist regimes of the right must turn on the same axis as discussion of statist regimes of the left: the monopoly of the means of power. By extension, this inevitably directs attention to the area of church-state relations. The state endeavours to include the church within its monopoly. However, it tries to do so at a point where the process of differentiation in the society at large gives leverage to the ancient symbolic tension between church and state, and allows it opportunity to express itself.

Furthermore the lesion between church and state is exacerbated by the fact that the Roman Catholic church at large, in Europe and elsewhere, has largely loosed itself free from statist entanglements, and exercises an external pressure on the pace of internal developments. Indeed, ecclesiastical leaders can easily draw appropriate lessons from the débâcles attending such entanglements, notably in France. A liberal regime becomes an acceptable option as compared with the fate awaiting the church under totalitarian regimes. The freedom of the spiritual arm is at least a possibility under liberal aegis, and the chief danger of liberalism is its tendency to offer opportunities for take-over by disciplined minorities.

Such a drift is particularly likely to occur in countries where all the processes have been damned up by a 'reactive organicism'. The fear of anarchy or of a disciplined take-over from the left holds back sectors which might otherwise embrace the liberal option and lends colour to the accusation that the church clings to the old organic Baroque connection. On the other hand, the same fear also inclines other sectors to make an immediate alliance with the left to prevent the classic polarization occurring yet again. And this fear is conjoined with a genuine idealism, especially among younger and lower clergy, which takes a politico-religious form. The fears of the right are thereby exacerbated, and the very alliances designed to prevent polarization then act to bring them into being. Yet these polar tendencies have not the force of the classic tension, because models of radical Catholicism are available to ameliorate them and because the enveloping atmosphere of religion can allow the early protests to utilize the church, and church buildings, as a symbolic and actual umbrella or refuge.

Since different parts of a country will be at different levels of development, the polarization will play up regional patriotism, some of an archaic, and some of a modern, variety. If large fissures are already present, based on regional sentiment, the polarization will partly turn on the axis of centre versus periphery. Spain provides the obvious instance, two of its regional areas being more developed than the centre, and one less.

The ideology of the right-wing conservative state tends to be an interim development and to occur as a reaction to an initial liberal phase or, more usually, phases. Each of these phases has exemplified accelerating hostilities between church and liberal state, in spite of major attempts to cross the divide. In the Spanish case, it was essentially the violence of the attack on the Church which sparked off the civil war. Once the organic state is restored, there cannot be a return to a straightforward traditional ideology, and there still has to be an interim hybrid form of legitimation incorporating a variety of tendencies, including the radical thrusts underlying the right-wing forces, as well as traditionalism. The uneasy alliance of the right is initially held together by the fact that its ideology turns less on ideas than on symbols and invocations. It is only afterwards that a central focus of power crystallizes out and clips both its traditionalist and its radical wings. However, this crystallization means that its power rests more specifically on control of the state apparatus and less on a broad base, and this in turn makes the internal manipulation of élites all the more crucial. At the same time, the mass of the population continue to note the invocation of familiar symbols, including religious symbols, and prefer any kind of stability to civil war and anarchy. The 'ideology' thus contains at least one plank which is largely accepted: stability. The familiar invocations join with the appeal to stability to create a form of mass support. Only a reckless misuse of force or violence will alienate this kind of support or else an egregious incompetence in the

I

handling of economic development. In Spain, the élite committed neither mistake: in Greece the élite committed both. The Spanish mistake was to identify opposition unequivocally as Marxist.

No analysis of fascist ideology is required here, nor of conservative organicism but one or two points are worth noting by way of contrast with statist ideology of the left. The chief distinguishing characteristic of left ideology is that it is an intellectual construct, and can even be regarded as an ideology of the intelligentsia in its bid for power. Certainly, its call to certain sections of the working class can be regarded as a useful gesture en route to supreme power, however marked by the guilt and romanticism of middle class intellectuals. But the kind of ideology animating right wing organization is not so much an intellectual construction as an invocation of certain attitudes and symbols believed to inhere in the nation and believed to be capable of saving that nation at historic crises. Since these virtues are essentially military there is already present an incipient tension with Christianity. In Nazi Germany the Christian aspiration towards peaceability was regarded as a weak religious sentiment sapping the warrior virtue of the German spirit. Behind this militarism lies a less stark, because a more Christianized, tradition of aristocratic chivalry. At any rate, it is the military who project themselves as unphilosophic guardians of the national soul and its martial spirit. They are 'called' by crisis to exercise their historic function and to banish the corruption and venality of liberal democracy. They speak for history, and in Greece they claimed to speak very specifically for Christianity. The rhetoric is based on notions of historic destiny toned by religion. Here there appears a further contrast with statist ideology of the left. The right sees itself as propelled by history whereas the left claims to act as its midwife and to propel it forward by conscious decision.

All statist ideologies demand public adherence to their rituals and dogmas, but the right seeks a lesser degree of inward assent. The élite are openly willing to act on behalf of the masses, whereas élites of the left retire behind a dogma of universal support to which they endeavour to give a measure of reality by total socialization. The right wing élite tolerates apathy in the mass, and indeed can approve of it, and also allows itself discreet scepticisms provided they are not trumpeted abroad in a disruptive manner. How people think is less relevant than how they act.

In Spain, for example, a degree of free speech and free circulation of books and ideas existed which compared very favourably with conditions obtaining in eastern Europe.

If leaders are forthcoming—and the right people in the right positions—then opinion need not be too grossly intruded upon. The crucial problem is the creation of a philosophy of development which will relate to the objective conditions and consequences of economic change and progress. Once models of modernity are available, especially through the impact of tourism, then development is essential. So there appear right wing approaches to modernity, endeavouring to promote industrialization within a traditionalist format. The most obvious contemporary example is Brazil, where an expanding élite of many millions subsists over a mass of many more millions. As in Spain, the trans-Lusitanian church has proved a major source of opposition to this policy both with regard to its political and its economic brutalism. The philosophy of development applied in Brazil is essentially that utilized in the Soviet Union: the sacrifice of a generation or so of workers now for posterity and—perhaps—liberty, later. The important point here is that all instances of 'reactive organicism', in Brazil, Chile, Spain, Portugal and to a lesser extent in Fascist Italy, and Greece, the Church has shuffled out of the ancient right wing alliance. And, in spite of frequent governmental pressure on higher appointments, the ecclesiastical protest has come in some degree from the episcopate itself. In 1971 the Joint Assembly of Spanish Bishops and Priests actually issued a scathing indictment of Franco.

One further important religious aspect of development has been the spread of Protestant attitudes partly through pietist sectarianism, as for example in the Pentecostal movement, and partly through functional equivalents of the Protestant Ethic within the Catholic Church itself. In Chile and Brazil, from about 1950 onwards, there has been a steady, indeed accelerating, growth of Pentecostalism, more particularly perhaps among migrant workers. In both countries Protestants now comprise some ten per cent of the population. In Spain, the *Cursillos de cristiandad* have worked on a psychological basis quite similar to Moral Re-Armament or the Wesleyan class meeting, and have formed cadres of local leaders and activists. In both Spain and Greece, ascetic lay orders operating among the highly placed, have penetrated the machinery of government: Opus Dei and Zoe. Opus Dei in particular was successful in providing a functional equivalent of the Protestant Ethic to channel the psychic energies for development and leadership. Indeed, the Spanish economic miracle, operative from about 1958 onwards, owed a great deal to the ideas of Opus Dei.

We now turn to the European cases of 'reactive organicism' which have been operative since the war, i.e. omitting Fascist Italy, and Nazi Germany, which are briefly covered in the 'Latin' and 'Mixed' categories respectively. Spain provides the most complex and sociologically interesting instance, and it is appropriate to begin by noting a crucial aspect of the Spanish case, the complex pull over centuries of centralism and pluralism, centralism and regionalism. Mediaeval Spain was, in a limited sense, pluralistic; Baroque Spain was a monolithic entity deriving from a drive to the unitary state. Indeed, Catholicism itself was thoroughly subordinated under the enlightened absolutism of Charles the Third. Hence the Protestants are very few (some 50,000) and mostly of foreign origin: they are concentrated somewhat in Catalonia and are primarily urban. Such proselytizing dynamic as there is can be found amongst such groups as Pentecostals and sectarians, operating amongst the poorer migrants in squalid urban areas (cf. Almerich 1972). But there are other sources of dissent, some old and some recent, operating within and without the Catholic Church and these may now be surveyed. Such a survey is best conceived within general remarks about the complex ambience of relations between religion and culture.

The traditional extra-ecclesiastical sources of dissidence are bourgeois rationalism, the spiritual illuminism of the freemasonry, Marxism (which is mostly not theoretical) and in the various forms of anarcho-syndicalism and anarchism, the latter rooted in notions of the autonomous village. Spanish freemasonry played the same important anti-clerical role in the nineteenth century as it did in France. The spirit of autonomous community (cf. Kenny 1961) (which one also finds, of course, in Russia and Greece) lies behind a variety of Christian humanism which is anti-clerical in its exaltation of the person and its opposition to all state absolutism. Perhaps one should emphasize that in a culture which is both orthodox and untheological intellectual dissent has traditionally had to express itself outside the Catholic Church, even though there are forms of historical romanticism (such as that of Menéndez y Pelayo) which emphasize the cultural role of the Church. The Spanish Church is historically not an intellectual church, any more than it is a lay church, and what is interesting about the present scene is the existence of progressive Catholic intellectuals and laity (Duocastella 1973b).

The layers of Spanish piety correspond roughly to those to be found in Poland and Italy as well, of course, as elsewhere, and some of them are in varying senses, 'secular'. Thus the layer of superstitious magic is secular in that it represents proto-scientific manipulations, and the layer of simple piety is secular in its attention to 'material' objects, albeit imbued with divine, efficacious 'stuff'. And the layer of Baroque Catholicism is secular in its complete assimilation to the *status quo* and the world as given. One makes this point here, though it could be made in most contexts, simply because the process of secularization is too often expounded by reference to orthodox, theologically adumbrated norms whereby not only are rather a small number of people classifiable as religious today, but very few can have been classifiable as religious in the ages of faith. Another point worth emphasizing in the Spanish context, since it is dramatically illustrated in the Spanish data, is that even reckoning by the usually accepted norms of institutional practice, secularization in parts of Spain is a process, indeed has been a constant *condition*, over two centuries.

The layer of superstition, popular, manipulative and utilitarian, is enormously important in Spain and not merely so in country districts. There are, according to Jesús Marcos Alonso (1965), two levels. The first is semi-magical and barely touched by Catholicism: the magic formulae of 'The Cross of Caravaca', and the spells, incantations and the like in which some Catholic element may be lodged, such as the sign of the cross. The second is best illustrated by the cult of the saints, and their respective fields of protective expertise. These are often survivals of older religions given a Catholic slant. Many people who are fanatically devoted to these patronal saints or procession societies are entirely unconcerned with communion, confessions or the moral precepts of the church. *Thus deviance from the moral precepts of the church, noted several times above, is no more a new phenomenon than is deviance from institutional practice.* Furthermore, even the more 'orthodox' rituals, devotions and spiritual associations are often recommended for 'secular' motives not far distant from those now so popular in the United States; peace of mind, family unity, relief of frustration.

A third level of ritual conformity and motivation exists which is less secular than sub-Christian: God is viewed as unapproachable, impersonal and capricious, especially in relation to untoward events. This leads to a propitiation of Him for basically utilitarian reasons, to the proliferation of less uncertain intermediaries, to excessive concern about the correct mechanics of the rite, to a disjunction between religion and morality, and to fatalism. In short, it has many characteristics in common with magic. It appears Catholic but is deficient by Catholic norms: its God is a disguise for the caprices of the phenomenal world and its ritual is a remedy limiting that caprice. The Church colludes in this because it colludes with an appearance of conformity, but under pressure of social change the exterior façade often collapses to the bare minimum of ritual acts involved in occasional conformity. Moreover, while internally incoherent it is also capable of subsisting with inconsistent ideologies, e.g. communism. A nontheological Catholicism can cohabit with a non-ideological communism.

A level of religiosity which may include some or even all of the above is cultural Catholicism, whereby a non-Catholic is not a Spaniard, and a non-Spanish Catholic is a Catholic of the second class. The Church becomes a cultural service station for the nation, as well as being defined as guardian of the national essence. Such a version of civic religion can easily be reduced to social conformities and pressures and involves a subjection of religion to the ethical norms of the particular community. This means in effect a strict application of ethical norms within the family and little application at all within the realms of economic and professional life: this is, of course, a phenomenon not confined to Spain and derives from a fundamental recalcitrance of social relations above the level of the intimate and personal to ethical regulation. It is the obverse of the inability of political norms, as for example in eastern Europe, to have resonance at the personal level. Such a sanctification of local standards (or a secularization and subversion of religious standards) makes all change equivalent to subversion. Hence the usefulness of this kind of religion to authoritarian regimes.

Such an identification of religion and caste is profoundly Durkheimian and breeds two dissident forms of religiosity: a non-church Christianity sitting loose to dogmas and institutions,[1] and a Christianity which sees the Church as a specific distinct community of believers in personal relationship to God and committed to a common way of life which translates as far as may be the imperatives of the gospel, first internally and then externally. More can be said of this below in the course of examining the transitions occurring in the recent past from the rigidities immediately succeeding the civil war to the relative flexibility and openness of the post-conciliar period. The end of the Civil War marked a return to the Baroque State whereby the Church was rewarded for its part in the War, more particularly by control of education and the prohibition of civil marriage. The Church licked its wounds after the violent explosions of anti-clericalism under the Second Republic (1931–36). With one or two episcopal exceptions conformity reigned and church adherence became an index of conformity. The radical Catholic movements in Catalonia (parallel to the French J.A.C.) were forced underground, as radical, separatist, and foreign-inspired. The Church however was not fascist: the fascists gestured towards it to secure support, but the Church remained simply conservative.

From 1950 to 1960 there were occasional and intermittent critical voices, sometimes of French inspiration: intellectual Catholics with more universalist perspectives, and movements within Catholic Action. Religious renovation worked through the 'Courses in Christianity' for local lay leaders, the development of a more specialized 'Catholic Action', movements of familial spirituality, and the organization called 'For a Better World'. All of these represented a desire for a more socially active religion, one which was more personal and thought out.[2] Nevertheless, the Concordat of 1953 between the Vatican and the state remained conservative.

The post-war period of inflation in religious practice and priestley vocations then reached a plateau. 1960 marked a new era: the impact of the economic miracle, of accelerated tourism and above all migration, of elements of liberalization, of the

Vatican Council, and then of the general stirrings of dissent abroad, especially in France. The Council itself fed additional inflammable material into the new situation and made the Pope and Rome appear to conservatives as another channel of foreign, meddlesome influence. Many Catholics began to feel the need of a degree of independence from the State, especially so amongst workers, students and members of the liberal professions. Those who accepted the ideas of the Council favouring pluralism, liturgical reform and the replacement of authority by pastoral dialogue found themselves embattled in a generational struggle which was even more marked within the priesthood than elsewhere. This struggle contained echoes of the Dutch situation and of the much more minor disputes in Croatia: vocations fell, defections rose, some lost their faith, a few became Marxists. Various factors contributed to this, amongst them the shocks sustained by priests in working class areas, and an even more general sense that the traditional psychology and role of the priest was too constricting. Hence young would-be priests interrupted their studies and shifted into industrial or intellectual avocations. Ordinations fell by one third; vocations which had climbed to a peak in 1967 also fell.[3] The crisis in ordinations and in vocations reflected a partial abandonment of the traditional anti-intellectual traditions of Spanish clergy and religious, a rejection of the principle of seniority, and an aspiration towards the expertise appropriate to specialist tasks. The latter ran pari-passu with a sense of displacement amongst the religious as the State absorbed their traditional functions in public health, social assistance and education. Underlying it all were new conceptions of humanity, of Christ and of personal realization which were seen as needing to be worked out through personal work and evangelical poverty within a communitarian setting. In short, the general crisis of identity and role in Western Europe, plus the aspiration to communal forms of existence, hit the Spanish Church a little later than elsewhere, but not much. Hence the disfavour into which the Concordat of 1953, tying the Church to the regime has fallen, even amongst moderate Catholics. Hence also, maybe, the statement by the new Prime Minister (1974), in his speech announcing a measure of liberalization, that interference by the Church would not be tolerated. Presumably the association of radical Catholicism and both Basque and Catalan separatism in part lay behind this warning.

Official uncertainty about the Church probably underlay the new 1970 education law giving the state an effective monopoly.

Opus Dei is a quasi-order, founded in 1928, operating a type of patronage system which has earned it the sobriquet 'Holy Mafia'. It is ascetic in discipline and aims to influence the world rather in the manner of Moral Re-Armament. The basic conception runs parallel to, and in imitation of, the Institución Libre de Enseñanza which was not only a seedbed of progressivism and agnosticism but also influential in distributing jobs. Though Opus Dei was originally unsuccessful the Civil War and its aftermath brought an opportunity to help fill the immense gap left by the exiled or liquidated Republican intelligentsia. The greatest success was in Catalonia. The Catalonian bourgeoisie was brought back to Hispanic piety and preferred the Opus, with its combination of the Catalan evaluation of hard work and loyalty to the regime, to the anti-capitalist slogans and centralist attitude of the Falange. Since then the Opus has infiltrated banks, bought shares in diverse companies, and has its members in key posts in industry and the ministries, though it is relatively unrepresented in the present government, (1974).[4] The important point is that Opus Dei has found means, temporary maybe, of reconciling modernization and hierarchy, religion and rationalization and the public recognition of certain forms of hedonism. It constitutes a theo-technocracy and as such is a partial equivalent of the Protestant Ethic, albeit working within the élite levels of a hierarchical, Catholic society and specifically dedicated to élitist ideals. And in its concern for education, signalized in the creation of the new university of Navarre, it grasped at one of the crucial levers of power and influence.

This then is the wide spectrum of Spanish religiosity, running from manuals of incantation to the left-wing guerrilla priest in the movement for Basque autonomy and the J.O.C., Juventud Obrera Católica.[5] Thus William Christian (1974) in his description of religious life in the Nansa Valley of Northern Spain, more especially the apparitions of the Virgin and St. Michael in the early 1960s, can describe the co-existence of these levels even in one area. The oldest layer probably antedates Christianity and manifests itself in the shrines which influence specific areas, such as province, valley or village, and it corresponds to the local sense of identity. These shrines also help to deal with concrete problems:

soliciting divine energy for human purposes and eliciting human energy for divine purposes. The next layer, deriving from the impulses of the Counter-Reformation, is characterized by a sense of sin and fear of purgatory and includes highly general devotions, such as the Sacred Heart and the Rosary, whose objective is personal salvation and the transformation of persons from one spiritual condition to another. The latest layer, barely laid down, derives from the initiative of young priests encouraging people to find God in one another rather than through inter-mediaries.

The situation may now be described in quantitative terms, recognizing the variety of meaning interpenetrating apparently similar ritual acts and seemingly identical institutional attachments. In making this quantitative assessment one must also remember the maldistribution of priests as between the practising north and the indifferent south, and the difficulty religious and priests, some old and many of rural origin, have felt in adjusting to the new urban conditions and needs of migrants. The same maldistribution affects the lay groups of 'Catholic Action', though there are certain dioceses in the centre and south where the social cohesion brought about by being a minority increases the relative strength of Catholic Action.

Some seven basic areas may be distinguished, following Duocastella 1965:

1. A region of high practice in Galicia and Asturias, broken by the mining basin, the industrial littoral, the fishing areas and the metallurgical complex of 'Ocho asturiano'.
2. A region of high practice (60–80 per cent per Sunday) adjacent to the above in Castile and León.
3. A further region of very high practice in Navarre and the Basque country, broken somewhat by the industrial segment of Bilbao.
4. An area of intensive practice in parts of Aragon and Catalonia, which is at its maximum towards the Pyrenees and diminishes to a very low level in the centre and south of the region.
5. The S.E. rural region of the Levante including the Catalonian littoral and southward, in which practice is fairly constant and invariant from area to area at about 38 per cent.

The offshore Balearics, being islands, have a practice of about 68 per cent.

6. The central region between the 40th parallel and Andulasia, where practice per Sunday oscillates from area to area between 20 per cent and 40 per cent. Parts of this area include the regions in constant dispute between the Christian north and Islamic south.

7. The area of Andalusia and of neighbouring Badajoz where practice stands at about 15 per cent per Sunday.

These seven areas can be collapsed broadly into a gradual transition from north to south whereby the north is a region of high practice and the south an area of low practice. It has already been pointed out that this division parallels the division between Christian north and Islamic south, but a crucial element may well be the fact that the north is an area of middling and small farms and the south an area of latifundia. Galicia is a region of stability, high practice and of poverty stricken minifundia: it is marked by traditional subservience, a sense of social awe and a low level of class consciousness. In Catalonia and the Basque country, where farms are of middling size, there is a greater degree of security and egalitarian sentiment: practice is very high in the Basque country and high in the north of Catalonia. It is worth emphasizing that unlike many peripheral areas or subordinate areas (e.g. Slovakia, Brittany, Quebec) they are the *most* developed and therefore their alienation from the centre is in terms of their relative deprivation of a political power complementary to their economic power. In the south, however, there is the area of latifundia extending into Portugal, where marginal land is worked by small owners who alternate their work with that seasonally rendered to the landlords. These landlords are often absentee noblemen or descendants of the nineteenth century bourgeoisie. The principal division is between landless peasants, often living in the Andalusian agrotowns and waiting for work, an upper class of grandees, and a class of servants, retainers and administrators. In this kind of milieu religion oscillates between fatalism and anarchistic millenarian atheism; conventional practice and church provision is very poor, and has been so for a very long time. Gradually, however, capitalistic values of efficiency and mechanization are altering the scene. Mechanization supplants the labour, which migrates to the towns, and this migration is as high in the latifundia as it is on the minifundia.

The great migrations are, of course, part of the process of rapid industrialization and urbanization. Madrid itself is now an industrial city, and many rural towns, including the agrotowns, have become partially industrialized. A classic proletariat has been created, though the proportion of skilled to unskilled continues to grow, as well as the proportion of service, technical and administrative personnel. The lower working class is augmented by the rural exodus; the middle class rapidly augmented by recruitment from the working class. Since the best paid workers are, as is generally the case, the most militant, the government must face dissent, (and Catholicism must face institutional defection) not only from Asturian miners, Catalan textile workers and Basque steel workers—a combination of class and regional alienation—but also from workers in industrial areas created by its own policies, such as the Madrid industrial belt and the I.N.I. plants. The revolutionary potential of the proletariat as a whole however is diminished by the fact that most workers are in small firms and have become, under the impact of the availability of consumer goods, more wages-minded than ideological (Giner 1971, Duocastella 1965, Almerich 1972).

These very broad characterizations could lead to more detailed ones, showing how religiosity would vary by occupation in accordance with historic alignments vis-à-vis the Republic, and the kind of contemporary factors already suggested: size of plant, degree of rural unemployment and anomie, scale of farms and personal ownership, proximity to administration and so on. The point about historical alignment could be illustrated by the absence of the health professions and relative absence of academics and journalists from recent cabinets, which reflects the leftist and laicist traditions which gave them influence in the Republic. So far as proximity to administration is concerned it is interesting that the highest practising group tends to be the 'clase media', i.e. the pre-industrial middle class, consisting of professionals, merchants, small vintners and servants, officers and so on, many of whom still own some land. (This perhaps parallels the *ir*religiosity of those within administrative cadres in Eastern Europe). However, even in such groups there may be variations in *type* of religiosity, that of the upper military being of an unreflective kind dominated by

notions of the correct behaviour appropriate for those who hold
the national destiny in their hands. Furthermore, in certain kinds
of area, where there is a gulf between gentry and the proletarianized labourer on large farms, the difference in practice sometimes
grows progressively wider, each element of polarity leading to a
reinforcement of polarization, until one cultural identity is coinci-
dent with church practice and the other antithetical to it.[6]

Some of these points emerge if we look at the distribution of
practice by occupation in different kinds of area. If we take our
third area designated above, we find the following situation in the
rural and urban parts of Vitoria, a partially industrialized Basque
town (1965). In both the town and the country property owners,
domestic servants, members of the liberal professions, administrators and clerks all showed nearly complete conformity to Catholic
norms of Sunday mass, but there were noticeable differences
between higher technicians and managers in the rural area (89
per cent) and in the urban area (55 per cent); similarly so with
public servants, tradesmen and transport workers; and the unskilled dropped from 81.2 per cent in the rural to 29.2 per cent
in the urban area. The unemployed, as everywhere, had a low
level of practice but not so low in the country as in the town. It
was also the case that migrants to Vitoria were pulled up towards
the general level of practice, but nevertheless remained more or
less practising according to the characteristic level of their place of
origin. This is the obverse of the fact often noted that people
leaving high practice areas for areas of low practice adopt the
norms of the locality.

A useful contrast can be made with practice in the diocese of
Albacete (1967) which comprises an area of little industry and
depressed countryside. Some two out of three amongst the liberal
professions and technicians are present at Sunday Mass, but only
one in five of employers and one in ten of labourers. Quite
another sort of area is represented by the mining basin of the
Nalón (1967) which has been much influenced by left-wing
ideology. Here only the technicians have a high rate of practice
(66.6 per cent), while even public servants and liberal professionals
sink to 27.0 per cent and 21.7 per cent respectively. Only 8.6 per
cent of farmers are present on a given Sunday, 5.9 per cent of
surface miners, 4.1 per cent of metal workers and 1.9 per cent of
transport workers and miners underground. Medium sized towns,

like Gerona and Mataró show rates of practice in between the above extremes. Thus in Mataró (1960) the big industrialists are 80.8 per cent present on Sunday, the liberal professions 51.3 per cent, public servants 30 per cent and labourers on farms or in industry 5 per cent. Studies made in 1957 concerning the working class in general indicate a low level of attendance at Sunday Mass (7.6 per cent) but higher levels for occasional practices (23.3 per cent) and for Easter duties (28.5 per cent). Over half the working class population declared itself indifferent to religious questions, and 40 per cent described themselves as *anti*-religious.[7]

Duocastella, from whom most of the material utilized above derives makes various observations of some interest. The unemployed, distanced from the social structure, are everywhere inclined to a low level of practice. He notes, what indeed is obvious, that practice is associated with power and prestige: if the farmers of the north are not so practising as those of the south this is because they are not grandees. Furthermore, much depends on relative status, so that particular social categories practise not simply in accordance with the general religious tone of their profession but in accordance with its relative rank in a given local context. Such facts are indicative of a form of religion based on conformity to social ethos and proximity to power.

There are other factors apart from professional and local 'tone': notably size of town and extent of migration, the two things being often positively related in contemporary Spain. In many towns less than half the population are of local origin and one must take account of the kind of practice existing where they came from. By and large uprooting works against religious practice. Towns vary according to the urban sector concerned: the central areas of Madrid and residential quarters had a relatively high rate of practice (30 per cent – 50 per cent) compared to the industrial suburbs. In the industrial suburbs ('obreras') of Barcelona the rate of practice sinks to 2.5 per cent, which is partly due to the fact that migrants are from the non-practising non-Catalan speaking south. An important and surprising fact to be referred to later in the context of France is that in certain areas of central Spain the level of practice in the towns exceeds that of the surrounding countryside. One partial explanation in certain cases may be that towns contain functionaries and members of the bourgeoisie, while the countryside consists of depressed seasonal labourers. On the whole practice diminishes with size of town, but this is qualified by two factors: the extent and type of the working class population within it, and the general tone of the region. Thus Vitoria and Granada are both towns of approximately the same size but have overall numbers at Sunday mass of 73.5 per cent and 12 per cent respectively, reflecting the religious tone of extreme north and extreme south respectively. But within each religious zone towns tend to achieve a level of practice diminishing with increase in size.

There are other indicators of religious practice: obedience to the Easter precept follows the line of Sunday practice already indicated: 80 per cent – 100 per cent in the north-east, 50 per cent along the Mediterranean provinces and in Catalonia, 37 per cent in Madrid, 10 per cent in the extreme south. With regard to the reception of communion, which is a general indicator of a more personal form of religious faith, it seems that the proportion rises where the total of those at mass is rather small. Two elements may be operative here: towns encourage an increase in an individually appropriated type of religion while minority status leads to a higher degree of fulfilment of religious norms. Where mass is a matter of social ostentation it tends to be anonymous and lack the more personal and direct forms of participation. As to the last sacraments over 90 per cent of those who died in rural areas received the last rites; in Madrid less than half did so. Family prayer is a practice much attenuated by urbanization, more particularly by the exigencies of children's schooling and the other attractions available: perhaps about a third of those attending Mass regularly say family prayers. Baptism is an almost universal practice, but there is often a much longer delay than previously between the birth and performance of the rite. It is perhaps a highly indicative statistic that 90 per cent of workers have their children baptized—and 90 per cent express anti-clerical sentiments.

There is not a great deal of information about belief except with regard to students. 83.2 per cent of the men students believed in God, and 97 per cent of the women; 71.8 per cent of the men believed in the divinity of Christ and 90 per cent of the women; 58.8 per cent of the men believed the Pope infallible in matters of faith and 84.5 per cent of the women. This last figure is clearly important and links with the spread of a pluralistic ethos in that the majority of men and women thought the relationship of church to state prejudicial, and preferred that the state should be religiously neutral. In Spain as a whole only 10 per cent of men and 15 per cent of women thought Catholicism should be the only religion permitted. A further significant indicator is to be found in the fact that only about half the total population took a rigorist attitude to birth control. This clearly must vary with the region: the Basque country has a higher birth rate than Catalonia.

It remains only to note data with respect to age. Amongst those under ten years of age practice is very high and after ten it drops rapidly, continuing to do so throughout adolescence, excepting only rural areas of high general practice. In some areas, notably in urban parishes where general practice is high, the level of attendance reaches a low point in the mid-twenties and slowly recovers towards the mid-fifties, but much depends on the historical experience of particular generations. In urban Catalonia, for example, those in their fifties have the lowest level of practice for all ages, reflecting the views of people whose crucial experience occurred during Catalonia's espousal of the left in the civil war.[8]

Spain has been treated in some detail because it serves to illustrate a number of complex interrelations for which data are not always available elsewhere: the relationships of occupation, place in the hierarchy of prestige, proximity to power and administration, type and scale of farming and of industry, and degree and type of urbanization. Portugal may be dealt with much more summarily from one point of view only: the repetition of precisely the same division between north and south, and for exactly the same reasons, i.e. the imperfect christianization of the Islamic south and the latifundia which the conquering Christians carved out for themselves. When the Portuguese South was reconquered the crown, the military orders and the nobility divided up the land between them thus bringing about an initial concentration of property. This frontier between north and south, roughly marked by the Tagus, is not merely an economic one, but can be traced along the whole march of Christian–Islamic coexistence and warfare, through southern Italy and Albania to the Bulgarian Black Sea coast.

The River Tagus is not merely a geographical but a social and religious boundary. A primary index of this difference is provided by the map of civil marriages. Civil marriage has been long recognized in Portugal, even between 1910 and 1926, and carried with it the legal possibility of divorce; those who were married canonically automatically renounced this legal possibility. Now divorce is open to those married in church. The map of civil marriages prior to 1974 therefore reflects faithfulness to the norms of official, institutional Catholicism though not necessarily religiosity *in se*. The whole of the north of Portugal constitutes a solid bloc in which Catholic marriage forms 90 per cent–100 per cent of the total. In the south by contrast there is quite a large area in which Catholic marriages run only at 40 per cent–60 per cent, and in one municipality they sink to only 20 per cent of the total. Infant mortality is higher in the north and the number of births per 1,000; illegitimacy is higher in the south. Communism and atheism are largely confined to the south, and both have drawn of the reservoir of radicalism laid down earlier by anarchism and anarcho-syndicalism.

The variations in moral style, of if you like degree of secularization, are related to basic differences in social structure. The family in the north is patriarchal and deeply attached by kinship ties and personal ties to small holdings. The family in the south has been proletarianized and its relatively unstructured constituent members work for low pay in large scale holdings organized on capitalist lines. The equipment used in the north is more primitive and unmechanized. The farming of the north is basically for subsistence whereas in the south there is a degree of unemployment which contributes to social disintegration. Although Portugal as a whole is primarily agricultural (47 per cent of its population works in agriculture) the industry of the north tends to be of the kind characteristic of the *first* industrial revolution (textile industries, personally owned, with a considerable artisanate) while the industry of the south is large-scale, impersonal industry. The latter is associated with a lower degree of practice than the former. Two further points are worth making since they bear on the issue of secularization. First, there is a layer of religion below the Church, operated by female adepts. Second, the religion of the north, though practised by the majority is essentially a folk religion, whereas the ecclesiastical religion of the south, *where* practised, is sometimes closer official Catholicism.[9] As in Spain some southern towns exhibit higher practice than the country: the towns contain the bourgeois, administrative and landed sectors.

These elements have, of course, all been reactivated by revolution. The church initially welcomed the regime in cautious terms,
and at least avoided any identification with the so-called Christian
party of the right. It attacked atheism and totalitarianism, not
agrarian reform or communist cooperatives. As the communist
attempts at hegemony grew in vigour and determination, the
Church was forced into a practical alliance with democratic
forces, drawing on its northern strength especially at parish level
to neutralize communist control of the levers of power. Thus the
socialists found themselves demanding freedom both for their own
paper and for Catholic radio. If the Portuguese struggle for
democracy proves successful, this unique alliance will have had
much to do with it. What one has above all to remember is that
the liberal regime of 1910–1926 acted against both the Church
and the left. This did not join them together, but it did provide a
common fate and thereby broke the worst spirals of left-wing-
Church antagonism. The revolution, even in its extremist phases
before November 1974 was *not* markedly anti-clerical. The
Bishops repaid moderation with moderation, whatever local
priests might say in their parish weeklies. Moreover, the corporatist union organization of the right-wing regime 1926–1974
ensured that there was no specifically catholic unionism to confront left-wing unionism. The struggle in the unions is between
a centralizing communist thrust and the socialist and extreme left
opposition. Church influence presumably leans towards the non-
communist forces.

When considering modern Greece, which is a country with
high levels of belief and even to some extent of practice, one must
remember history[11] Whereas Spain was divided in two by the
Muslims, in Greece the Turks were dominant for several hundred
years. However, the Greeks were not only dominated by the Turks
but themselves became an instrument of Turkish domination
through the Patriarchate of Constantinople and its relation to
other Christian millets. The Greek hierarchy became *more* powerful and centralized under the Turks: it monopolized the highest
offices and fully participated in the corruption of the Porte. The
Turks effectively controlled appointments and a corrupted
simoniac Church became assimilated to national interests almost
without remainder. Since in the period of national awakening the
nation came to be conceived in terms of Hellenism the Church

became a defender of non-Christian values including the lay and enlightened spirit of the Phanariot aristocracy. It was therefore triply secularized: by its identity with the nation, by secular power and corruption, and by the promotion of Hellenism. There remained the monastic tradition of spirituality and the liturgy, the former bitterly attacked and restricted by the 'enlightened'. And even these remains went into slow decline. The Church of independent Greece became helplessly dependent on the state and supported the government in the task of shaping Greece according to urban and middle class values. There is however a continuing sentiment at village level, also to be found in Spain, which comprises a tradition of human equality and brotherhood expressed in communal and economic forms.[12]

Two points are crucial for the present argument: the role of Zoe, parallel to Opus Dei, and the continuing struggles over appointment which carry on the age-old Byzantine and Turkish tradition. Zöe was founded in 1913 as a monastic order in the world, dedicated in part to liturgical reform and especially to the elimination of the kind of priestly isolation symbolized by the iconostasis, and dedicated also to militant social action. This social action includes a notion of Graeco-Christian civilization which compounds the earlier conjunction of Orthodoxy and Hellenism. The role of Zoe became increasingly controversial with the appointment of Hieronymos Kotsomis, one of its members, as Archbishop of Athens, and the penetration of the government of the colonels by other members of the organization. Dissident bishops were removed and the Ecumenical Patriarch in Constantinople was attacked in order to create a mini-Vatican in Athens. Indeed, these attempts are similar to those of the Moscow Patriarchate in trying to extend is ecumenical control, so that political ambition can be pursued in a wider context. What is interesting in the debate between governmental supporters and dissidents is the fact that the latter appeal to ancient precedent. As the ultramontane liberals in nineteenth century France appealed to the Pope against Gallican subservience so the Greek dissidents appeal to the ancient rights of the Ecumenical Patriarch: 'the bonds between the Church of Greece and the Patriarchate are unbreakable and sacred'.[13]

The Colonels corruption of the Church could not do away with the age-long identification of the Church and the Greek and Byzantine spirit. Yet it did contribute to a youthful alienation which saw the new appointees of the regime as puppets of reaction. Only a very few dissident priests attracted torture at the hands of the regime, and the 'true' tradition perhaps passed into the hands of Makarios. As is well known, the Colonels and Makarios were more and more in conflict. His deposition and the Cypriot tragedy followed directly on this conflict, accelerated by the final desperate moves following the polytechnic events in Athens. Once the northern army removed the Colonels, after refusing to move against the Turks, the appointees of the right were mostly retired, and the tarnished image of the Church hierarchy at least improved to some degree. What remained indestructible was the rural cycle of festival and rite, both personal and communal, carrying forward the heart of Greek culture in a manner almost Jewish in its intimate linkage of family, community, and religion. The Paschal Lamb in Greece symbolizes exactly what the Passover signifies in Israel.

At this juncture, and before attempting any more general summary, it is appropriate to refer more specifically to a local level of festival and rite which persists not only in Greece but all over the Mediterranean. This 'social' religion compounded of superstition and a tincture of Christian symbolism and meaning exists in a complex relation to the official institutional church and the wider world of which the church is also a part. In the microcosm of local life the resistance to Christianity of the old gods, of ideals of prestige and manliness, and of semi-magical manipulations is clear. Whether the institutional church penetrates the microcosm depends on its wealth, on how the wealth affects the ordinary man i.e. in the form of property relations and status identifications, on the degree of intimate association between priesthood and locality, and on how it transcends the divide between local culture and impinging external structures. Not only is it important to examine this layer of local bond and ritual, but also to suggest its current fate at the hands of modernity.

Four studies by J. K. Campbell (1964), J. Cutileiro (1971), J. Pitt-Rivers (1954) and J. Boissevain (1965) each provide something of the range of alternatives and they show societies at very different levels. Nevertheless all these societies have their being within a common Mediterranean culture which northern Protestants too easily identify as typically Catholic. As Michael Fogarty has pointed out the heartlands of Christianity are further north and represent the first recovery of Christianity from centuries of invasion from the east. From northern Spain to Poland Christianity is an institution implanted over a millenium. Along the Mediterranean littoral however it is much less securely rooted and the institutional church stands in ambiguous relation to local culture. So something further is worth saying about 'southern' religion, partly because it is often para-Christian or pre-Christian and because it illustrates all levels from a family religion centred on the hearth to a well-organized church in straightforward confrontation with modern secular (and secularist) politics. I have, of course, already alluded to these levels in the discussion of Spain.

J. K. Campbell's study of transhumant shepherds entitled *Honour, Family and Patronage* (1964) is about a society where religion turns around the hearth, and where the basic Christian symbolism works in direct relation to everyday life. Bread and Wine are the everyday and the sacramental expression of shared life and brotherhood. The Lamb is the sacred animal of the society and the bleeding sign of God's reconciliation with men, and of men. Time turns not in rational divisions but within a human and divine continuum of activity in family and in flock. Religion is based on the family and clusters around its concepts of honour. There is no individuality aside from membership of the family and brotherhood is realized in family and kin to the partial exclusion of wider ties. The attenuation of those wider ties and the emphasis on prestige heightens a difference between the easy passage granted to Christian symbols and a resistance to their meaning insofar as they recommend poverty and humility and universal ties of blood among all men. Hence the woman bears the mark of Christian humility and simultaneously bears the mark of the Devil. She is Mary, humble and obedient, and Eve, whose seductive cunning threatens male honour and nobility. Since man is inherently noble in spite of the 'weight' of sin the Devil plays a large role as the basic source of evil. And since life is hard in spite of the inherent goodness of God fate plays a large role in fixing the frame of human destiny. Man protects himself against evil by divine grace and this is focused in magic substances, words, rituals, the icon corner in his hut, and the sign of the Cross. Apart from the Easter ritual, Christmas and the Feast of the Assumption, the Church plays little part. Religion resides in the images and the imagination of the shepherds and sets up the archetypal holy family above, which guides the human family below and provides its heavenly pattern. The father in heaven is all powerful above, and patronage relationships, particularly the spiritual ones set up by virtue of being a godparent, are very powerful below. It is divine patronage which makes the link with heaven, and human patronage which establishes the link with the external bureaucratic world of administration. Patronage makes God flexible and makes bureaucrat flexible.

In J. Cutileiro's study *A Portuguese Rural Society* (1971) the same substratum of patronage and of superstition remains present, and the church is similarly part of the world 'out there'. But here the ownership of the land is the key to prestige though even that is giving a way to professional certification and mobile skills. The stratification system is still tied to ownership of land, and whereas this was once ecclesiastical and aristocratic or communal it is now largely in the hands of latifundists who rose by skill in business. The last century inaugurated a rival régime which concentrated land in the hands of men who were not seen to be legitimate; and the collateral incidence of unemployment and of poor yields and pay has led to migration, either to the factories or abroad. This is the economic background and the latest stage is neatly summed up in a shift from a tradition of cheating employers, especially large ones, and waiting for the millenium, to leaving for work in industry.

Degrees of literacy correspond to degrees in society and administration works by the power of the word. The major radical role operating a contrary power of the word used to be that of schoolmaster. The cohesive force linking outer power and local community was patronage: advancement in return for respect and conformity. God the Father watches over baptism and the godparents over the child's future. Spiritual kinship supplements natural kinship. But it has been declining and (pre-1974) paternalism gave way to corporatism. Country-wide welfare provision and wider job opportunities have undermined paternalistic responsibilities and 'all idyllic patriarchal relations'. An impersonal framework leaves the labourer isolated, while private voluntary associations, like religious brotherhoods, become moribund. This in turn pushes people back on the search for friends and favours. The Church is part of this system of favours, alongside the professional men and latifundists. So too is the left.

The latifundists have a Marxist view of the Church i.e. that the poor need it. They go themselves, along with their wives, the wives of local officials, small shopkeepers, domestic personnel. But since they don't live in the fregnesia they can't impose the conformity on the labourers which they impose on domestic servants. Overall religious participation is small except at Christmas and Easter and then there are two levels: family supper and mass. The picnic should include a lamb, though the meaning of this is largely forgotten even when it can be afforded. The old religious plays of the past, which used to provide the principal entertainment, have declined with the advent of modern communications media. Baptism is the most important rite: children should not be allowed to 'remain Moors'. As to marriage a comparison of Republican periods and later ones suggests that most people adapt to whatever is officially approved, whether civil or religious. The church is largely for externals, for the ceremony rather than for the intimacies of life. The evidence is, as suggested earlier, that this situation is of very long standing, certainly long antedating the Revolution of 1910. The priests are administrators like other administrators, collect their rents as others collect rents and—maybe —they lie with women as other men do. Few people want to confess to a man whose worldly roles predominate over his spiritual ones. Yet anticlericalism of a cosmopolitan kind is rare and when it exists it persists alongside systematic appeals to the saints. Pious women despise the indifferent priest and so do landless labourers: he is a prisoner of the structure.

However if he moved outside the structure the negative reactions might be more overt. As it is the infrastructure of religion has to be carried by priestesses seeking the favours of the saints. Life is a matter of luck and and invocation of the saints: the One Above is too far away for immediate purposes. The women look after the black virgin or the holy cross; they bless and heal and are agents of the evil eye. Children must be protected against the evil eye by medallions, prayers, amulets. Women dress the dead, empty the spirit-laden earthenware jars of water in the house of the bereaved, and join in the priest's prayers—if he is called in.

The women are dangerous during menstruation, and there is an uncertain connection between the pollution involved in menstruation and jealousy. At the same time the advent of science and of more mobile, less dense, relationships, has attenuated at least some of the superstitious and pious practices. Basically religion is a set of personal bargains—like patronage—between individual believer and individual saint: society is neither seriously protected nor condemned.

Julian Pitt-Rivers in *The People of the Sierra* (1954) emphasizes the same infrastructural resistance as it operates in a southern village on the border. For each external, formal institution there is an informal equivalent, from bandits to women with 'arts'. Pitt-Rivers also stresses the historical background and differences in various regions of Spain. Once the Church was the largest landowner: there were common lands and no absentee landlords. Political powers were diffuse and multi-centred and the agents of administration were sons of the pueblo. But with the Liberal era church lands were confiscated, a new landowning class took over, religious legitimacy gave way to bureaucratic illegitimacy, and state appointees penetrated the community. When the church lost its properties it lost its organic connection with the values of the pueblo, and anti-clericalism moved from its cosmopolitan centres and intelligentsia to the local people. The Anarchists, many of them craftsmen, affirmed the values of local autonomy and personal morality and provided an atheistic analogue to Puritanism. Anarchism in the south, like Carlism in the north-west, was a local protest against state interference, the one looking forward to atheism, the other back to God and the Old Laws. The different politics followed the lines of different economics. In the south the rulers were absentee landlords and new rich who bought up church lands and were associated with the state and national upper class. When the church was deprived of its wealth it became dependent on this class and forfeited the allegiance of the pueblo. In the north however the good lands were divided into small holdings and no such new class emerged. Moral leadership resided in traditional local rulers: the clergy and a modest upper class. The result was Carlism, and when Carlism was crushed a movement for regional autonomy. However the relinquishment of regional autonomy by Carlist Aragon was followed by the emergence of anarchism: thus Carlism and anarchism acted as functional alternatives, the one a geographical division, the other a vertical and class division. In Andalusia the Federalist movement represented a transitional phase and as soon as agrarian anarchism became a threat the social carriers of Federalism i.e. the urban middle class, made peace with the state. And this in turn accelerated the progress of anarchism. The Church then became the visible focus of anarchist rebellion and violence; in the village the left killed priests, sacristans, members of the professional classes. The failure of anarchism led in two directions: the national syndicalism which grew up in the towns, and communism. Since the civil war all opposition in the area studied by Pitt-Rivers became communist.

This finally introduces another factor illustrated by J. Boissevain in his study of Maltese villages *Saints and Fireworks* (1965). He describes a situation where the church stands in for the state as guardian of all identity and culture against alien rule. Moreover, the cramped ecology of the islands prevents the formation of centre-periphery relationships. So conflicts occur *within* the Church. The Church is the authority which hands down decisions and against which the disappointed must rebel. It provides the corporate structure of almost all village associational life, the prestige of a village is coextenive with the prestige of its feast and each village competes with its neighbour. Competition and status tension within the village also take a religious form through the rivalry of the 'festa partiti' which commenced in the mid-nineteenth century. The origins of these are instructive because they foreshadowed the clash of the Church with the Maltese Labour Party. The supporters of the feast of the titular saint are in general of higher status than the supporters of the 'rival' saint. Anticlericalism is expressed in relation to the non-establishment festa. The competing celebrations, and competing brass bands, arose in conditions of economic prosperity in Malta, when voluntary associations expanded and when schools (and schoolmasters) made their appearance. Many feasts were dedicated to St. Joseph, patron saint of workers. They thus laid a slip-way for the subsequent conflict between the Church and the Malta Labour Party, in which professional white collar workers and farmers largely supported the Church against industrial workers. The Church by its intransigence increased the class alignment of political divisions. But whereas 'festa partiti' are localized and formalized disputes with acknowledged peace makers, the church–state conflict was continuous and appealed to no agreed arbiters. What that dispute also did was to provide an understood role for those who rejected the church, few though these were, and to modify the traditional system of patronage in the direction of the professional politicians, except that they were in any case largely drawn from the older patrons in the professional classes. Plus ça change.

Boissevain in his original *Saints and Fireworks* and in subsequent reworkings of his broad thesis has provided a framework which has been extended in a more directly sociological manner by M. Vassallo.[14] Vassallo has set the case of Malta within the available frames of secularization theory. It will be appropriate and useful therefore to conclude this section with his formulations since in these matters all the regions of the northern Mediterranean basin are as one, whether or not they have exemplified 'reactive organicism'. What happens now in Malta, a society rooted in localized ritual bonds, is in the course of becoming true for the islands and mountains of Greece, for isolated Bragança in northern Portugal, and for the remote villages of the Sierra.

As Vassallo points out, language (Maltese, and Italian in the 20's and 30's) and religion have provided distinctive rallying points of Maltese identity in its role of convent-fortress. Religion was the bond of each tight knit community, and this was imaged in the huge rival churches dominating every village. But the second decade after the ending of the war brought further education and the beginnings of indigenous industrial development: factories supplemented by tourism. Learning, work and play were together the agents of secularity. New work patterns meant new roles and attitudes for women as well as for men. Thus, as S. O. Mizzi has illustrated, a system of dowry, restricted contact and family choice gave way to free mixing and to choice based on personal experiment; and from 1961 on the number of children began to drop, more especially where television was established, and where the husband had access to higher education.[15] A key role belongs therefore to 'communications of all kinds', to the fresh use of time and to the perception of new possibilities.

The new processes meant a loosening of the grip of village on the individual and a loosening of personal dependency, even though patronage remains strong within the organizations and parties created by industrialization. Malta is yet another instance of the universality of patronage in the Mediterranean and of how the left advances as an alternative system of patronage not as an ideology. Developments move now at the macro-level of the society as a whole. Even the festas perhaps acquired something of a conscious character and a further role as tourist attractions. The impact of differentiation can be traced in the sphere of overall legitimations, and in all branches of education: the church ceased to be sole purveyor of knowledge. At the same time welfare tended to develop within the church itself, since when the church is all-encompassing the process of differentiation initially takes place inside the church rather than outside it. And of course there were movements within the Church itself, not only the impact of the Ecumenical Council, but the Cana Movement (concerned with the family's new role) and the Social Action Movement. Some scholars claim a very important role for the Council: Roma locuta, causa finita.

As elsewhere education created a new élite, simultaneously hungry for power and inclined to the various modes of withdrawal or nostalgia or utopianism traditionally characteristic of the European intelligentsia. Daniel Massa (1976) has nicely described the secularizing trends in the new élite, more especially as it developed outside the nexus of traditional 'professionals' which had dominated Malta for some two centuries. The older literature of epic and historic celebration or unified affirmation gave way to uncertainty and variety. The usual attacks were made on national sentiment, the 'establishment' and established mores, the idea of eternal and changeless law. Intellectuals explored various syndromes of romantic and subjective isolation, retreat from society, role-rejection, gestures towards relevance. Yet there remains a paradox: the aspiration towards a free genuine individual perfectly conjoined to his fellows, and towards a free, independent community perfectly conjoined to the community of mankind is highly religious in character. It is as if the Ninth Symphony should be reality and not art. The foral community and the Roman oekumene become potent anticipations continuous with the utopian future. As a Maltese poem puts it with Marxist overtone and unintentional irony 'I have dreamt of the ending of dreams'. These dreams are inherent in reactive organicism, even though embedded in hierarchical forms and historical nostalgias. They provide part of the radical thrust within the reaction of the right and give it continuity with radical aspirations to community without hierarchy, and to oekumene without dependence or spiritual colonization. The local communitas and Rome are genuine anticipations.

The three oligarchic and—until recently (1974)—conservative cultures just discussed have characteristics which enable one to emphasize points of key importance. The first two points are about history. The rhetoric of Spanish nationalism is in terms of historic destiny and identity; the rhetoric of Greek face to face with Greek is in terms of an appeal to ancient practices and rights, including the practices of Byzantium. And just as the language of such cultures refers back to the past and mystical doctrines of the meaning of the past, so too the historic frontiers of the past underlie the patterns of contemporary religiosity, above all the age-old frontier with Islam. The strong religiosity of Cyprus (and indeed of Malta) is nourished by the existence of that frontier. The third point concerns the range of meaning behind the term secular in that it may denote assimilation to established power, an overtly materialist doctrine, hedonistic indifference, religious propaganda based on psychic utility, or manipulative, proto-scientific practices designed to conjure responses from nature. Such a range of definition allows one to see how beneath the apparently identical outward garment of religion, modern and ancient, there may be highly secular substrata, depending of course on the definition one chooses to employ. The Greek case is particularly dramatic insofar as the Greek Church, seemingly devoted to Orthodox spirituality, became quite soon after the achievement of independence, closely identified with Hellenism, in many respects a secular doctrine and certainly one at odds with its own deposit of faith. Of course, the face of 'secular' will vary with the religion under review. When the religion is Christian, then there arises a contrast between a faith in 'signs' relating to God's Kingdom and magical manipulations for one's own benefit, so that faith in 'signs' is 'religious' and magicality 'secular'. Similarly for a religion whose fundamental deposit of faith puts secular authority under divine judgement, separates the community of faith from the ethnic or local community and reverses the status order in favour of the 'offscourings of the earth' most of the data presented above constitute secularization. They do so because religion becomes almost isomorphic with social structure, local identity and secular moral and status evaluations. It is precisely this secularization, whereby the institutionalization of faith accelerates its assimilation to the world as given, which sparks off—in certain circumstances—the rejection of institutional Christianity *in se* and all its structures of authority. It is therefore arguable that 'progressive' forms of Christianity in (say) Spain are more religious than the ancient faith of that country.[16] Indeed, there is one further point of interest here: in Spain and in Greece, and for that matter Tsarist Russia, there existed and exists today a local level of equality, communal sensitivity and democracy, which stretches back, like the foral traditions of the Basques, to medieval times and earlier. These very old traditions of communalism link with some of the progressive sectors of the church, but since such traditions occur within very hierarchical overall structures, the underlying impulse finds its modern realization in 'communautes de base', reclaiming derelict areas and setting up self-selected groups of radical dissenters. In so far as such groups are explicitly political, they can be labelled as 'secularized' but they are hardly more political than was the Baroque church and their relation to the foundation documents of Christianity is arguably closer. We have the paradoxes of secularization always with us. What more materialistic, in one sense, than agricultural magic, and what more materialistic, in another sense, than the total collusion of the church with the imperatives of power?

NOTES

1. Cf. for example the para-Christian influence of the minor German philosophical current associated with Karl Krause. Carr 1966, gives an account of this, and underlines the mixture of Protestant Ethic motifs and subjective mysticism. What one finds especially interesting is the way the innovators reflect the structure and mode of traditionalism. As Carr puts it, 'The danger of Krausism lay precisely in that it was a quasi-religious movement with professors as its priests.' (p. 303).

2. Duocastella 1973b. On the period of 'personal religion' in the 1950s, cf. Orensanz 1974b. The *Cursillos de cristiandad* represented

a version of the Wesleyan class meeting plus various social-psychological techniques. It is as if Spain passes through hints of Protestantism very rapidly, as it were en passant, as it shifts between traditionalism and radicalism. Protestantism is implicit in aspects of Opus Dei, Krausism, and the *Cursillos* but never achieves full expression on classic Reformation lines. There are further references to the Cursillos and to Catholic Action in Orensanz 1974a.

3. Duocastella 1973b. For a survey indicating the degree of recent radicalization among the clergy, cf. Cazorla 1975. This showed that over one third of the priests surveyed were socialistic in approach. On a comparative note, one has the feeling that the tension which gradually developed in Fascist Italy between Church and State after the Concordat could have developed further along the lines now evident in Spain.

4. According to a report in *The Times*, 3 January 1974. Cf. various works which comment on the relation of politics and religion in Spain: Tusell 1975; Linz 1970; and Giner 1971. Giner discusses such matters as the unrest among higher-paid workers and students, as well as the clergy (p. 149). Giner describes the Church as implicated in the political system and ruling élite up to 1951, and definitely split after 1968, more particularly along generational lines, between *conciliares* and *integristas*. He stresses the skill of Opus Dei in blending *integrismo* and *desarrollismo*. J. J. Linz provides an interesting analysis of the Spanish cabinet from 1938 to 1962 (p. 276). His reference to the acquiescent attitudes of technical élites fits in with the passive attitudes of such élites in many social contexts, left, right or liberal. Technological Universities are a good investment against radicalism. For a comparison of Spain and Holland, cf. Alfonsi and Pesnot 1973.

5. Orensanz 1974b, p. 53. "El movimiento jocista trata de aprehender la realidad del mundo obrero en su interna conformación 'sin' mediatizacíones estructurales'.

6. Lison-Tolosano 1966. Pages 112–115 are worth quoting at length. 'These women organize the charity campaigns, the tombola during the festivals, represent the town at regional catholic meetings, look after the cleaning and decoration of altars, and directly second the projects initiated by the ecclesiastical hierachy. They go to church every day, and always occupy their favourite seats; they may bring in a priest from outside to administer first communion solely to their own children, or invite several priests to solemnize a baptism or a wedding. Their funerals and anniversary services are of the most solemn possible; in the former the priest accompanies the funeral procession right to the cemetry. In general a first-class funeral is the mark not only of the pious élite but of the economic power of the family, for it is another of the social forms that go with a definite style of living, and one with a history of over 400 years as we have seen. Finally, it is interesting to note that the religious élite feel a certain responsibility and obligation towards the needy, being time and

again splendidly generous in their donations. In consequence they provide the poor to some extent with a share of the communal wealth and through this personal contact reduce the social distance separating the two extremes of the hierarchy.

The religious conduct, attitudes and observances of the socially inferior groups indicate the reverse. They have a specific conception of religion on which I shall comment later; for the present I shall confine myself to the connexion between stratum and religion. Many of them observe only the rites of baptism, first communion, marriage, the last sacraments, and church burial. If there are missions in the parish they may attend one or other of the meetings. These people almost make up the number of those who do not observe Easter, though some may attend mass on Easter Day, New Year's Day, and the feast of the Immaculate Conception. Their participation in the religious life of the community during the rest of the year is nil, because even if they are not at work on Sundays they do not go to mass. They do not, however, directly impede the religious practices of their children if they wish to perform them and it appears that they prefer their children to have religious beliefs.

The anti-religious attitudes of these minor sections of the community take two different forms, one ideological and the other comparative. They affirm that they 'do not go to mass because the priests are those who are in command but do not practice what they preach'. They continue with the well-worn themes: 'nobody has come from hell. If they (who practise) are so afraid, why aren't they better than they are?' This direct allusion to those at the highest levels—'they'—lays a finger on the wound. 'The rich go to mass but they exploit the workers'. They cite examples in which they have been passive protagonists: once they worked over the agreed hours for a land-owner, 'one of those who go to mass of Sundays', and he refused to pay them for the extra work. On another occasion, at the end of the war, when there was a bread shortage, a pudiente, notorious for his religiosity, deducted from wages the price of the bread he had supplied for them to eat. Employers have on occasion sent their men to work on a Sunday without worrying whether or not they had time to go to mass, etc.

In this way they identify superior status with religion; from the antagonism of interests it is very easy to slip into the antagonism of ideas, so easy that many in trying to explain the essential differences between the two political groups during the civil war told me 'some attacked the church and others defended it'. To these informants the political ideology was secondary, or rather confusel with the religious. If political party and religious practice are identified with the economically powerful strata, the antagonistic, economically weak strata will be likely to reject not only the political ideas of the former but their religious attitudes too. More briefly, membership of a given social group will influence the attitude towards religion, whether positive or negative, of those included in it. As we have seen, attendance at Sunday mass may for some be a function of their way of life, rather than a result of religious conviction. Similarly in the groups less well endowed economically some people do not practise religion because it is not the custom among them: as they say 'they know what behoves them', and it behoves them, obviously, not to go to church.

Political power is harmoniously linked with certain religious practices. The mayor and corporation occupy the pews of honour in the church at high masses and to them the preacher addresses the first greeting of the sermon. Processions end with the Council accompanying the clergy. This harmony of powers shows itself also in the invitation to the parish priest to attend certain meetings of the Council. We have already seen that the Council was invited to the meeting which decided upon the creation of a parochial centre. This subject, rich in historical data, will be considered separately.

Finally, do religious practices contribute to the raising of the social status of those who practise them? The correlation between religion and standing is evident, but is the practice of religion a facet of the style of living or a new contribution which brings with it the increase of social status? More concretely, if two pudientes have the closest possible affinity in economic 'situation', but one is more devout than the other, will the devout one gain greater social status? In this case religion is neutral. Indeed the inverse might be thought to apply to men because the most pious are sometimes the object of irony. Indirectly it could help to adorn personal status since if a *pudiente*, for example, did not practise like the rest and attacked religion in earnest this would be violently out of keeping with his style of living and in present circumstances would injure his personal prestige. Some of the *propietarios* may serve as an indication in this respect: they never practise for personal reasons, nor do they attack religious principles, and neither their social status nor their personal prestige has suffered on this account.

7. Duocastella 1967. Duocastella also has extensive analyses area by area, as for example, Catalonia.

8. Duocastella 1967 has been extensively drawn upon for all the above information.

9. The data cited above are located in Querido 1972. Cf. Cutileiro 1971. There is further background in H. Martins, in Giner and Archer 1971. I am most indebted to Dr Cutileiro for a paper given at L.S.E. and originally read in Rome, May, 1976.

10. I rely here on reports from *The Times*; on Hastings 1975; and Monteiro 1975. It seems likely that the strength of northern Catholicism did, in the end, contribute to the relaxation and (perhaps) the end of communist hegemony in the summer of 1975. The situation also shifted further and more crucially in a non-communist direction in November 1975.

11. For the history, cf. Campbell and Sherrard 1968, Chapter 6.

12. Cf. Campbell 1964, which gives an excellent account of con-

cepts of honour and the role of religion in a mountainous area of Greece.

13. Cf. 'Greek Report', April, 1969, *Shadow over the Greek Church*, which discusses the role of *Zoe* (or Zoi). I rely partly on information provided by Dr N. Kokosalakis. There has been material from time to time in the Eastern Churches Quarterly, and a special issue dedicated to Greece in *Social Compass*, xxii, No. 1, 1975. This issue contains a short history of Zoe, including its divisions, and an article by A. Goussidis on the Greek priesthood. The sociographic account of the priesthood shows it to be drawn more particularly from isolated island and mountain areas, where is exercises a clear and broad leadership role and provides a channel of mobility. The recruitment of priests declines with increasing size of town and is negatively associated with education. (It is perhaps of interest that Greece is the most 'believing' of European nations, more especially with respect to the existence of the Devil. Few countries rival Greek deference to the existence of the Devil, though Americans are much seized of his diabolic reality and have shown marked increases in their belief over the past decade.)

14. Vassallo, 1976 and 1974. Vassallo argues that Boissevain's analysis applies largely to the villages.

15. Mizzi 1976. Women exercise considerable power in their traditional roles. There is an interesting comparison with Sardinia where industrialization has actually weakened the power of the matriarchate. For the religious aspects of this cf. Matthias 1976, and *The Times* 'Sardinia', June 28, 1976. Mrs Matthias argues that ecological necessity dictates a division of labour whereby men are engaged pastorally and women agriculturally. This induces both mutual dependency and a general segregation of roles. The rituals surrounding death are one important instance of this more especially the singing of the *attitu*. The twenty hour wake becomes the collective representation of female unity and a mainspring of tradition and of information. The female chorus plays Greek chorus to the familial tragedy, and honour, and continues the community tradition.

16. Cf. Norman Cooper's account of contemporary Spanish Catholicism in Preston 1976.

K

VII

Crisis amongst the Professional Guardians
of the Sacred

This chapter is concerned to describe the development of the clergyman according to a process of social differentiation and to rotate its elements in that process with respect to the varied categories outlined in my argument.

Christianity is itself an aspect of social differentiation in that it distinguishes an earthly kingdom from a heavenly kingdom, and by extension distinguishes Church from State.[1] This differentiation is always maintained at the symbolic level, and usually at the organizational level. However, Christianity encounters a vigorous Durkheimian pull towards a total unity of Church and State, and even when that unity has been broken, there remains a pull towards collusion between fundamental social and religious values.

The tension and collusion between Christianity and Society passes through various phases. Phase one consists of the collusion of Church and State, which still persists today as a collusion over fundamental values.[2] These values are only partially Christian since they comprise layers of superstition, the validation of local social continuities, and limited reciprocities at odds with the universality of Christianity. The integration of religion and society characteristic of this phase is based not so much on regular attendance at church or communion, both of which may be very infrequent, or on strict adherence to Christian precept, as on an acceptance of Church and clergyman as ontologically part of the social order.[3] Even in the contemporary period, when attitudes towards the institutional church have become largely passive and when the process of further differentiation has generally separated church from state, this persists in that the presence of the clergy at times of communal or personal mourning and rejoicing, e.g. birth, death and marriage, is taken for granted.[4]

In phase two, however, Christianity and its professional guardians are partly winkled out of the structure of legitimation and become more marginal to local and national élites.[5] The clergy either presides over an explicitly voluntary association and its leisure activities or over an implicitly voluntary association within what appears to remain an established church. If clergy are in a Catholic society they often experience an intermediate stage when they are integral to one *half* of an organic society confronted by an openly secularist opposing half. Initially the voluntaristic associations of phase two may expand church activities, particularly in the sphere of education and welfare (cf. Heasman 1962), but gradually various sectors are removed from religious aegis, and differentiated, leaving the Christian community as one leisure association among others.[6] With such increasing differentiation the sectors which are removed become 'secularized' while the church and its clergy become more religious. The pragmatic secularity and multiple secular roles of clergy under phase one disappear (magistracy for example) and there is an emphasis on the specifically religious aspects of the clerical role. This takes two forms: a sanctification of the church, of clerical orders, of ritual technique, or a sanctification of individual persons. Both forms stress the importance of a specifically theological training. Furthermore, the bureaucratization of the increasingly differentiated ecclesiastical institution results in specialized agencies, at local and at national levels, some of which acquire a utilitarian approach at odds with the 'sacred'.[7]

In phase three the voluntary associations of Christians, segmented and partial in their influence and often concentrating at particular status levels, become attenuated, along with most other associational aspects of social life.[8] The increased religious component in the clerical role, whether it be ritual technique, or psychic expertise in the domain of the soul, seems less relevant in view of a diminished *active* constituency.[9] At the same time the secular responses of phase two, the social gospel evolving from individualistic evangelicism and the semi-socialistic medieval organicism of the ritualists, both appear unsuccessful in terms of their own hopes and aspirations.[10] Three responses are possible, each interconnected. First, the committed Christian can leap out

of the boundaries of the specific denomination, out of ecclesiastical
language and buildings, and out of the clerical role, to confront
social structures and people globally. So doing he may reject all
social structuring, and translate Christian concepts into secular
equivalents: communion-community, sin-alienation, holiness-
wholeness. This is characteristic of the progressive upper middle
class and the higher specialized agencies. Or, alternatively, he
may re-create a close, all-in, face-to-face group on the model of
the New Testament, translating secular concepts like healing and
power *back* into spiritual terms. The charismatic invocation of the
Holy Spirit parallels the emphasis on existential spontaneity found
among 'secular' clergy, eliminating denominational boundaries,
blurring role structures, absorbing traditional norms under the
general rubric of the 'spirit', and transcending specific concepts
and language. This is more characteristic of local and provincial
congregations.[11] Between these two possibilities lies the *social work*
alternative, concentrating on limited social criticism and re-
creating the clerical role on the model of a therapist within the
encounter group. All these developments parallel changes in the
university: first the differentiation from élite culture, followed by
a bifurcation into specific technicality (ritual technique) or cultivation (the soul), which then breaks down under the pressures of
bureaucratization and massification into either a complete confrontation with the world and the elimination of any boundary
between university and society, or into an intense, internal life,
anarchic and spontaneous, similarly devoted to eliminating all
boundaries based on organizational structures, roles and languages.[12]

This much by way of summary. I now want to develop the scheme
just outlined and to describe the different elements as they need to
be rotated for the different categories.

The differentiation written into Christianity itself, and a fortiori
into the role of Christian clergy, is irreducible, but it constantly
encounters the centripetal power of society, either converting the
body of the church into the body of citizens without remainder,
or making Christianity merely the vehicle of local continuities,
reciprocities and values. In less 'developed' societies this centripetal power expresses itself in attempts to unite church and state;

in more developed societies it expresses itself in a marked tendency to make religious and social values one and the same. Thus the pressure against Christian differentiation may occur in varied types of society: in the Ethiopian empire, in medieval Norway, in Joseph the II's Austria, Peter the Great's Russia, Hitler's Germany.[13] And when the differentiation is well established with regard to church and state as in the U.S.A. the pressure is renewed in the realms of values. Indeed, where the differentiation is most great organizationally, as in parts of Eastern Europe, the pressure towards unity in the sphere of values—and onto-logy— may reach the point where Christianity has to be eliminated.

In what follows various categories or phases are distinguished related to the degree of social differentiation in society. It is perhaps important to stress that these 'phases' are not a set of evolutionary stages through which a society or Christianity *must* pass. They are heuristic devices: phase one can persist alongside phases two and three, phase two can revert to phase one, though on the balance the phenomena of this phase or that phase vary very loosely, with the degree of social differentiation.

The first category, or phase, must be delineated both in its classic form, signalized by the collusion of church and state, and in its mutated form, characterized by a collusion over basic values. The classic form was dictated by the fact that Constantine made Christianity the official religion, and the spread of Christianity thereafter was often through its acceptance by a king or emperor. From the fourth century to the eighteenth certain elements characterized the situation of religion and therefore of religious professionals. These elements did *not* involve universal obedience to religious precepts or universal attendance at divine service, though there are examples of the latter at different times and in different places. They did involve an almost ontological assump-tion of membership whereby the ecclesiastical organization de-fined the limits of society, with the clerk defined as ontologically necessary to that society. He was integral to it, and his legitimating function indispensable even when supplemented by other legiti-mations. The parson (or 'person') might be corrupt, hated, des-pised or even physically an absentee, but he was not, conceptually, a dispensable adjunct of the social order. So there *could be* no social orders without holy orders: the clerk was locked in to the

social order at each level from local parish to the whole community, and neither local élite nor the wider élite questioned his
place, even though they might question his power and/or his
interpretation of the clerical function. In pragmatic terms the
priest might be almost wholly absorbed in secular functions, e.g.
administration, or in secular extensions of his religious functions.
In short, his secularization was practical, and in that respect it
could be, and often was, nearly total. Perhaps the most dramatic
instance of secularization in this sense is the case in which a bishop
or cleric was also a warrior.

The mutated form of this situation found in the contemporary
world is interesting. Very broad, semi-consensual orientations
continue to exist in whole populations, and these *do not* differ in
certain basic respects from those existing in the situation just
described. I mean that there remains an extensive formal acceptance of the title 'Christian' allied to a feeling that church and
parson are an accepted part of the social scene. There exists, as
there did in previous periods, a very partial absorption of Christian norms and a very tenuous understanding of the symbols
which carry those norms. This point is a very complex and de-
batable one, but I am trying to underline an ignorance, only
intermittently interrupted, in every kind of social order, an
acceptance of 'natural', localized reciprocities and loyalties, only
partially ameliorated by wider Christian perspectives, a pool of
non-natural orientations never eliminated at the level of everyday
praxis by such scientifically efficient knowledge as might exist.[14]
This semi-coherent but extremely widespread set of orientations
includes the church and the clerk, as equally 'natural', and as
taken for granted. He is the most visible and tangible, though not
necessarily the most crucial, sign of its existence. When he performs the rites of passage, which belong to these reciprocities,
non-natural beliefs and unarticulated continuities, he becomes
their tangible and necessary representative. When the community
is visited by overwhelming threat, or facing either disaster or
triumph, he is a natural vehicle which *must* be included in the
complete response. At the birth of a child, in a moment of disaster,
whether personal or communal, in times requiring the evocation
of a collective memory or mourning or celebration he is 'taken for
granted' as an appropriate part of the response, perhaps even its
principal focus. The annual meeting of the British Legion is one

occasion which illustrates the situation. You *need* a bishop to preside on such an occasion, and the broader the social involvement implicated in such an occasion the more necessary he becomes. At the death of Kennedy, Pompidou, General de Gaulle, the solemn mass is an essential element.

For very many clergy this combination of folk religion and civic piety still provides a full-time and completely satisfactory role. This is particularly so when it involves multiple chaplaincies: to hospitals, to the military, to the local mayor, or to a particular professional organization (e.g. seamen) or an institution. The role is supported by almost universal popular approval, and it is significant that uncertainty over the role often begins within its clerical incumbent. In the modern situation the cleric is subjected to a more specifically religious and more directly Christian socialization than in the past. This leads him to be dissatisfied with ritual performance as the main criterion of his Christian duty, especially where this is defined as ancillary rather than central to whatever activity may be involved, e.g. fighting or being ill. Furthermore, he may come from, or be in contact with, those sectors of the progressive middle class and of the educational system which stress authenticity at the expense of role performance and this clouds his internal commitment to civic ritual. Alternatively, he may be in contact with that very large sector of the working class which defines civic ritual and rites de passage as the *sole* components in his role, thereby leaving his aspiration towards more 'genuine' Christianity without an outlet.

So far as the 'progressive' middle class itself is concerned there is a double problem: they prefer authenticity to ritual, but recognize that the consequence of authenticity is banality. The traditional language and defined role of the cleric at least exclude the banality, unless the cleric himself succumbs to explicit, open, personal expression in the approved extempore manner. Those who celebrate or mourn desire the 'fitness' of the language, but do not know what to do with its manifest content, whereas the cleric himself grows uncertain about conforming to the criterion of 'fitness'. These points will be developed below, because the increased component of 'religion' in the clerical role is associated with the second category now to be analysed, while the desire for open, authentic confrontation with the world belongs to the third category. Within that third category it will be useful to compare the parallel developments affecting both student and cleric, university and church.

The second category is based on an accentuation of the specifically religious element in the clerical role. This accompanies increased social differentiation and involves a curve of involvement in leisure and welfare activity, which initially expands and then contracts. It does so because the new situation first implies fresh functions and then progressively reduces them down to the crisis point which marks the boundary with the third category.

Increased social differentiation involves several possible developments realized in varying degree according to complex socio-historical circumstance. Free Churches are differentiated from society as a whole and often related to relatively localized sectors of a differentiated social system. The clergyman becomes the nub, less of a local 'natural' community, than of a self-selected group, even though this voluntarism can easily evolve back again into forms of natural local community in which self-selection is pretty nominal. Indeed, to the extent that the free church or voluntaristic concept becomes widely disseminated in a given area, or dominant, two things tend to happen. There is a partial exclusion of explicit and especially particularized religious attachments at the level of the state and maybe also of the education system, while the voluntary associations themselves tend to take on Durkheimian roles, i.e. their ministers speak for the local community as a whole and represent it. The Durham mining villages described by Robert Moore exemplify precisely this development from association to community.

Wales provides an obvious example of a dissent so widespread as to constitute a new establishment, and the U.S.A. exemplifies a *formal* exclusion of religion from state and education which masks both heavy identification with religion-in-general at the subjective level, and heavy religious socialization outside the presumed neutrality of the school system. Indeed, in the extreme instances religious socialization in the family is supported by religious secondary socialization in a network of higher educational and even medical institutions internally divided according to denomination. However, this extreme development is generally avoided, and the voluntaristic principle is restricted to networks of leisure institutions built up on denominational lines. Paradoxically, where the voluntaristic principal is *less* widespread, as in England, the formal dissociation of religion and education does not occur, and this then allows a partial absorption of all educational institutions, except some élite ones, along lines of denominational loyalty. This lasts until the state reintegrates the educational system under its own wing.

Now, clearly the voluntaristic principle is not universally established: it is most developed in the U.S.A., and strongly developed in Britain and in cultures of British origin. Thus clergy with second category features abound most in American and British contexts. But the voluntary principle also corrodes important sectors of the older system internally, by making inclusive churches, like the Church of Sweden or the German Lutheran Church, into de facto voluntary associations. This even happens in Catholic countries, but at a very late stage in the differentiation process, which occurs after an initial gestation period largely absent in Protestant cultures. In those Catholic countries where social development occurs relatively early, there appears, not free churches, but an almost complete secular sector in opposition to an almost complete and organic Catholic sector, both of which fight for *total* control of the socialization and educational process and of the central organs of state. The clergy are shock troops in this battle.[15] Only in those instances where the secularists secure overall command does the tension eventually subside leaving the church as a voluntary association possessed of strong educational bastions on the condition they are not used to advance Catholic 'integriste' ideas. Where the Catholic Church wins there is an initial complete re-clericalization of education, which only gradually succumbs to the processes whereby the church grows closer to the voluntary associational model and the state takes over a formal responsibility for education which is distinct from specifically clerical concerns and powers. These points about Catholicism are important since a French situation, rooted in a Catholic dominance explicitly reduced by secularists, creates different crises in the clergy to a Spanish situation where—so far at least—reclericalization gradually succumbs to progressive increments of voluntarism and associational organization.[16] In communist societies, of course, it is normal for clerical education to be replaced by the compulsory reduction of *all* religious bodies to the formal and sometimes the actual status of voluntary bodies, and these moreover of a very restricted kind.

What are the more characteristic roles of clergy within the second category, and their more usual problems? Clearly, there are very large sectors of modern society where the voluntary principle is implicitly or explicitly operative. The Church of England, still partially inclusive in the nineteenth century, can provide examples of the process of accelerating voluntarism and its social concomitants, including internal differentiation. In this it provides richer material than the inclusive Protestant churches of the continent which remained more monolithic and retained more functions initially, before collapsing into *de facto* voluntarism. Perhaps this is a weaker echo of the Catholic situation: initial blockage, followed by a slide into voluntarism. Let us examine the English case.

The early attempts of the Church of England to retain its monopoly, either practically in the Act of Uniformity, or theoretically in the line of thinkers from Hooker to Coleridge and Gladstone gradually collapsed. It accepted large sectors of voluntarism outside certain key positions in the upper élite system (Parliament, the judiciary, the ancient universities) and then accepted strong elements of voluntarism and pluralism inside itself. One should pause here to distinguish voluntarism and pluralism: Anglo-Saxon cultures exemplified both, whereas the Protestant and Catholic state churches on the continent eventually moved towards voluntarism without any substantial element of pluralims, outside that is the dichotomy brought about by clericals versus organized anti-clericals. In short, the very limited pluralism of Catholic countries was rooted in straight division of clericals and anti-clericals, and this is a situation which for a period hardened the role definitions of Catholic clergy in a way which still trails some consequences for them today. Protestant functionaries have never had to face the role problem and role *consolidation* resulting from violent ideological opposition nor have they had to face the accelerating difficulty of self-understanding which arises when the Church mutes this opposition for its own part, and confronts apathy rather than hatred.

The Church of England became differentiated internally and externally: dividing into parties within, and gaining some degree of self-government, which limited the outside interference deriving from the state connection. What happened during this process is in the highest degree instructive and not only applies to the whole category of voluntarism under discussion, but also sets the scene within which the third category can be understood. The various elements in the English situation can easily be rotated to comprehend developments in other cultures and I will myself suggest preliminary rotations necessary for the continuum of which the English example is obviously a part, i.e. situations where there is no inclusive state church (America); where there is a semi-inclusive state church (England); and where there is a totally inclusive state church (Scandinavia and parts of Germany).

Let us begin by developing the formal elements of external and internal differentiation just referred to. As external control loosened leaving church-state integration largely at the level of symbolism, the church developed its *own* bureaucracy and specific requirements of professional socialization. Previously it simply shared the socialization of the élite in the classics, or if not in the classics, at least in gentlemanly manners, and then it developed a role-specification stressing the specifically religious element. As the clergy were partly separated off from the pragmatic secularity of their role in the local and national élite, so they developed a pattern stressing the differentia specifica of priesthood and the special technicalities inhering in priesthood or in ministry. With regard to matters *within* the clerical sphere there was a decrease in secularity matching the increase in secularity in all those sectors gradually being detached from the church: secular administration, legitimation as such, medical care, and so on. Thus the sacredness of Sunday, of the church, of the priest himself, were all emphasized, and a specifically theological education devised to ensure adequate attention to the *specifically* ecclesiastical elements in the clerical style of living. (Too many schemata having taken this accentuated religiosity as the base line for inferring tendencies to secularization).

This articulation of the enlarged religious component in the clerical role also gave rise to variant conceptions of that role, i.e. articulation and differentiation. Those adhering to the older conceptions now formed one *party* alongside other parties stressing either ecclesiastical autonomy and ritual technique (the Anglo-Catholics) or a specific charter to supervise the personal religious lives of the converted and charge the batteries of the individual soul (the evangelicals).

At the local level, there might or might not be a partial

severance from the integral links with local élites, depending on the nature of the social context, but the role of the clergyman increasingly became that of coordinator of a particular kind of voluntary community. He supervised leisure and welfare within that community, and some of the charity and welfare outside it. He became more an active supervisor of an association and less an integral and 'passive' participant in an organic community. A. J. Russell has described the immense proliferation of activities, partly concerned with leisure, but also concerned with local organization in general, in which the parson became engaged, and also how the rising technical requirements of specific church activities downgraded the involvement of all the local population (Russell 1970). Within the church the expert control of the parson increased; outside the church the parson's participation in a system of control diminished to the mere exercise of influence, which in turn eventually affected only a sector of the population.

The latter development belongs to a later stage in the process whereby the established church and its priesthood increasingly approximated the voluntary associational model of Protestant dissent. Eventually the parish churches and chapels grew closer to each other and to a common model of associational life *actively* affecting only a specific sector of the community, internally differentiated according to a bureaucratic paradigm of functions allocated in accordance with specified expertise, and then in time progressively devoted to one specific sector of social existence: leisure. Thus there had been a series of proliferating differentiations each occurring across and within each other, church from state, church from local community, parson from élite—national and local, specifically clerical education from general education, and party from party within the church according to different views of what that specific clerical education should be. Then the local church had approximated specifically leisure functions in relation to the world outside and actively catered only for a specific social sector, while within the local church itself roles had been allocated according to specific expertise. Society without experienced a successive loosening of institutional religious attachments sector by sector, beginning with science and industry and gradually moving towards the most sensitive redoubts of social sacredness: civil ritual, law and education.[17]

As the local church differentiated so the structure of the Church as a whole gave birth to specialist agencies organized on a national basis and attracting clergy away from such diffuse local involvements as existed into specialist enclaves: industrial mission, missions to seamen, railwaymen, etc. on the lower levels, and agencies for social responsibility, public relations, communication, and so on at the higher levels. This latter type of development gradually extended further into international bureaucracies employing the ecclesiastical equivalents of entrepreneurs in multinational companies, e.g. W.C.C. officials.[18] The central and international officials grew steadily divorced from local constituencies, while in the localities themselves larger-scale groupings evolved in which 'area teams' of clergymen collaborated less on a basis of common cloth than complementary expertise.

Now, it is necessary to supplement the above model of the second category with an account of certain processes of social conflict and mobility operating with a clothing of religious difference and language. Let us return to the old élite, containing as it did an accepted and integrated clerical segment. This élite easily succumbed to stoic and classical concepts of virtue and enlightenment views of the world and whether these attitudes built up against the church or simply corroded the Christianity of the clergy from inside (or both) depended very much on historical context. In eighteenth century England, Sweden and Poland there was an internal corrosion but for various reasons no explosion against the church; in France there was both a process of corrosion and an explosion. In England in particular we must enquire what happened after (a) the partial differentiation of church from social élite, (b) the differentiation of voluntary bodies according to specific social sectors, and (c) the growth of parties inside the church.

The increasingly religious sectors of the church itself, emphasizing their clerical role, either as ritualists or evangelicals, clashed with the indifferentism of the élite, as did also the religious intensity generated in the voluntary associations outside the established church. Within the established church the more enthusiastic and lower class evangelicals could frequently be kept in the lower echelons or else encouraged to become ecclesiastical migrants to the mission fields.[19] Outside the established church the vigorous individual piety of dissenters was confronted by a division of society not in terms of class warfare but in terms of the religious styles of different statuses. The eventual compromise involved a partial evangelicalization of a sector of the élite and a hypocritical acquiescence in other sectors, balanced by an amelioration of evangelical intensity with each penetration further and higher into the old élite areas of society. Education provided the ground on which the old élite and new arrivals worked out a common, genteel acceptance of a semi-christianized stoicism, and this was often supervised by clergy. At lower levels the compromise derived from a double source: the educational motivation, ability and background of religious dissenters gave them differential social mobility and therefore differential access to humanistic culture, which in turn ameliorated their religious intensity and smoothed out their style in a manner more in conformity with élitist concepts. So far as Anglo-Catholic tendencies were concerned they became associated with a fairly radical penetration of working class culture which altered the image of the priest favourably without attracting large-scale working class adherents; and they were also associated with a revival of national folk culture, including dancing, carols and customs.

Obviously all these varied developments produced a very varied social and role profile amongst the clergy; the devoted seeker after souls or radical priest in the slums, the local parson tending his regular flock, the church administrator, the international ecclesiastical bureaucrat, the expert parson with the specialized ministries and so on. And these varied tendencies, involving increasing variety of clerical role, increasing technical specialization, increasing involvements over wider areas of cultural space in the local, national and international context, all worked together in a complex mesh of developments until those crises occurred which gave a stimulus to the third category.

Before examining the third category and pin-pointing its social incidence at different levels of church organization and as between different social and historical contexts it is worthwhile relating the elements just described for England so as to suggest how they might work in an analogous context: America. In the American context the second category is explicitly and early universalized: the denominational minister presiding over a voluntary association is the classic norm. Moreover, the élite culture was rapidly penetrated by dissenting fervour and the eventual compromise was much less in the élites' favour than it was in England. Indeed, dissenting practicality and incipiently utilitarian notions of culture pushed back élite humanism to such an extent that a sharp antagonism persisted and manifested itself in élitist rejections of the American way of life.[20] As in England a progressive middle class developed, drawing sustenance from the individualist notions of Protestant evangelicism, yet deeply suspicious of its social consequences, enamoured of more organicist views of culture and of more humanistic criteria as to what the context of culture should be. The persistence of a minority élitism in the United States sitting loose to dominant Protestant styles runs parallel to a much more resistant élitism in England and a much more widespread English attachment to and admiration for élitist culture. The scene was set in America for a battle of styles in the higher educational institutions which also involved the clergy. As in England, so in America, the clergy were to be involved in a battle between humanistic institutions which had partially absorbed the best of the educationally mobile dissenters (along with their emphasis on social conscience) and the rawer, utilitarian world of an older dissent rooted in science and industry. The stage was therefore prepared for the developments associated with the third category in which the humanist élite fought the older utilitarian professional and business sector of the middle class, and in which the clergy came to collaborate more with the former than the latter. (If one wants a Catholic variant of this battle it is to be found in Holland).

It is now appropriate to describe the third category in which now occurs the major crisis among the professional guardians of the sacred. The contemporary crisis occurs in conditions of very marked differentiation, although obviously there are other factors at work as well. Broadly the crisis is rooted in a reaction to and extension of certain aspects of phases one and two already described. Phase one, as has been indicated, embodies very prevalent semi-coherent series of orientations loosely grouped under the label 'Christian' joined together with elements of civic ritual: rites de passage augmented by state piety. Clergy affected by the conditions attaching to phase three are not willing just to be respected public figures engaged in purely ritual activity or performing in a social round with people who have a largely passive attitude to church loyalty and attendance. Phase two involves an increase in the specifically religious element in the clerical role: either evangelical enthusiasm or a stress on religious technique and validation, i.e. ritualism as distinct from the performance of *rites de passage*. It lays stress on theological training, on the care of the community of committed Christians and on a specifically Christian approach to mundane knowledge and mundane society. It asks: what is the *Christian* view of X, whether biological knowledge or international relations. Clergy in phase three have often been deeply impregnated by the presuppositions of phase two but find them largely irrelevant in the new conditions. There is little point in stressing the special technique of the cleric and the special validity of holy orders, or in emphasizing the importance of sound theological training if people are just not there to receive the blessed sacrament, or benefit from the sound training. In other words not only have the broad social orientations of phase one become too passive and implicit to offer a springboard for an active clerical role, but the accentuation of the specifically religious elements in that role appropriate to phase two finds itself without a supporting structure of active members within which to operate.

However, certain elements in the previous phases can be retranslated to cope with the conditions in phase three. But before outlining how this occurs it is necessary to state what the conditions of phase three are. Bureaucratization continues apace and more and more specialized agencies arise at the local, regional, national and international levels. This means that the role of the generalist is diminished, though those who do remain in the local parish ministry find themselves overwhelmed with a range of demands on their time and capacities which are very general in character. They are often still committed to running this, that and the other, and wonder what precisely these things have to do with the purposes for which they were ordained; or else there is specialization of function even at the parish level which leaves the priestly 'core' of the system somewhat uncertain as to what the cleric, qua priest or minister, has to offer.

Specialization of agencies and specialization of role together breed a vigorous demand for a loosening of *all* constricting structures and for a re-definition of role which allows the cleric to come out of the diminishing enclave of the faithful and face the world. It is here that he draws on elements from roles developed in phases one and two. He develops the *general* role of priest characteristic of phase one and endeavours to confront society as a whole, no longer from the standpoint of a member of an élite but radically. Yet he uses such respect as appertains to his cloth and his public position to hammer home his general critique of society, and is sometimes motivated further in this direction by a sense of declining status and social indifference. In so doing he draws on the tradition of the social gospel developed in phase two which he mutates into a thoroughgoing critique of all social arrangements, including the very concept of role-structuring; and he also draws on the organicist, semi-medievalist assumptions of phase one to underwrite an aspiration towards a new organicism and new communitarianism, recast along socialist lines. Clearly this extension of the liberal social gospel and espousal of socialistic communitarianism is not without serious tensions. In addition the radical cleric feels that to be *truly* religious he must reject the tendency to make his role more religious in the manner characteristic of phase two: it is just this irrelevant theological knowledge, and this emphasis on ritual validity, etc., which now provides a major constriction. So just as phase two was in a sense more religious than phase one, so phase three is in a sense more religious than phase two. He must become a total 'man' facing the whole structure of society with a radical criticism. And if he still possesses a congregation which expects certain extensive but constricting types of performance from him then he becomes doubly irked and charges his flock with ingrained apathy or even pharisaism with respect to the urgent world outside. They, for their part, of course, are thoroughly confined to their own mundane tasks, and expect the clergyman to look after the sacred for them on Sunday. His exaltation of their 'lay' priesthood, his denigration of his own role and his call to go out to talk to what they regard as a deaf world all appear profoundly perverse. So a chasm begins to widen between pastor and flock. They do not conform to his view of their exalted role and vice versa. His ideology of communal participation is irrelevant to them.

However, the chasm is widened by certain other developments at the regional and international level which enable the radical clergyman to escape his flock and confront the world globally in a much more congenial way. He may, of course, accept his own theory of lay priesthood, and simply give up orders to become a radical Christian layman. He then pin-pricks the congregation internally instead of from the altar or the pulpit. Or he may join a specialist agency in which he confronts the world as a missioner to the down and outs or the racially despised and so on. Usually he does this ecumenically, partly because this is the efficient way to do it, and partly because his pan-human radical ideology disdains denominational boundaries, or even the boundaries of Christianity itself. Engaged in this way he may start to translate notions like the communion of the church into community, adapt concepts like sin to the vocabulary of alienation and convert the image of Christ into a paradigm of revolutionary (or existenial) man. At any rate quite a sector of traditional theology may be dismissed as irrelevant or ripe for demythologization. The same doctrinal tendencies and the same politicization occurs with respect to those who enter specialized agencies like those of public relations and the media: radical clergy, like radical students, hone in on the media and on the means of communication, and so the content of the messages given out becomes highly unrepresentative. The media's endemic need of novelty in turn makes such people doubly welcome. Meanwhile the flocks at home are confused by the new roles and messages of their erstwhile shepherds; and since the radicals have left the local ministry and dropped out of the theological colleges those left in the ranks of the clergy become disproportionately conservative. Indeed, moderate liberals find themselves squeezed between radicals in the command posts of metropolitan communication and theological conservatives manning the local churches in the provinces. The dichotomy breeds a deeper conservative reaction, increasing the radicals' suspicion of the organized church, and making theological colleges rather uneasy about their new recruits. Such recruits are sometimes too enthusiastic and fundamentalist for comfort, but those who run theological colleges know that in a situation of decreasing recruitment (and lower educational standards) they are the main single source of new clergy.

The situation of the World Council of Churches is just another aspect of this and makes still worse the relationship between the 'centre' and the provincial periphery, as well as squeezing out the moderate, old-fashioned liberals yet further. Naturally, the W.C.C. bureaucrats are highly unrepresentative, both in their style and their politics; and their ecumenist assumptions are thoroughly out of tune with the deep rooted attachment to particular forms and localities found amongst most ordinary Christians. The interests of such bureaucrats lie in canvassing support in the third world, in problems of racism and the like, and their whole theology and vocabulary has decreasing contact with the home constituency. At one and the same time they bureaucratize and standardize and manage to wield an existentialist-cum-Marxist vocabulary of liberation, dialogue, significant encounter and the like. Feeling their own loss of roots they lean ever more heavily towards third world politics, condoning whatever is illiberal in the third world (or indeed in communist countries since they want the prestige deriving from the participation of the Orthodox) while campaigning vigorously against every blot on the social record of their own countries. (Nairobi 1976, was significant for a break in the silence over communist persecution). One further characteristic of this higher itinerant ecclesiastical bureaucracy is its espousal of a bureaucratic version of existential language, which issues at the local level in the emasculation of traditional Christian speech, notably the Bible and the liturgy. The mythological elements in Christianity are actually accentuated, *because* they are treated as myths, and then incongruously joined to a flat, official prose style which is regarded as congruent with modernity. The faithful are thus doubly deprived: forced to put up with myth emphasized for its double meaning and made to accept forms of language without rhythm, power or the capacity to evoke. There is one additional difficulty. Both the bureaucratic modernizations of language and the restructurings of organizational forms emanate from *different* bureaucratic sources, thus creating accelerated confusions as to channels and to forms of communication. Nobody knows what to do and everything has to become extremely explicit. Both in clergy and congregations the innovations breed an initial interest, quickly followed by exhaustion.

Thus far one has been analysing in terms of the paradoxical consequences of bureaucratization and of specialization at every level. Plainly there is a further accelerating factor working at the point where the clerical profession overlaps the progressive middle class and the world of higher learning. In the universities and the expressive professions the results of bureaucracy and specialization have been similar to those among the clergy: an emphasis on technology parallel to that on ritual technique, and an emphasis on 'cultivation' parallel to the saving of souls. The first comes to be regarded as spiritless and the second as irrelevant. In the universities and the churches there issues a complementary pan-human, radical critique of society, which then expands through the education system and the media to confuse whole sectors of 'normal' society. At the point where church and university meet, e.g. in colleges of education and university chaplaincies, these tendencies are extremely marked. It is in this upper middle class milieu that the radical cleric makes most use of a traditional status to declaim against traditional society. Furthermore, he utilizes his position in the old élite to assist the progressive middle class in its war against the old middle class of business and the more staid professions. He attacks the old virtues of the Protestant ethic (or Catholic discipline) with exemplary vigour and increases a sense of marginality and alienation both in himself and in those he attacks. Less radical clergy, bothered and distressed by these developments, either explicitly align themselves with movements like the Festival of Light, directed against 'moral pollution', or else perhaps become immersed in the charismatic movement which has the virtue of combining a transcendence of role and language and denominational boundary with a reassertion of old-time religion. Many do adopt this option, combining the techniques and virtues of encounter groups with the content of traditional evangelical religion. The results are often both spectacular and evanescent, producing initial excitement and eventual disillusion and fission. Even so the charismatic movement is an authentic point of renewal. Bryan Wilson has even identified this as the beginning of a fourth clerical phase: the presidency of the sectarian group.

This analysis has concentrated on Protestant versions of the crisis: suffice to say that Catholic radicalism is more extreme and more explicitly political and that Catholic reaction to radicalism is more intense. Clergy, Protestant and Catholic alike, become divided into very clear parties (or join the party of those who vigorously reject parties) and the unity of the pastorate is broken. A radical priest operating without visible ecclesiastical plant in a working class district, or in an upper middle class metropolitan area is totally divorced from a traditional priest ministering in the hinterland of Brittany: each type of ecclesiastic will have his distinct pressure group designed to press his views on an episco-

pate leaning slightly but clearly in a liberal election. The episcopate itself, partly winkled out of its élite connections and out of
the structure of traditional legitimation, increasingly takes a
critical view of its social context or else attempts to reconcile
elements inherently resistant to reconciliation.

One version of moderate liberal/radicalism among phase three
clergy is perhaps worth noting, particularly as it characterizes a
good deal of Anglo/American culture. This comprises a position
in which the precepts of psychotherapy are employed to approximate but also to modify the radical position and allow the cleric
to adopt modernist and 'committed' stances which stop short of
revolutionary political challenge to the structure of society.
Freudian and Jungian psychological mythology partly replaces
and partly parallels the tenets of Christian theology; the special
mystique of the phase two clerical role finds its shadow and
mirror in the mystique of the psychoanalyst. Moreover, it is easy
for the clergy uncertain of the legitimacy and ontological primacy
if their liturgical function to develop the traditional pastoral role
to converge with that of the secular social worker. This combines
the individual 'cure of souls' (psychotherapy) with a modicum
of phase one concern for the integration and welfare of the
community. The techniques of psycho-therapeutic pastoral care
tend therefore to concern themselves at one level with helping the
neurotic and the misfit to adapt better to their expected social
roles and at another level with pursuing welfare activities for the
relatively deprived, provided this does not seriously over-step the
society's and the congregation's sense of the fine distinction between non-political 'good-causes' and politically controversial
meddling outside the clergy's 'proper' sphere.

Now one may ask, by way of conclusion, where the tendencies
described as belonging to phase three are likely to be most marked
and where they are likely to be muted or non-existent.

From what has been argued above it is clear that tendencies
belonging to 'phase three' are most like to occur amongst clergy
recruited from, educated amongst and operating with the progressive middle class. In this context religion is assimilated to the
expressive arts and the cleric acquires the free-wheeling moralism
and critical stance of the intellectual. By the same token he is freed
from the actual constraints of practical politics: his politics are
assimilated to theatre, and liturgy is his preferred form of theatre.

Ritualists of the old school frequently gravitate towards this political theatricality. Phase three tendencies are least likely to occur in provincial sectors where church-going is still an important habit: the clergy in such areas retain an adequate role which combines civic ritual and the care of sizeable voluntary communities of committed Christians of the lower middle or respectable working class. These retain the old Protestant ethic of achievement and personal discipline, and their radicalism, such as it is, retains the presuppositions of an older liberalism. In these sectors one finds both the conservative evangelical and the moderate liberal. In some rural areas there remain milieux where the clergy are still major figures in social life and are integrated into the local social structure: they perform the rites, civic, ecclesiastical and personal. However such areas mostly occur where there is a tradition of a long-established state church: England and Scandinavia.

There are certain societies where phase three tendencies are most unlikely in any sector, though the educated class always retains a certain susceptibility to them. For example, in communist societies the clergy are legally restricted to a phase two role minus any component of social criticism: they are simply forced to be pastors of their flock. Such phase three tendencies as do occur arise in those areas where the younger clergy may espouse a 'New Left' wing decentralizing variety of socialism, which links them with the younger intelligentsia. This is possible for example in contemporary Croatia and is at odds with the traditional role of nationalistic guardian of a peasant culture. Elsewhere the normal role is precisely that of a guardian of the peasant way of life, and this guardianship is somewhat weakened by industrialization and migration. If the national culture is under persistent external pressure and there is a traditional Catholic association with national resistance there is a strong current against any encroachment of phase three: the church forms of fairly solid bloc, dedicated to its traditional role, as in Poland and Lithuania.

In societies noted for extreme traditionalism there is often a vigorous and sudden transition to phase three, unless there is a factor of contemporary or recent identification between Catholicism and a persecuted or dispersed nationality: Southern Ireland. Even this may not prevent the phase three tendencies: in Holland for example the approach of near parity with the Protestants plus the over-emphatic integration of the 'minority' culture around the symbol of Catholicism produced a violent reaction in which the old structures have partly disappeared. Something similar and milder has occurred in the United States. In other societies where the old antagonism between secularist left and clerical right weakens, as in Spain, Italy and France, and parts of Latin America, there appears a Catholic left of some importance. This joins existentialist objections to constricting roles with a Marxoid critique of society. It contributes to general confusion in the ranks of Catholicism and accentuates both generational differences amongst clergy and the inflexibility of the traditionalist right. The radical tendency reaches maximum strength where it combines both local integration and revolution in a sub-national community seeking autonomy, e.g. the Basque country. Since Catholicism is international these various semi-revolutionary developments cross over national borders and affect areas which one might expect to be less susceptible to them, e.g. Canada. This contagion combines with the impact of the Vatican Council to bring about severe disorientation, especially among those Catholic sectors traditionally most disciplined, e.g. the religious orders. These are very inclined to inaugurate a period of constant innovation and to engage in various egalitarian and communitarian experiments. When a vast, rather inflexible organization like the Catholic Church shifts from right to middle and from traditionalism to innovation it is bound to spawn a large number of extremist movements and experience sharp internal conflicts. Clearly Catholic clergy, except in places like Ireland and Poland, are very much more confused and likely to fly to extremes than the Protestant clergy. Catholic countries are in any case usually conditioned to more violent conflict as part of social life and the inflexibilities of the past breed more intense fissions and disagreements. Indeed, there is a paradoxical analogue with the past: whereas there used to be sharp conflict between two integrated systems, clericalist and anti-clericalist, the conflict now appears *within* the church. In other words whereas the church was united and integral in relation to the traditional sector it is now disunited and marginal to all sectors.[21]

In sum the tendencies of phase three are noticeable as a covert undertow in certain parts of eastern Europe wherever left-wing or liberal critiques of the regimes are possible and where the Church is not pushed into a completely defensive stance by what the population conceives as alien power.[22] They are present too where sub-national communities approach near-parity with national Protestant majorities since this weakens the need for a purely integrative, defensive Catholicism. And they are present where the right-left dichotomy weakens and a substantial Catholic left becomes possible. In Protestant countries clerical radicalism is largely part of the revolt of the 'progressive' middle class and works against the old, traditional virtues and disciplines of the provinces and the 'respectable' Christians in the lower middle and upper working class. Much depends here on whether there is a large enough provincial sector to organize against the metropolitan centre: Festivals of Light, movements for local cultural defence, rejections of metropolitan media of communication, small 'Christian' parties as in Scandinavia.

There is nothing to suggest that phase three tendencies are destined to be dominant. In many societies the phase two organization of voluntary religious association remains vigorous and active, e.g. Protestant America. In others the phase one elements, rooted in civic and folk religion, retain considerable importance, e.g. England and Scandinavia. But everywhere, as the church becomes less central to local integration and less implicated in the structure of local and national élites, and as levels of participation fall—as they do with respect to *all* voluntary associations—the radical tendency makes its appearance. One stresses that all voluntary associations are under pressure just as almost all close, small face to face groups flourish: religious associations provide the most resilient examples of voluntary associations, just as they provide the most successful examples of face to face groupings. Through the process of differentiation the cleric may cease to be either prop of the local establishment or pastor of a voluntary community and to the extent that this happens he approximates the position of the radical intelligentsia.[23]

NOTES

1. An important contribution on differentiation within Christianity and on Christianity itself as an instance of differentiation is to be found in Parsons 1968. Cf. Stark 1966–72. Stark's study is pecu-

liarly concerned with the varieties of church-state tension and collusion, and with such modern developments as messianic nationalism and American civic religion. The Catholic Church has never totally capitulated to the state, but its symbolic witness to alternative values has always—and *necessarily*—been weakened by fighting the state in terms of its own power base or of some defunct ancien regime.

2. Cf. Herberg 1955. Herberg's book is a classic statement of how the separation of church from state can actually facilitate a religio-political collusion over values. On the other hand, this 'secularization' of Christian values is historically endemic. The tension can be maintained only by minorities and individual prophets, and through the medium of symbolism. The church-state distinction is just one such symbol. Coleman 1970 has a useful discussion of 'Civil Religion'. He distinguishes church-sponsored civil religion (e.g. Orthodox Greece), secular nationalism (e.g. Ataturk's Turkey; the Third French Republic), and religion-in-general, partially distinct from both church and state (e.g. the U.S.A.).

3. Cf. K. Thomas 1971. This very important study challenged the extent of pre-industrial christianization, particularly at the level of folk concepts. The work of other social historians has also thrown doubt on the extent of pre-industrial belief and practice. In some areas there may indeed have been near-universal practice, sometimes because the law required it. For example, Principes 1959 shows total uniformity. Cf. Obelkevich 1971.

4. For material on the attitude to baptism, cf. Salomonsen 1971, and 1972. These findings would thoroughly document Kierkegaard's contention that baptism had become Christian circumcision, i.e. a badge of community membership. Cf. Pickering 1974.

5. Cf. Morgan 1963, and 1969; and Towler 1970, and 1972. The article by Leslie Paul in the same volume (Towler 1972) should also be consulted.

Cf. K. Heasman, *Evangelicals in Action*, London: Bles, 1962.

6. Russell 1970. My account of 'phase two' leans on Dr Russell's excellent research. Cf. Pickering 1968. Dr Pickering emphasizes the shift towards entertainment and relaxation in nonconformist bodies during the late nineteenth century. There is also material in Inglis 1963.

7. Cf. Thompson 1970, and 1968; Rudge 1968 sets the church within the typologies offered by the sociology of organization.

8. Cf. Yeo 1971. Dr Yeo's painstaking and exhaustive account of the churches and other associations in Reading sets the decline of the churches within the context of an overall decline of active associational activity and of personal civic involvement. It has now appeared as Yeo 1976.

9. Cf. Absalom 1971, and Daniel 1968. Both these authors emphasize the tendency of ritualists to slide across into the radical fold once their traditionalist world comes under severe pressure.

10. Cf. Niebuhr 1949. A point made by Yeo 1976, and in Handy 1971, is that the social gospel really aspired to a christianized society, and it was in the light of such an aspiration that the Protestant conscience judged itself a failure. For an account of the operation and frustration of the Protestant conscience in relation to war, cf. Martin 1965a, and Yinger 1946. It is important to consult Semmel 1974, since this revives Halévy, and regards Methodism as a mobilization of democratic possibilities within a religious frame. His analysis is entirely consonant with Lipset's account of the role of Arminian theology in America. One can, if one likes, see contemporary radicalism as a second stage of the social gospel, or otherwise as a response to the social-structural limitations encountered by the social gospel.

11. Cf. Zaretsky and Leone 1974, which gives an account of most of the fringe religions currently operative in America. In so far as it deals with neo-Pentecostalism, it stresses the variety of social locations where it may be found. Catholic Pentecostalism probably needs to be treated separately, since there are specific factors travelling in the wake of Vatican II, such as the dislocations both of rite and authority. At any rate, Virginia Hines's contribution casts some doubt on the relevance of theories stressing deprivation. I am hypothesizing that the Charismatic Movement and Neo-Pentecostalism are more clearly provincial in Britain than in the United States. The Jesus movement is much less important in Britain. It seems that Jesus people are often returning to religion after a period in the counter-culture, and in Britain fewer return to religion because fewer began there in the first place. Cf. Richardson 1974. If Professor Richardson is right, the Jesus movement depends on the counter-culture, and will cease rapid growth with the slowing down of the counter-cultural impulse.

12. Cf. Martin 1973b. This attempts to criticize these tendencies in the university contexts. A useful book which sees the University as a 'functional equivalent' partly displacing the Church is H. Barnes 1970.

13. There is a problem here which relates to notions of the 'power' of the Church at different times. In the early middle ages for example, religion was powerful in that it provided a comprehensive backdrop of conceptions, but kings constantly subordinated the Church to the imperatives of secular power. Then there occurred the struggle of which à Becket provides the most dramatic instance. The Reformation can be seen simply as making the domination of the secular power more direct and explicit, by turning the Church into a department of state, and integrating the clergy more directly with the secular hierarchy. The enlightened despots of the next two centuries then brought the Catholic Church (and the Orthodox Church) to heel in similar manner, using it as a vehicle of centralization. It can be argued that it was precisely these 'secularizations', whereby religion was made a vehicle of monarchical ideology and

state power, which sparked off the alienation of the people at large. Their conformity represented social obedience; and their nonconformity then represented social revolt. Secularization in one sense— the attenuation of the Christian tension—accelerated secularization in the other sense—of popular withdrawal from ecclesiastical participation. Some of the paradoxes written into this complex history of the church-state relation are nicely shown up in Starkey 1973. Dr Starkey documents the increases in mystical 'religious' aura sustained by the monarch after the secularization of the church, i.e. after it was made explicitly subordinate. The royal ideology 'collected' the fund of mystical energy which must hedge a king or a president, or, for that matter, a Lenin or a Stalin.

14. R. Towler has developed the concept of 'Common Religion' in Towler 1974, chapter 8.

15. Dansette 1948 and 1951 provides a classic treatment of this. The period of practical reconciliation after the First World War is fully treated in H. W. Paul 1967.

16. The evolution of the Spanish Church and clergy is described in Orensanz 1974b.

17. Szasz 1975 has interesting comments on law in America which he sees as formally separate from religion yet subserving a religious function in circumscribing the bounds of sanity and madness and of what is permissible in the realm of what he calls 'ceremonial chemistry', i.e. drugs. Cf. also Martin 1975c.

18. Cf. Lewis 1973, which treats particularly of faith and order but also nicely illustrates the divorce of ecumenical idealism from social-structural considerations. In that respect it exhibits another facet of the frustration of liberal Protestant idealism. There is also an underlying tension between 'locals' and 'cosmopolitans'.

19. Semmel 1974 makes this point with regard to the export of Methodist enthusiasm to the Empire, thereby lessening the tension at home. Potter 1975 makes the same point about the artisans who became evangelical Anglican priests, and whose destiny was in some foreign mission field, not at home. Metropolitan élites have often been happy to see enthusiasm directed elsewhere, leaving the green pastures of the homeland to be grazed by more docile sheep under more liberal shepherds. Holland provides evidence of the same phenomenon, and even secularist France was sometimes not unwilling for French civilization to be carried by Catholic missions providing they did not trouble the sacred homeland.

20. Lipset 1969 has pinpointed the role of the Established Church in Canada and England in underwriting a more humanist and élitist conception of civilization than could prevail in the United States. I assume that part of the nostalgia amongst American intellectuals for Europe, and especially France, stems from the embattled defensiveness of humanist culture, relative, that is to available resources. Hofstadter 1964 also documents the dominance of Puritan utilitarianism in the United States.

21. Perhaps it is appropriate to refer to the special position of Catholic communities in Protestant countries. Traditionally, these communities have been characterized by high integration and practice. Now there has emerged a left wing and a right wing, disputing issues of authority and ritual, and the faithful have become seriously disgruntled. A generation gap has emerged of considerable dimesions, and practice has fallen quite sharply. A.E.C.W. Spencer has documented a sharp fall among English Catholics: recent Australian and American polls show the same tendency. These falls seem to occur after Vatican Two, whether or not there is an open contretemps on the Dutch scale. They relate to post-Council disorientations without necessarily reflecting any rejection of the Council by the majority of Catholics. Indeed, to take but one instance, the majority of Catholics in England and Italy are known to approve of the shift to the vernacular. To put the matter paradoxically: most Catholics approve the changes and more Catholics leave the Church, or at any rate, cease regular practice. Cf. B. Martin 1968; Kokosalakis 1971, and 1969; Brothers 1964; C. Longley, an article in *The Times*, 14 April 1975; and A. E. C. W. Spencer, an article in *The Month*, April, 1975.

22. Petešić 1972. The following quotation provides a summary of issues not only in Yugoslavia, but elsewhere. 'The central issue is the approach to the implementation of the conclusions of the Second Vatican Council on which the Croatian hierarchy is shown to be split right down the middle. The cases, which are given to illustrate this, show that while the younger clergy are predominantly enthusiastic about the reform, the older and upper hierarchy are firmly opposed to any change, claiming that in local conditions, where the majority of believers are poorly educated people, the spirit of the reform will only be misunderstood and harm the reputation of the Church. There is conflict on the following issues: the position of the modern priest within the Church; the demand for greater specialization of the clergy according to the type of duties they require to perform; a more open attitude towards the secular world; matters concerning the administration of dioceses (i.e. decision-making by a collegium of all the clergy in dioceses, instead of by the bishop alone); participation of laymen in church affairs; education in religious institutions; the role of the religious press; celibacy; the translation of the Dutch Catechism into Serbo-Croat in 1969 (which created a turmoil of protests and approvals and involved the intervention of Cardinal Šeper, who tried to stop its publication), etc.'

23. I have attempted another treatment of the confusion over roles, norms, in contemporary English Christianity in Martin 1975b. This essay relates the confusion in the Church to the confusion in education, more especially with regard to the cult of spontaneity and the issue of so-called middle-class values and language. Just as the erosion of active church-going also affects most active attachment to voluntary association, so the confusion of clerical role is shared with

the secular clerks. Clerics are confused, teachers are confused; teachers of religion are doubly confused. Cf. Martin 1977a.

I have also attempted a brief treatment of the contrast between those clergy whose sense of moral responsibility is achieved in civic roles and those who approximate the condition of the alienated intelligentsia. This treatment was a response to the interesting outcry over the rival statements of the Archbishop of Canterbury and the Bishop of Southwark concerning British society. It is appended here and was originally printed in *The Times*, 15 November, 1975.

In this connection I would like to draw attention to G. H. Moyser's recent paper 'The Political Organisation of the Middle Class; the case of the Church of England' (privately circulated in 'Papers in Religion and Politics', Manchester University, Summer 1977.) This bears out my general analysis.

Dr Moyser shows first that active members of the Church of England are 50 per cent 'middle class', but its General Synod is almost entirely middle class, indeed upper middle class. That is not surprising. He shows secondly that the General Synod has *very* marked liberal opinions on such matters as migration and the death penalty, much more so than the middle class generally, and very much more so than the working class generally. Only on such matters as nationalisation are Synod members characteristically middle class, though on this issue the working class does not differ so very much in attitude from the middle class. He makes the additional point that the Church tends to act as a pressure group only in relation to the 'moral' issues like migration and not in relation to such issues as nationalisation. In other words it is a specialised pressure group.

When the Archiepiscopal Trumpet Sounds

For a churchman to sound the moral trumpet is a hazardous undertaking. A trumpet needs to be loud rather than subtle and only makes the required impact when it comes in at exactly the right moment. Moral trumpeters easily hit the wrong note and critics soon claim they are playing thinly disguised versions of old political tunes. The contemporary moralist faces a further difficulty. When Joshua encompassed Jericho the priests all blew the trumpet together and the people shouted simultaneously. But that was wartime.

Hitting the wrong note is so easy because the vocabulary of morals has been worn smooth and bland by time, while the vocabulary of politics is stained by misuse, dishonesty and conflict. Justice, mercy, love and peace are good words, but they are not news; other words are more newsworthy but are on the Index. If you talk of 'class' you may be labelled a class warrior or else somebody who has just noticed the unpleasing existence of the lower orders. When Sir Keith Joseph sounded the moral trumpet he took part of the score from a left-wing pamphlet and bluntly referred to social classes 4 and 5. Millions of people immediately echoed Joe Gormley 'Does he mean us?' Sir Keith had ignored the political echo-box and the orchestration he would receive from the media. Dishonest politicians get a bad press but not so bad as honest ones.

An ecclesiastical moralist usually tries to sound above the confused arena of politics. He wants to strike a broad, common chord and this immediately cuts down his repertory. The common chord cannot include specific detailed analysis of evils. The task is far too complicated and the solutions merely reflect or even exacerbate existing divisions. Any focus of criticism will be plausibly attacked as selective and the critic will be accused of having raised his telescope either to his left eye or his right eye. A moral appeal has to be simple if it is to be heard when in fact the essence of the problem partly resides in it enormous complexity. To talk about the 'system' in general is as naïve as to use the straightforward moral vocabulary. Every system is an incredibly complicated balance of moral and practical opportunity costs. Equality is at odds with freedom and tolerance and local autonomy, the popular will is in tension with expertise, individual spontaneity clashes against consistent rules and secure expectations, collective participation threatens individual autonomy, justice threatens efficiency. For most problems there is no morally satisfactory solution. For example, to judge a juvenile delinquent by a fixed menu of punishments ignores differences of social circumstances. But to tailor treatment precisely to circumstances is to abolish equality before the law and to dislocate the consistency of judgements. The juvenile is handed over to therapy and this may mean long term control in the interests of social conformity.

Most ecclesiastical moralists and social critics accept that individual morality is shaped by a variable social experience, but are uneasy about attributing everything to environment. If people are simply creatures of environment it is difficult to see what is the point of a moral criticism or what is the basis of moral language. Everybody is handed an excuse, and that goes for rich goose as well as for poor gander. It seems better to push up to that mined and delicate frontier between individual morality and social justice, on the assumption that collective ills are susceptible to individual initiative. A clergyman feels able to locate and stigmatize an evil without adopting a party political solution. He points but does not prescribe. If a clergyman *did* prescribe he would then have to accept the limitations of the political role: mutual labelling, murky compromise, indiscriminate blaming, obligatory collective righteousness, misrepresentation and the posing of false alternatives. You need *some* people who are not continually obliged to do these things.

The office of a bishop is peculiar in several ways. Its moral terms are rooted in simple models of 'family' and 'community' which are partly false and yet partly appealing at the same time. They have a very partial fit. In wartime the threat from outside does indeed create a family and makes almost everybody a brother-in-arms. Peacetime is different and internal crisis often deepens divisions as much as external warfare diminishes them. Yet internal crisis creates a pressure for the same vocabulary of family solidarity even when that is precisely the point at issue. A bishop should 'speak out' but what can he say?

There remains a sense in which even a democracy at peace remains a family. British democracy even projects some of its sense of self on to a particular family: the monarchy. The obscure, inchoate ambivalent identities and partly conflicting ideals are unified at a level of symbol and sentiment. The Church or Kirk and even more the word 'Christian' belong in this sacred area of semi-shared history and identity. But this sharing in symbol, myth, civic rite, memory and sentiment can only endure provided it is not made explicit in programmes and precise statements. The shared symbols have to be roped off from the divisions of everyday. When a bishop speaks he does so either at the level of acceptable generality or he unties the rope and speaks at the level of unacceptable specificity.

Clergy are custodians of two treasures. One is the common civic sense of British people and the other Christianity. As long as they are amongst the representatives of civic sentiment they have been trapped and controlled by the very importance of their role. But in the contemporary world they have become marginal to that role and many of them are anxious to walk out of the trap. Once out of that trap they have tended to speak more in terms which awake echoes in the third world and even to adopt the utopian freedoms and hopes of the alienated intellectual. They have drifted away from their little, local flocks and from moorings in the establishment. Their flocks define them in one way, they define themselves in another. For some the old civic role is the basis of responsibility; for others it is the major barrier to it.

Bibliography

One or two comments on the bibliography may be useful. The immediate ancestors to the kind of treatment utilized in this book are the political sociologists. I owe a major debt to Lipset, Dahl, Rose, Alford and Rokkan because they have assembled massive materials which take into account the religious factor and because they have engaged in large-scale, comparative empirical theorizing. At a slightly greater distance in time and intellectual pedigree I owe a debt to Almond and Verba's *The Civic Culture*. A work in a different mode which nevertheless connects religion to social structures, comparatively and historically, is Michael Fogarty's *Christian Democracy in Western Europe 1820–1953*. It is an invaluable resource. Allied to the political sociologists are those who have engaged in overall analysis of total structures, for example Goudblom's *Dutch Society* and Steinberg's *Why Switzerland?* I wish there were more such. A series of essays of the desired kind are to be found in M. Archer and S. Giner *Contemporary Europe* (1971). Another series of useful essays is located in the collections of the European Consortium for Political Research. Robin Williams' essay on religion in his *American Society* could serve as a model for work relating religion to the basic institutional set of a culture. An important and neglected attempt to do this on a comparative basis is to be found in J. M. Yinger's *The Scientific Study of Religion*.

Macro-relations are reflected at the micro-level. I have consulted a large number of community studies, some of which are very useful for charting the role of religion in the overall network, e.g. Margaret Stacey's study of Banbury, and Brennan, Cooney and Pollins' study of South Wales. Only a few of these are listed here apart from some very useful works in the field of Mediterranean studies. I have left out the whole field of sectarian studies:

L

Pentecostalists in France, Witnesses in England, Mormons in Merthyr Tydfil, though I have read most of it. Some works on Russian sectarianism are included since they have special interest in the Russian context. Even so I have not listed the Russian ethnographers.

Eastern Europe has presented many problems. The literature of comment is very large, but it remains impressionistic. There is an extensive literature on religion in Russia, more especially from Kolarz onward, but I have not listed much of it. Such work is easily located by consulting G. Simon, B. Bociurkiw, E. and S. Dunn, M. Bordeaux and the recent work of Christel Lane. I was particularly lucky to have Mrs. Lane as my student over this period. I was lucky in having Lucian Blit as a colleague: his knowledge of Poland was most valuable.

Symposia like T. Beeson's *Discretion and Valour* and H. Mol's *Western Religion* illustrate the immense range in the availability of empirical material. Catholic countries are, of course, well served by Catholic research agencies, and these provide a storehouse of materials, especially for France, Belgium, Holland, Spain and Poland. Would that the pioneering work of A. E. C. W. Spencer and L. Paul in England had received similar support. Much of the sociographic material is to be found in *Sociologia Religiosa*, the *Archives de sociologie des réligions*, *Social Compass* and the *Sociological Yearbook of Religion in Britain* variously edited by myself and M. Hill. I suspect there is more work on Germany and Hungary than linguistic competence has spurred me to search out. I know that Roumania and Greece are poorly served; the Albanian situation is as obscure as it is bleak.

I anticipate that the advances to come will emanate from the kind of social history pursued by John Walsh, James Obelkevich, E. P. Thompson, R. Moore, Hugh MacLeod, Stephen Yeo, Clive Field, Keith Thomas, A. A. MacLaren and others. I also know the kind of thing an E. P. Thompson might say of this work: witness the *British Journal of Sociology* for September 1976. Nevertheless I have largely omitted historical materials apart from indicating the occasional standard history where this happens to have proved especially valuable, as for example Raymond Carr's *Spain 1808–1939*. Some of the French historical material is, of course, peculiarly rich for understanding basic processes and I have derived much ancillary pleasure from works by such authors

as A. Vidler, A. Dansette, E. Weber and Harry Paul. But my aim
is not history but sociology. Historical particulars act as a basis
for a control over sociological generalization. If the sociological
sketch I have attempted were to take in the relevant history,
especially the intellectual history, it would have to be ten times
as long. Owen Chadwick's *The Secularisation of the European
Mind in the Nineteenth Century* (1975) is, of course, a distinguished contribution to the intellectual history of secularization.
Martin Marty's *The Triple Schism* would fit in with my analysis
very well.

Just as I assume the historical materials so also I assume the
American literature and the sociological literature past and
present. I trust my various debts to Berger, Luckmann, Eisenstadt,
Parsons, Bellah, Yinger, De Tocqueville, Herberg, Coser, etc. are
as obvious as they are great. It was my misfortune to read Shils'
Center and Periphery and Bell's *The Cultural Contradictions of
Capitalism* too late in the day to incorporate their major insights,
though much had influenced me in their earlier writings. I also
owe a large debt to Bryan Wilson, in discussion, through his
extensive published works on secularization and on sectarianism,
and through the researches of his students.

AARFLOT, A. (1969), 'Tro og Lydighet', Oslo: University Press
(with English summary).
ABSALOM, F. (1971), 'The Anglo-Catholic Priest' in M. Hill (ed.),
A Sociological Yearbook of Religion in Britain, No. 4, London:
SCM Press.
ADORNO, T. (1964), *Minima Moralia*, Frankfurt: Suhr Kampf.
ALEKSEEV, N. P. (1974), 'Reasons for the Retention of Religiosity
in the Psychology of the Kolkhoz Peasantry', *Social Compass*,
Vol. 21, No. 2.
ALEXANDER, S., Forthcoming, *Church and State in Yugoslavia.*
ALFONSI, P., with P. PESNOT (1973), *L'Eglise contestée*, Paris:
Calmann-Lévy.
ALFORD, R. R. (1964), *Party and Society*, London: John Murray.
ALLARDT, E. (1962), 'Factors explaining variations and changes
in the strength of Finnish radicalism', in *Proceedings of the
Fifth World Congress of Sociology*, Washington.
—— (1964), Patterns of Class Conflict and Working Class con-
sciousness in Finnish Politics', in E. Allardt and Y. Littunen

(eds.), *Clearages, Ideologies and Party Systems*, Helsinki: Transactions of the Westermarck Society, Vol. X.
—— with S. ROKKAN (1970), *Mass Politics*, New York: Committee on Political Sociology.
ALMERICH, P. (1972), 'Spain', in H. Mol (ed.), *Western Religion:* the Hague and Paris, Moutón.
ALONSO, J. M. (1965), 'Layers of Piety in Spanish Religion', *Social Compass*, No. 3.
ANTHONY, D. with T. ROBBINS (1974), 'The Meher Baba Movement' in I. I. Zaretsky and M. P. Leone (eds.), *Religious Movements in Contemporary America*, Princeton N.J.: Princeton University Press.
AQUAVIVA, S. S. (1957), 'Sezione Cartografica', *Sociologia Religiosa.*
—— (1975), 'Religion and Cultural Change', Padova. Privately circulated.
——, with G. GUIZZARDI (1971), *Religione e irreligione nell'età postindustriale*, Roma: Ave.
——, with G. GUIZZARDI (1973), *La secolarizzazione*, Bologna: Il Mulino.
——, with G. GUIZZARDI and G. MILANESI (1975), 'Nouvelles formes de religiosité et et développement socio-économique en Italie', *Acts of the 13th Conference of the Sociology of Religion*, C.I.S.R.
APTEKMAN, D. M. (1965), 'Causes of the Vitality of the Ceremony of Baptism under Modern Conditions', *Soviet Sociology*, Vol. IV, No. 2.
ARCHER, M. S., with M. VAUGHAN (1971), *Social Conflict and Educational Change in England and France 1789–1848*, London: Cambridge University Press
ARDAGH, J. (1970), *The New France. A Society in Transition, 1945–1973*, Harmondsworth: Penguin.
ARGYLE, M. with BEIT-HALLAHMI (1975), *The Social Psychology of Religion*, London: Routledge.
ARTIGUES, D. (1971), *El Opus Dei en España.* Ruedo iberico: Paris.
AUBERT, R. (1973), 'L'église catholique et la vie politique en Belge depuis la seconde guerre mondiale', *Res Publica*, No. 2.
AVER, E. (1970), 'Pratique religieuse et comportement électoral', *Archives de Sociologie des Religions*, No. 29.

BAAN, M. A. (1966), 'Structural and cultural changes in the Dutch Franciscan Province', *Social Compass*, Vol: 13, No. 3.

BAHTIJAREVIC, S. (1971), 'Some characteristics of the religiosity of secondary school attendants', *Actes de la 11ième Conférence internationale de sociologie religieuse, Opatija*, Lille: C.I.S.R.

BALTZELL, E. DIGBY (1964), *The Protestant Establishment*, New York: Random House.

—— (1972), 'To be a Phoenix—Reflections on Two Noisy Ages of Prose', *The American Journal of Sociology*, Vol. 78, No. 1, July.

BANGO, J. (1968), 'Convictions religieuses de la jeunnesse hongroise scolaire et étudiante', *Social Compass*, 15/5.

BARNES, H. (1970), *The University as New Church*, London: Watts.

BARNES, J. (1971), 'The Righthand and Lefthand Kingdoms of God' in BEIDELMAN, T. O. (eds.) *The Translation of Culture*, London: Tavistock Publications.

BARNES, S. H. (1966), 'Italy: Oppositions on Left, Right and Center', in R. A. Dahl, *Political Oppositions in Western Democracies*, New Haven and London: Yale University Press.

BAUMAN, Z. (1971), 'Social Dissent in the East European Political System', *Archives Européennes de Sociologie*, Vol. 12, No. 1.

BAXTER, J. (1974), 'The Great Yorkshire Revival 1792–6', in M. HILL (ed.), *Sociological Yearbook of Religion in Britain*, No. 7, London: S.C.M. Press.

BECKFORD, J. (1973), 'A Korean evangelistic movement in the West', *Actes de la 12ième Conférence internationale de sociologie religieuse*, Lille: C.I.S.R.

BEESON, T. (1974), *Discretion and Valour*, London: Fontana.

BELL, D. (1975), *The Cultural Contradictions of Capitalism*, New York: Basic Books.

BELLAH, R. N. (1965), *Religion and Progress in Modern Asia*, New York: Free Press.

——(1968), in R. N. Bellah and W. G. McLoughlin (eds.), *Religion in America*, Boston: Houghton Mifflin.

BELLAH, R. N. and GLOCK, C. Y. (eds.) (1976), 'The New Religious Consciousness' Berkeley: University of California Press.

BENSIMON, D. (1971), 'Aspects de l'abandon de la practique religieuse en milieu juif francais', *Social Compass*, Vol. 18, 3.

BERGER, P. (1961), *The Noise of Solemn Assemblies*, New York: Doubleday.

—— (1969), *The Social Reality of Religion*, London: Faber.

——, with B. BERGER and H. KELLNER (1973, *The Homeless Mind*, New York: Random House.

——, with T. LUCKMANN (1966), in J. Matthes, *Internationales Jahrbuch für Religionsoziologie*, No. 2.

BILLIET, J. (1973a), 'Secularisation and compartmentalisation in the Belgian Education System', *Social Compass*, Vol. 20, 4.

—— (1973b), 'Changement religieux et système scolaire en Belgique', *Actes de las 12ième Conférence de Sociologie Religieuse*, Lille, C.I.S.R.

BINCHY, D. A. (1970), *Church and State in Fascist Italy*, Oxford: Oxford University Press.

BLACKWELL, W. (1965), 'The Old Believers and the rise of private industry in early nineteenth-century Moscow', *Slavic Review*, Vol. 24, No. 3, September.

BLOCH-HOELL, N. (1964), *The Pentecostal Movement*, Oslo: Universitetsforlag.

BOCIURKIW, B. R. (1973), 'Church–State Relations in Communist Europe', *Religion in Communist Lands*, Vol. 1, Nos. 4 and 5, July and October.

——, with J. W. STRONG (1975), *Religion and Atheism in the U.S.S.R. and Eastern Europe*, London: Macmillan.

BOCOCK, R. (1974), *Ritual in Industrial Society*, London: Allen and Unwin.

BOGENSBERGER, H. (1972), 'Austria' in H. Mol (ed.), *Western Religion*, The Hague and Paris: Mouton.

BOISSEVAIN, J. (1965), *Saints and Fireworks*, London: The Athlone Press.

BORDEAUX, M. (1965), *Opium of the People*, London: Faber.

—— (1968), *Religious Ferment in Russia*, London: Macmillan.

—— (1970), *Patriarchs and Prophets*, New York, SCM.

BOSERUP, A. with C. WERSØN (1967), 'Rank analysis of a polarized community', Institute of Peace and Conflict Research, Copenhagen.

BOULARD, F. (1971), 'La "déchristianisation" de Paris. L'évolution historique du non-conformisme', *Archives de sociologie des religions*, No. 31.

—— (1960), *An Introduction to Religious Sociology*, London: Darton, Longman and Todd.

——, with J. REMY (1968), 'Urban cultural regions and religious practice in France', *Social Compass*, Vol. 15/6.

BOVY, L. (1969), 'La vie religieuse à la péripherie de Paris', *Rivista di Sociologia*, Gennaio-Dicembre.

BRAGA, G. (1957), 'Tipologia delle sottostrutture delle parrochie Siciliane', *Sociologia Religiosa*.

BREISTEIN, D. (1955), *Hans Nielsen Hauge, Merchant of Bergen, Christian Belief and Economic Activity*, Bergen: Grieg.

BRENNAN, T., with E. W. COONEY and M. POLLINS (1954), *Social Change in South-West Wales*, London: Watts.

BROGAN, D. W. (1940), *The Development of Modern France 1870–1939*, London: Hamish Hamilton.

BROTHERS, J. (1964), *Church and School*, Liverpool: Liverpool University Press.

BRUNT, L. (1972), 'The "Kleine Luyden" as a Disturbing Factor in the Emancipation of the Orthodox Calvinists (Gereformeerden) in the Netherlands', *Sociologica Neerlandica*, Vol. VIII, No. II.

BUDD, S. (1973), *Sociologists and Religion*, London: Collier-Macmillan.

BULL, E. (1958), 'Arbeider Miliø', Oslo: University Press.

BUTLER, D. with R. STOKES (1969, 1974), *Political Change in Britain: the evolution of electoral choice*, London: Macmillan.

BUTLER, S. (1918), *The Notebooks*, London: Fifield.

CALDAROLA, C. (1975), 'Religion and Voting in Canada' [Quebec], *Actes de la 13ième Conférence internationale de Sociologie religieuse*, Lille: C.I.S.R.

CAMPBELL, C. (1971), *Toward a Sociology of Irreligion*, London: Macmillan.

CAMPBELL, J. K. (1964), *Honour, Family and Patronage*, Oxford: Clarendon Press.

——, with SHERRARD, P. (1968), *Modern Greece*, London: Ernest Benn.

CAMPICHE, R. (1971), 'La Sociologie de la Religion en Suisse', *Archives de Sociologie des Religions*, 32.

—— (1972), 'Switzerland', in H. Mol (ed.), *Western Religion*, The Hague: Mouton.

—— (1975), Stratification sociale, participation et sociabilité religieuse dans quatre contextes Suisses', *Actes de la 13ième Conférence internationale de Sociologie religieuse*, Lille: C.I.S.R.

CARR, R. (1966), *Spain 1808–1939*, Oxford: Clarendon Press.

CARRIER, H., with E. PIN (1956), *Essais de sociologie religieuse*, Paris: P.U.F.

CAZORLA, J. (1975), 'Consensus et conflits dans l'Eglise espagnole sous la régime de Franco', *Actes de la 13ième Conférence internationale de Sociologie religieuse*, Lille: C.I.S.R.

CHADWICK, O. (1975), *The Secularisation of the European Mind in the Nineteenth Century*, Cambridge: Cambridge University Press.

CHARLTON, D. (1963), *Secular Religions in France*, Oxford: Oxford University Press.

CHARPIN, F. (1964), *Pratique religieuse et formation d'une grande ville: Marseilles 1806–1956*, Paris: Editions du Centurion.

CHRISTIAN, W. (1974), *Person and God in a Spanish Valley*, New York and London: Seminar Press.

CHRYPINSKI, V. C. (1975), 'Polish Catholics and Social Change', in B. R. Bociurkiw and J. W. Strong (eds.), *Religion and Atheism in the U.S.S.R. and Eastern Europe*, London: Macmillan

CIMIC, E. (1971), 'Structure de la conscience religieuse dans les milieux ruraux et ur bains, in *Actes de la 11ième Conférence de Sociologie Religieuse*, Lille: C.I.S.R.

CLIFFORD-VAUGHAN, M. (1972), 'Poland' in M. Archer (ed.), *Students, University and Society*, London: Heinemann.

COBBAN, A. (1961), *A History of Modern France*, Vol. 2, Harmondsworth: Penguin.

COLEMAN, J. A. (1970), 'Civil Religion', *Sociological Analysis*, Vol. 31, No. 2, Summer.

CURRIE, R., with A. GILBERT (1978), *Churches and Church-Going*, Oxford: Oxford University Press.

CUTILEIRO, J. (1971), *A Portuguese Rural Society*, Oxford: Clarendon Press.

CUTLER, R. (1969), *The Religious Situation*, London: Evans Brothers.

CVIIC, C. (1973), 'Recent Developments in Church-State Rela-

tions in Yugoslavia', *Religion in Communist Lands,* Vol. 1, No.
2, March-April.
CZARNOWSKI, S. (1956), *Works,* Vol. 1, Warsaw.

DAALDER, H. (1966), 'The Netherlands: opposition in a Segmented Society', in R. A. Dahl, *Political Oppositions in
Western Democracies,* New Haven and London: Yale Uni-
versity Press.
DAHL, R. (1966), *Political Oppositions in Western Democracies,*
New Haven: Yale University Press.
DAHRENDORF, R. (1959), *Class and Class Conflict in Industrial
Society,* Stanford: Stanford University Press.
—— (1963), 'Conflict and Liberty: Some remarks on the structure
of German Politics' *British Journal of Sociology,* Vol. XIV, No.
3, September.
—— (1967), *Society and Democracy in Germany,* New York:
Garden City.
DANIEL, M. (1968), 'Catholic, Evangelical, and Liberal in the
Anglican Priesthood', in D. Martin (ed.), *A Sociological
Yearbook of Religion in Britain,* No. 1, London: S.C.M.
Press.
DANSETTE, A. (1948 and 1951), *Histoire religieuse de la France
contemporaine,* 2 vols., Paris: Flammarion.
—— (1962), *The Religious History of Modern France,* New
York: Herder and Herder.
DATUNASHVILI and others (1974), 'Sociologie de la religion en
u.r.s.s.', *Social Compass,* Vol. 21, No. 20.
DAVIE, G. (1975), *The Protestant Right in France with particular
reference to the Association Sully,* unpublished Ph.D., London
University.
DAVIES, C. (1975), *Permissive Britain,* London: Pitman.
DAVIES, E. T. (1965), *Religion in the Industrial Revolution in
South Wales,* Cardiff: University of Wales Press.
DAVISON, W. PHILLIPS (1954/5), 'A Review of Sven Rydenfelt's
Communism in Sweden, Public Opinion Quarterly (18)
Winter.
DE KADT, E. (1970), *Catholic Radicals in Brazil,* London: Oxford
University Press.
DEMERATH, N. J. (1965), *Social Class in American Protestantism,*
Chicago: Rand McNally.

—— (1968), 'Trends and anti-trends in religious change' in E. B. Sheldon and W. E. Moore (eds.), *Indicators of Social Change*, New York: Russell Sage Foundation.

DUNN, S., with E. DUNN (1964), 'Religion as an instrument of cultural change', *Slavic Review*, No. 3.

—— (1967), 'Religion as an instrument of culture change: the problem of the sects in the Soviet Union', *Slavic Review*, Vol. 26, No. 1.

—— (1975), 'Religious Behaviour and Socio-cultural change in the Soviet Union', in B. Bociurkiw and J. W. Strong (eds.), *Religion and Atheism in the U.S.S.R. and Eastern Europe*, London: Macmillan.

DUOCASTELLA, R. (1965), 'Géographie de la pratique religieuse en Espagne', *Social Compass*, Vol. XII, Nos. 4–5.

—— (1967), *Análisis sociológico del catolicismo español*, Barcelona: I.S.P.A.

—— (1973a), 'Actitud y mentalidad religiosa en la archdiocesis de Barcelona', 3 vols., Barcelona.

—— (1973b), 'Espagne: Societé et Eglise en processus de change', *Actes de la 12ième Conférence de Sociologie religieuse*, Lille: C.I.S.R.

EISENSTADT, S. N. (ed.) (1968), *The Protestant Ethic and Modernization*, London and New York: Basic Books.

—— (1972), 'Intellectuals and Traditions', *Daedalus*, Spring.

—— (1973), 'Continuity and Reconstruction of Tradition', *Daedalus*, Winter.

ELIOT, T. S. (1939), *The Idea of a Christian Society*, London: Faber.

ELLIOT, R. S. P., with J. HICKIE (1971), Ulster: *A Case Study in Conflict Theory*, London: Longman.

ENCEL, S. (1970), *Equality and Authority: A Study of Class, Status and Power in Australia*, Melbourne: Cheshires; London: Tavistock.

ENGELMANN, F. C. (1966), 'Austria: The Pooling of Opposition', in R. A. Dahl, *Political Oppositions in Western Democracies*, New Haven and London: Yale University Press.

ESSIEN-UDOM, E. (1962), *Black Nationalism*, Chicago: University of Chicago Press.

FAG, J. E. (1976), 'Republican Politics in the reign of Isabel II', in M. Vassallo (ed.) Mediterranean Studies, Malta University Press.

FENN, R. K. (1969), 'The Process of Secularisation: a post-Parsonian view', *Journal for the Scientific Study of Religion*, Vol. VIII.

FEUER, L. S. (1963), *The Scientific Intellectual*, London: Basic Books.

FIAMENGO, A. (1962), 'Croyances religieuses et changements technologiques en Yougoslavie', Archives de Sociologie des Religions, Vol. 15.

—— (1972), 'Yugoslavia', in H. Mol (ed.), *Western Religion*, The Hague: Mouton.

FIELD, C. (1975), *Methodism in Metropolitan London 1820–1920. A social tnd sociological study*, unpublished Ph.D. thesis, Oxford.

FIELD, C. (1977), 'The social structure of English Methodism', *British Journal of Sociology*, Vol. XXVIII, No. 2, June [important bibliography].

FIRESIDE, H. (1971), *Icon and Swastika. The Russian Orthodox Church under Nazi and Soviet Control*, London: Oxford University Press.

FISCHER, H., with A. HOLL (1968), 'Enquête auprès soldates de l'armée autrichienne', *Social Compass*, Vol. 15/1.

FLETCHER, W. C. (1965), *A Study in Survival: The Church in Russia 1927–1943*. New York: Macmillan.

—— (1971a), *The Russian Orthodox Church Underground, 1917–1970*, Oxford: Oxford University Press.

—— (1972), 'U.S.S.R.' in H. Mol (ed.), *Western Religion*, The Hague: Mouton.

—— with D. A. LOWRIE (1971b), 'Kruschev's Religious Policy', in R. H. Marshall (ed.), *Aspects of Religion in the Soviet Union, 1917–1967*, Chicago: University of Chicago Press.

FLANAGAN, T. (1972), 'Social Credit in Alberta. A Canadian Cargo Cult?' *Archives de sociologie des religions*, No. 34.

FLINT, J. T. (1968), 'Historical Role Analysis in the Study of Secularization. The laity-clergy ratio in Norway 1800–1950', *Journal of the Scientific Study of Religion*, Vol. VII, No. 2, Autumn.

FOGARTY, M. P. (1957), *Christian Democracy in Western Europe 1820–1953*. Notre Dame, Indiana: University of Notre Dame Press.

FREND, W. H. C. (1971), 'The Rumanian Church rides high', *The Times*, 20 November.

FÜR, F. (1952), 'Frikyrklighet och socialgeografiska regioner i Smaland', *Svensk Geografisk Arsbok*.

GAASHOLT, Ø. (1975), 'Religious Belief and Political Orientations in Yugoslavia', European Consortium for Political Research. (Paper available from the University of Essex).

GALLI, G. with A. PRANDI (1971), *Patterns of Political Participation in Italy*, New Haven: Yale University Press.

GAY, J. D. (1971), *The Geography of Religion in England*, London: Duckworth.

GELLERSTAM, G. (1971), 'Fran Fattigrard till Forsamlingsvoord', unpublished Ph.D thesis, Lund University.

GELLNER, E. (1964), *Thought and Change*, London: Weidenfeld and Nicholson.

―― (1974), *Contemporary Thought and Politics*, London: Routledge.

GINER, S. (1971), 'Spain', in S. Giner and M. Archer, *Contemporary Europe*, London: Weidenfeld and Nicolson.

GUISEPPE, B. (1957), 'Statistica Religiosa in Italia', *Sociologia Religiosa*.

GLASNER, P. (1977), *Secularisation*, London: Routledge.

GLOCK, C. Y., with R. STARK (1965), *Religion and Society in Tension*, Chicago: Rand McNally.

―― (1968), *American Piety*, Berkeley: University of California.

――, with B. B. RINGER and E. RABBIE (1967), *To Comfort and to Challenge*, Berkeley: University of California.

GODDIJN, W. (1973), 'La minorité catholique aux Pays-Bas: analyse sociologique de différents types de "survival"', *Actes de las 12ième Conférence internationale de sociologie religieuse*, Lille: C.I.S.R.

―― (1974), *The Deferred Revolution*, Amsterdam: Elsevier.

GOGUEL, F. (1966), 'Religion et politique en France', *Révue Française de Science Politique*, Vol. 16.

GOODE, E. (1968), 'Class Styles of Religious Sociation', *British Journal of Sociology*, Vol. XIX, No. 1.

GOODRIDGE, R. (1975), 'The Ages of Faith—Romance or Reality?', *The Sociological Review*, Vol. 23, No. 2.

GOUDSBLOM, J. (1967), *Dutch Society*, New York: Random House.

GOUSSIDIS, A. (1975), 'A Statistical Analysis and Sociography of Ordinations in the Greek Church 1950–1969', *Social Compass*, XXII, 5.

GREELEY, A. (1969), *Religion in the Year 2000*, New York: Sheed and Ward.

—— (1973), *The Persistence of Religion*, London: S.C.M. Press.

GREINACHER, N. (1963), 'L'évolution de la pratique religieuse après la guerre' [West Germany], *Social Compass*, Vol. 4/5.

GRUMELLI, A., with R. CAPORALE (1973), *Religione e Ateismo nella società secolarizzate*, Bologna: Il Mulino.

GRUNER, E. (1969), *Die Parteien in der Schweiz*, Berne: Francke Verlag.

GUIZZARDI, G. (1974), *New Religious Phenomena in Italy*, Presented at the 8th World Congress of Sociology, Toronto 1974, Padova: edition C.S.S.R.

GUSFIELD, J. (1966), *Symbolic Crusade*, London and Urbana: University of Illinois Press.

—— (1957 and 1971), *Svensk Kyrkogeographi*, Malmö: Gleerups Förlag.

GUSTAFSSON, B. (1966), 'People's view of the minister and the lack of ministers in Sweden', *Archives de Sociologie des religions*, No. 22, July-December.

—— (1968), 'Sin in Sweden', *Social Compass*, Vol. 15, No. 2.

—— (1970), *Svenske folkets böner*, Stockholm: Verbum Aktiebologet Tryckmans.

GUSTAFSSON, G. (1967), *Religion och Politik*, Lund: mimeo Sociologiska Institutionen.

HADDEN, J. K. (ed.) (1971), *Religion in Radical Transition*, Transaction Books.

HAGEN, E. E. (1962), *A Theory of Social Change*, Homewood: Dorsey.

HALL, J. (1976), *The Edwardian Intelligentsia*, unpublished Ph.D thesis, London University.

HANDY, R. (1971), *A Christian America*, New York: Oxford University Press.

HARGREAVES-MAUDSLEY, W. N. (1977), 'Centralism and Regionalism in the Eighteenth Century', in M. Vassallo (ed.) 'Mediterranean Studies', Malta University Press.

HARRIS, C. C. (1973), *Facing the Future Together*, Bangor: The Diocesan Office.

HARTMANN, P. (1976), 'Social dimensions of occult participation: the Gnostica study', *British Journal of Sociology*, Vol. XXVII, No. 2, June.

HASSING, A. (1973), 'Methodism in Norwegian Society', unpublished Ph.D. thesis, Northwestern University.

HASTINGS, A. (1975), 'A Church in Isolation', *The Tablet*, 12 and 19 April.

HAUGLIN, O. (1969), *A Study of the religious life of a community near Oslo*, unpublished Ph.D. thesis, Oslo.

HAZELRIGG, L. (1972), 'Occupation and Religious Practice in Italy: the Thesis of "Working Class Alienation"', *Journal of the Scientific Study of Religion*, Vol. II, No. 4, December.

HEASMAN, K. (1962), *Evangelicals in Action*, London: Bles.

HEER, F. (1962), *The Medieval World*, London: Weidenfeld and Nicolson.

HELMREICH, E., (ed.) (1964), *A free church in a free state?*, Boston: Heath.

HERBERG, W. (1955), *Protestant—Catholic—Jew*, New York: Doubleday.

—— (1964), 'Religion in a secularized society: some aspects of America's three-religion pluralism', in L. Schneider (ed.), *Religion, Culture and Society*, New York: Wiley.

HERVIEN, D. (1973) 'Protestation religieuse, protestation sociale: le cas des communautés de jeunes en France', *Actes de la 12ième Conférence de Sociologie Religieuse*, Lille: C.I.S.R.

HICKLING, M. (1969), 'The Churches in Hungary', B.A. dissertation, Sheffield University.

——, (no date), *Church–State relations in Eastern Europe*, Ph.D. commenced at London University, and most unhappily cut short by Michael Hickling's death. I would like to record my indebtedness to his extensive research.

—— (1973), 'Worse Church–State relations feared in Yugoslavia', *British Weekly*, 27 April.

HIGHET, J. (1960), *The Scottish Churches*, London: Skeffington.

HILL, M. (1970–75), *A Sociological Yearbook of Religion in Britain*, Nos. 3–8, London: S.C.M. Press.

—— (1973a), *The Religious Order*, London: Heinemann Educational.

—— (1973b), *The Sociology of Religion*, London: Heinemann Educational.

HOBSBAWN, E. J. (1969), *Primitive Rebels*, Manchester: University Press.

HOFSTADTER, R. (1964), *Anti-Intellectualism in American Life*, London: Jonathan Cape.

HOUTART, F. (1972), 'Belgium', in H. Mol (ed.), *Western Religion*, The Hague and Paris: Mouton.

——, with E. PIN (1965), *The Church and the Latin American Revolution*, New York: Sheed and Ward.

——, with J. REMY (1969), *Eglise et société en mutation*, Paris: Maine.

HOUTTE, J. van (1964), 'Pratique dominicale urbaine et ages en Europe occidentale', *Archives de sociologie des religions*, No. 18.

INGLIS, K. S. (1963), *Churches and the Working Classes in Victorian England*, London: Routledge.

ISAMBERT, F.-A. (1961), *Christianisme et classe ouvière*, Paris: Casterman.

—— (1975), 'Les ouvriers et l'église catholique', *Revue française de sociologie*, No. 1.

JAROSZEWSKI, M. (1965), 'Pratiques et conceptions religieuses en Pologne', *Recherches Internationales à la lumière du Marxisme*.

JEMOLO, A. C. (1960), *Church and State in Italy 1850–1950*, Oxford: Basil Blackwell.

JENKINS, D. (1975), *The British. Their Identity and their Religion*, London: S.C.M. Press.

JENKINS, R. (1969), 'Religious Conflict in Northern Ireland', in D. Martin (ed.), *A Sociological Yearbook of Religion in Britain*, No. 2, London: S.C.M. Press.

JIOUITSIS, B. (1975), 'Religious Brotherhoods', *Social Compass*, Vol. XXII, No. 5.

JOHNSON, B. (1964), 'Ascetic Protestantism and Political Preference in the Deep South', *American Journal of Sociology*, No. 69, January.

JONES, E. (1956), 'The Distribution and Segregation of Roman

Catholics in Belfast', *Sociological Review*, Vol. 4, No. 2, New Series, December.

—— (1960), 'Problems of Partition and Segregation in Northern Ireland', *Journal of Conflict Resolution*, Vol. 4, No. 1.

KADLECOVÁ, E. (1965), 'Recherche sociologique sur la religiosité en Tchecoslovaquie', *Recherches internationales a la lumière du Marxisme*.

—— (1972), 'Czechoslovakia', in H. Mol (ed.), *Western Religion*, The Hague: Mouton.

KASER, G. (1966), 'L'eveil du sentiment national. Rôle du piétisme dans la naissance du patriotisme', *Archives de sociologie des religions*, Vol. XXII, pp. 59–80.

KEHRER, G. (1972), 'Germany: Federal Republic', in H. Mol (ed.), *Western Religion*, The Hague: Mouton.

KENNY, M. (1961), *A Spanish Tapestry. Town and Country in Castile*, London: Cohen and West.

KERR, H. H. (1974), *Switzerland: Social Cleavages and Partisan Conflict*, London: Sage Publications.

KJAER, K. (1968), 'Free Churches in Denmark', unpublished Master's thesis, University of Copenhagen.

—— (1971), 'Religious Minority Groups in Denmark, unpublished Licentiat thesis, Copenhagen University.

KLIBANOV, A. (1965), 'The Dissident Denominations in the Past and Today', *Soviet Sociology*, Vol. III, No. 4.

—— (1970), 'Fifty years of the study of Religious Sectarianism' and 'Sectarianism and the Socialist Reconstruction of the Countryside', *Soviet Sociology*, Vol. VIII, Nos. 3–4.

——, with L. M. MITROKHIN (1974), 'The Schism of Contemporary Baptism', *Social Compass*, Vol. 21, No. 2.

KOKOSALAKIS, N. (1969), *The Impact of Ecumenism on Denominationalism*, unpublished Ph.D. thesis, University of Liverpool.

—— (1971), 'Aspects of conflict between Authority and the Laity in the Roman Catholic Church', in M. Hill (ed.), *A Sociological Yearbook of Religion in Britain*, No. 4, London: S.C.M. Press.

KOLARZ, W. (1962), *Religion in the Soviet Union*, New York: St. Martin's Press.

KOSKELAINEN, O. (1968), 'Religiosity in Helsinki', *Temenos*, No. 3.

KRAUSZ, E. (1971), 'Religion and Secularization', *Social Compass*, Vol. XVIII, No. 2.

KREITERLING, W. (1966), 'Les Catholiques allemands et la social-democratie', *Projet*, November.

KRIANEV, I. V., with P. S. POPOV (1963), 'The emotional effect of religious ritual and the process of overcoming it'. Voprosy filosofii, No. 9, 1963.

KUBIAK, H. (1970), *Religiosity and Social Milieu*, Warsaw: Polish Academy.

KUSTERS, W. J. J. (1971), 'From a Universal Church to a local church', Actes de la 11ième Conference internationale de sociologie religieuse', Lille: C.I.S.R.

LANE, C. (1974), 'Some Explanations of the Persistence of Christian Religion in Soviet Society', *Sociology*, Vol. 8, No. 2, May.

—— (1975a), 'Socio-political accommodation and religious decline: the case of the Molokan Sect in Soviet Society', *Comparative Studies in Society and History*, Vol. 17, No. 2, April.

—— (1975b), 'Russian Piety among Contemporary Russian Orthodox', *Journal for the Scientific Study of Religion*, No. 14.

—— (1977), *Christian Religion in the Soviet Union: A Sociological Study*, London: Allen and Unwin.

LARKIN, G. (1974),'Isolation, Integration and Secularisation: A Case Study of the Netherlands', *Sociological Review*, Vol. 22, No. 3, New Series, August.

LAEYENDECKER, L. (1967), The development of sociology of religion in the Netherlands since 1960, *Social Compass*, Vol. 14, No. 1.

—— (1972a), 'The Netherlands', in H. Mol (ed.), *Western Religion*, The Hague: Mouton.

—— (1972b), Sociologia Neerlandica, Vol. VIII, No. 11.

LE BRAS, G. (1955), *Etudes de Sociologie Religieuse*, 2 vols., Paris: Universitaires de France.

LEHNBRUCH, G. (1975), 'Religion, cleavages, political behaviour and conflict regulation in Germany', Workshop on Language, Religion and Politics, L.S.E., April. (Obtainable from Essex University.)

M

LEMIEUX, R. (1973), 'Projets et nouvelles expériences du catholicisme quebecois', *Actes de la 12ième Conférence internationale de sociologie religieuse*, Lille: C.I.S.R.

LENNON, J., and others (1972), 'Survey of Catholic Clergy and Religious Personnel 1971' [Eire], Social Studies, March.

LEONARD, E. G. (1953), *Le Protestant français*, Paris: P.U.F.

LEONI, A. (1972), *Sociologia and Geographia di una Diocesi*, Rome: Gregorian University Press.

LÈS, B. (1975), *Secularisation: a comparison of Britain, Poland and France*, unpublished Ph.D. thesis, Cracow.

LEVITTE, G. (1966), 'Vers une étude des mutations de la population juive en France et du judaisme français', *Archives de sociologie des religions*, No. 22.

LEWIS, C. A. (1973), *A Sociological Approach to Faith and Order: Methods of Reaching Unity*, unpublished D.Phil. thesis, University of Cambridge.

LIEBMAN, C. S. (1975), 'Religion and Political Integration in Israel', *Jewish Journal of Sociology*, Vol. XVII, No. 1, June.

LIJPHART, A. (1971), *Class Voting in the European Democracies*, Glasgow: University of Strathclyde.

LINZ, J. J. (1970), 'An Authoritarian Regime', in E. Allardt and S. Rokkan (eds.), *Mass Politics*, New York: Committee on Political Sociology.

LIPSET, S. M. (1963), *The First New Nation*, New York: Basic Books.

—— (1969), *Revolution and Counterrevolution*, London: Heinemann.

—— (1972a), 'The End of Ideology and the Ideology of the Intellectuals' revised version (1976) of an article in *Encounter* 39, December.

—— (1972b), *Rebellion in the Universities*, Boston: Little, Brown.

—— (1975), 'Social Structure and Social Change' in P. Blau (ed.), *Approaches to the Study of Social Structure*, New York: Free Press.

——, with S. ROKKAN (eds.) (1964), *Party Systems and Voter Alignments*, New York: Free Press.

LISON-TOLOSANA, C. (1966), *Belmonte de los Caballeros*, Oxford: Clarendon Press.

LORWIN, V. R. (1966), 'Belgium: Religion, Class and Language in National Politics', in R. A. Dahl, *Political Oppositions in Western Democracies*, New Haven and London: Yale University Press.

LUCKMANN, T. (1967), *The Invisible Religion*, New York: Macmillan.

MCCAFFERY, P. C. (1973), 'A sociological analysis of the concerns of pressure groups in the Roman Catholic Church in the Netherlands and in England', *Actes de la 12ième Conférence internationale de sociologie religieuse*, Lille: C.I.S.R.

MCGUIRE, M. (1975), 'Religion and Socio-Economic Change in Western Ireland', *Actes de la 13ième Conférence internationale de sociologie religieuse*, Lille: C.I.S.R.

MCINNES, N. (1975), *The Communist Parties of Western Europe*, London: R.I.I.A.

MACINTYRE, A. (1967), *Secularisation and Moral Change*, London: University Press.

MACKIE, T. T. (1975), 'Generational Change in Italian Politics: the Democrazia Christiana', Workshop on Language, Religion and Politics, L.S.E. April.

MACK SMITH, D. (1959), *Italy, a Modern History*, Ann Arbor: University of Michigan Press.

MACLEOD, H. (1974), *Class and Religion in the late Victorian City*, London: Croom Helm.

MCLOUGHLIN, W., with R. N. BELLAH (1968), *Religion in America*, Boston: Houghton Mifflin.

MADELEY, J. T. S. (1974), 'Churches, Cleavages and Confessional Parties', Workshop on the Comparative Study of Contemporary Switzerland, privately available, Department of Politics, University College, Cardiff.

—— (1975), 'Scandinavian Christian Democracy: throwback or portent?' Workshop on Language, Religion and Politics, European Consortium for Political Research, obtainable from Essex University.

MAJKA, J. (1963), 'La sociologie de la religion en Pologne', *Social Compass*, Vol. 10, No. 6.

—— (1968), 'The Character of Polish Catholicism', *Social Compass*, Vol. 15, Nos. 3–4.

—— (1972), 'Poland', in H. Mol (ed.), *Western Religion*, The Hague: Mouton.

MARCILHACY, C. (1964), *Le diocese d'Orléans au milieu du XIXième siecle*, Paris, Sirey.

MARCUS ALONSO, J. (1965), 'A Social and psychological typology of religious identification in Spanish Catholicism', *Social Compass*, Vol. XII, Nos. 4–5.

MARSHALL, R. H., (ed.) (1971), *Aspects of Religion in the Soviet Union, 1917–1967*, Chicago: University of Chicago Press.

MARTIN, B. (1968), 'Some Comments on Gallup Poll Statistics' in D. Martin (ed.), *A Sociological Yearbook of Religion*, No. 1, London: S.C.M. Press.

MARTIN, D. A. (1962), 'The Denomination', *British Journal of Sociology*, Vol. XIII, No. 1, March.

—— (1965a), *Pacifism: a sociological and historical study*, London: Routledge.

—— (1965b), 'Towards Eliminating the Concept of Secularisation' in J. Gould (ed.), *Penguin Survey of the Social Sciences*, Harmondsworth: Penguin.

—— (1966a), 'Utopian Elements in the Concepts of Secularistion' in J. Matthes (ed.), *Internationales Jahrbuch für Religionsoziologie*, No. 2.

—— (1966b), 'The Unknown Gods of the English', *Advancement of Science*, June.

—— (1967a), 'Religion in Bulgaria', *Theology*, November and December.

—— (1967b), *A Sociology of English Religion*, London: S.C.M. Press.

—— (1968), 'The Secularisation Process in England and Wales' in G. Walters (ed.), *Religion in Technological Society*, Bath: Bath University Press.

——, (ed.), (1968–70), *A Sociological Yearbook of Religion in Britain*, Nos. 1–3, London: S.C.M. Press.

—— (1969a), *Anarchy and Culture*, London: Routledge.

—— (1969b), *The Religious and the Secular*, London: Routledge.

—— (1969c), 'Notes towards a General Theory of Secularistion', *European Journal of Sociology*, December.

—— (1971), 'The Secularisation Issue', *Encounter*, April.

——, with C. CROUCH (1971b), 'Modern Britain' in M. S. Archer and S. Giner, *Contemporary Europe*, London: Weidenfeld and Nicolson.

—— (1972), 'Church, Denomination and Modern Society' in M. Hill (ed.), *A Sociological Yearbook of Religion in Britain*, No. 5, London: S.C.M. Press.

—— (1973a), 'England' in H. Mol (ed.), *Western Religion*, The Hague: Mouton.

—— (1973b), *Tracts against the Times*, London: Lutterworth Press.

—— (1973c), 'The Secularisation Question', *Theology*, February.

—— (1973d), 'Institutionalism and Community', *Actes de la 12ième Conférence internationale de la Sociologie religieuse*, Lille: C.I.S.R.

—— (1974a), 'Patterns of Secularisation', *The Times*, 16 February, 2 and 16 March.

—— (1974b), 'Christianity, Civic Religion and Three Counter-Cultures', *Human Context*, Vol. VI, No. 3, Autumn.

—— (1974c), 'The Church: the familiar: unknown quantity', *Crucible*, January–March.

—— (1975a), 'Polymorphous Pieties', *Times Literary Supplement*, 13 June.

—— (1975b), 'All Cultures and Sub-Cultures are Equal', *Contemporary Review*, September.

—— (1975c), 'Doctors of the body or leeches of the soul', *Times Higher Education Supplement*, 1 August.

—— (1976a), 'The Prospects for Non-Scientific Belief and Ideology' in G. Suffert (ed.), *Les Terreurs de l'an deux milles*, Paris: Hachette.

—— (1976b), 'Mutations: Religio-Political Crisis and the Collapse of Puritanism and Humanism' in P. Seabury (ed.), *Universities in the Western World*, New York: Free Press.

—— (1976c), 'Traditional Religion and the traditional transitions to the tradition of the new', paper given at the Centenary of the Hebrew Union College, Jerusalem, Easter.

—— (1976d), 'Dr. Adorno's bag of tricks', *Encounter*, October.

—— (1977a), 'Religious Education in the Secular City', *Learning for Living*, October.

MARTY, M. (1969a), *The Triple Schism*, London: S.C.M. Press.

—— (1969b), *The New Shape of American Religion*, New York: Harper and Row.

—— (1970), *Righteous Empire: the Protestant Experience in America*, New York.

MASSA, D. (1977), 'Contemporary Maltese Literature', in M. Vassallo (ed.), *Mediterranean Studies*, University of Malta Press.

MATTHIAS, E. (1977), 'Funeral laments and female power in Sardinian Peasant Society', in M. Vassallo (ed.), *Mediterranean Studies*, University of Malta Press.

MATTHIESON, T. (1966), 'Religion in Norway', in N. R. Ramsøy (ed.), *Det Norske Samfunn*, Oslo: Sociological Institute.

MAYER, P. (1966), *The Pacifist Concience*, London: Rupert Hart-Davis.

MEHL, R. (1965), 'Traité de sociologie du protestantisme', Neuchatel: Delachaux and Niestlé.

—— (1970), *The Sociology of Protestantism*, London: S.C.M. Press.

MERMET (1971), 'Les fonctions politiques des organisations religieuses dans les régimes à pluralisme limité', *Revue Française de Science Politique*, Vol. XXIII, No. 3, June.

MILLAR, J. R. (1971), *The Soviet Rural Community*, Urbana: University of Illinois Press.

MILLETT, D. (1975), *The Age of Organised Religion in Canada*, Toronto: Macmillan.

MIZZI, S. O. (1977), 'The Changing Status of Women in Malta', in M. Vassallo (ed.), *Mediterranean Studies*, University of Malta Press.

MOBERG, D. (1962), *The Church as a Social Institution. The Sociology of American Religion*, Englewood Cliffs, N. J.: Prentice Hall.

MOL, H. (1966), *Religion and Race in New Zealand*, Christchurch: National Council of Churches.

—— (1969), *Christianity in Chains*, Melbourne: Nelson.

——, (ed.) (1972), *Western Religion*, The Hague: Mouton.

MONTEIRO, J. S. (1975), 'O dilema da Igreja em Portugal', *Expresso*, 19 April.

MOORE, Barrington (1966), *Social Origins of Dictatorship and Democracy*, Boston: Beacon Press.

MOORE, R. S. (1974a), *Pitmen, Preachers and Politics*, Cambridge: Cambridge University Press.

—— (1974b), 'Religiosity and Stratification in England', *Sociological Analysis and Theory*, Vol. IV, No. 3, October.

MORGAN, D. H. J. (1963), 'The Social and Educational Back-

ground of English Diocesan Bishops of the Church of England 1860–1960, M.A. thesis, University of Hull.
—— (1969), 'The Social and Educational Background of Anglican Bishops', *British Journal of Sociology*, Vol. xx, No. 3, September.
MURASKIN, W. A. (1976), *Middle Class Blacks in a White Society: Prince Hall Freemasonry in America*, Berkeley: University of California Press.

NICHOLLS, D. (1967), *Church and State in Britain since 1820*, London: Routledge.
NIEBUHR, H. R. (1949), *The Kingdom of God in America*, New York: The Shoestring Press.
N.I.P.O. (1971), 'Foi, religion, morale et vie familiale dans dix pays d'Europe', *Social Compass*, Vol. 18, No. 2.
NOWAKOWSKA, L. (1961), 'The Outlook of the Man of Learning', *Argumenty*, Vol. 5, No. 32.
NUIJ, T. (1973), 'La subculture religieuse dans la ville d'Amsterdam', *Actes de la 12ième Conférence internationale de sociologie religieuse*, Lille: C.I.S.R.

OBELKEVICH, J. (1971), *Religion and Rural Society in South Lindsey 1825–1875*, Ph.D. thesis, Columbia University.
O'BRIEN, D. J. (1969), *American Catholics and Social Reform*, Oxford: Oxford University Press.
OCHAVKOV, J. (1972), 'Bulgaria' in H. Mol (ed.), *Western Religion*, The Hague: Mouton.
O'DEA, T. (1966), *The Sociology of Religion*, Englewood Cliffs, N.J.: Prentice Hall.
O'DONOGHUE, D. (1972), 'Religious Gaps in Ireland', *Social Studies*, October.
ORENSANZ, A. (1974a), *Crisis Rural y Sociedad del Ocio*, Zaragoza: Prensa Aragonesa.
—— (1974b), *Religiosidad Popular Española, 1940–1965*, Madrid: Editoral Nacional.

PARISI, A. (1971), *La matrice socioreligiosa del dissenso cattolico in Italia*, Bologna: Il Mulino.
PARKIN, F. (1968), *Middle Class Radicalism*, Manchester: Manchester University Press.

PARSONS, T. (1968), 'Christianity' in D. Sills (ed.), *The International Encyclopedia of the Social Sciences*, New York: Macmillan and the Free Press.

PAUL, H. W. (1967), *The Second Ralliement*, Washington: The Catholic University of America Press.

PAUL, L. (1964), *The Deployment and Payment of the Clergy*, London: Church Information Office.

—— (1968), *The Death and Resurrection of the Church*, London: Hodder and Stoughton.

—— (1973), *A Church by Daylight*, London: Chapman.

PAWELCZNSKA, A. (1961), 'Les attitudes des étudiants varsouiens envers la religion', *Archives de Sociologie des religions*, No. 12.

—— (1966), *The dynamics of religious changes in the country*, Warsaw: P.W.N.

PAWLEY, M. (1973), *The Private Future*, London: Thames and Hudson.

PEEL, J. (1971), *Herbert Spencer*, New York: Basic Books.

PETEŠIĆ, C. (1972), 'What is going on in the Catholic Church in Croatia', *Stvarnost*, Zagreb; summarised in ABSEES, April 1973.

PICKERING, W. S. F. with J. L. BLANCHARD (1967), *Taken for Granted*, Winnipeg: The General Synod, Anglican Church of Canada.

—— (1968), 'Religion—A Leisure-time Pursuit?', in D. Martin (ed.), *A Sociological Yearbook of Religion in Britain*, London: S.C.M. Press.

—— (1974), 'The Persistence of the Rites of Passage', *British Journal of Sociology*, xxv, 1, March.

PIN, E. (1956), *Pratique religieuse et classes sociales dans une paroisse urbaine: Saint Pothin à Lyon*, Paris: Spes.

PITT-RIVERS, J. (1954), *The People of the Sierra*, Chicago and London: University of Chicago Press.

PIVOVAROV, W. (1969–1970), 'The Religious Group of Parishioners in the system of the Church Parish', *Soviet Sociology*, Vol. 8, Nos. 3–4, Winter–Spring.

PIWOWARSKI, W. (1971), *Urbanization of rural communities and changes in religious life*, Warsaw.

—— (1974), L'influence de l'industrialisation sur la religiosité populaire en Pologne, *Actes de la 13ième Conférence internationale de Sociologie religieuse*, Lille: C.I.S.R.

Poeisz, J. J. (1963), 'Déterminants sociaux des inscriptions dans les séminaires', *Social Compass*, Vol. 10, No. 6.
—— (1967a), 'The priests in the Dutch Church Province: number and functions', *Social Compass*, Vol. 14, No. 3.
—— (1967b), 'The Parishes of the Dutch Church Province 1966', *Social Compass*, Vol. 14, No. 3.
Poggi, G. (1967), *Catholic Action in Italy*, Stanford: Stanford University Press (O.U.P.)
Potter, S. (1975), *The Social recruitment of missionaries*, unpublished Ph.D. thesis, University of London.
Poulat, E. and others (1972), 'L'église catholique et la vie publique en France', *Archives de sociologie des religions*, No. 34.
Preston, P. (ed.) (1976), *Spain in Crisis*, London: Harvester.
Prifti, P. (1975), 'Albania—towards an Atheist Society', in B. P. Bociurkiw and J. W. Strong (eds.), *Religion and Atheism in the U.S.S.R. and Eastern Europe*, London: Macmillan.
Principbes, Q. (1959), 'Diocesi di Padova: Practica religiosa, 1744–53', *Sociologia Religiosa*, Vol. 3, Nos. 3–4.
Pym, B. (1974), *Pressure Groups and the Permissive Society*, Newton Abbott: David and Charles.

Querido, A. (1972), 'Portugal', in H. Mol (ed.), *Western Religion*, The Hague: Mouton.

Ranulf, S. (1964), *Moral Indignation and Middle Class Psychology*, New York: Schocken Books.
Raynor, H. (1976), *Music and Society since 1815*, London: Barrie and Jenkins.
Richardson, J. T. (1974), 'The Jesus Movement', *Listening: Journal of Religion and Culture*, Vol. 9, No. 3, Autumn.
——, with R. S. Simmonds and M. W. Harder (1975), 'The Evolution of a Jesus Movement Organization', presented at the American Sociological Association annual meeting.
Ringren, H. (1967), *Fatalistic Beliefs in Religion, Folklore and Literature*, Stockholm: Almquist and Wiksell.
Roberts, D. A. (1971), 'The Orange Order in Ireland', *British Journal of Sociology*, Vol. 22, No. 3.
—— (1975), The Orange Order, unpublished Ph.D. thesis, University of London.

ROBERTSON, D. R. (1968), 'The Relationship of Church and Class in Scotland' in D. Martin (ed.), *A Sociological Yearbook of Religion in Britain No. 1*, London: S.C.M. Press.

ROBERTSON, R. (1970), *The Sociological Interpretation of Religion*, Oxford: Blackwell.

—— (1971), 'Sociologists and Secularisation', *Sociology*, Vol. 5, No. 3, September.

ROKKAN, S. and H. VALEN (1964), 'Regional Contrasts in Norwegian Politics', in E. Allardt and Y. Littunen (eds.), *Cleavages, Ideologies and Party Systems*, Helsinki: Transactions of the Westermark Society, Vol. x.

ROSE, R. (1971), *Governing without Consensus*, London: Faber and Faber.

ROSZAK, T. (1968), *The Making of a Counter Culture*, London: Faber.

ROTER, Z. (1971), 'Nature et Structure de la Religiosité en Slovenie', in *Actes de la 11ième Conférence de Sociologie Religieuse*, Lille: C.I.S.R.

RUDGE, P. (1968), *Ministry and Management*, London: Tavistock.

RULE, J. (1971), *A social history of the labouring miners in Cornwall, 1740–1870*, unpublished Ph.D. thesis, Warwick University.

RUNCIMAN, S. (1971), *The Orthodox Churches and the Secular State*, Auckland: Oxford University Press.

RUSSELL, A. J. (1970), *A Sociological Analysis of the Clergyman's Role, with special reference to its development in the early nineteenth century*, unpublished D.Phil. thesis, University of Oxford.

RYDENFELT, S. (1954), *Kommunismen i Sverige*, Lund: Gleerupska Universitetsbokhandeln.

SALISBURY, W. S. (1964), Religion in American Culture, Homewood, Ill.: The Dorsey Press.

SALOMONSEN, P. (1971), *Religion i dag*, Copenhagen: C. E. Gad.

—— (1972), 'Attitude Measurement', *Social Compass*, Vol. xix, No. 4.

—— (1973), 'Contemporary Religious Attitudes in Denmark', in *Actes de la 12ième Conférence de Sociologie Religieuse*, Lille: C.I.S.R.

—— (1975), 'Religion in a welfare state', *Actes de la 13ième Conférence internationale de Sociologie religieuse*, Lille: C.I.S.R.

SARASIN, C. (1954), *German Protestants Face the Social Question*, Notre Dame, Indiana: University of Notre Dame.

SARLVIK, B. (1970), 'Socioeconomic position, religious behaviour and voting in the Swedish electorate', *Quality and Quantity*, Vol. IV, No. 1, June.

SCHNEIDER, L. (ed.) (1964), *Religion, Culture and Society*, New York: John Wiley.

SCHRAM, S. R. (1954), *Protestantism and Politics in France*, Alençon.

SCHREUDER, O. (1970), 'Trends in the Sociology of Religion in the Netherlands, 1960–1969', *Sociologia Neerlandica*, Vol. VI, No. II.

SEGUY, J. (1956), *Les sectes protestantes dans la France contemporaine*, Paris: Beauchesne et ses Fils.

SEMMEL, B. (1974), *The Methodist Revolution*, London: Heinemann.

SEPPANEN, P. (1966), 'Religious Solidarity as a Function of Social Structure and Socialisation', *Temenos*, No. 2.

—— (1968), *Finland. A country of Conformist Religion and Secular Protest of the Working Class*, Institute of Sociology, Helsinki University.

—— (1971), 'Finland' in H. Mol (ed.), *Western Religion*, The Hague: Mouton.

SHEEHY, M. (1969), *Is Ireland dying? Culture and the Church in Modern Ireland*, New York: Taplinger.

SHILS, E. (1972), *The Intellectuals and the Powers*, Chicago: University Press.

—— (1975), *Center and Periphery*, Chicago: University Press.

SHORTER, E. (1976), *The Making of the Modern Family*, London: Collins.

SILLS, D. (ed.) (1968), *International Encyclopedia of the Social Sciences*, T. Parsons.

SIMON, W. M. (1963), *European Positivism in the Nineteenth Century*, Ithaca, N.Y.: Cornell University Press.

SKORZYNSKA, Z., with M. SZANIAWSKA, (eds.) (1960), *The Outlook of Youth and the Membership of Youth Organizations*, Polish Radio.

SMITH, T. L. (1965), 'Revivalism and Social Reform', New York: Harper Torchbooks.

SPENCER, A. E. C. W. (1966), 'The Catholic Church in England' in J. D. Halloran and J. Brothers (eds.), *The Uses of Sociology*, London: Sheed and Ward.

STACKHOUSE, M. L. (1968), 'Christianity and the New Exodus', in D. Cutler (ed.), The Religious Situation; Boston: Beacon.

STANLEY VARDYS, V. (1971), 'Catholicism in Lithuania', in R. H. Marshall (ed.), *Aspects of Religion in the Soviet Union, 1917–1967*, Chicago: University of Chicago Press.

STARK, W. (1966–72), *The Sociology of Religion*, 5 vols. London: Routledge.

STARKEY, D. R. (1973), *The King's Privy Chamber*, 1475–1547, unpublished Ph.D. thesis, University of London.

STARON, S. (1969), 'State-Church Relations in Poland. An Examination of Power Configuration in a Noncompetitive Political System', *World Politics*, Vol. 21, No. 4.

STEEMAN, T. (1967), 'L'église d'aujourd'hui, *Social Compass*, Vol. 14, No. 3.

STEINBERG, J. (1976), *Why Switzerland?*, Cambridge: Cambridge University Press.

STEINER, E. (1973), *The Slovak Dilemma*, Cambridge: Cambridge University Press.

STIGANT, E. P. (1968), 'Methodism and the working class, 1760–1821', unpublished M.A. thesis, Keele University.

STOOP, W. (1971), 'Quatre enquêtes sur la signification de la vie religieuse parmi quatre groupes différents de religieux aux Pays-Bas' *Social Compass*, Vol. 18, No. 1.

STOUTHARD, P. with W. E. MILLER (1975), 'Confessional Attachment and Electoral Behaviour in the Netherlands'. European Consortium for Political Research, (Paper available, University of Essex).

SWANSON, G. E. (1970), *Religion and Regime*, Ann Arbor: University of Michigan Press.

SWIECICKI, A. (1973), 'Les origines institutionelles du movement "Znak"', in *Actes de la 12ième conférence de sociologie religieuse*, Lille: C.I.S.R.

SZASZ, T. (1975), *Ceremonial Chemistry*, London: Routledge.

TAZHURIZINA, Z. A. (1974), 'Les superstitions, mystifications des rélations quotidiennes', *Social Compass*, Vol. 21, No. 2.

THOMAS, K. (1971), *Religion and the Decline of Magic*, London: Weidenfeld and Nicolson.

THOMAS, W. J., with F. ZNANIECKI (1958), *The Polish Peasant in Europe and America*, New York: Macmillan.

THOMPSON, E. P. (1968), *The Making of the English Working Class*, Harmondsworth: Penguin.

THOMPSON, K. A. (1968), 'Bureaucracy and the Church' in D. Martin (ed.), *A Sociological Yearbook of Religion in Britain*, No. 1, London: S.C.M. Press.

—— (1970), *Bureaucracy and Church Reform*, Oxford: Clarendon Press.

THURLINGS, J. M. G. (1971), 'The case of Dutch Catholicism: a Contribution to the Theory of a Pluralistic Society', *Sociologia Neerlandica*, Vol. VII, No. II.

TIEGLAND, G. (1970), 'Study of the Haugean Movement as a case study of mobilisation', unpublished Ph.D. thesis, Bergen University.

TOMASSON, R. F. (1968), 'The Religious Situation in Sweden', *Social Compass*, Vol. XV, No. 6.

—— (1970), *Sweden: Prototype of Modern Society*, New York: Random House.

—— (1971), 'Religion is Irrelevant in Sweden', in J. K. Hadden (ed.), *Religion in Radical Transition*, Chicago: Transaction Books.

TOWLER, R. (1970), 'A Sociological Analysis of the Professional Socialization of Anglican Ordinands', Ph.D. thesis, University of Leeds.

—— (1972), 'The role of the clergy today', in C. L. Mitton (ed.), *The Social Sciences and the Churches*, Edinburgh: T. and T. Clark.

—— (1974), *Homo Religiosus*, London: Constable.

TRACY, M. with D. MORRISON (1976), 'Opposition to the Age: a study of the NVALA', Leicester University, privately circulated.

TREVOR-ROPER, H. (1965), 'Religion, the Reformation and Social Change', *Historical Studies*, Vol. 4.

TRINDER, B. (1973), *The Industrial Revolution in Shropshire*, Phillimore, Chichester.

TRUZZI, M. (1972), 'The occult revival as popular culture', *Sociological Quarterly*, No. 13.

TURNER, R. H. (1960), 'Sponsored and Contest Mobility in the School System', *American Sociological Review*, 26 (6), December.

TUSELL, J. (1975), *Historia de la Democracia Cristiana en España*, Madrid: Cuadernos para el Dialogo.

VAN TILLO, G. (1973), 'Redefinition of religion in the Shalom Movement', *Actes de la 12ième Conférence de Sociologie Religieuse*, Lille: C.I.S.R.

VARGA, I. (1972), 'Hungary', in H. Mol. (ed.), *Western Religion*, The Hague: Mouton.

VASSALLO, M. (1973), *Men in Black. A Report on Malta's Diocesan Clergy*, Malta: P.R.S. Publication.

—— (1974), *Religion and Social Change in Malta*, unpublished D.Phil. thesis, University of Oxford.

—— (1977), 'Religious Symbolism in a Changing Malta', in M. Vassallo (ed.), *Mediterranean Studies*, University of Malta Press.

VEINBERG, A. (1971), 'Lutheranism and Other Denominations in the Baltic Republics', in R. H. Marshall (ed), *Aspects of Religion in the Soviet Union, 1917–1967*, Chicago: University of Chicago Press.

VERBA, S. with G. ALMOND (1963), *The Civic Culture*, Princeton: University Press.

VERDONCK, A. T. (1971), 'Réorientation ou désintégration? Une enquête sociologique sur une congrégation religieuse masculine au Pays-Bas', *Social Compass*, Vol. 18, No. 1.

VERDOOT, R. with D. RAYSIDE (1975), 'The Splitting of the Belgian Social Christian Party along language lines', Workshop on Language, Religion and Politics, L.S.E., April.

VIDLER, A. (1954), *Prophecy and Papacy*, London: S.C.M. Press.

VINCENT, J. (1966), *The Formation of the Liberal Party*, London: Constable.

WALLIS, R. (1975), *Sectarianism*, London: Peter Owen.

—— (1976), 'Moral Indignation and the Media', *Sociology*, Vol. 10, No. 2, May.

WALSH, J. (1975), 'Elie Halévy and the Birth of Methodism', *Transactions of the Royal Historical Society*, 5th Series, Vol. 25.

WARNER, W. J. (1930), *The Wesleyan Movement in the Industrial Revolution*, London: Longmans Green.

WEARMOUTH, R. F. (1937), *Methodism and the Working Class Movements of England 1800–1850*, London: Epworth Press.

WEBER, E. (1962), *Action Française*, Stanford: Stanford University Press.

WEBER, W. (1975), *Music and the Middle Class*, London: Croon Helm.

WERBLOWSKY, Z. (1975), *Beyond Tradition and Modernity*, London: The Athlone Press.

WHITE, J. (1976), *Minority Report: The Protestant Minority in the Irish Republic*, London: Gill and Macmillan.

WHITWORTH, J. M. (1975), *God's Blueprints*, London: Routledge.

WHYTE, J. H. (1971), *Church and State in Modern Ireland 1923–1970*, Dublin: Gill and Macmillan.

—— (1975), 'The Catholic Factor in the Politics of Democratic States', European Consortium for Political Research (Paper available University of Essex).

WICKHAM, E. R. (1957), *Church and People in an Industrial City*, London: Lutterworth.

WILHELM, B. (1972), 'Germany: Democratic Republic' in H. Mol (ed.), *Western Religion*, The Hague: Mouton.

WILLEMS, E. (1965), 'Religious Pluralism and class structure: Brazil and Chile', in J. Matthes (ed.), *International Yearbook for the Sociology of Religion*, No. 1.

—— (1967), *Followers of the New Faith*, Nashville: Vanderbilt University Press.

WILLIAMS, R. M. (1960), *American Society*, New York: Knopf.

WILSON, B. R. (1966), *Religion in Secular Society*, London: Watts.

—— (ed.) (1967), *Patterns of Sectarianism*, London: Heinemann.

WILSON, B. R. (1968), 'Religion and the Churches in contemporary America' in R. N. Bellah and W. G. McLoughlin (eds.), *Religion in America*, Boston: Houghton Mifflin.

—— (1970), *Youth Culture and the Universities*, London: Faber.

—— (1974), 'The Anglican Church and its decline', *New Society*, 5 December.

—— (1975), *The Noble Savages*, Berkeley: University of California Press.

WINTER, G. (1962), *The Suburban Captivity of the Churches*, New York: Macmillan.

YALMAN, N. (1973), 'Some Observations on Secularisation in Islam: the Cultural Revolution in Turkey', *Daedalus*, Vol. 102, No. 1, Winter.

YEO, S. (1971), *Religion in Society: a View from a Provincial Town in the late nineteenth and early twentieth centuries*, Ph.D. thesis, University of Sussex.

—— (1976), *Religion and Voluntary Organisation in Crisis*, London: Croom Helm.

YINGER, J. M. (1946), *Religion in the Struggle for Power*, Durham N.C.: Duke University Press.

—— (1957), *Religion, Society and the Individual*, New York: The Macmillan Company.

—— (1970), *The Scientific Study of Religion*, New York: The Macmillan Company.

ZARETSKY, I. I., with M. P. LEONE (1974), *Religious Movements in Contemporary America*, Princeton: Princeton University Press.

ZATKO, J. J., (ed.), (1967), *The Valley of Silence*, London: University of Notre Dame Press.

ZDANIEWICZ, W. (1968), 'Le problème des vocations religieuses en Pologne', *Social Compass*, Vol. 15, Nos. 3–4.

ZLOBIN, N. S. (1965), 'Le Baptisme contemporain et son idéologie', *Archives de Sociologie des Religions*, Vol. 20, July–December.

ZURCHER, L. A., with R. G. KIRKPATRICK (1976), *Citizens for Decency*, London and Austin: University of Texas Press.

OTHER SOURCES

THE GALLUP POLL,
Release Sunday, December 24, 1972:
'Decline in Churchgoing levelled off in 1972'. [U.S.A.]
'U.K. Catholic Profile, 1980'.
'Religious Denomination analysed by region', 1966.
'La pratique religieuse et la satisfaction', 1975.

'Fewer Australians are going to church'. Releases No. 2373–7, December 1972, January 1973.

DOXA 'Religione e Partiti', No. 14, 30 Luglio, 1974.

DOXA 'Partecipazione degli Italiani adulti alla vita religiosa', No. 17–18, 7 Settembre, 1973.

Centre for the Study of Religion and Communism, 34 Lubbock Road, Chislehurst, Kent.

HOWARD JOHNSON, X. (ed.), 'Religion in Communist Lands', *Journal*, London School of Economics.

Institute of Faith and Secularity Bulletins. Madrid: Universidad "Comillas", 1970ff.

Index of Names

Index of Subjects